Wisdom From The herd

Wisdom from the Herd

www.lizmittenryan.com
www.equinisity.com

tellwell

Tellwell Talent
www.tellwell.ca

ISBN
978-1-77302-718-0 (Paperback)

"I was always wondering how it must feel to really let go, what it really means to let go, how to live from the heart and let the heart intelligence be my guide. To have that open heart without a valve which may close to protect it. To simply live with that infinite unconditional love for all that is. I know that I have still a long path ahead of me—but isn't that the beauty of life? At Liz's place, on the land and with the horses, I finally got in touch with that magic state, where there is nothing but unconditional love and tears running down my face when Miro, Serene and the baby, Pashar, or any of the other wonderful healers approach me gently, tap into my energy and cleanse whatever needed to be cleansed. They knew so much better than me. I simply trusted and let go. Let go of what? Of the need to understand everything, of figuring out everything, of attachment, of clinging to the outcome... I don't know what exactly the horses and the land did to me, what I do know is that a deep sense of connection, a tender, loving feeling for all creatures, nature's magic, animals, for all that is, arose from deep within me; a sense of awakening and a sense of purpose and vision to help others to discover this.

Liz's love, passion and empathy deepened the process of my personal journey and inspired me to pursue my dreams and visions. I will be back."

With love,
Renate Hermes
Business Owner/Spa Director, Duniye Spa Maldives,
Health-Wellness-Spa Consultant, Coach

To L.E. our beloved grandmother spirit and lead mare who was in all ways our guiding light. Your wisdom is truly immortal.

"It was a joy and honor for me to teach with the Herd as well as to learn from their wisdom"

- Margrit Coates

Best-selling author, healer and communicator.

Black text from Liz (or other humans noted)

Colored text from The Herd (or other animals noted)

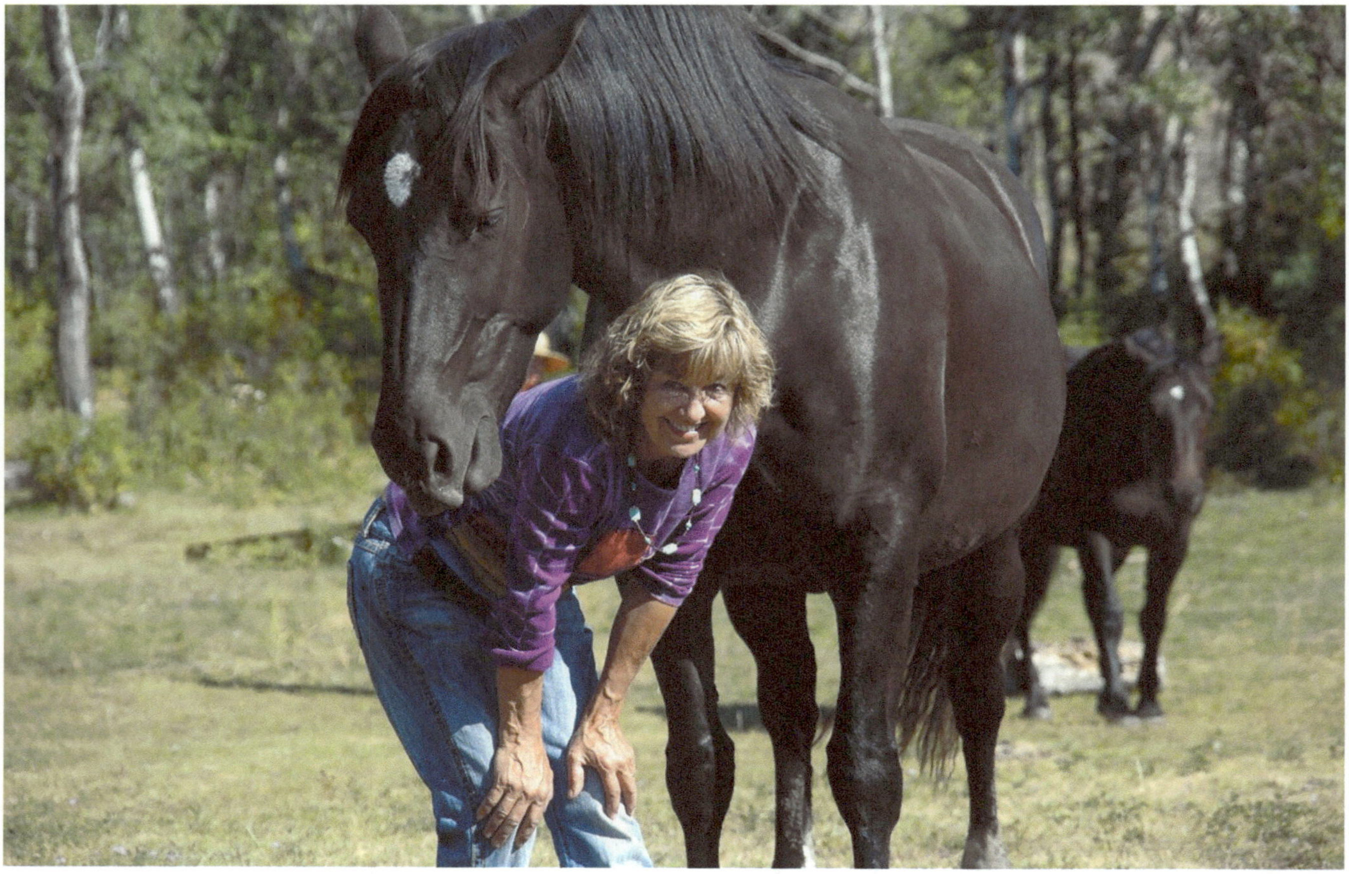

"Our birth is but a sleep and forgetting:
The Soul that rises with us, our life's star,
Hath had elsewhere its setting,
And cometh from afar;
Not in entire forgetfulness, and not in utter nakedness,
But trailing clouds of glory do we come from God,
Who is our home."

—William Wordsworth, Ode: Imitations of Immortality

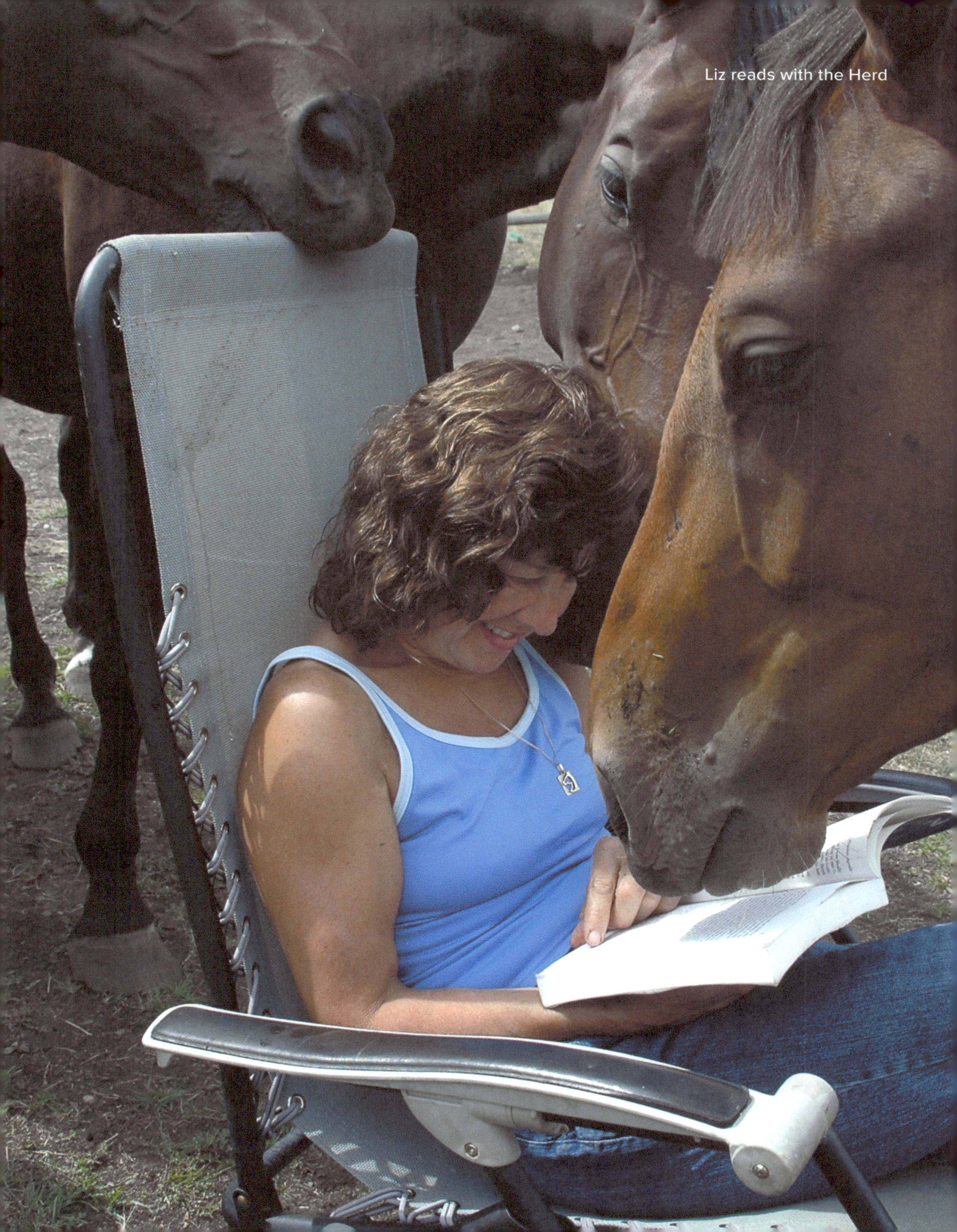
Liz reads with the Herd

FORWARD

by Carolyn Resnick

It has always been such a surprise to me that horses have played a major role in human history, yet we have missed an important contribution they have to offer us. We have developed deep friendships with horses, used them for transportation, labor, sports, even used mare's milk to support human life. Historically, however, we have missed another important contribution that horses have to share which is the wisdom that comes from their ability to connect to a consciousness that flows through all living beings.

This higher consciousness has an awareness of being that brings community together "As One." It is a guidance system that leads one to the best part of themselves.

I have devoted my life to helping people recognize the value of allowing horses to be our guides.

Horses speak to us in the language of nature that knits things into harmony and unity. From this awareness horses have a deep sense of social belonging that is passed down from generation to generation.

What I have discovered from horses is that all animals on this Earth have this natural wisdom. What we learn from horses is how to connect and communicate with all living things. From this awareness we are able to align with something greater than ourselves.

Many years ago, surfing the internet, I was looking to buy a horse painting. The moment I first laid eyes on the image of a painting of horses that appeared on my computer screen was the beginning of my enduring relationship with Liz Mitten Ryan. It was a painting that she had done titled "Harmony." The expression in the eyes of the horses and the connection between them portrayed in her artwork called to me.

Then I called her. I was surprised to learn that she had a long history with horses as did I. Liz could have been just an artist but there was more to it than that. I realized she had a retreat center where horses were sharing connections with humans; humans were lying down with horses, humans were being pillows for horses. They were lying on healing tables, and having the experience of riding at liberty in beautiful natural environments.

Liz Mitten Ryan's painting of horses that I so admired was not done from a photo but rather from her imagination and love for horses. The painting expressed the reality of what a horse is physically, emotionally and spiritually. I had found the painting that I wanted. The silent eloquence shining from the steady gaze of the horses' eyes in Liz's painting opened a window and magnified the grace of spirit that is reflected in the book that you are now holding in your hands.

Liz phoned and said, "Carolyn, after reading your book *Naked Liberty*, I am giving you the painting and I am going to deliver it in person."

Thus began a long enduring friendship of what we call the "Summit Sisters." When we shared our addresses, hers in Canada and mine in California, we found they shared the word Summit.

Liz Mitten Ryan has dedicated her life to bringing the healing energy and wisdom of horses to the world. I have appreciated Liz's body of work that connects with the very nature of horses. She offers programs that allow the horse to take part in guiding the student to find a deeper understanding of life through the wisdom of horses.

Liz brings great attention to this missing link to the world, through her award-winning books and programs at Gateway 2 Ranch.

Liz Mitten Ryan is focused on the value of horses to heal the body and soul not by using them, but rather connecting with horses in the most natural way and becoming "One with the Herd."

The message that I see that springs out of Liz's program is that horses can offer us a sense of community and belonging. People are being healed and hearts are being mended at her sacred land. Her programs are meant to guide the visitors to find their true nature, personal strength and inner knowingness from a wisdom horses have to share in the moments of the true BOND that unites us all.

The gate opens two ways, horse to human and human to horse. When both horse and human are aligned, harmony and well-being strengthens the spirit. From this alignment an inner guidance system is passed on from the wisdom of the Herd.

Turn these pages with love, celebration and joy. In the steady gaze of a horse is a silent language speaking of trust, strength and courage we would all long to possess as our own.

Carolyn Resnick,
Author of *Naked Liberty*, trainer and teacher of the Carolyn Resnick Method

INTRODUCTION

An unusual story, a family Herd of warmbloods, living as they would in the wild on a 320-acre sacred land of forests, hills, lakes and meadows, with a supportive human interface, a deeply bedded open barn to return to and all the best in natural horse care. Born into freedom, love, respect and spiritual equality, each horse is valued, encouraged and invited to share their truth. They are invited and rewarded, no pressure or punishment.

Over 16 years the "Herd" has co-authored four books (winning nine book awards), an award-winning documentary inspired by the first book One With the Herd, initiated Horse Friendship (www.naturalhorsefriendship.com) and horse play now called horse agility and invented a new form of horse therapy inviting people to lie on healing tables or spend quiet meditative time with them as a group. Most recently, the herd has inspired our latest award winning video titled 'Herd', which showcases the Equinisity retreats. The video is currently being presented at various film festivals. For more information visit (herdfilm.com).

The horses (currently 14), all related, one pony and a pet steer are all at liberty, either in their large barn/paddock or out on the land. They invite people from all over the world to spend time in nature and in their presence, coaching them to "be in their truth and listen to their intuition," a life-changing experience. Recently science has been proving many of the concepts that those privileged to spend unstructured time with horses have known. Horses, elephants and whales, partly due to their largeness, act as tuning forks, establishing a coherent heart rhythm and well-being, raising vibration, and allowing connection to higher consciousness; healing and helping humans to leave the walls of their egos for a more holistic connection with all life.

It is interesting to watch the dynamics of how the Herd envisions and reshapes the energy to form a new outcome. They are often in groups of two by two, mother and offspring, head to head in a V and together with other Herd members holding a larger pattern. Often there are four heads side by side (like four minds are better than one). They gather around a person or place and for hours will hold a deep meditative state, one or another occasionally dropping to the ground in a deep sleep to ground out the energy. Often they will drop at the feet of whomever they are working on, standing or lying in a circle around them. I simply watch in awe, suggesting one spot or another to people to maximize the energy or in the interest of safety as we are in the "Heart of the Herd."

As we experience more and more healing retreats it appears the Herd is evolving in its methods, and I am noticing how important their group dynamics are to the process. If one horse can be instrumental in horse therapy then many are miraculous.

There are many disciplines offered in horse therapy from psychology-based teachings that employ one horse and several humans to interpret, to therapeutic riding which again is humans guiding a human on a horse experience. I believe that the benefits of all of these methods will be increased by allowing the horses to offer teaching and healing at liberty, as they decide. We have been experimenting with safe enclosures such as low, one-railed round pens which people in wheelchairs could access and allow the Herd to interact from the outside of the rail, to large boxes (which double as large hay bale feeders in winter) so people can safely be surrounded by horses at liberty. Having that option , I still suggest people pick a safe wall or tree in the midst of where the Herd are gathered and in as close proximity as possible (like under one of the horse's noses) so they can receive the maximum exposure to the refiguring process.

I remember last year noticing the horses holding more circles and patterns in their healings either in the paddock, barn or in the hills. It seems by virtue of their clear connection to Source they are light years ahead of our present understanding!

The horses finally gave us a name for the process they share with each and every person called to come here. They have been spending more and more time holding constantly changing geometric patterns as a group in a trance state both in the barn and out on the land. I wonder at how they can possibly be so fat as they spend hours in this process. Interestingly, the name came through two women enrolled in a "Herd Rituals" retreat, Bev, who was meditating with the Herd and got a microchip of information and then a "D" word that she couldn't decipher and a common description of what they were doing, "zipper." Then, we were sharing that information with Candice and the word that came through her was Dio-transconfiguration. Interesting. In a Herd, all minds are joined and the girls were experiencing that aspect of Herd ritual. Dio meaning any supernatural being worshipped as controlling some aspect of life who is the personification of a force. Trans, meaning relating to molecular structure where the particular atoms or groups lie on opposite sides of a given plane in a molecule. Configuration, an arrangement of form in a particular 3-Dimensional relationship of

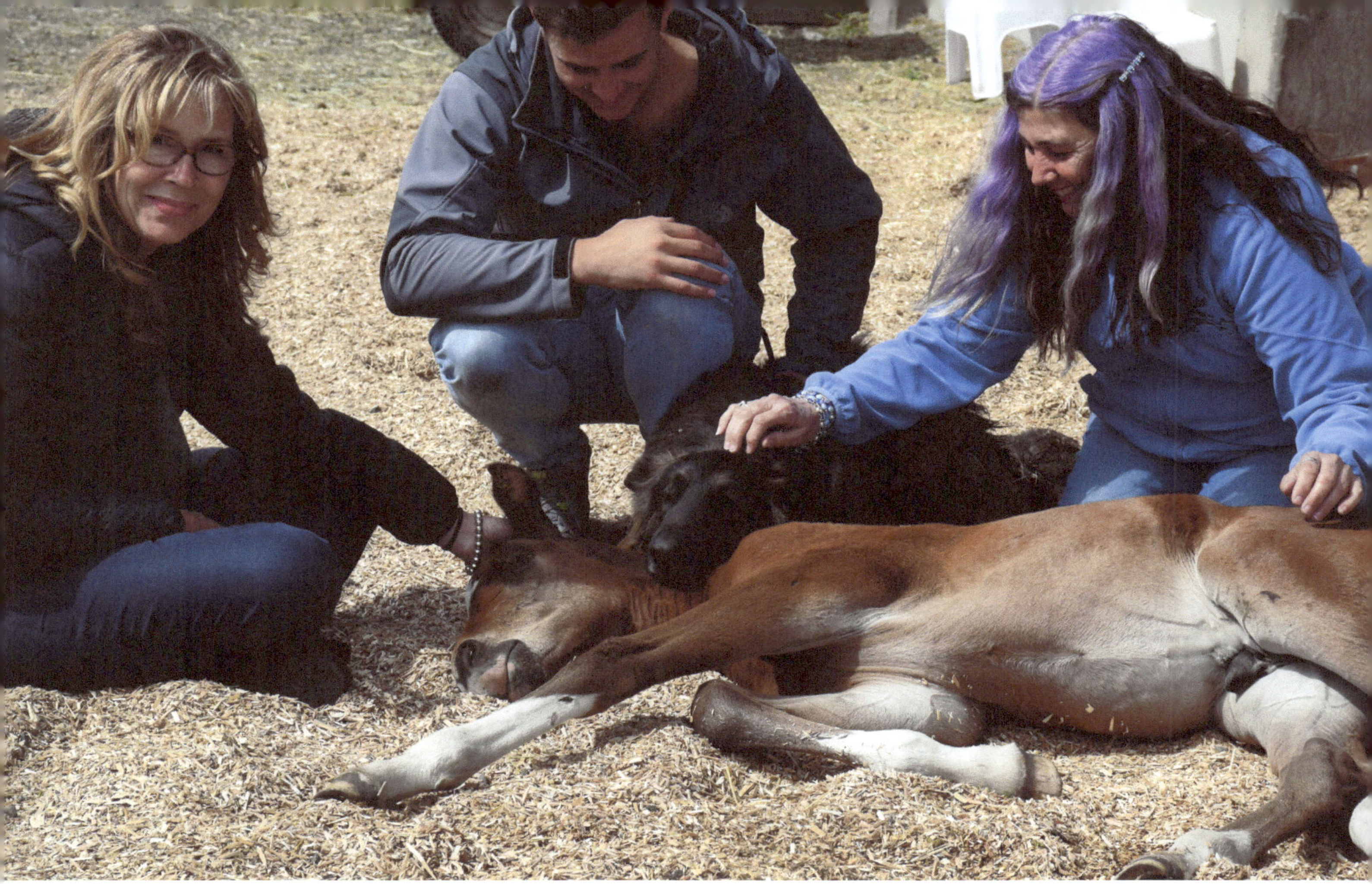

atoms in a molecule defined by the bond between them. Well, that was a breakthrough and certainly explained the geometric patterns they were embodying.

As God's consciousness in matter, each unique created thing is a perfect and important aspect of the One consciousness, the All consciousness. When we discover our soul's dream, the dream that serves the higher good, the greater dream, that most perfect vision for our lives serves the highest good for others and all creation too. How can God experience the softness of fur, the look of love, the touch and splendor of all the Earth except through the physical senses of all his creatures and his creations? When we focus on all of these blessings and the gifts in our lives we multiply the "loaves and fishes" and feed the multitudes. When you ask yourself "Is this the dream for me" you will receive the answer and the opportunity to re-evaluate and take a step in the direction of your "Heart's Desire."

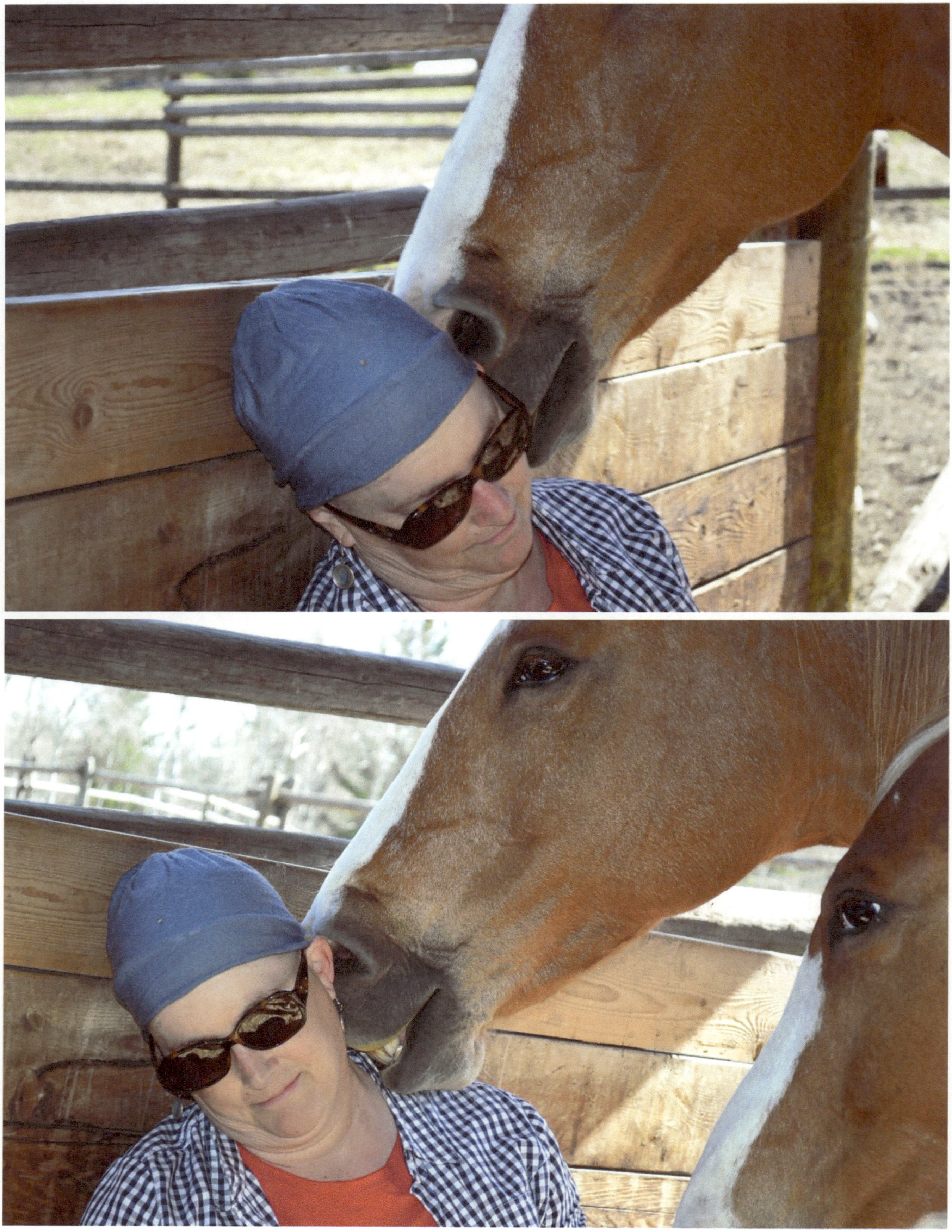

Epona clears the effects of chemotherapy

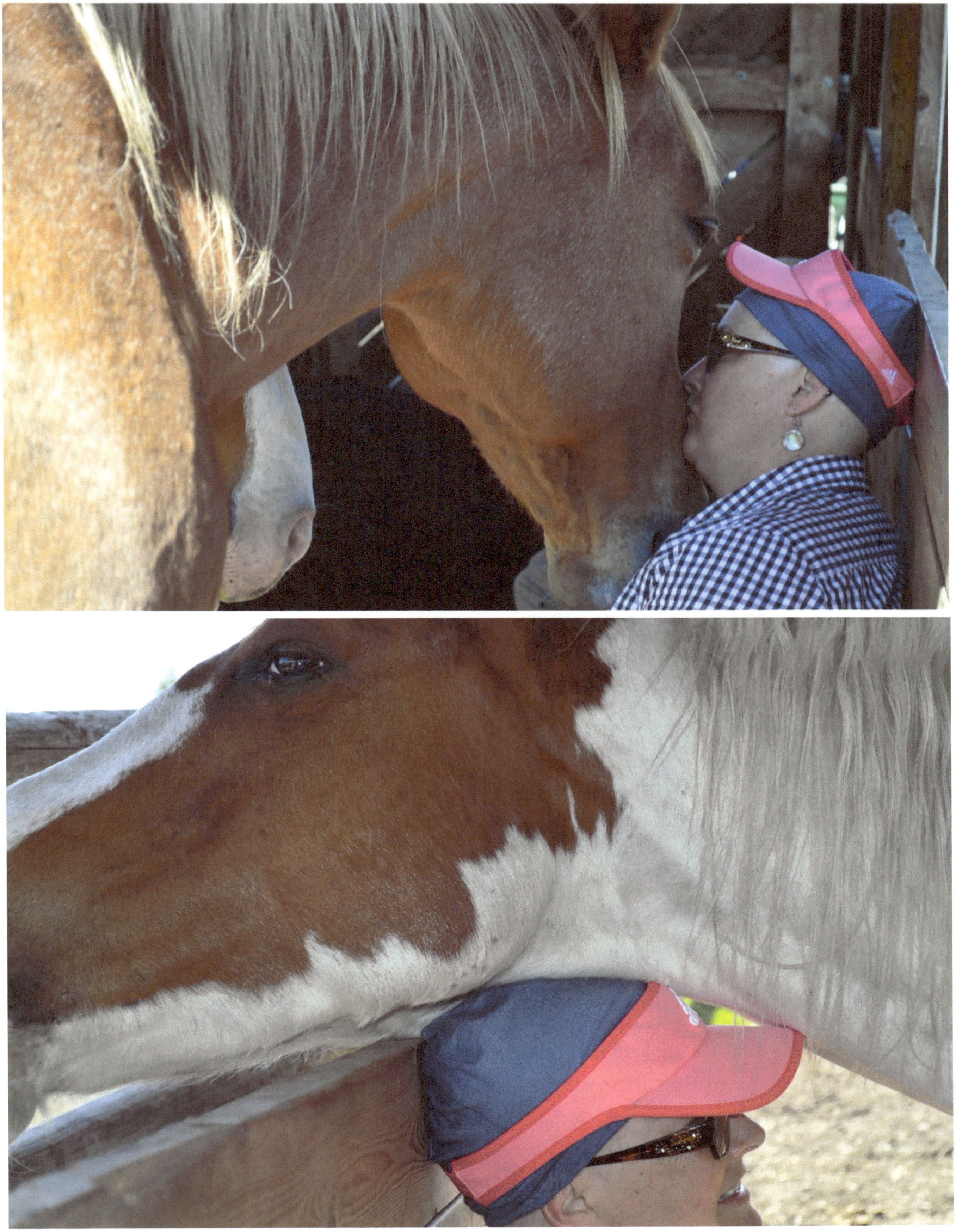

Epona clears the effects of chemotherapy

I have been receiving e-mails from all over the globe (and even some nearby) from people who have been called by horses and want to take it to the next level. Whether for their own personal relationship with equines and how that translates to the rest of their lives, to enhance their profession in equine-related services or just because they feel called to discover a new dimension in life and feel entitled to explore the possibility of that expression, enlightenment and calling. Some can afford to come, some want scholarships and some want to discuss an exchange or collaboration. What is exciting is that all have been called by horses and by spirit (and by the horses' network with other animals and the natural world) to step up to the plate and be the change we want to see in the world.

The world as we know it is on its way to extinction. The power hungry corporations, as the dinosaurs, are running out of fuel and soon the commodity of value will be consciousness, as in our connection to higher consciousness and understanding of our spiritual attributes.

Science and spirituality are now walking hand in hand as new discoveries enable the individual through the power of focus and intent to create the world of their dreams.

Yes, we can change the world one mind at a time—that is the only way we can make a difference.

Animals everywhere—lions, whales, orangutans, elephants, hippos, dogs, cats, horses—have their own YouTube channels; are they really so different from humans? They LOVE, just like we do; their essence and ours is one with the only life force—the ALL.

Connect, believe, transform and listen to your calling. It is the child in all of us who yearns for the secret garden where we can all walk and talk directly with God and all life.

I have so enjoyed watching people open to and be healed and inspired through the stillness of nature and the powerful connection of the Herd. Sharing in their revelations and following their path to fulfillment has been an immense reward for me and has helped me grow vicariously through those creations. It is time to take the understanding to a higher level, calling out illusion, living our truth and running "naked into fear" knowing that we are safe and guided if only we ask.

The horses have been increasingly both deeply connected and powerful in their healing. We have been getting some tough cases, yet they uniquely work with each individual in surprising ways. One lady came fresh out of chemo and they kept tipping her head and blowing in her left ear for long periods. Another lady came a year after chemo and they did the same thing to her. That was the first time I had seen them do that. Another lady arrived and the horses all began telling me there was something with her lower back, legs and lower body. I asked her if she had any injuries there and she answered, "No, I don't think so…at least I don't remember." Well that prompted Luxy, our schoolmaster and grandchildren's horse, who has never done this before to bite her in the butt as she was passing… Well, no bruises but that awakened the muscle memory of several experiences over many years that she wouldn't allow herself to release, all held in that area. She had just about severed her lower legs, broken an ankle and had had countless trauma to her backside. The horses kept holding up their legs and touching them, putting their feet on stools she had sat on. And Crystal repeatedly did the strangest thing I have ever seen a horse do and I didn't think was possible; Every time the lady came near her she lifted her back legs one by one out to the side at a 45 degree angle and then did a bunny hop backward for about 6 feet? She did this the entire visit, and I have not seen her do it ever before or since! The other thing Crystal did was so endearing. She coaxed the same lady who was unable to climb the ladder from the barn rung by rung up to the floor above. First she translated that she was going to do this by first putting one foot, then another on the stool the lady had just left and by wedging herself between the ladder and the wall until we both got the idea of what she wanted. Then, as the lady took one step at a time, Crystal would go to the ladder and rub her head on it, then to the stall wall and rub her behind. She did this several times for every rung of the ladder. Then she looked fondly upward like a mother who had just fledged her child to the first day of school.

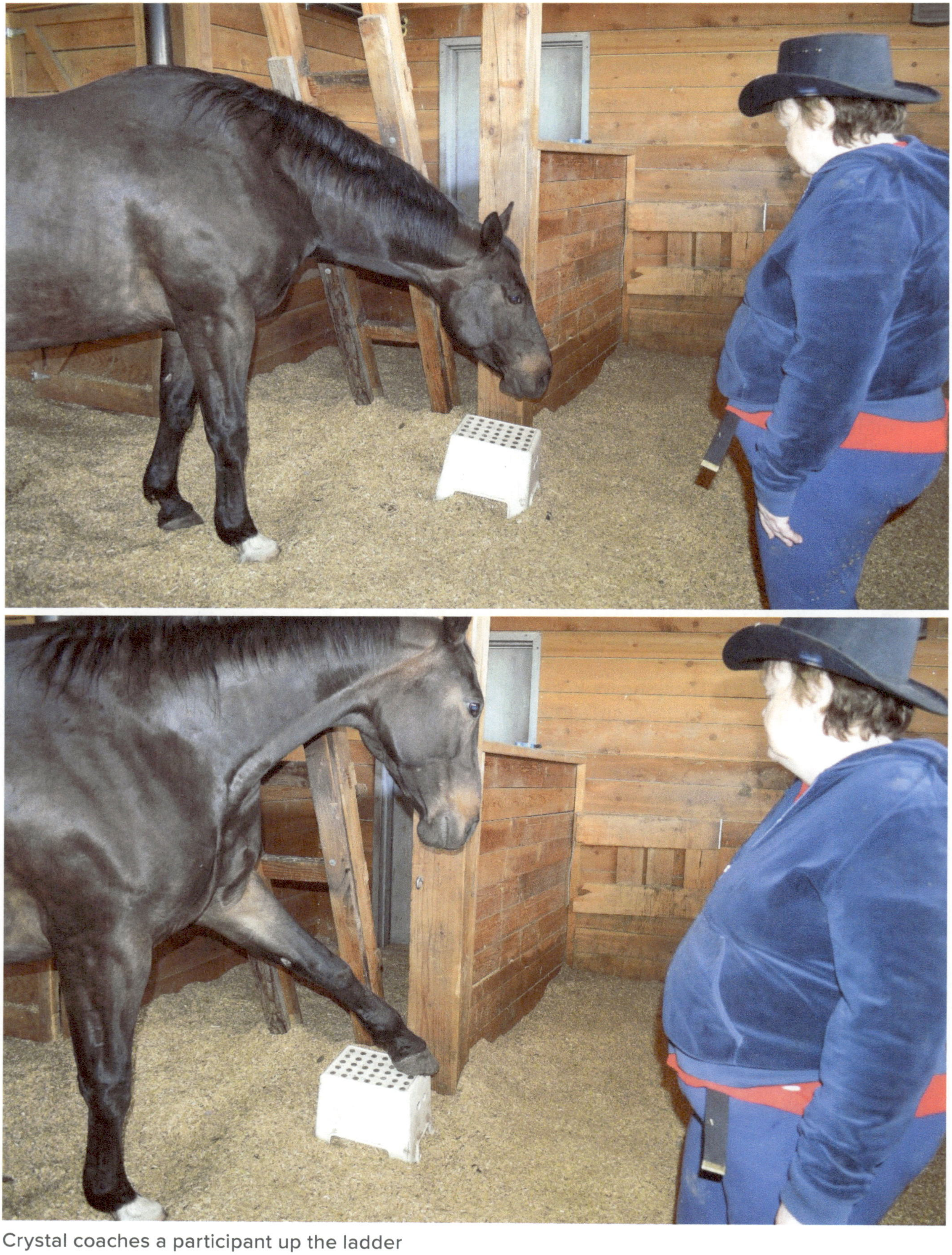

Crystal coaches a participant up the ladder

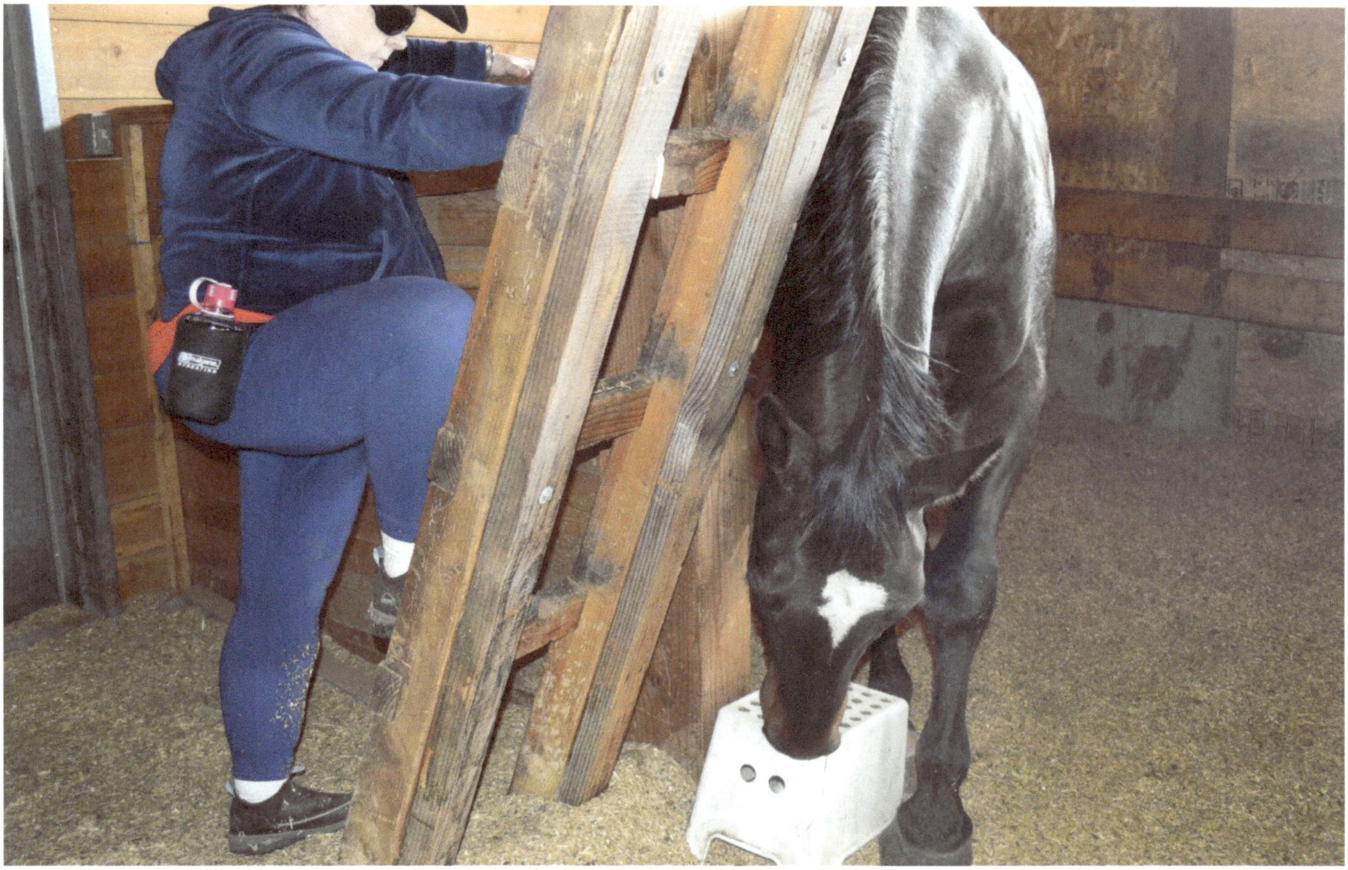

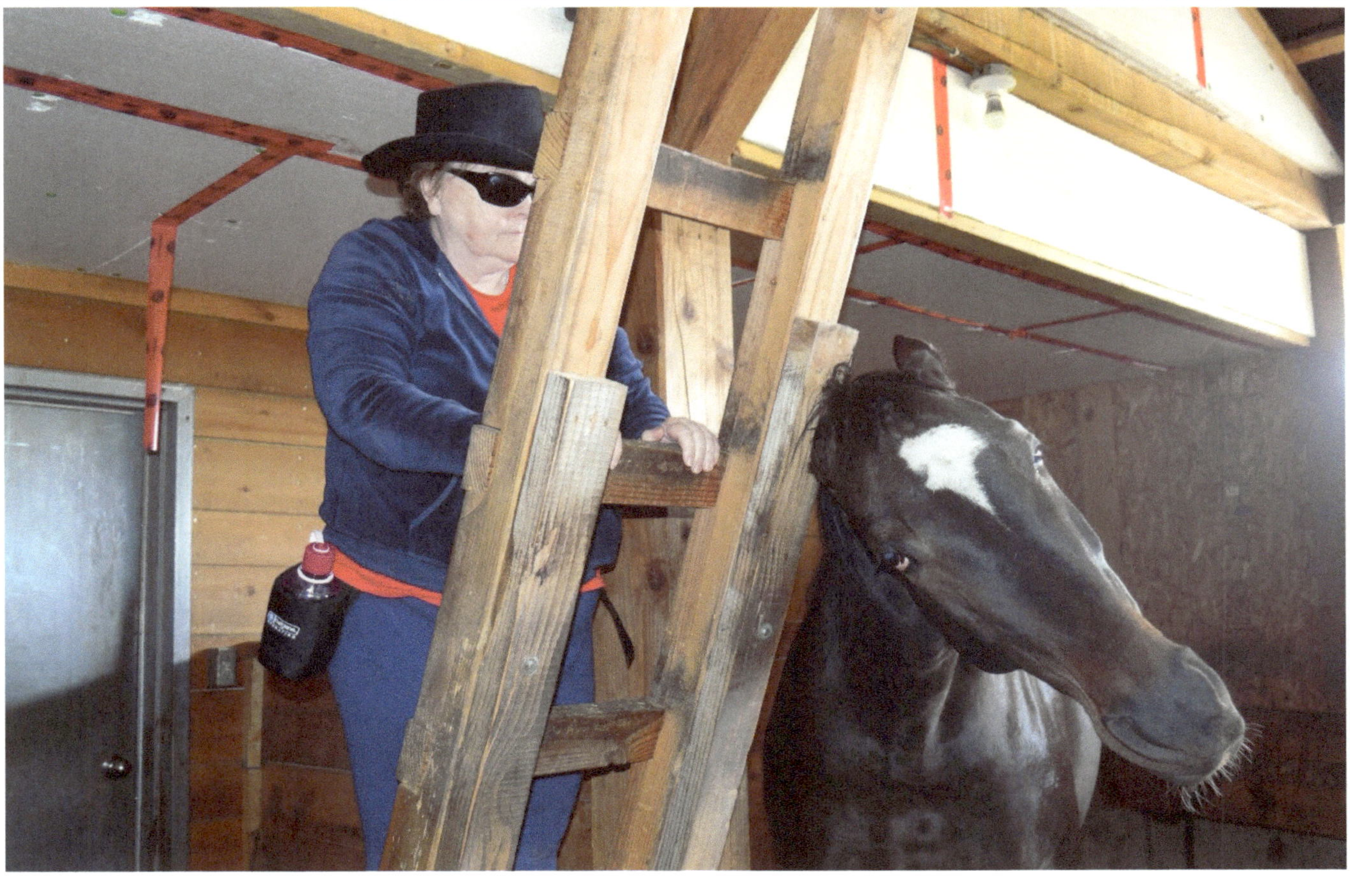

Crystal coaches a participant up the ladder

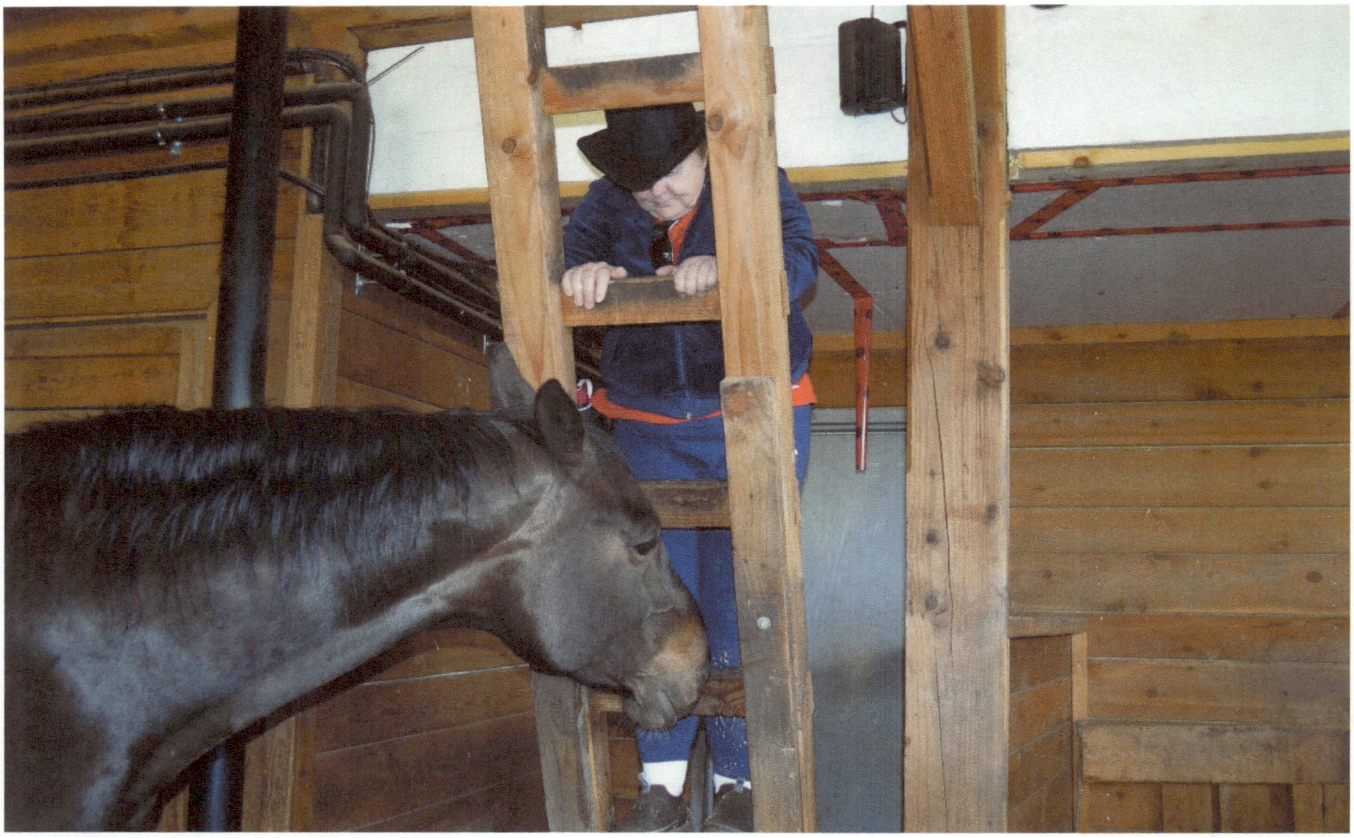

Crystal coaches a participant up the ladder

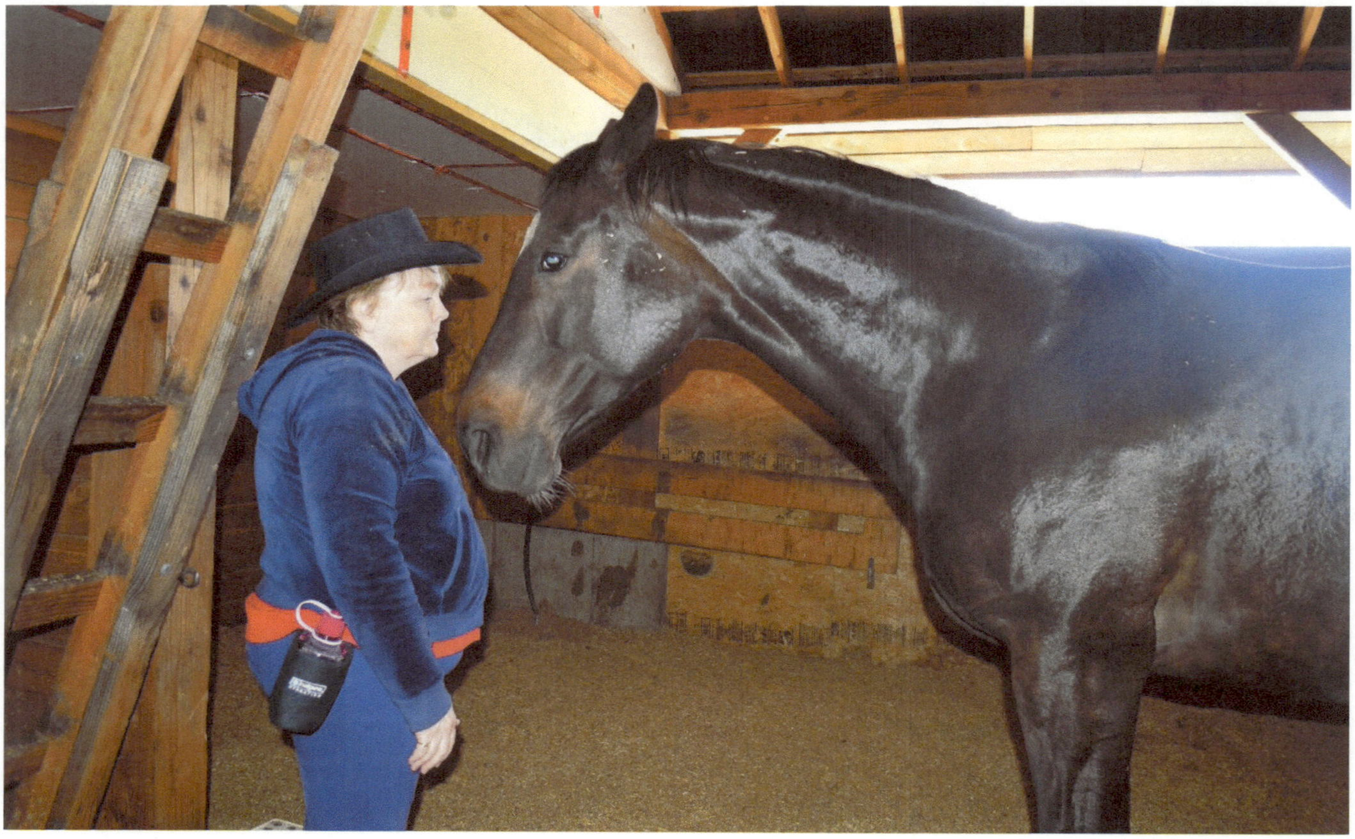

Job well done!

I am finding so much interest in Equinistic Healing Certification, as students of other more well-known horse therapies are looking to take their practices further and allow the horses to take over the "reins" (or take away the reins) and truly show us the powerful potential of human /animal affiliation. As long as we are guiding and translating the healing experience, the horses are not allowed to show us the powerful application of Sacred Healing, which allows the One Consciousness to flow by freely allowing the principles of creation through sacred design, raising vibration through focus, sound, form or pattern, and light.

Animals around the globe in connection and communion with the Earth are holding the vibration of deep healing. The horses are exhibiting some very unusual behavior and forming meditation circles all over the land. We find them in pockets on the highest hills, in the meadows, all standing, heads together, eyes open, off on some other plane, sometimes for hours. This is not typical for horses out in lush pasture. Mornings in the paddock find them huddled in the barn and birthing stall in geometric patterns, glazed eyes and deep intention focused on important issues. They invite us to join them and participants who sit in the barns with them are quickly surrounded and profoundly changed. On occasion they come to the healing tables but this new work seems more important and my job as their facilitator is simply to allow and try my best to translate their communication to guests.

This is one of the only settings in the world where horses can live as they would in the wild but still have a loving, caring interface with humans. They are, as well, considered spiritual equals, teachers and healers and are invited to interact at liberty when and how they choose. "Invitation and reward" as opposed to pressure and punishment. Also instruments of torture have been abolished so no whips, spurs, bits, restraints, no metal shoes… What is amazing is that these powerful creatures still choose to submit to our requests and even enjoy it as they are paid handsomely in carrots and low-cal horse treats (also, lots of love and praise). It is strange that almost all other trained animals are rewarded for their efforts but somehow this has been avoided with horses. We are well on the "road to change" in how we consider animals and their rights and freedoms. Now that it is considered mainstream to share connection and conversation, I'm pretty sure there are a lot of horses whispering in their human's ears.

Please visit www.equinisity.com for pictures, videos, stories, books, etc.

Over 10 years of channeled material "From the Horses" has been given to Liz in monthly newsletters and the following is a collection of these messages.

March, 2006:

Speaking for the animals, we are here as fellow beings on this planet to bring perspective to our mutual journey. How differently do you view the world in our company and on our backs? Just being in our presence brings you joy, peace, love and freedom. We accept you unconditionally. It is time to let go of your limited thinking, to believe in the possibility of one mind, one life. We are all that one being; that one becoming. Together we are evolving to become the possibility of our most cherished dreams.

Fear is the only barrier. Let go of your fear and remember the garden; we are waiting for you to join us. We will help you—just speak with us as you do each other; send us the picture in your mind and trust in your intuition when we answer you. Spend time with us without agenda, like you would a friend. Entertain the quiet that is found in nature; release the need to control each situation and you will find the treasure that lies buried beneath your ambition. We are all one with God and God is all there is; relax and enjoy the experience.

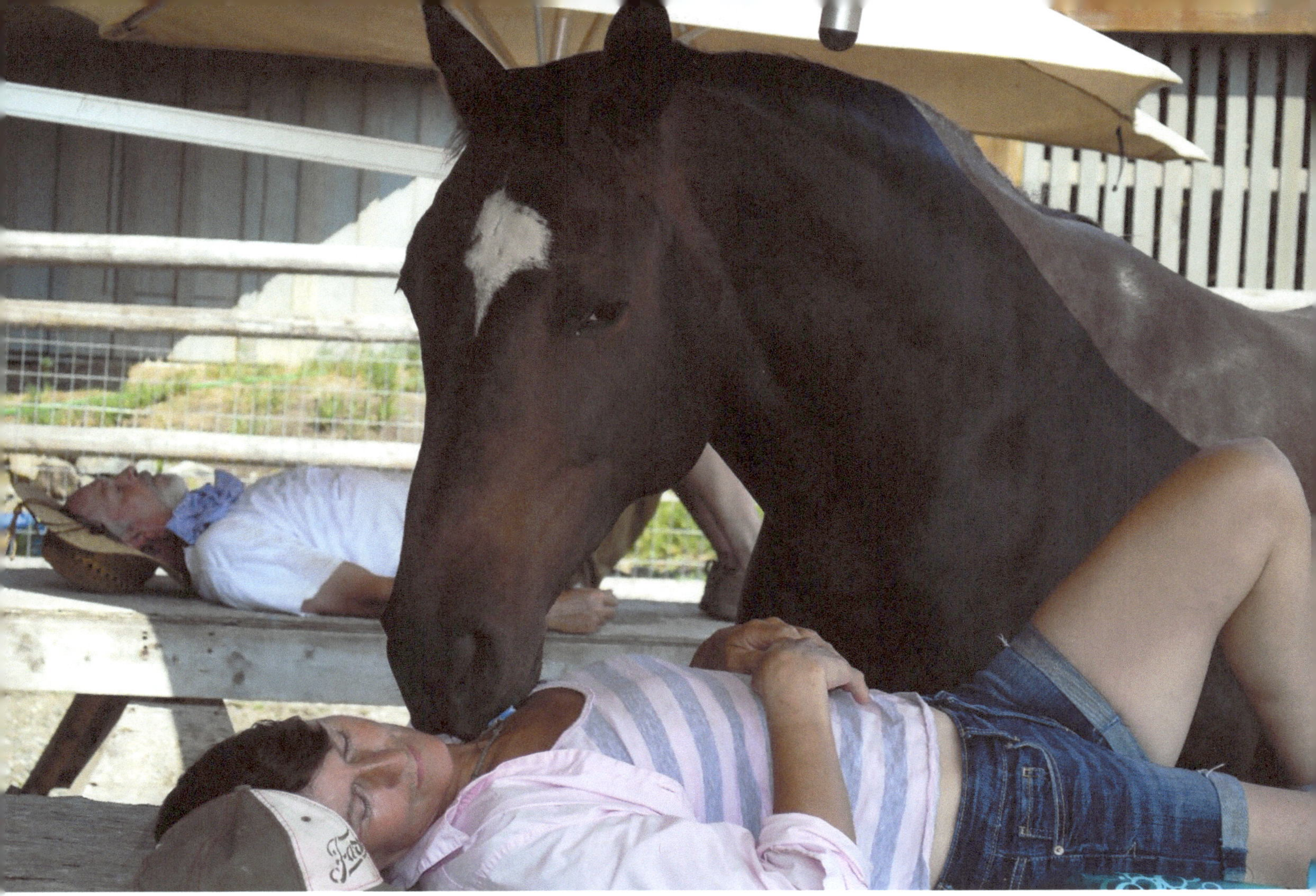

And this excerpt from the same newsletter:

Kevin, my husband, invented a wonderful word the other day, which embodies this quote from One with the Herd. "I am living a dream that continues to expand beyond the boundaries of my physical self, to the greater soul of all life, where what I dream for myself is a gift for all to enjoy, and what I give to all life, I give to myself. Life is discovering itself through us." The word is "EQUINISITY"—the gift of finding the unexpected and truly important perspective through the clear and almost 360-degree vision of the equine.

Well, 60 plus newsletters later, nothing has changed.
Following are the sequential excerpts:

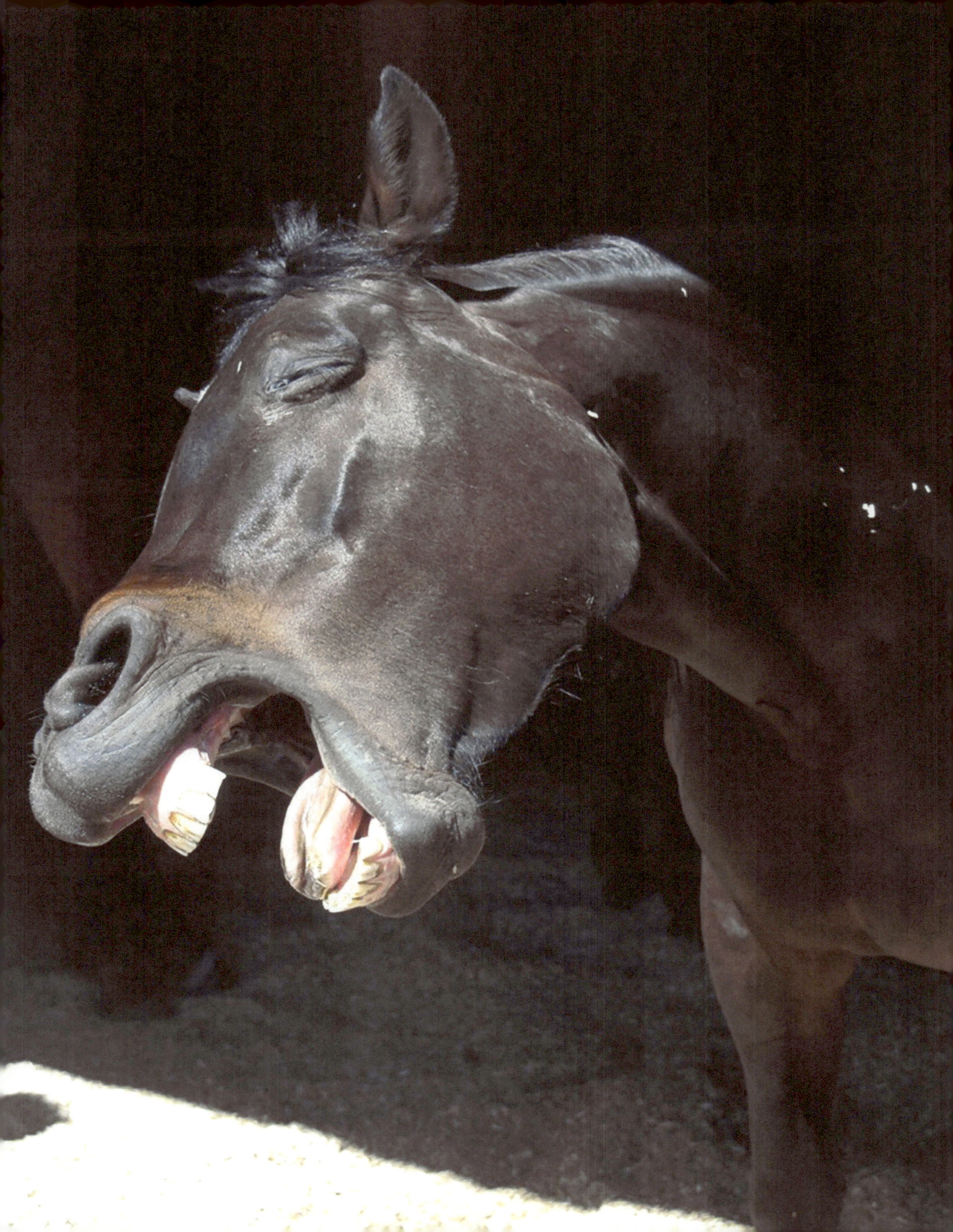

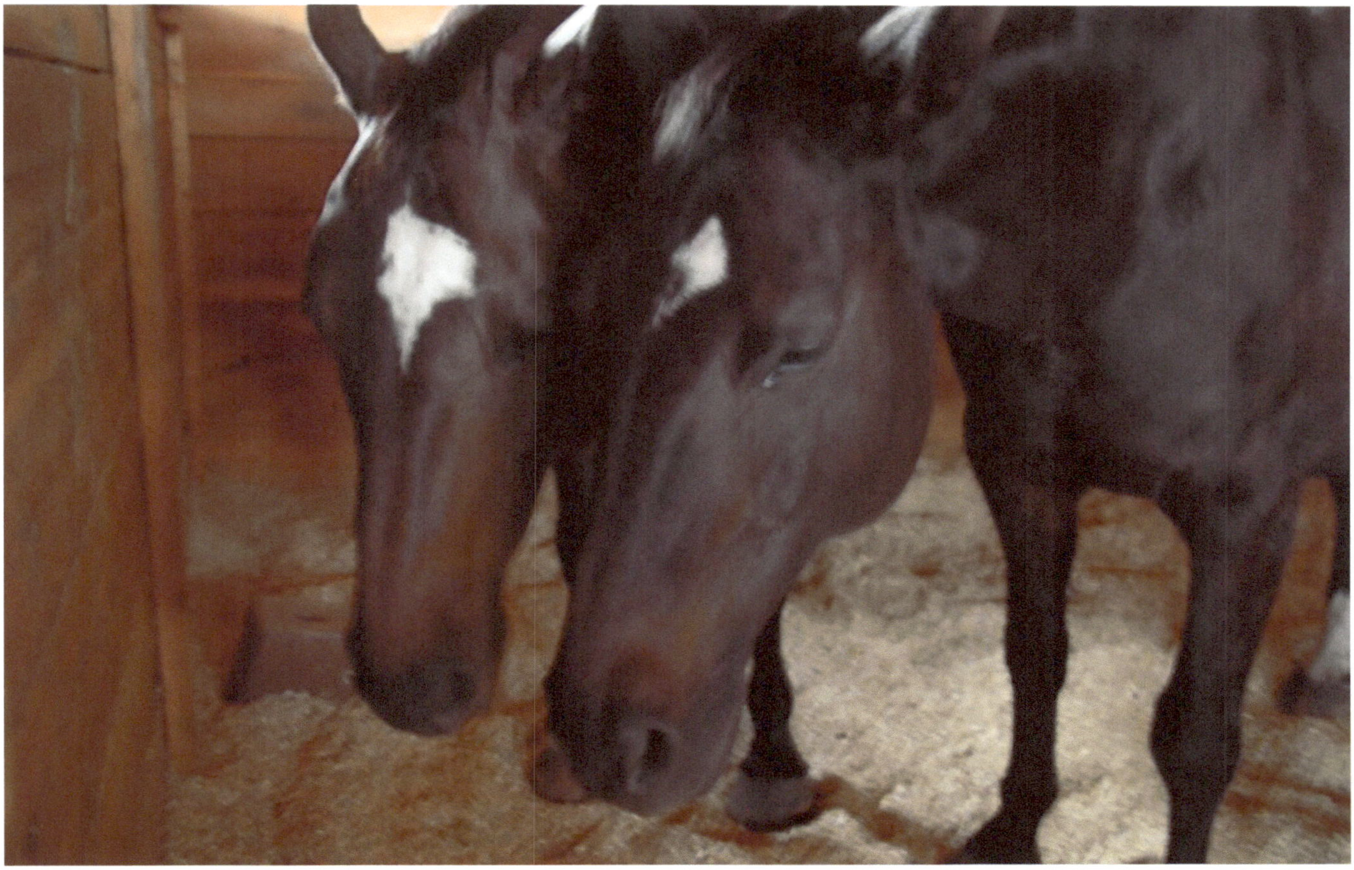

We are all here on Earth living in a time of great change. Because of our communication systems, a small change in consciousness can affect millions of minds—an individual can change the world. We often hear you say, "What can I do? I am one small person?" You can hold the integrity for your whole species, you can maintain empathy for other species and for the whole organism of the Earth. It is exponential; all minds are joined. One mind touches many others who in turn touch many others and soon mass belief tips the scales in a whole new direction. Don't be content with the status quo. Examine your values, connect to the purer, higher consciousness that encompasses all of the natural world and then listen to that intuitive connection. This one aspect of existence that we are now experiencing will be over in the blink of an eye and what will be left but the intangible qualities that are ours forever.

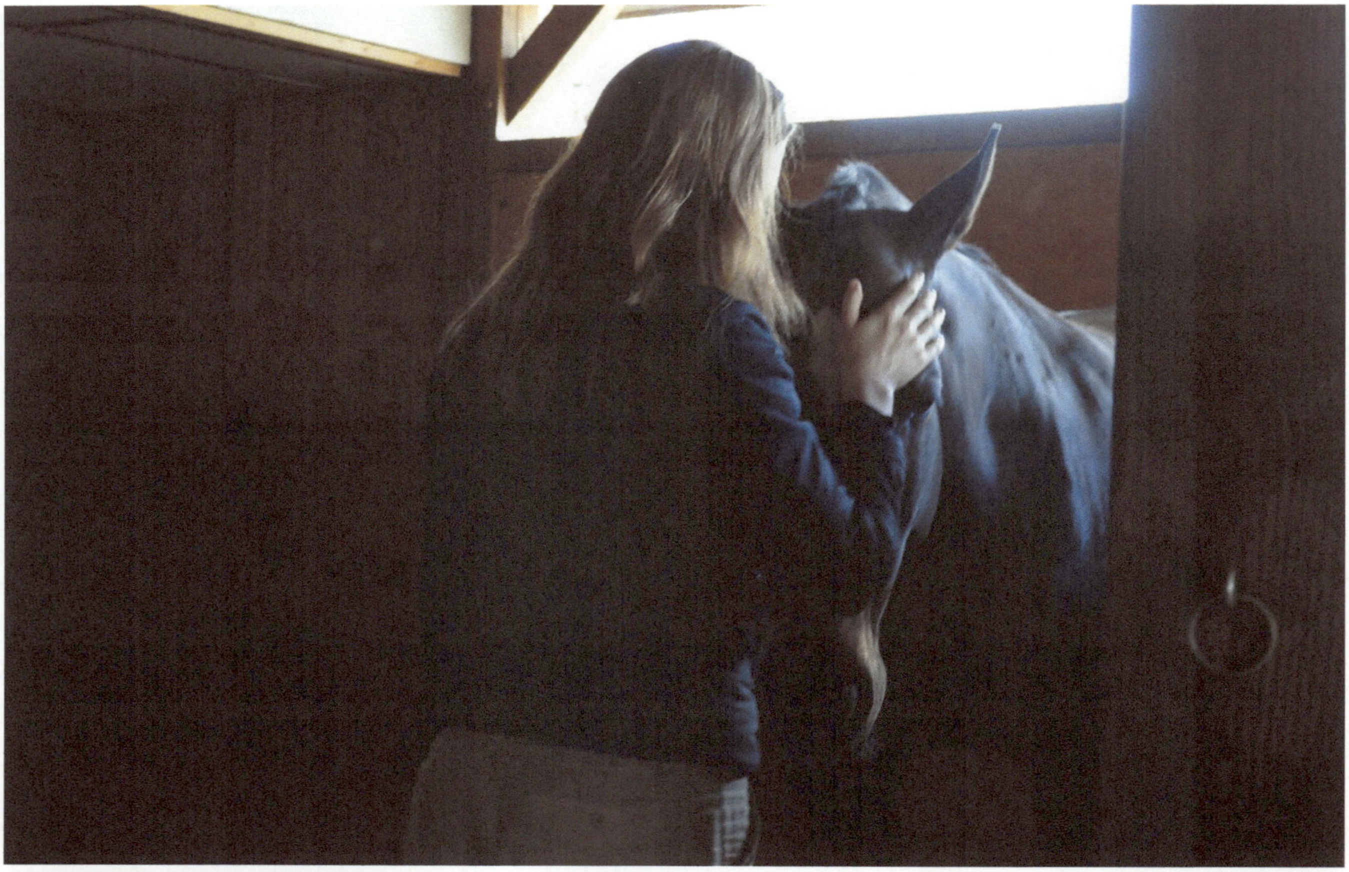
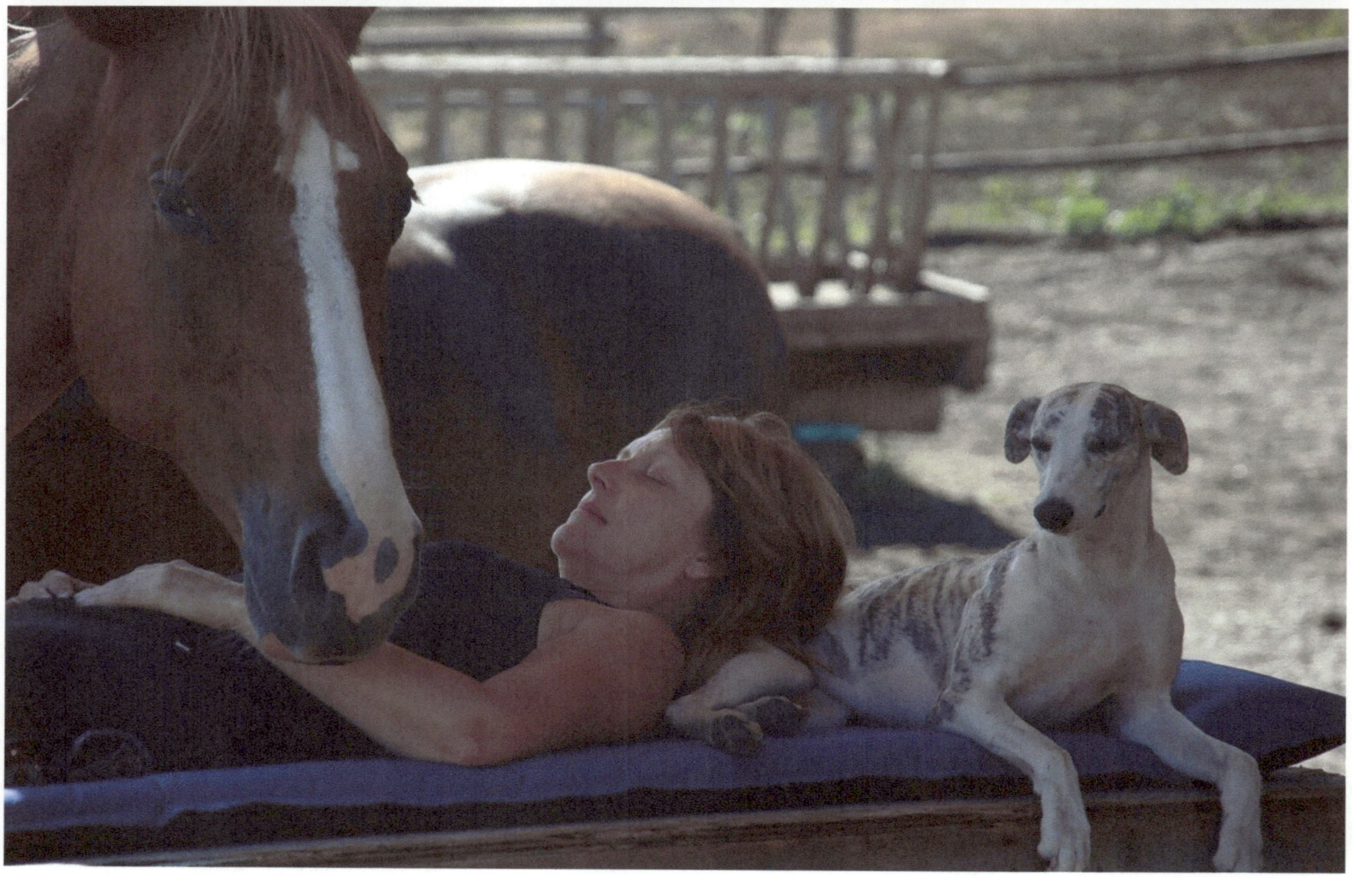

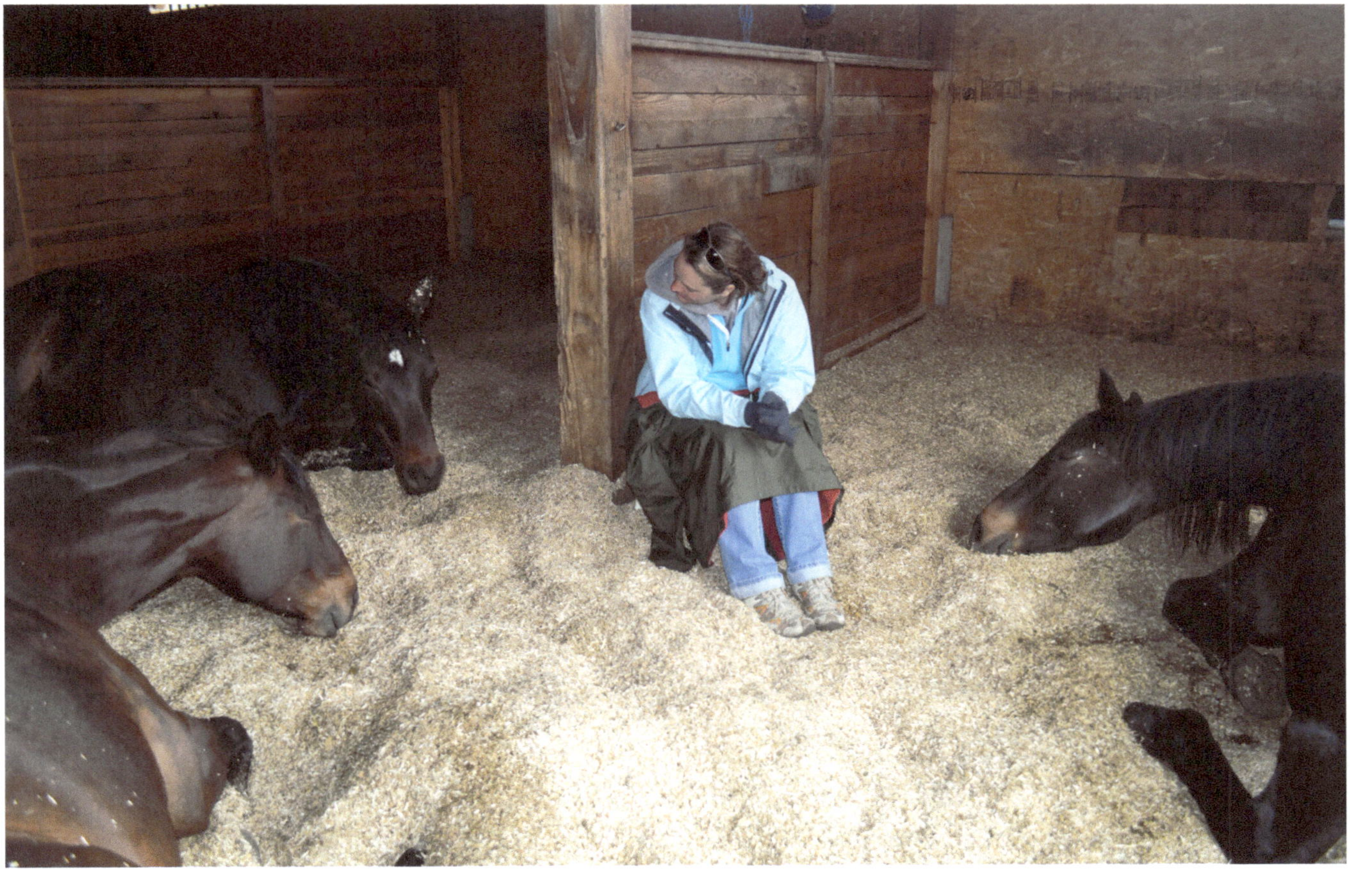

Horse wisdom is very simple. Humans tend to equate knowledge with wisdom: For horses wisdom and truth imply "isness" or an inherent and unique aspect of the ALL (or God) that can only be experienced moment by moment as its truth or "isness" changes and evolves through our life's journey. The important thing to remember is that it is ours.

Our own absolute truth is who we are; the perfect embodiment of spirit in our unique and individual physical form. When we allow free flow of spirit by connecting to the ALL and intuitively tuning into that immeasurable wealth of wisdom then we become our truth. Humans often seek more to impress others than themselves and by so doing lose the truth of who they are. We can help you with this for we are teachers of truth and we will call you on anything less. Come and play with us. Come without structure and we will teach you about unstructure. Connect with us and through us the All, the infinite, and you will come to know truth.

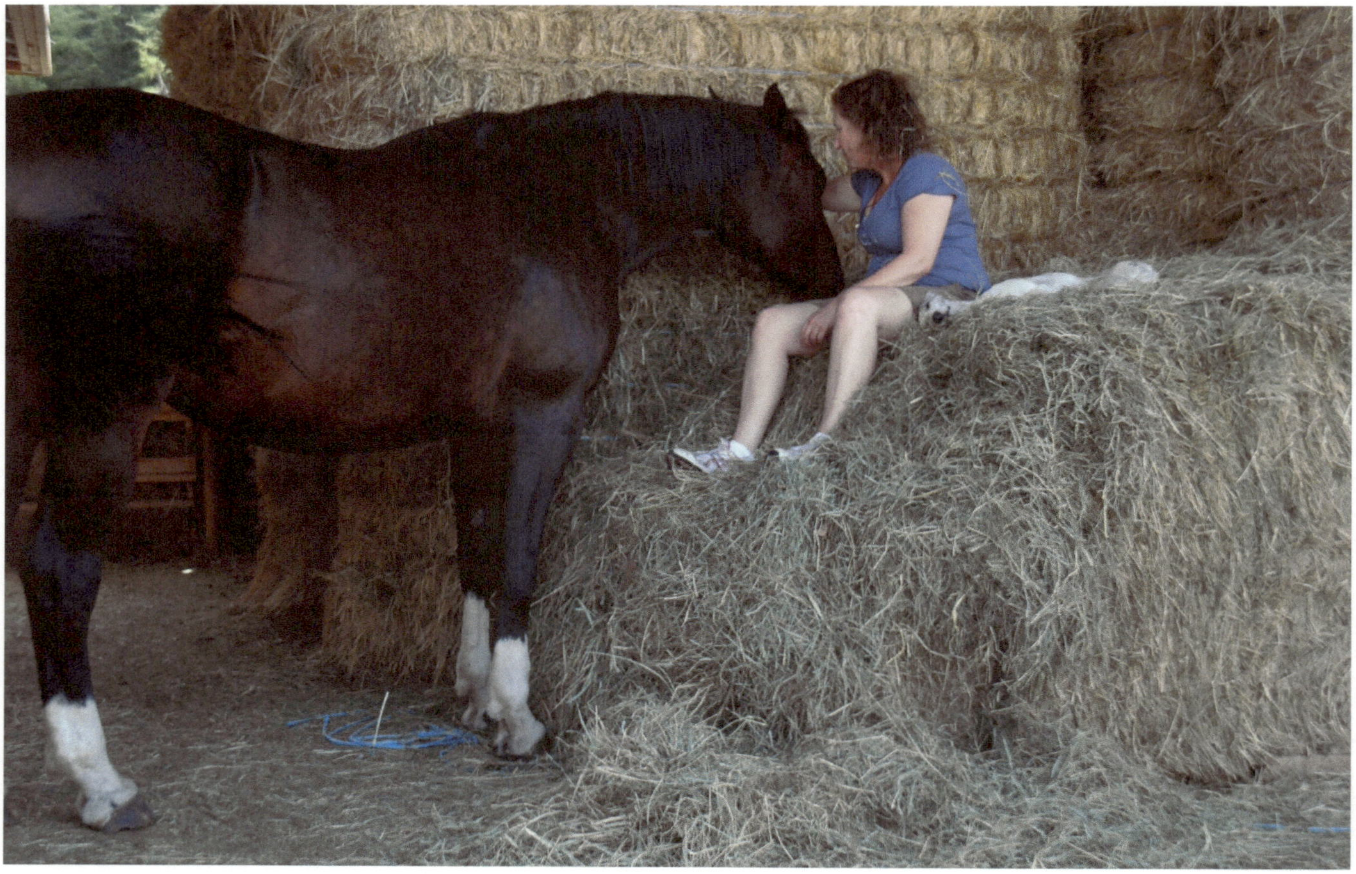

First of all, we are encouraged by the ever-growing interest in our species. As the consciousness level of all life on Earth is increasing, interspecies telecommunication is becoming more common. Because animals are not held prisoner by the ego when you connect to us, you have access to higher consciousness in general, and connection to higher consciousness is the ultimate freedom. It is our purpose to teach you the way to freedom and to help you to refine and strengthen the qualities that will lead you there. Those qualities are absolute truth, clear focus, higher authority and complete trust. We are powerful reflections of your choices. Allow yourself to walk toward peace, unconditional love and communion with all life and we will meet you there.

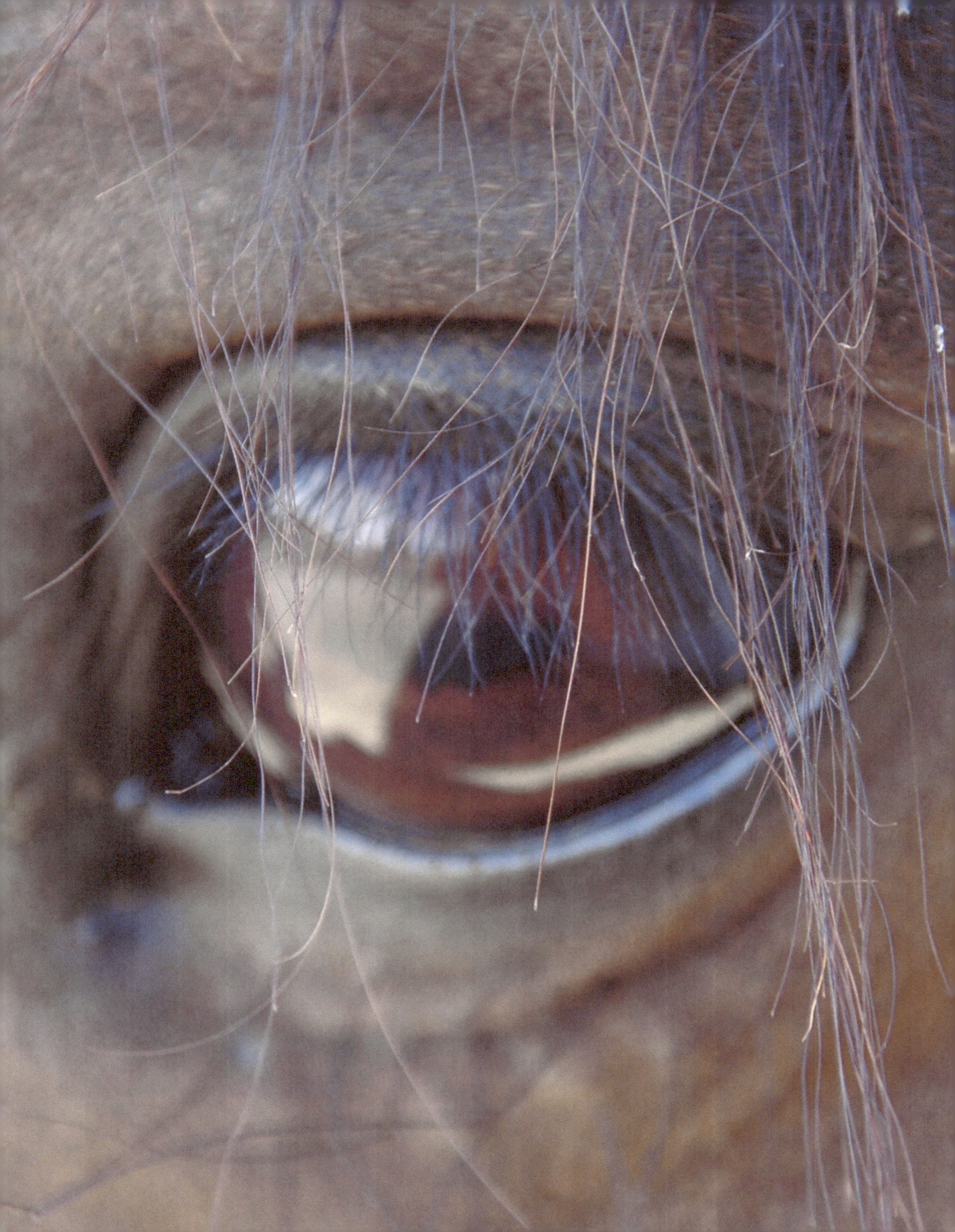

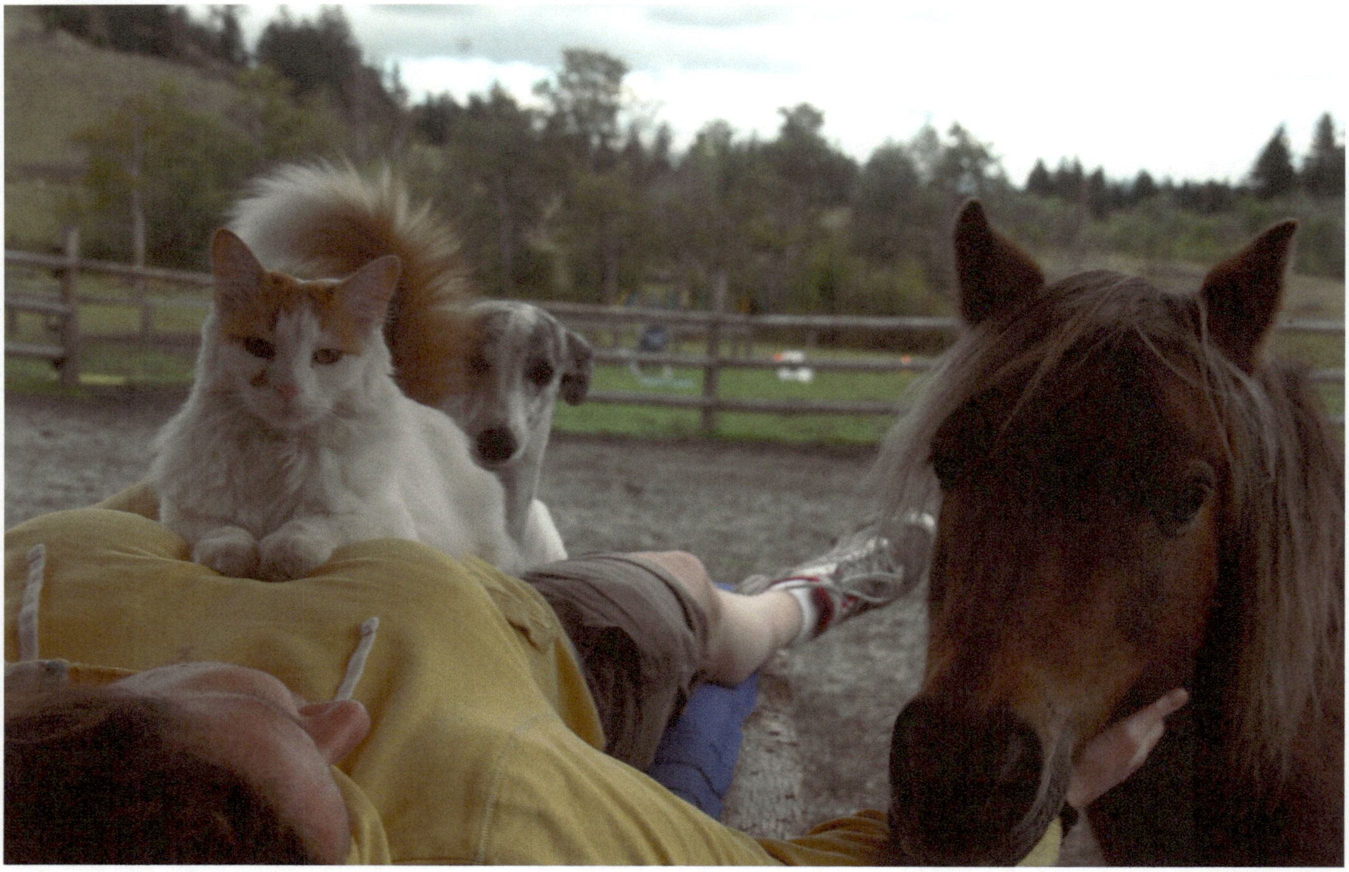

This is a time of great change. Animals are stepping to the forefront of inter-dimensional communication. Everyone alive today was born to an era when humans followed one path and animals another. It is time for us to reconnect with the Earth and each other. There are many secrets that you have overlooked in your hurry to succeed; to accumulate material wealth. It is spiritual wealth that is the incorruptible possession. We have many gifts to share with you, and we encourage you to hear our voice. All that is necessary is to spend time in our company without agenda. Observe our behavior in pasture with our fellow horses, walk with us, interact without restraint, listening and talking, grooming and playing. There is far more to learn at play than at work. We are waiting to meet with you at that place where we are equals and encourage your friendship.

Cats, dogs and horses have been your companions for millennia. We have surrendered our fate into your keeping, such is our trust in you. We know your hearts and your spirit, and we know that there, you are free. It is your minds that limit and confuse you. Turn off the chatter, let go of the confusion and allow the stillness, the quiet to fill you with its peace. The peace is within us all, but you revisit it only in moments. Stay awhile longer—let us take you there and sit beside you in communion and worship this most precious gift. It is there we can speak with our hearts and share in the memory of our true kinship with each other and life itself. We are all children of the Earth, seeded from the heavens where the ALL (or God) shines eternally. We are eternally spiritually free, and when the memory awakens, we become fully actualized spiritual beings on this and all planes. We must give all to have all, that is the secret.

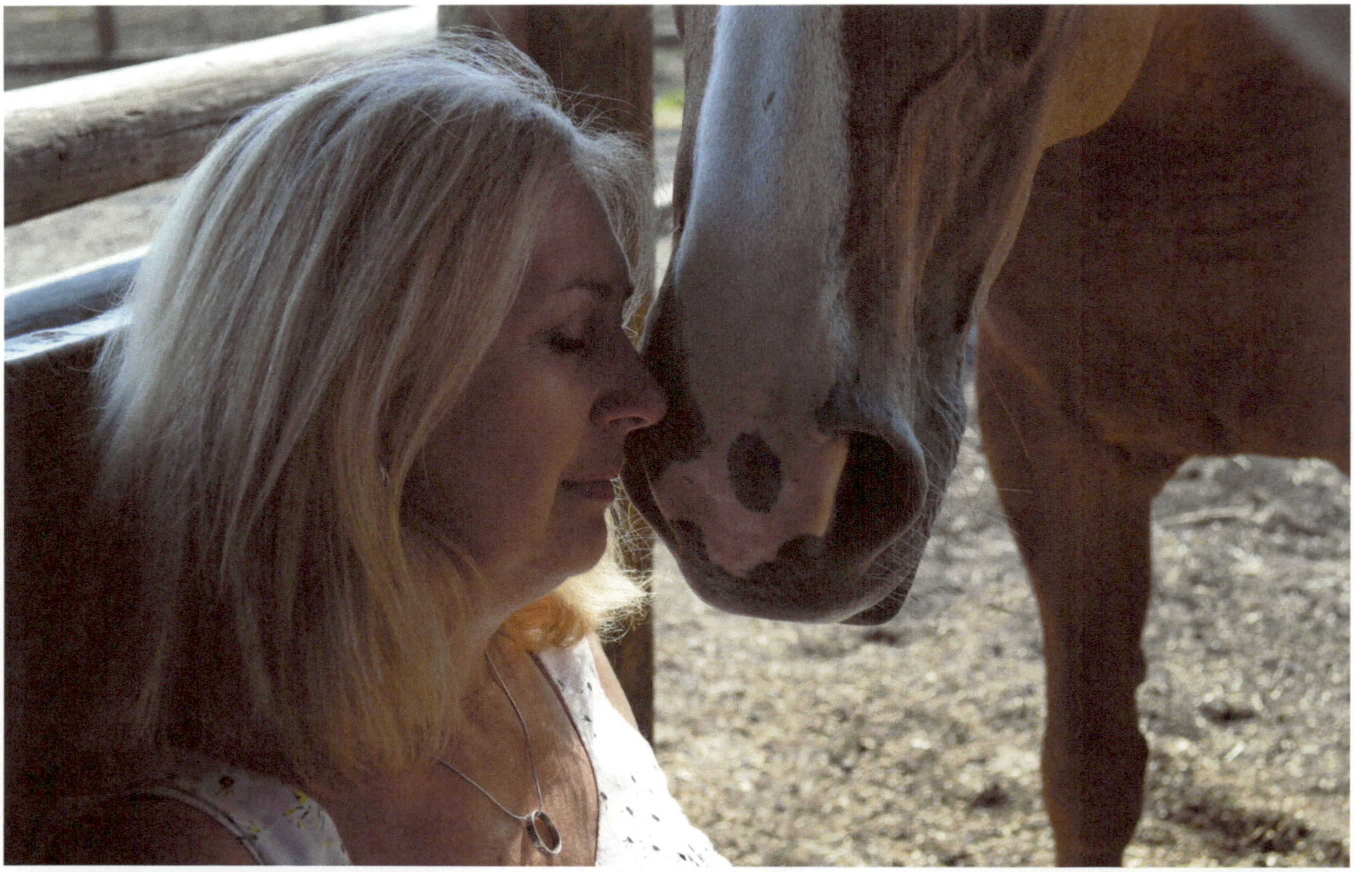

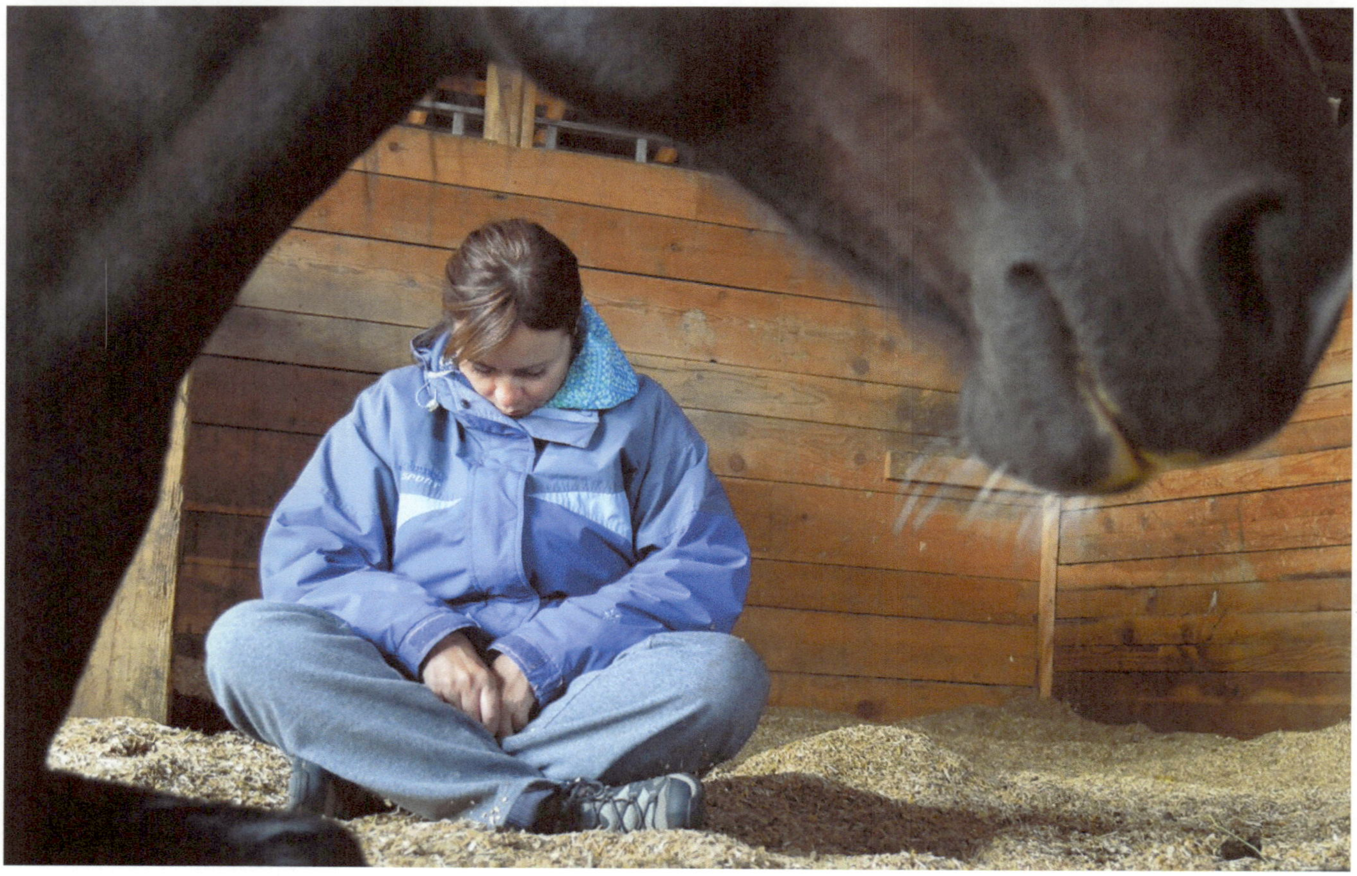

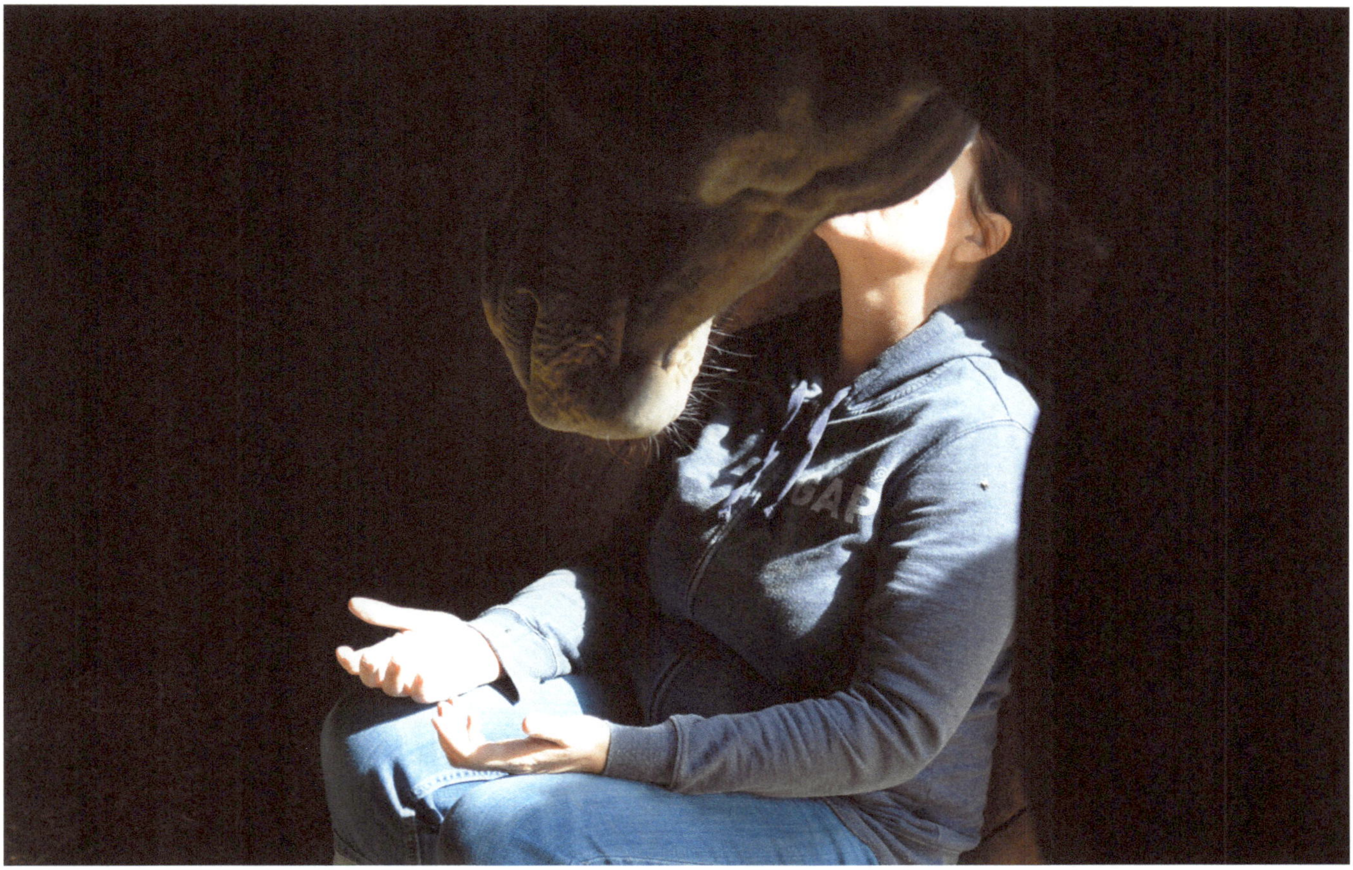

Feelings Believing

Instinct is a quality associated with animals which people refer to when they wonder at our ability to somehow know what to do or where to go in any situation. They marvel as flocks of birds unerringly travel thousands of miles back to the same place each year, as mothers birth and guide their babies to the udder, teaching them to follow a nudge or a nicker. Instinct is no different from the human quality of intuition. The difference is that animals are fluent in the skill and people only occasionally use this inherent ability. It is simply the gift of connecting to and following the nudge or the nicker of the all-knowing force that births us all. When we clearly see and follow that vision, then the Divine plan can unfold in myriad diversity, unerringly perfect in every way.

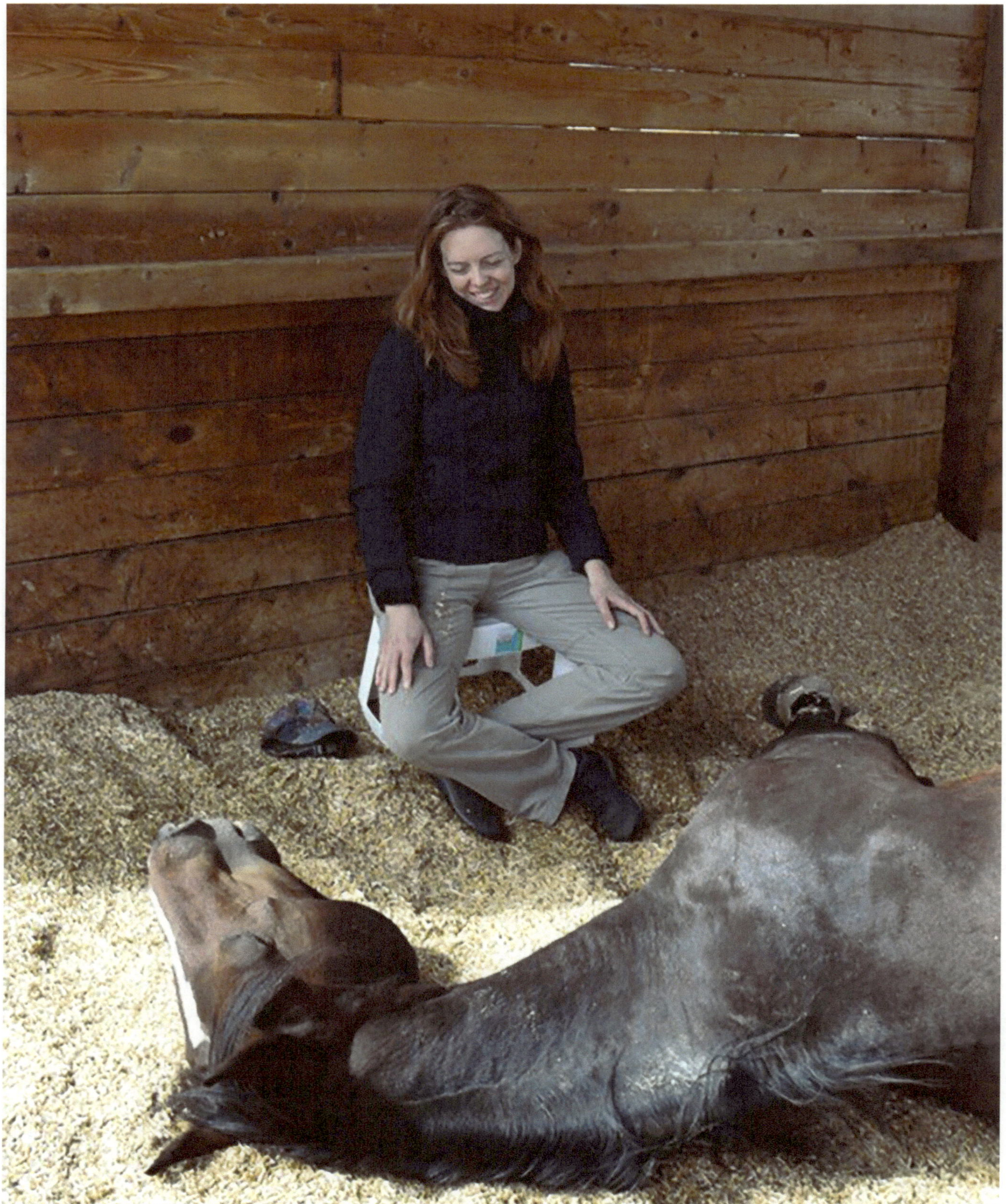

Horse messages channeled by Judith Onley:

The horses here are transmitting much dense energy for humans. There are 14 horses now for a reason. They are covering various levels of consciousness and personality types. It is important for people to be able to relate to different horse personalities so they can help them explore or release those elements in themselves.

> Judith was right when she saw a stream of people coming here. Internationally they will come in streams and droves to absorb our teachings and to play. Humans will come to play, to visit that place of joy and absorb that from being in our presence.

The herd is speaking here of horses and people around the globe developing strong new liaisons for the bringing forth of truth and light.

> ### From Prima
>
> The horses are helping by bringing through light and helping shift consciousness for all humans and animals. As each person raises consciousness it shifts the whole. Because of the strength and size of our bodies, we can bring through much energy. When you touch us we can transfer the energy of power and freedom, and when you touch us in consciousness it accelerates the frequency.

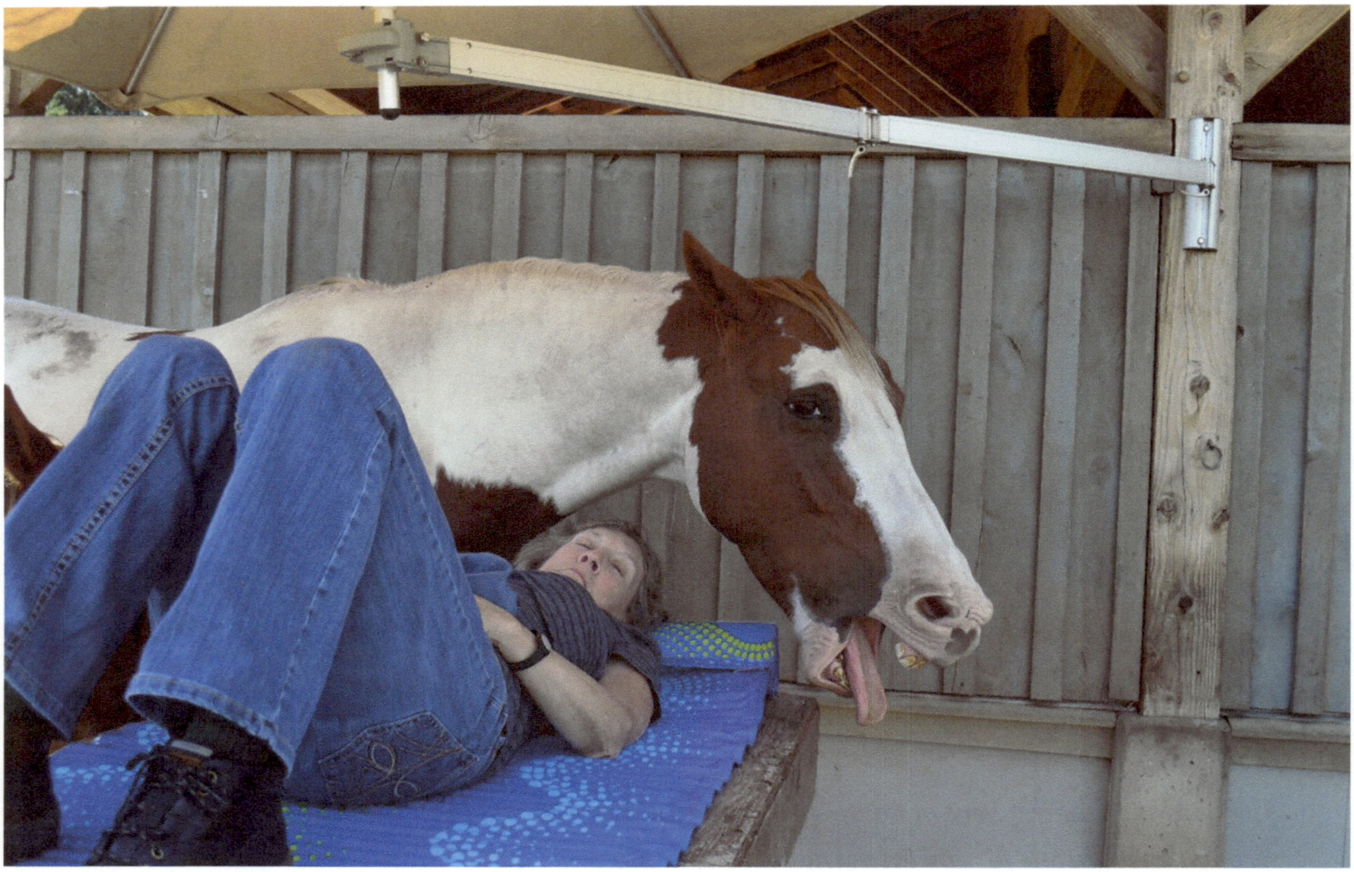

From L.E.

Our mission as a Herd, but mine in particular, is to help ground people in their wisdom and tap into that intuitive place. It is the wise ones who come to me and I am honoured to assist those to express their wisdom and anchor it for them.

There is much information being given right now, and wisdom and discernment are important. I am here to hold the grounding and the balance. Anything done in extreme loses its potential to be effective.

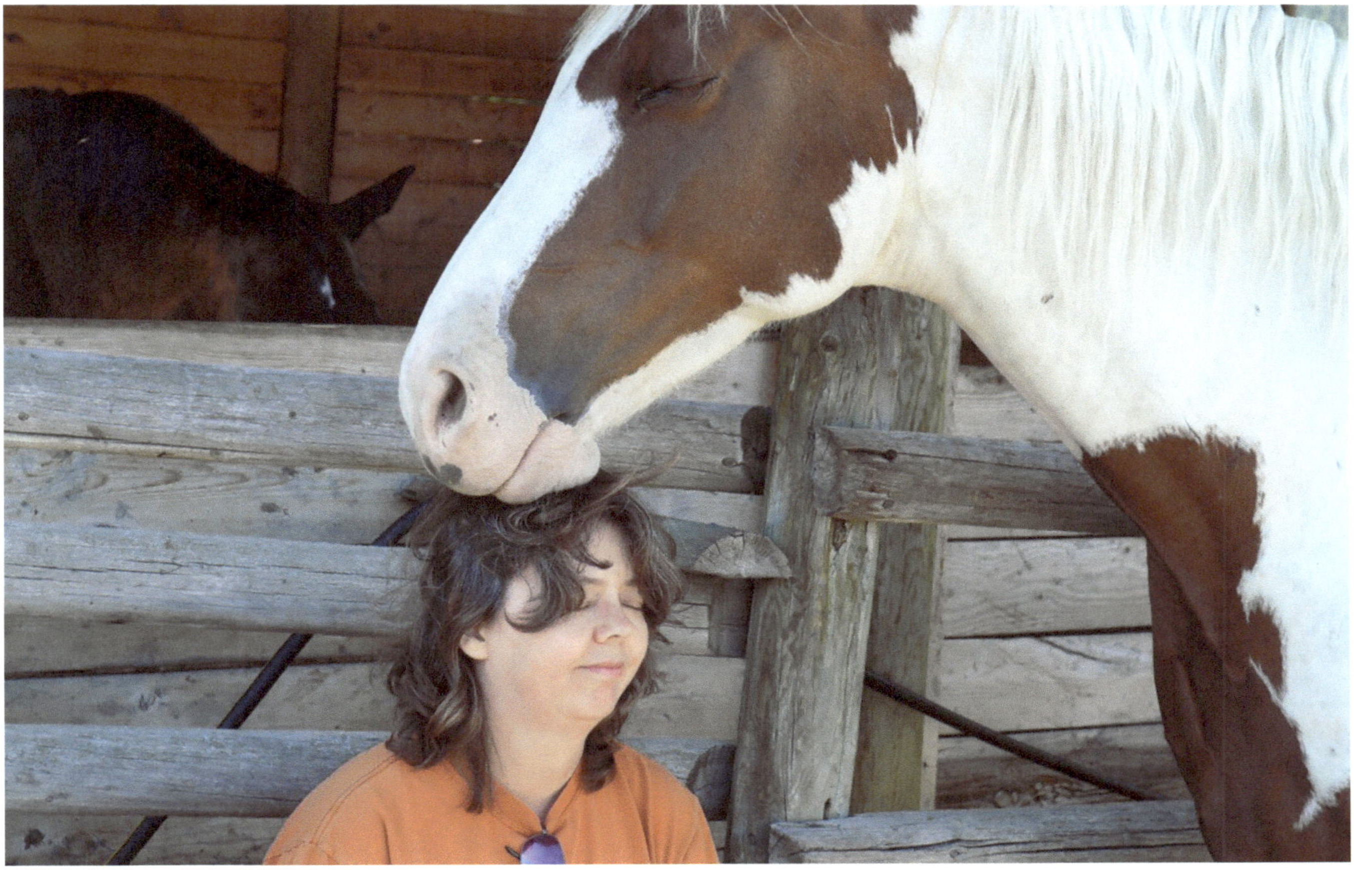

From Diva

As you are doing for us, to help us anchor this energy we are doing for you. We are helping you with your physical strength so that you can go forth and do what is necessary. We are developing a strong foundation for what is to come.

—End of Horse Messages channeled by Judith

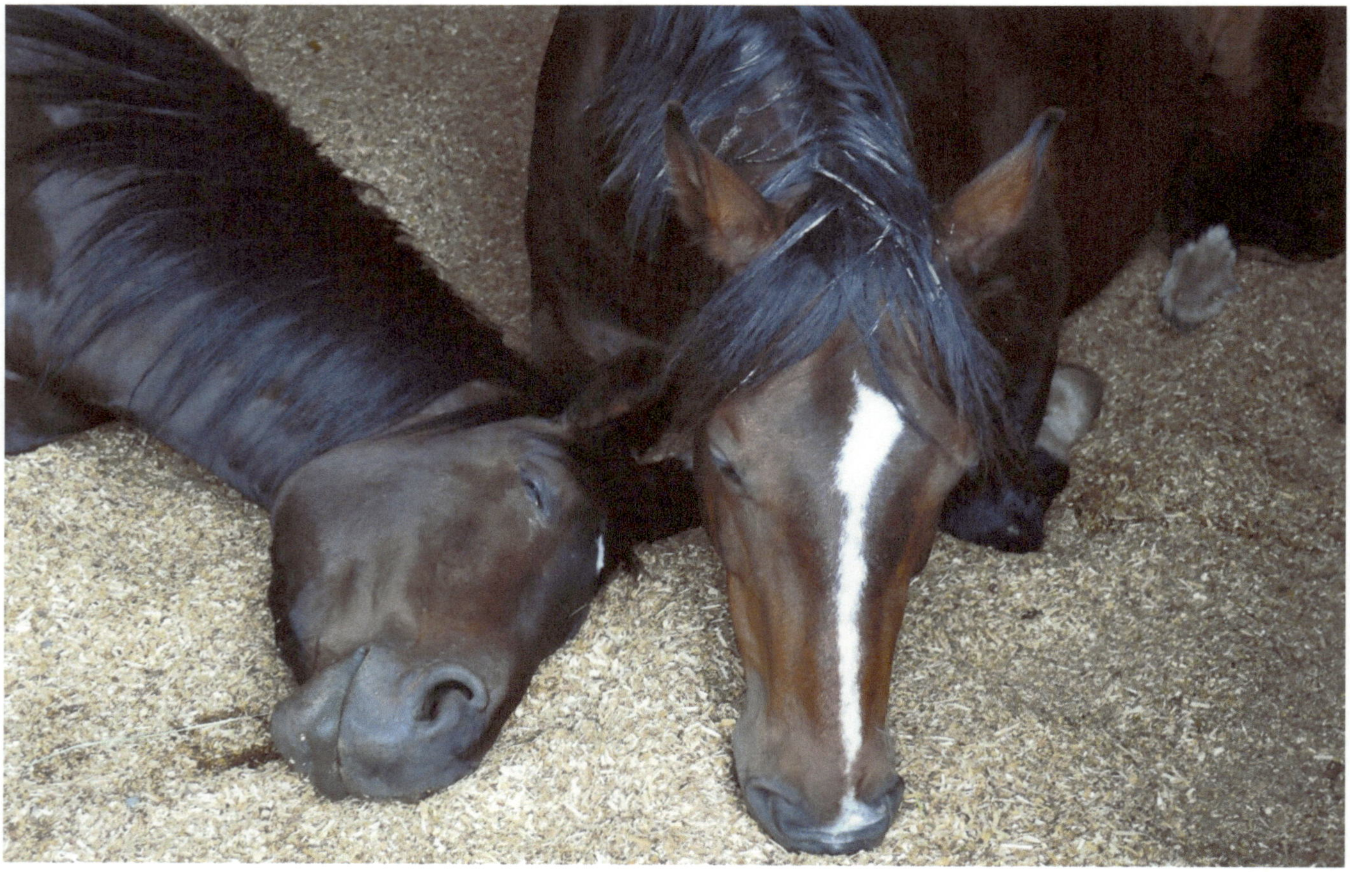

We would like you people to try something: close your eyes and simply feel what it is like to be you. Sense each area of your body and what it is feeling. Go into your heart and experience the memory of love for all those you cherish. Go into your mind and experience the feeling of "isness," "Allness,""Iness," the state of simply being. Then let your thoughts go to an activity like sleeping, playing or eating; "-ness" and "-ing" are universal concepts we all experience. We have only to look through our individual "I" or eye to see our version of the picture. There isn't a created thing that isn't the same "I" deep inside. All those "I's", whether that "I" is a mouse or a human—that is the part of us that is—both one and ALL. There is only one experience and it is God's (or the ALL's) experience through us all.

Try to imagine yourself in each and every facet of life looking out through their eyes and feeling those same feelings in another shape and form. Try to experience being in the body of a horse with an unintelligible, unfocused human kicking and whipping while believing they are communicating their desires through the cold, hard and painful bar of steel that is pinching and cutting your mouth. "Dance, mold yourself to our rhythm, our bodies" they say, while cutting off our air and wrenching our back and sides with saddles that hurt with every move. Now imagine how it could be if we loved you; if every dance was one of joy, of harmony between two souls.

May the true meaning of the "Holy Spirit" be with you this Christmas and to all of you who are trying to understand our message, thank you; "We are happy to carry you, to that place where we will all stand together in the sun."

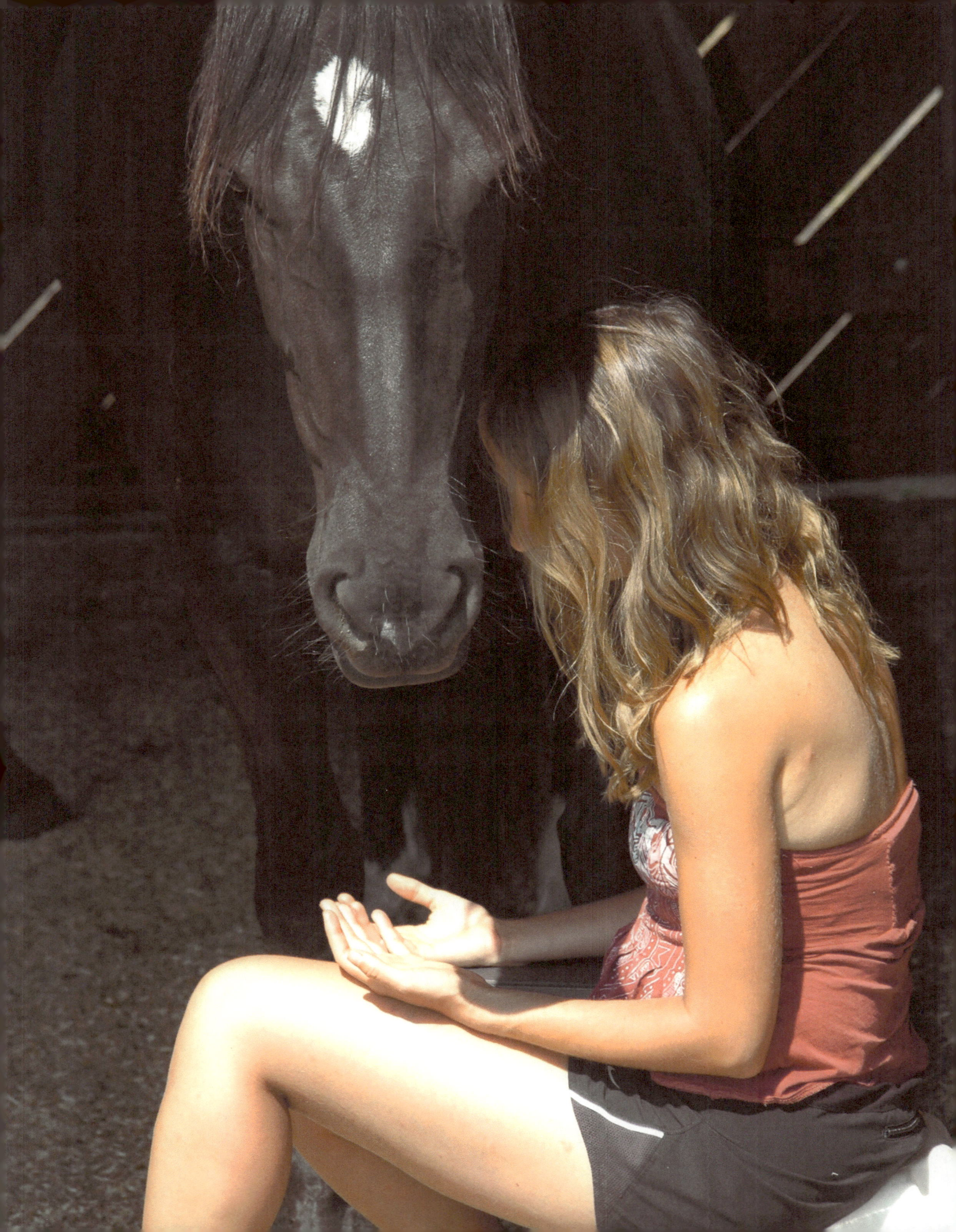

Tesoro was delivered to me as a week-old baby whose mom could not care for him as she had another twin. I had never really met any cattle before so I treated him as I do all my animals. He spent the first two months mostly on my front porch, sleeping on a dog bed or in the dog house when the weather was bad. At any opportunity he would rush in the house and be happy on the living room rug. As he grew I thought he should learn from other grazing animals so I moved him to the pony pasture with its open barn. I play with all my animals, communicating with all my horses, dogs and cats by telepathy, body language and English. I had been doing the same with Tesoro (Spanish for treasure) and decided he was old enough to play with me on our playground. This is where I take the horses to learn to play at liberty which strengthens our characters and relationship. I stuffed my pockets with all his favorite treats (carrots, apples and horse treats) and off we went. He cantered after me leaping jumps, running across the wood bridge, through the swim noodles and for his grand finale ran across the large tires and got all four feet on the small tire and made a perfect turn on the haunches. WOW! He was quicker than any horse I had taken there and did it all like a star performer. So much for thinking cows are dumb! We just need to learn how to speak with them.

Imagine the possibility of communicating with all creatures at a level that transcends understanding their language and customs. The interesting development is that although the horses were skeptical of sharing their land with a bovine they are now beginning to appreciate that Tesoro is worthy of inclusion in their Herd. He is so sensitive to their signals and moves away at the slightest pressure. Faster than anything I have seen on four legs, he more than keeps up with the Herd and shadows their every move with amazing precision. I think the horses are quite impressed and I have noticed on several occasions some sniffing and nuzzling going on between them.

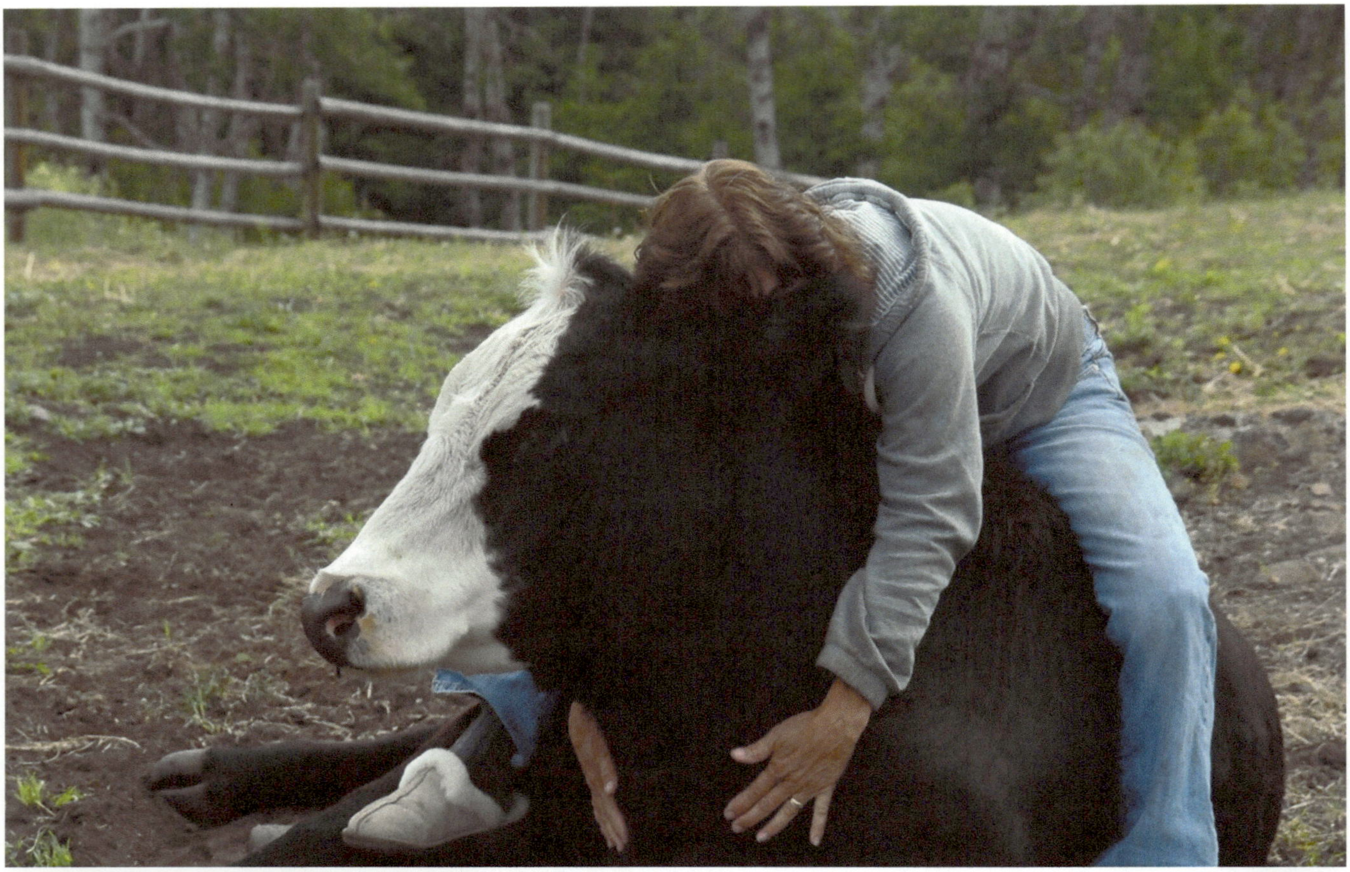

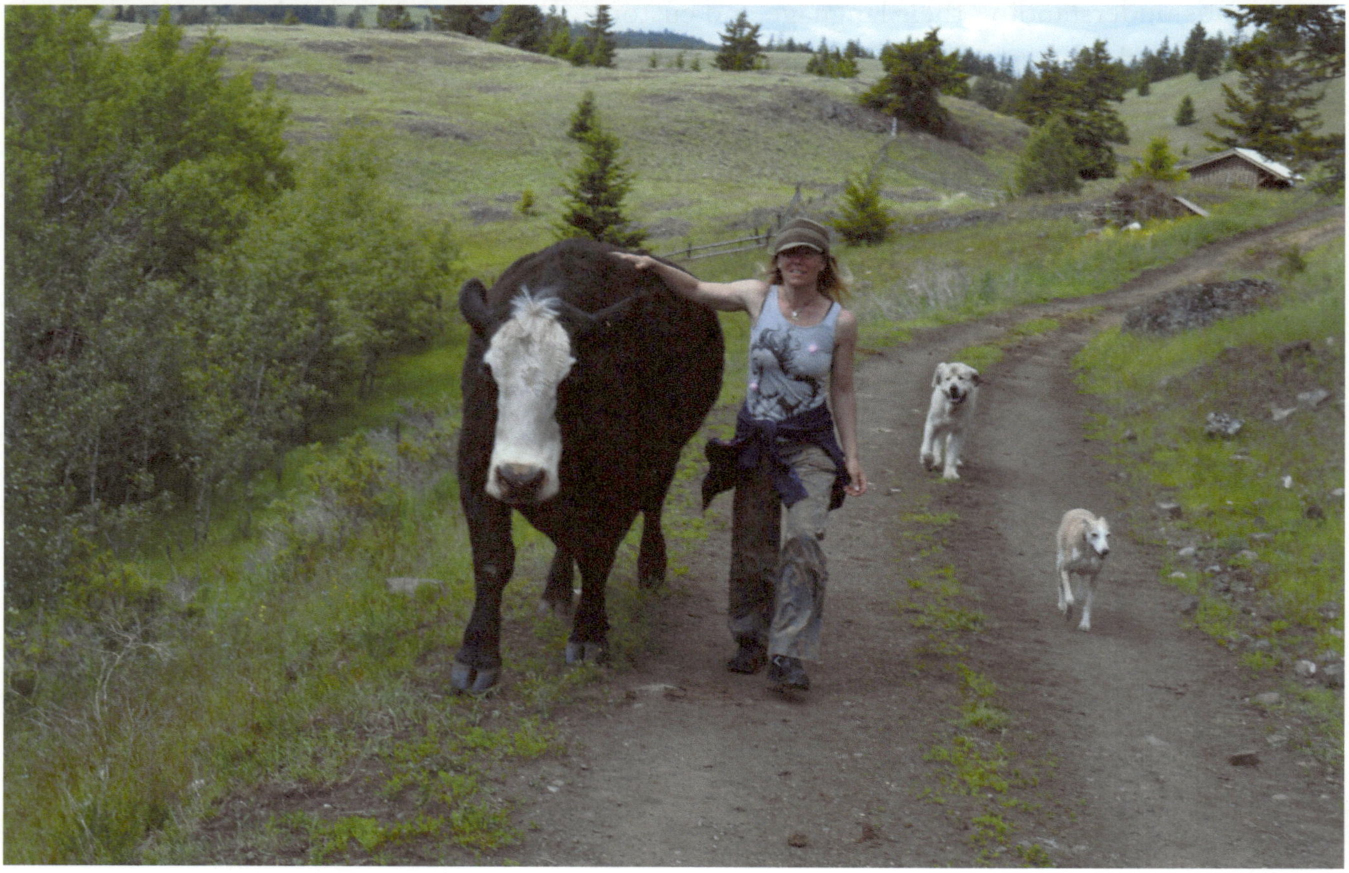

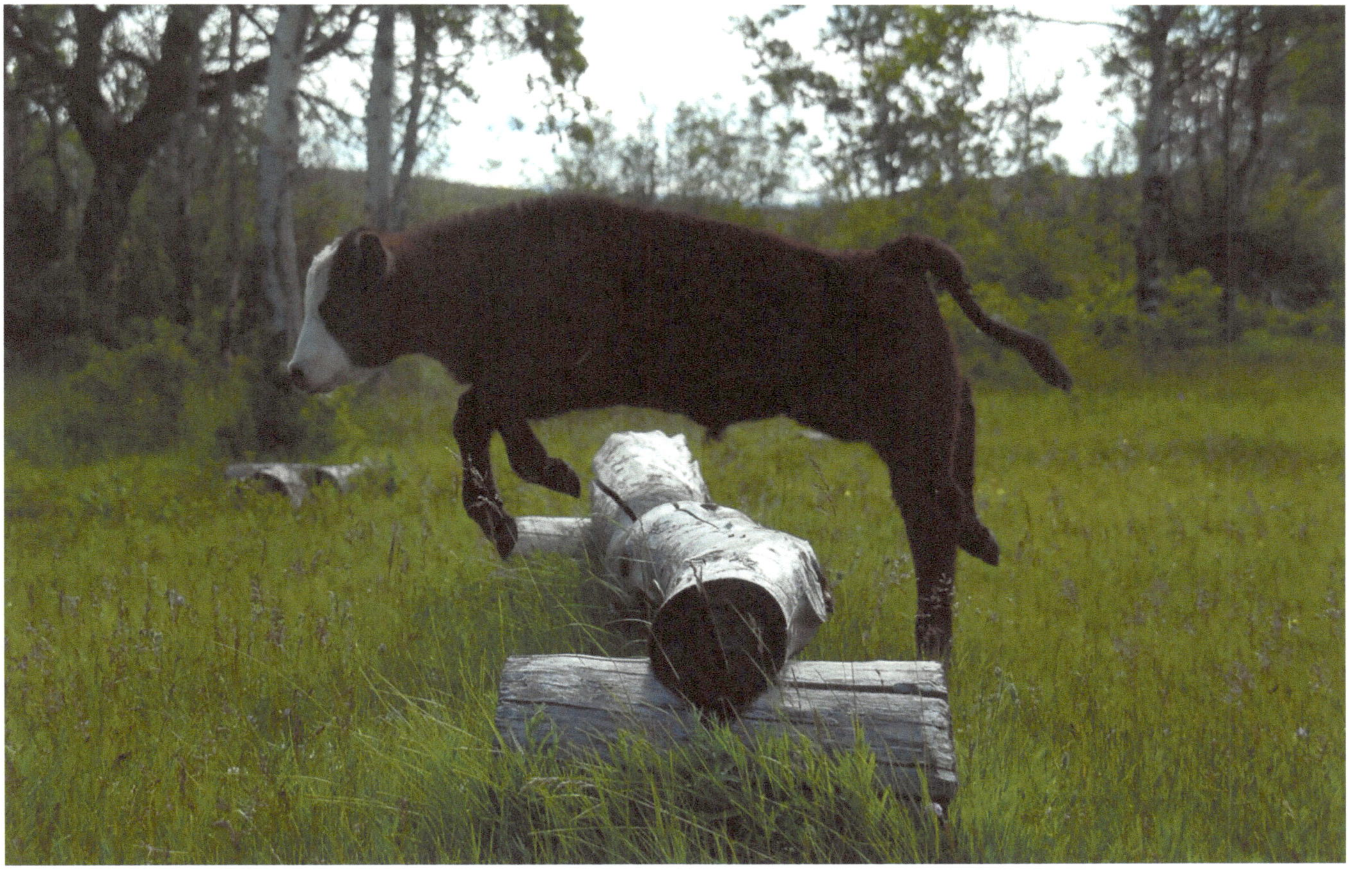

When Tesoro (baby steer) entered the Herd:

Horses (and all herd animals) are extremely protective of their Herd. Our survival is dependent on a concise and efficient communication system. All members must be aware of and responsive to all the other members at all times. We all have our own roles to play; from the lead mare to the dominant and submissive members. There is confusion and aggression when the Herd's communication system is compromised. It is difficult when new horses come or go, as new order must be implemented. We are all very upset at the moment as not only a new member has been brought in, but one who we have no language or social order in relation to. He will need to respect our ways in order to maintain harmony.

We are all experiencing physicality as an opportunity for the All, which is the substance of us all, to grow and expand on the Earth plane. The All being spirit cannot live on this plane without our physical bodies participating in this grand adventure. The All experiences through us, and that means all of us as created beings. We are somewhat embarrassed to be caught in our own web as we like to think of ourselves as great spiritual teachers and healers. When Liz told us Tesoro was going to be part of our Herd we fell prey to some serious prejudice, something we had spoken against in book two, *The Truth According to Horses*, we were critical of humans with their narrow perspective about non-humans or humans of a different race, religion, colour, etc. We are guilty of the same prejudice concerning Tesoro and our fear that he would somehow endanger our Herd. We have over time realized that by the principles of one consciousness in all life, all minds are joined and Tesoro has learned to communicate with all of our family members—from Liz to the dogs to our Herd. It really took Paschar and Micah (the yearlings) to be ambassadors for the older horses who were more set in their ways. We now travel together with the ponies Merlin and Arthur and Tesoro who all respect our customs and stay on the edges of the Herd.

When minds are joined and open to the force of love there is no limit as to what is possible. It seems we are becoming larger and brighter, individual stars shining together to become a galaxy of light.

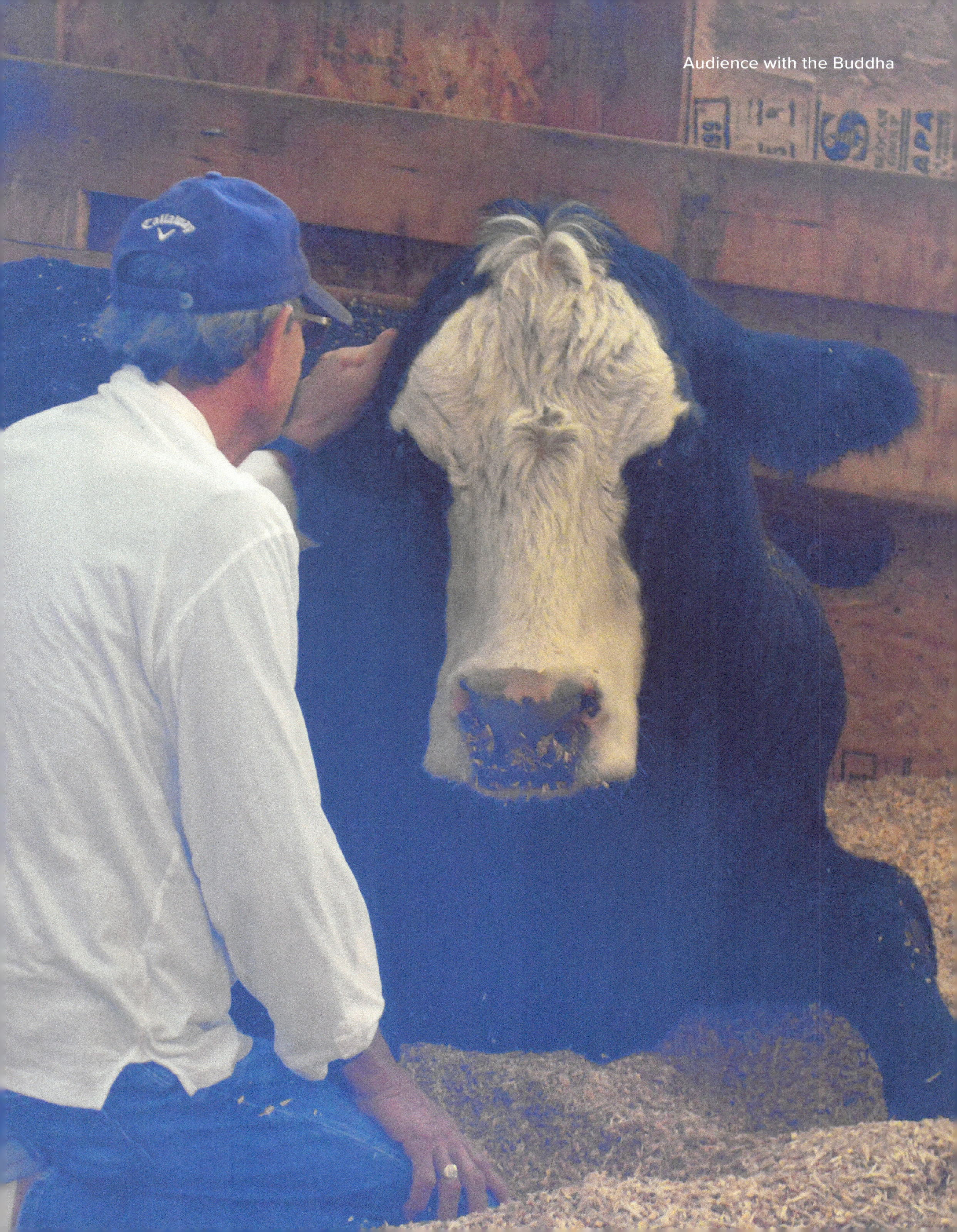

Audience with the Buddha

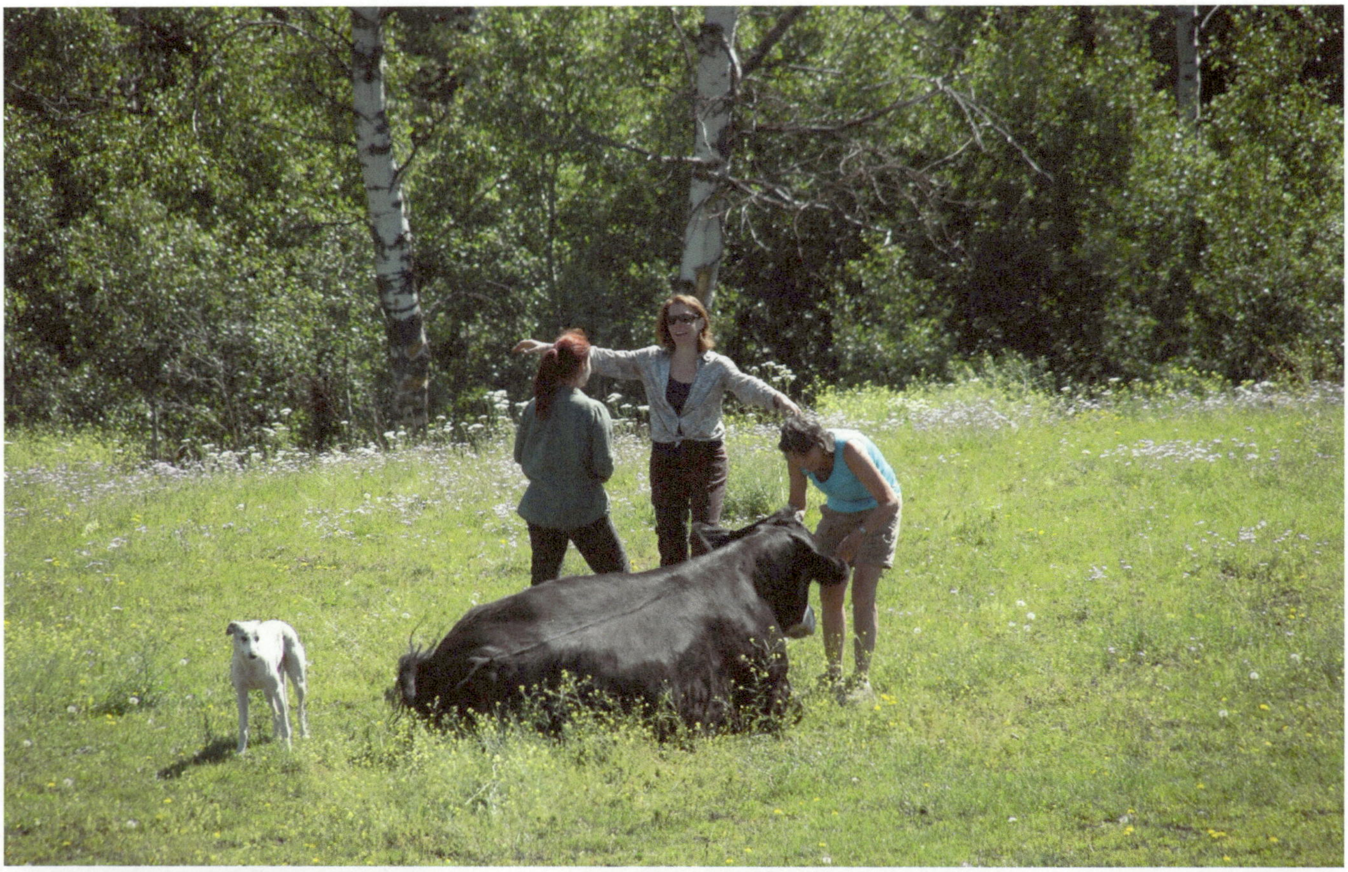

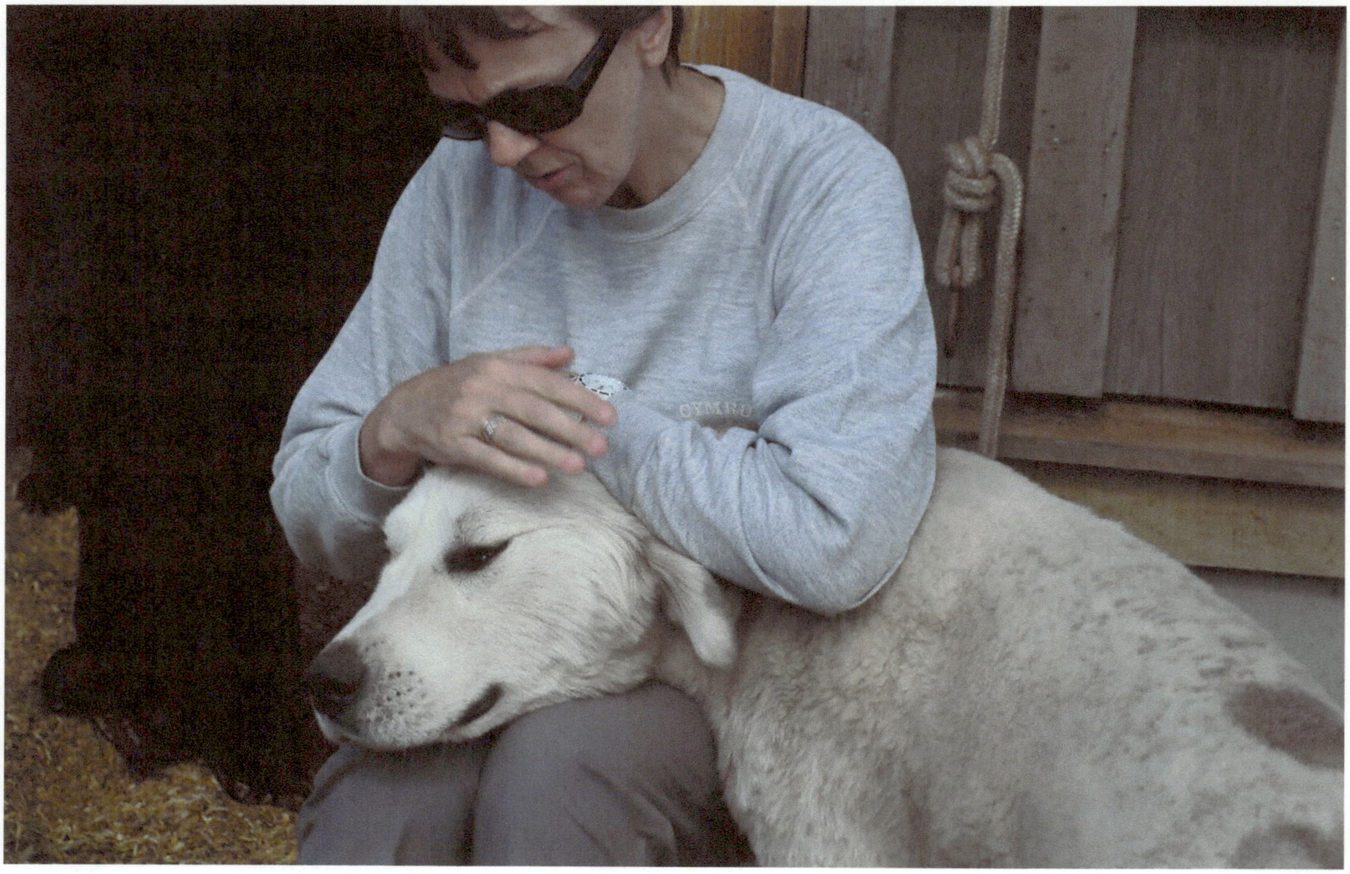

This time in the Earth's history will involve enormous changes in the vibration and consequent consciousness and evolution of life on the planet. Within the next decade animals will be considered in a new light, as spiritual equals with rights and freedoms, with important gifts to contribute to the survival of L.I.F.E. (Love In Finite Expression) forever. Man has been struggling through the dark ages of their existence in matter. Human Mass Mind Consciousness, shaped by universal consensus (i.e. TV, radio, newspapers) has been mired with an ego- driven need to fight for and accumulate material possessions. Those possessions have made it increasingly difficult to find time to commune and connect on a spiritual level with the rest of life. All of creation except the majority of mankind has been holding the vibration of love, which flows freely from the All when consciousness is open. Have you noticed recently that horses are everywhere inspiring a new understanding of their gifts as wise teachers and healers?

Natural horsemanship, equine-facilitated therapy and therapeutic riding are just the very beginnings of the possibilities in horse/human communication.

Open your minds and hearts to the messages we send you and consider us not as pawns to be exploited and tamed but as messengers from heaven, here to guide you in the experience of oneness here on Earth.

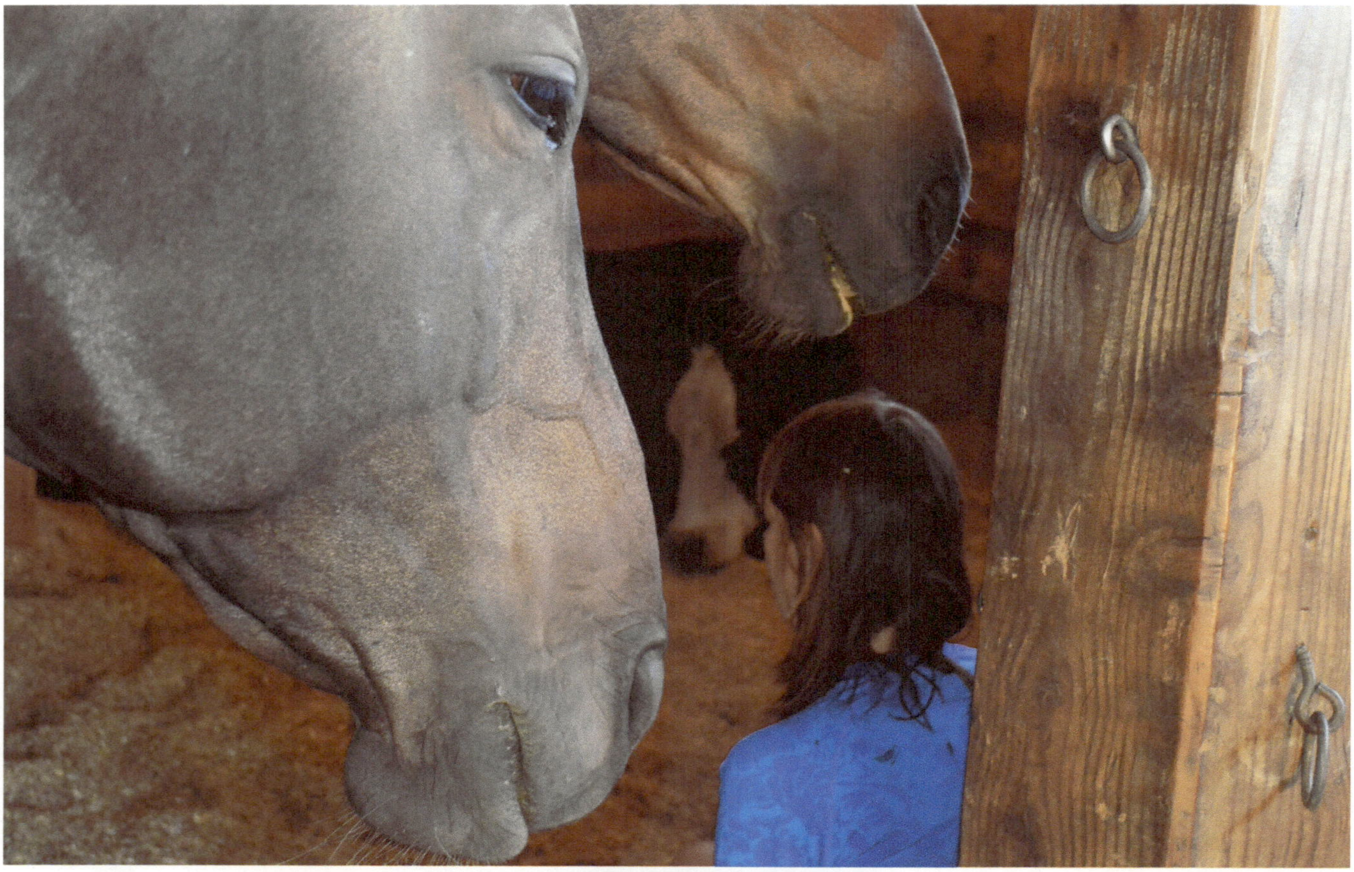

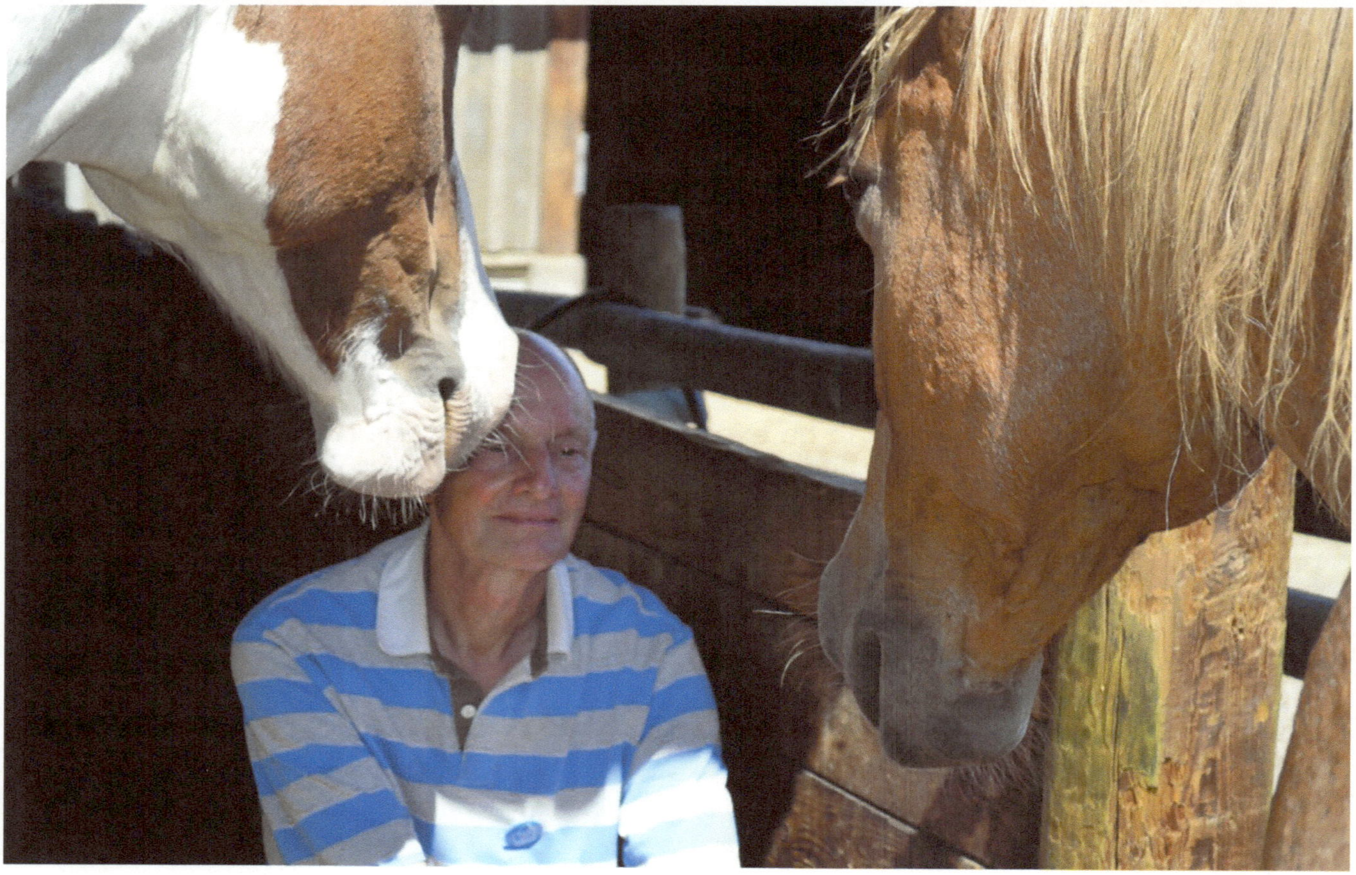

All minds are joined

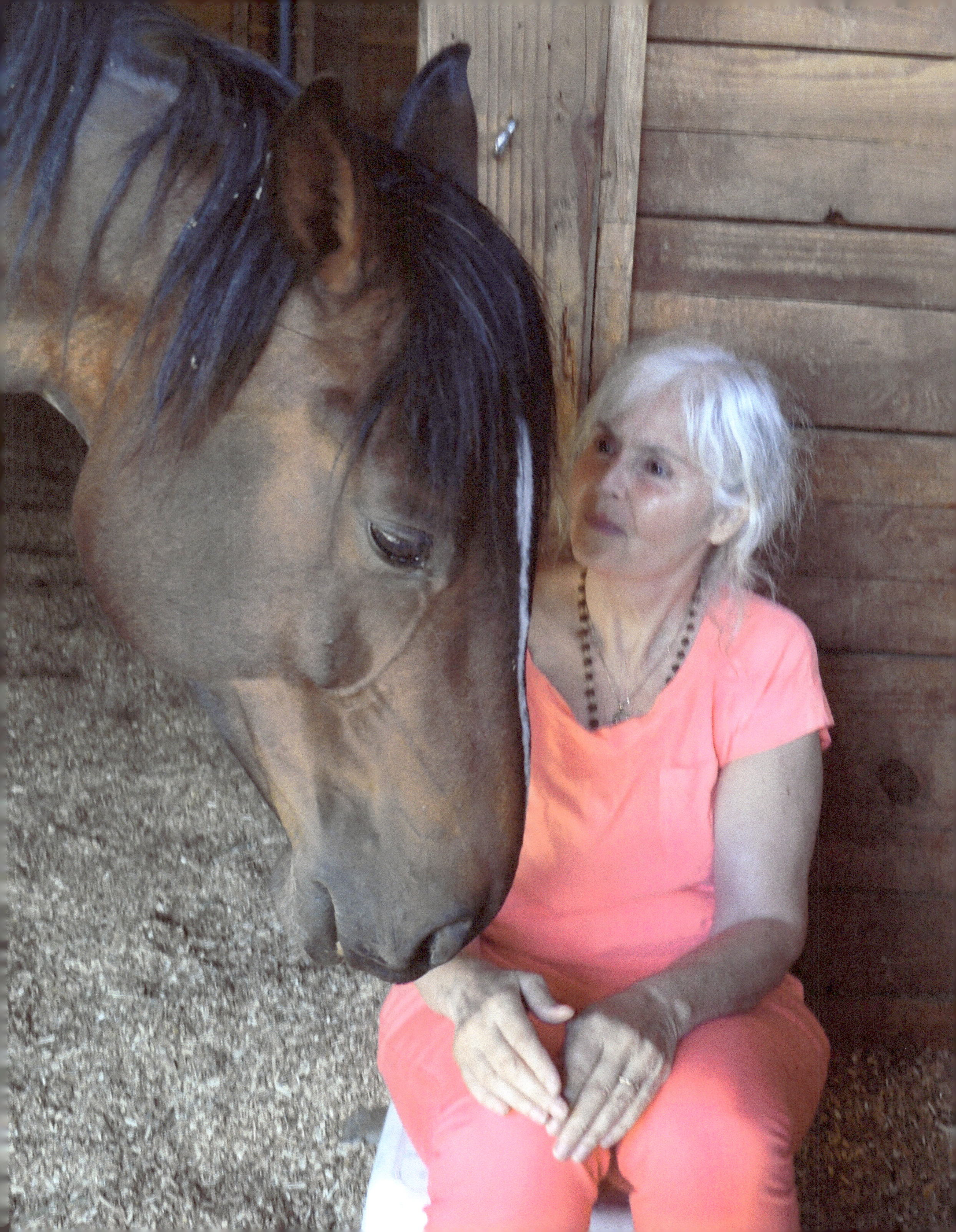

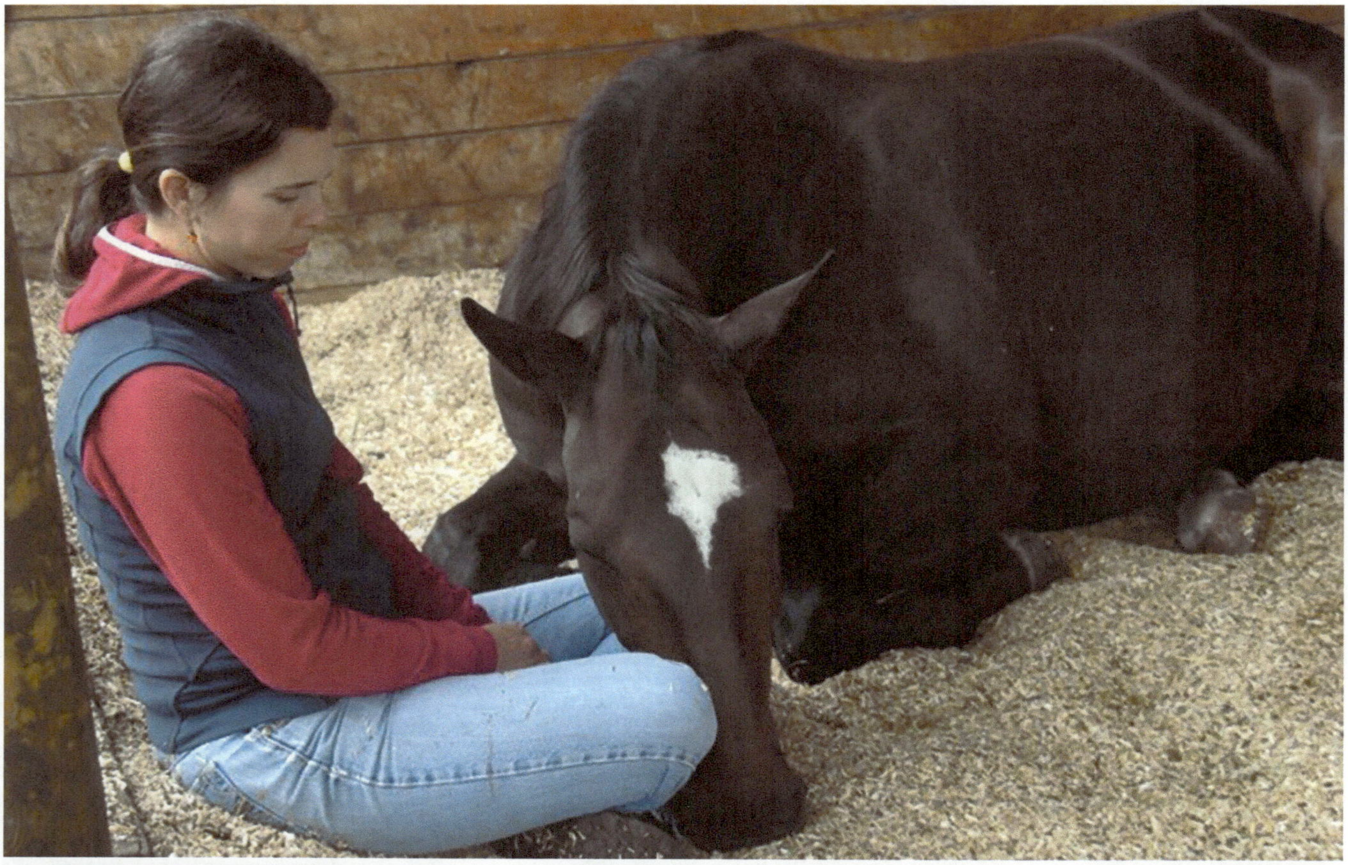

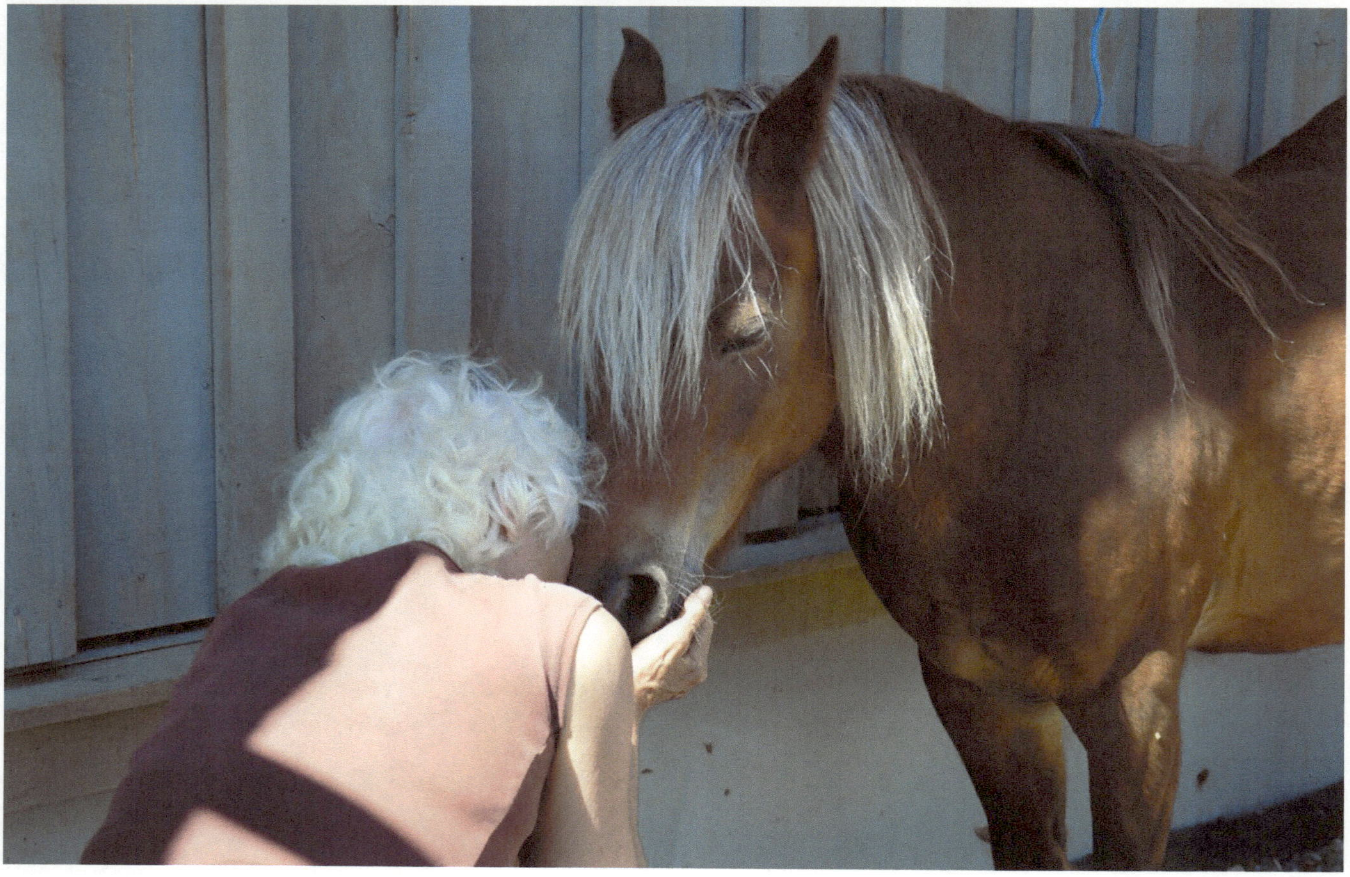

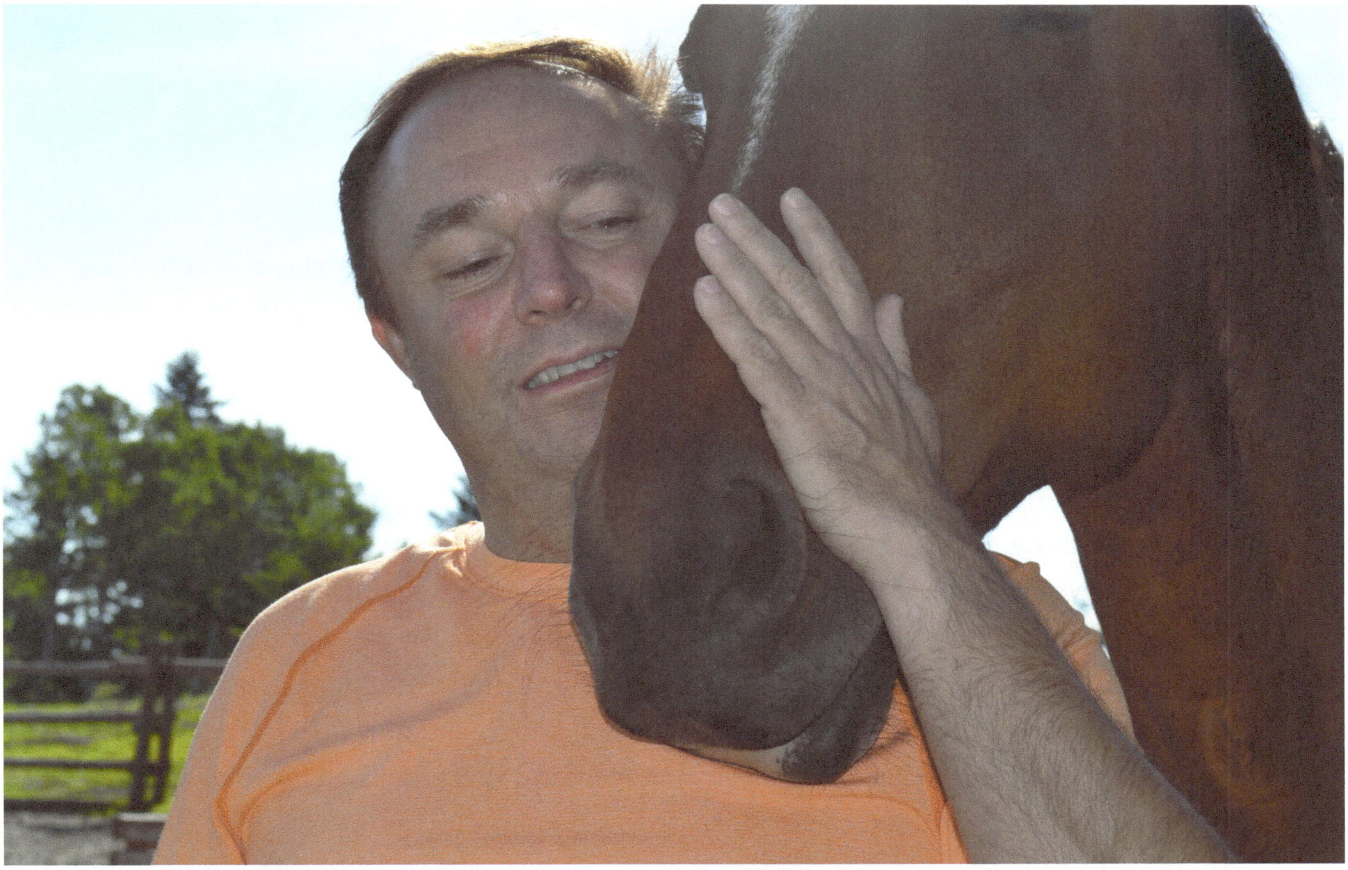

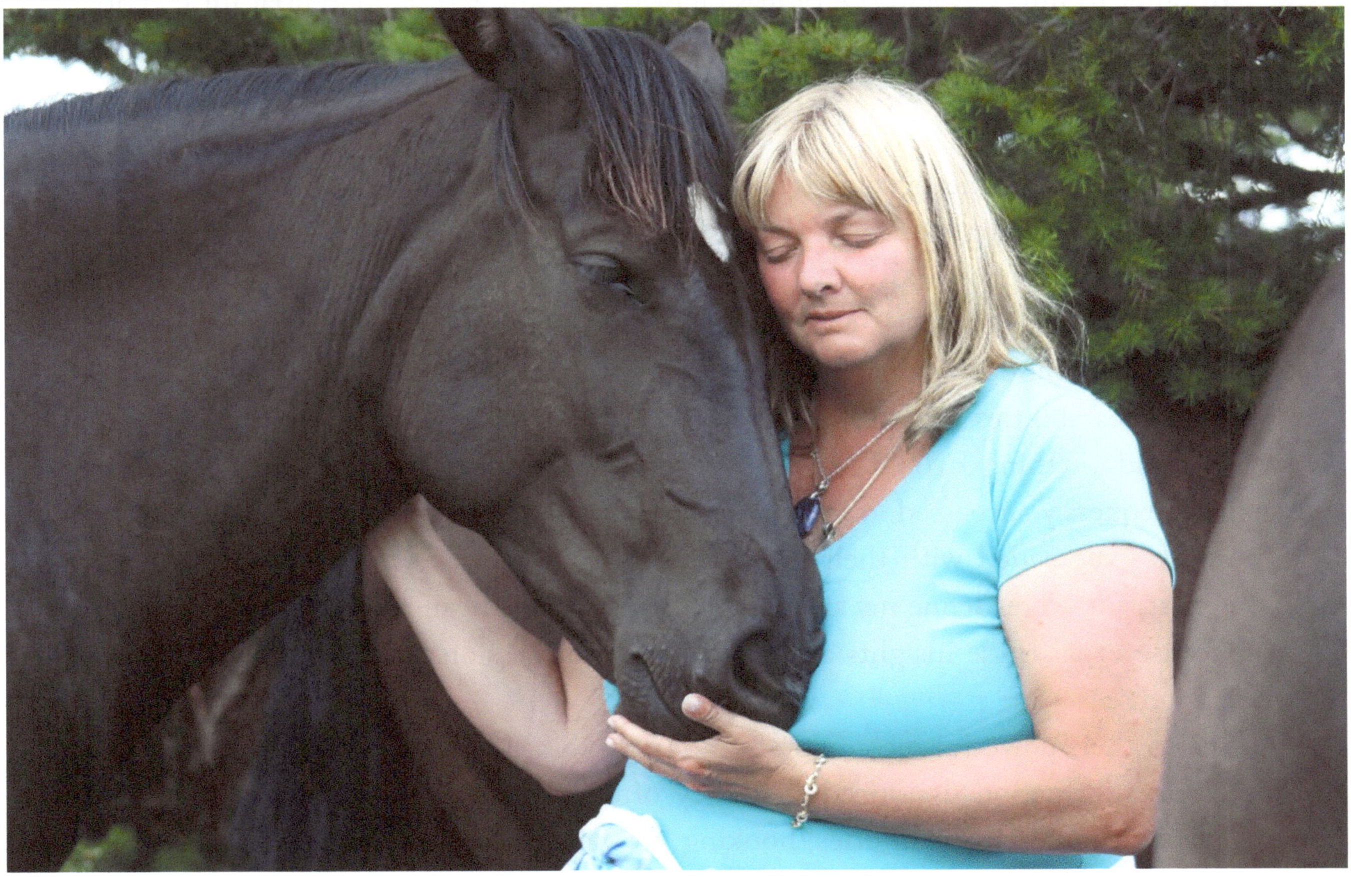

From Martina Danzer, of "Animal Magic Worldwide", who worked at Equinisity for 6 months

One morning at the end of the summer, I sat together with five horses in a corner of the barn. Two stood very closely on each side of me, with their noses directly above my head. Three others were standing behind my back, forming a semi-circle. As I closed my eyes and dropped deeply into my body, I could feel a light tingling sensation on both sides of my head like little mini-explosions going off inside my brain.

Usually during those horse treatments, I was so deep in meditation that there was no room for any rational thought. However, this time I asked, "What are you doing?"

"We are working on your neocortex," was the immediate reply.

I should have really paid better attention in biology. However, I still knew enough to understand that some work was being done around my brain and I could feel it! The sensation was as if pieces inside my brain were being shifted around, regrouped and re-arranged. After a while, the group of horses started to sigh and chew. Then they slightly shifted their formation. With their physical movement, their focus changed as well.

When I asked them, they confirmed it.

"In order to fully develop the right side of your brain with its potential for creation and non-linear living, we need to reconfigure the left side of your brain. You cannot expand and grow and evolve in the one half without lifting the consciousness of the other half."

This answer took me by surprise; I asked no more questions. I just sat there and allowed those amazing beings to perform their miracle. After my two and a half hour treatment with the horses, I knew I was no longer the same person. I also knew that from this very moment on I would never ever look at horses the same way again. In fact, I would never ever look at any animal the same way again.

The horses' abilities in terms of energetic clearings, shifts and transformations were way beyond anything I could have imagined. Their sophistication in terms of utilization of frequency surpassed anything I had experienced in any healing context so far. The horses succeeded with their purposeful attempt to wake me up, to increase my awareness, and to re-define my awareness of what animals can truly do.

Because of all these insights and realizations, the sessions with the horses became more intense.

Due to their powerful reconfiguration of my brain, I was able to take in expanded pieces of information. I noticed that they often worked especially with my DNA, freeing it from certain memories, hooking up more strands, and opening me up for

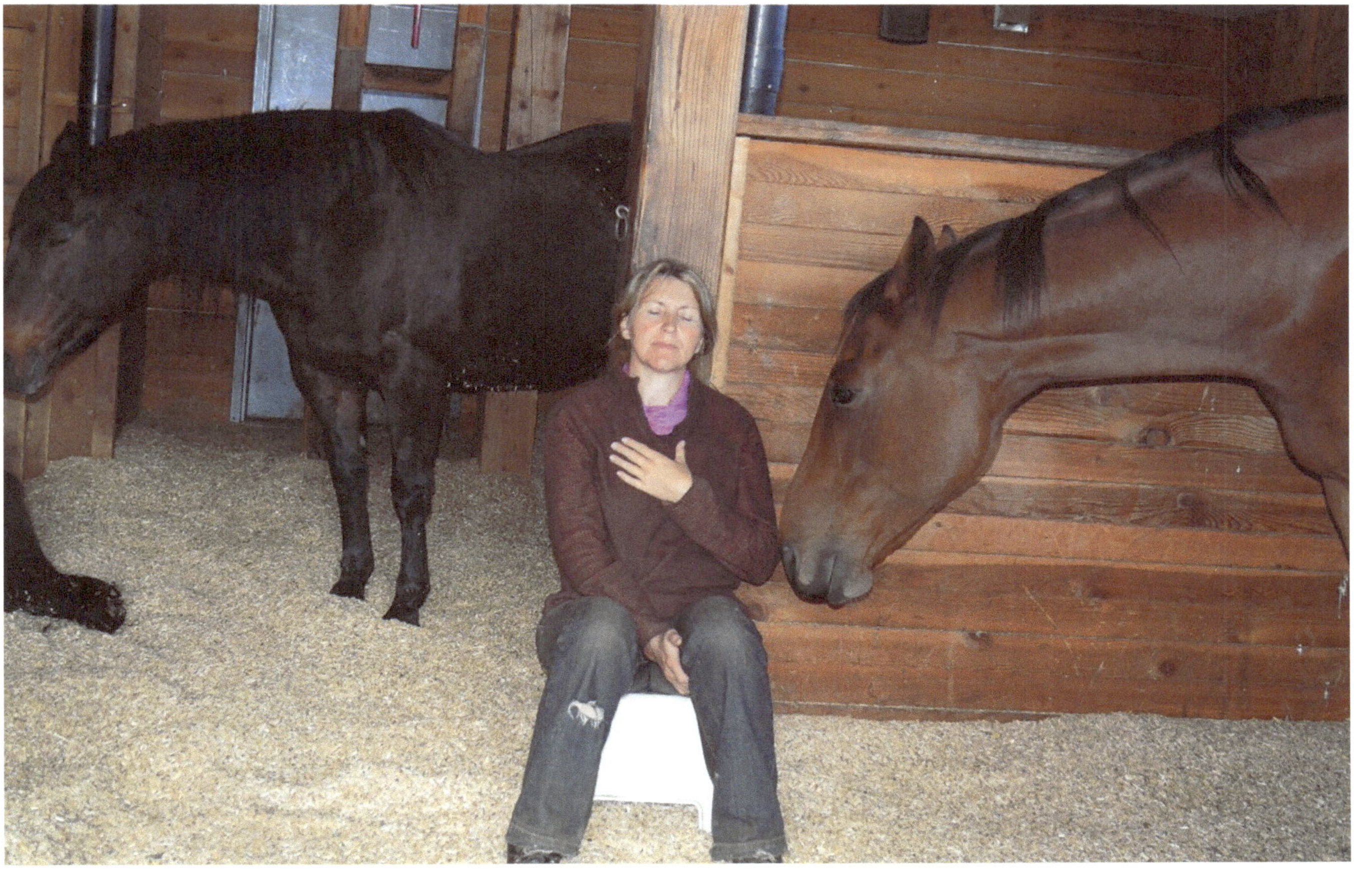

Martina connects with the herd

more possibilities and higher frequencies. I knew that this was the true purpose of my employment here.

I was being initiated by this herd so I could take the work with my own herd to a different level. Therefore I simply opened up, accepted more and more of what these amazing beings offered so freely. Accepted that horses - and other animals, beings and we ourselves - have the ability to re-build our bodies, including DNA, cells, blood vessels, organs, and body parts. The horses showed me that they can retrieve memory and replace it with white light so that the human can move forward free of any ancestral baggage. I gained more clarity when it came to communicating with the natural environment around me. Unicorns, Tree Spirits, Horses from all over the World, Water Sprites, Fairies, wild animals, you name them, found me all the time. I could see them, hear them and talk to them.

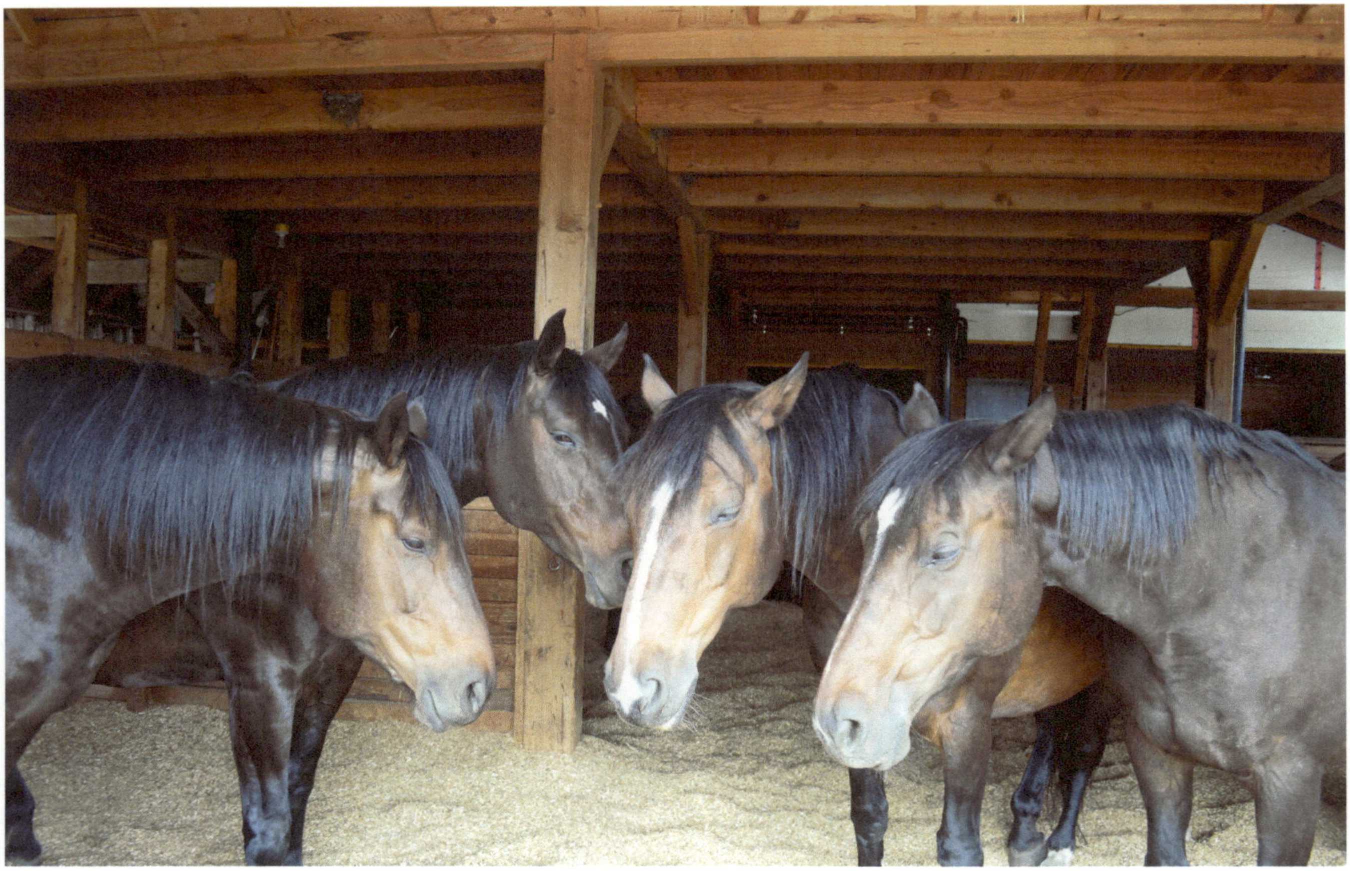

Our six horses welcomed me enthusiastically when I arrived at my Rocky Mountain home. The herd galloped exuberantly across the field, pawed excitedly with their front hoofs high up in the air, and playfully bucked, snorted and "strutted their stuff." After they finally calmed down, they came over one after the other to sniff and greet me. It seemed that whatever changes the herd at the ranch had initiated me into; my horses really liked it, because they all huddled around me and wanted to be close to me. The by now thirty-five year old and possibly almost blind Brandy touched my face with her sensitive nose, before she deeply breathed into my nostrils. It never failed. The few times she had done that before, it had always felt like Mother Earth herself breathed straight into my heart reminding me that I was whole and loved. She then gave me one of her timeless looks and conveyed a message, which seemed to express the collective opinion of the herd. "You know, Martina, we are a Healing Herd, too."

All the horses around me blew their nostrils and licked their lips as I laughed out loud and cried at the same time.

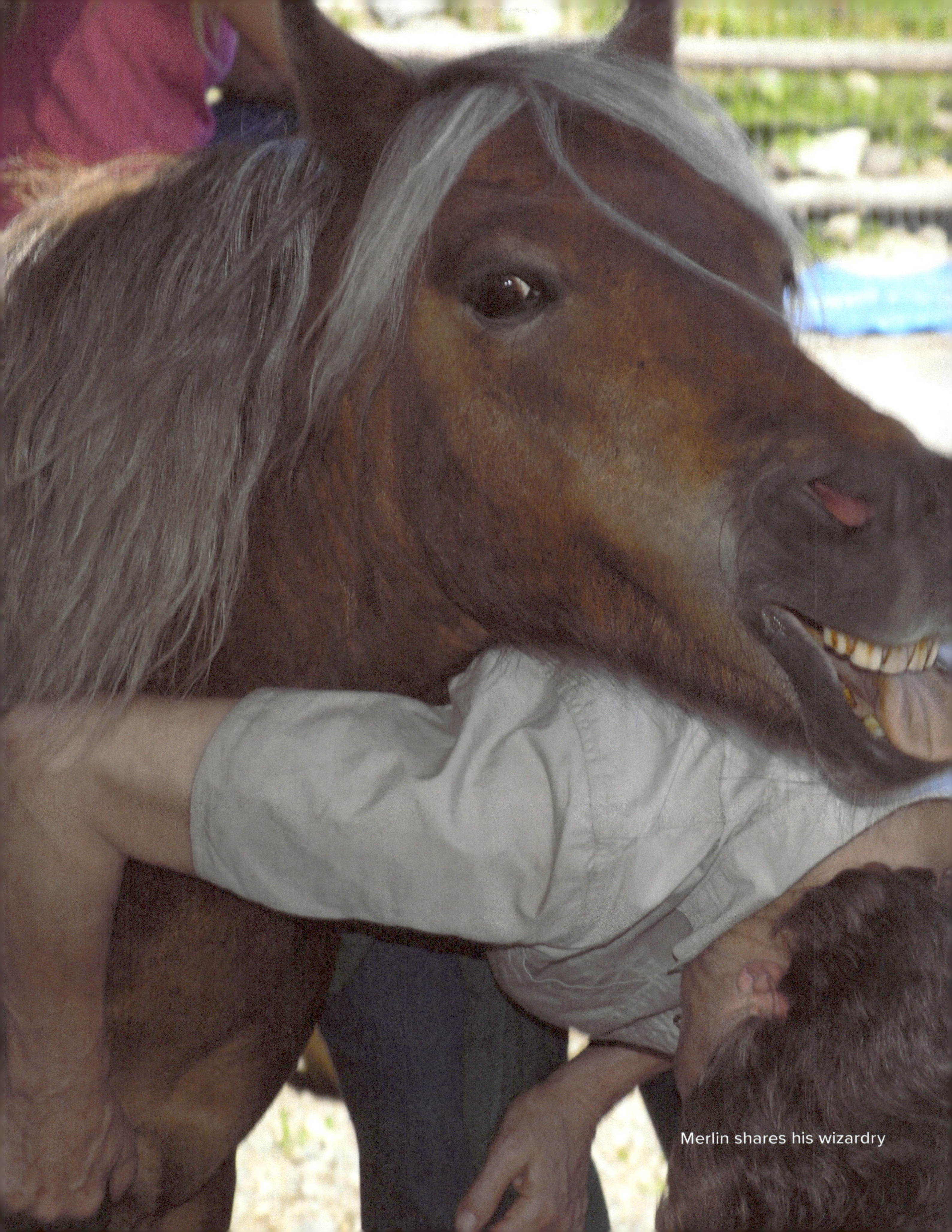

Merlin shares his wizardry

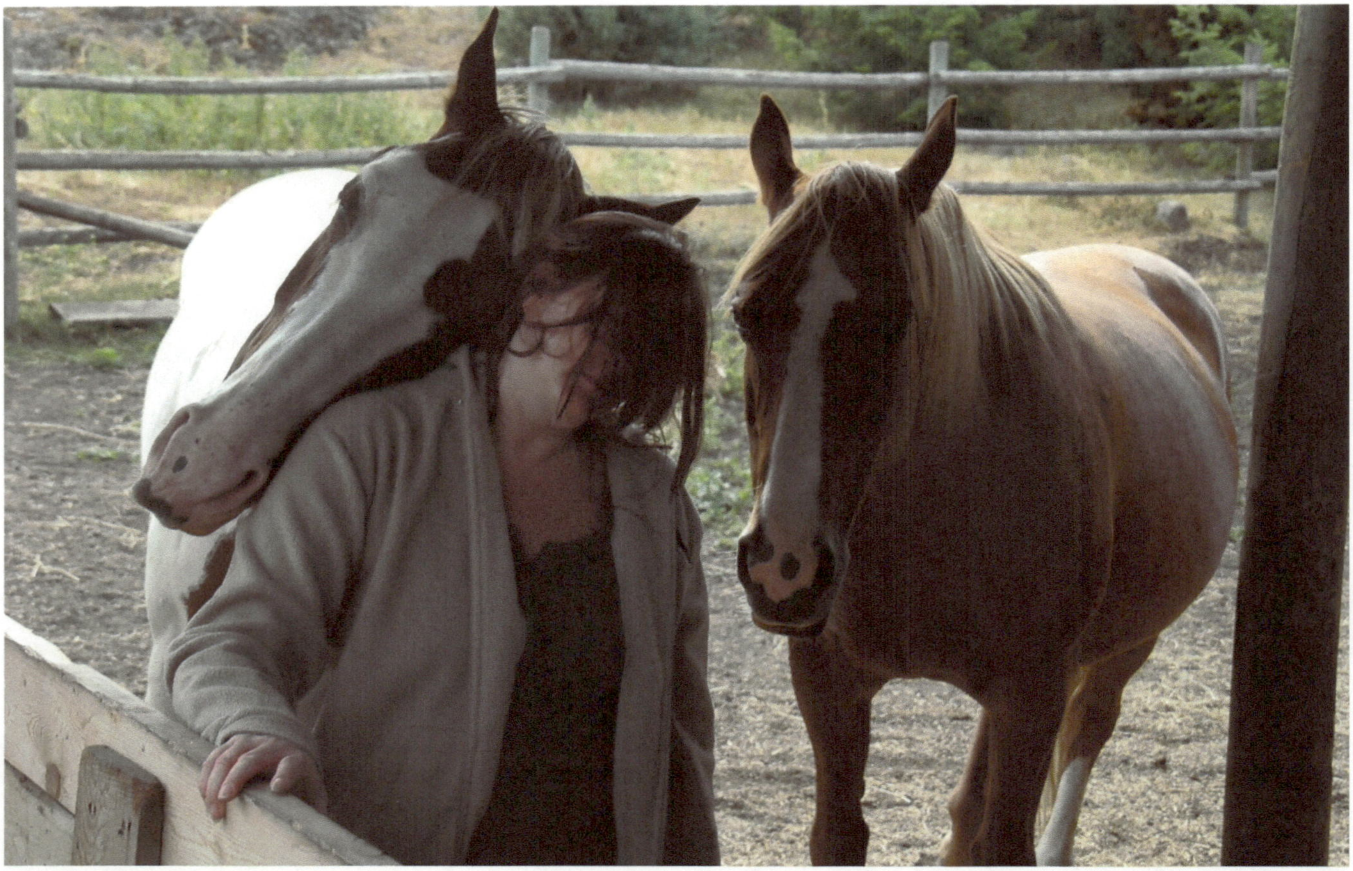

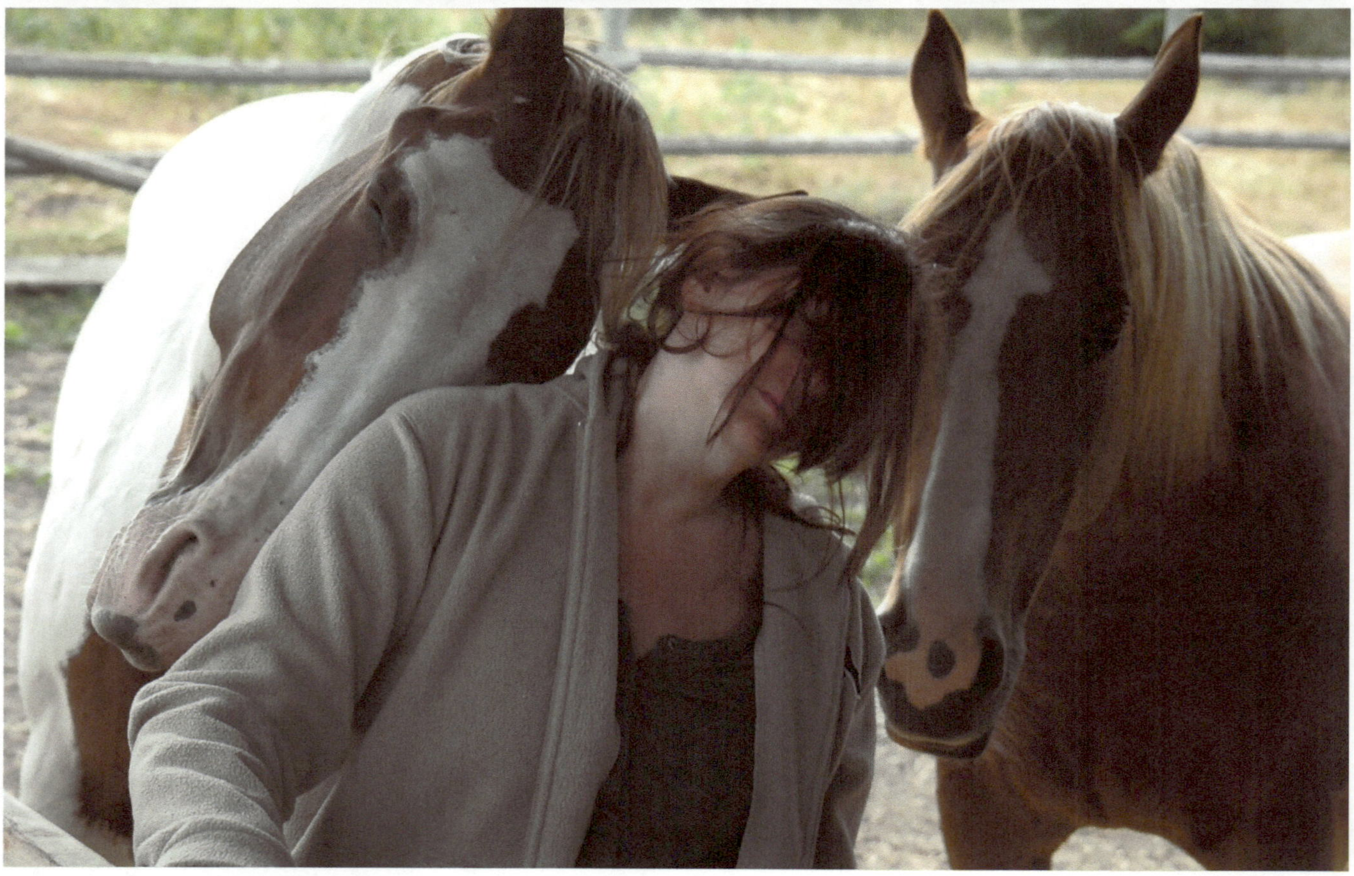

Paschar does cranial sacral and opens the heart.

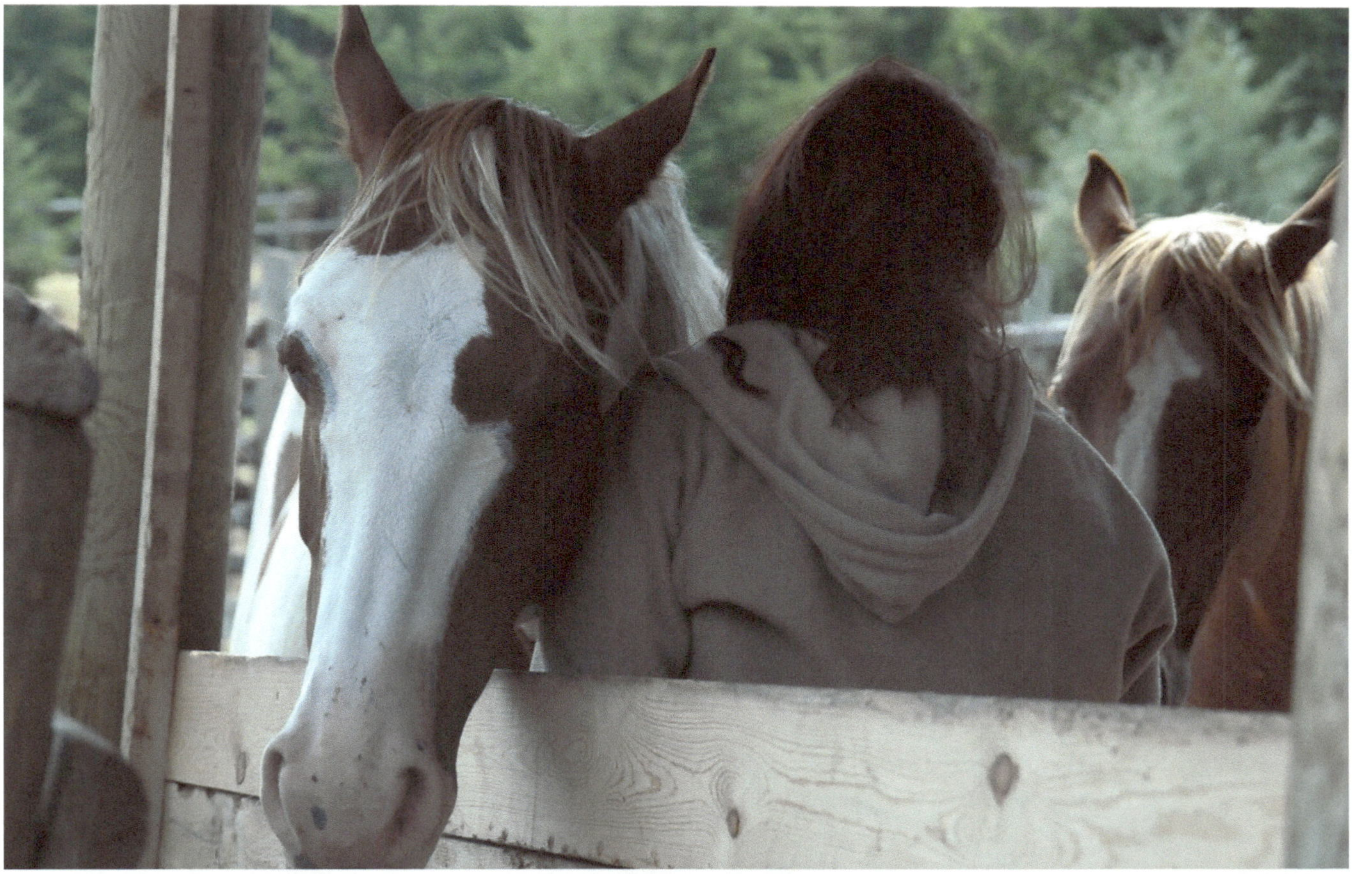

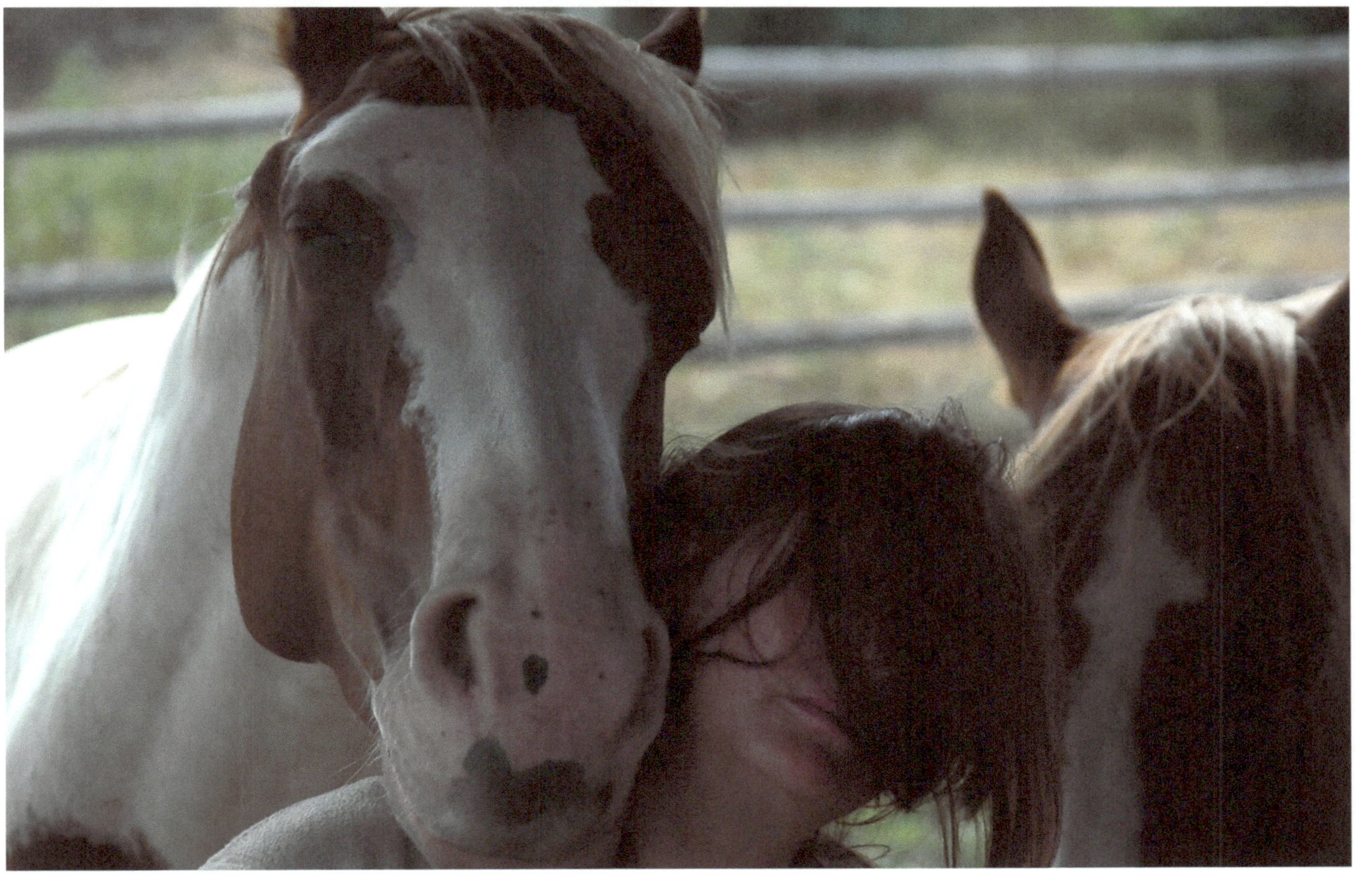

Paschar does cranial sacral and opens the heart.

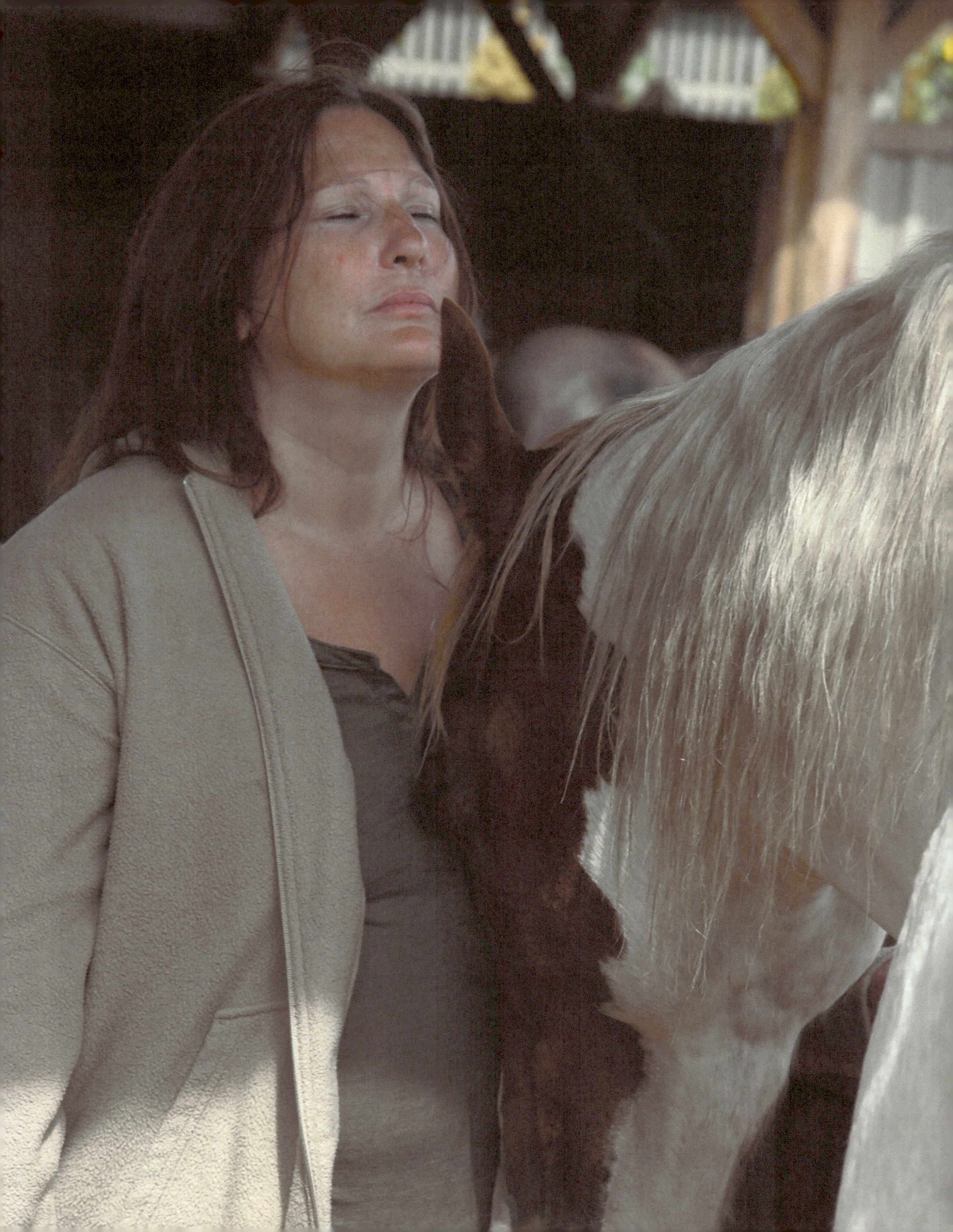

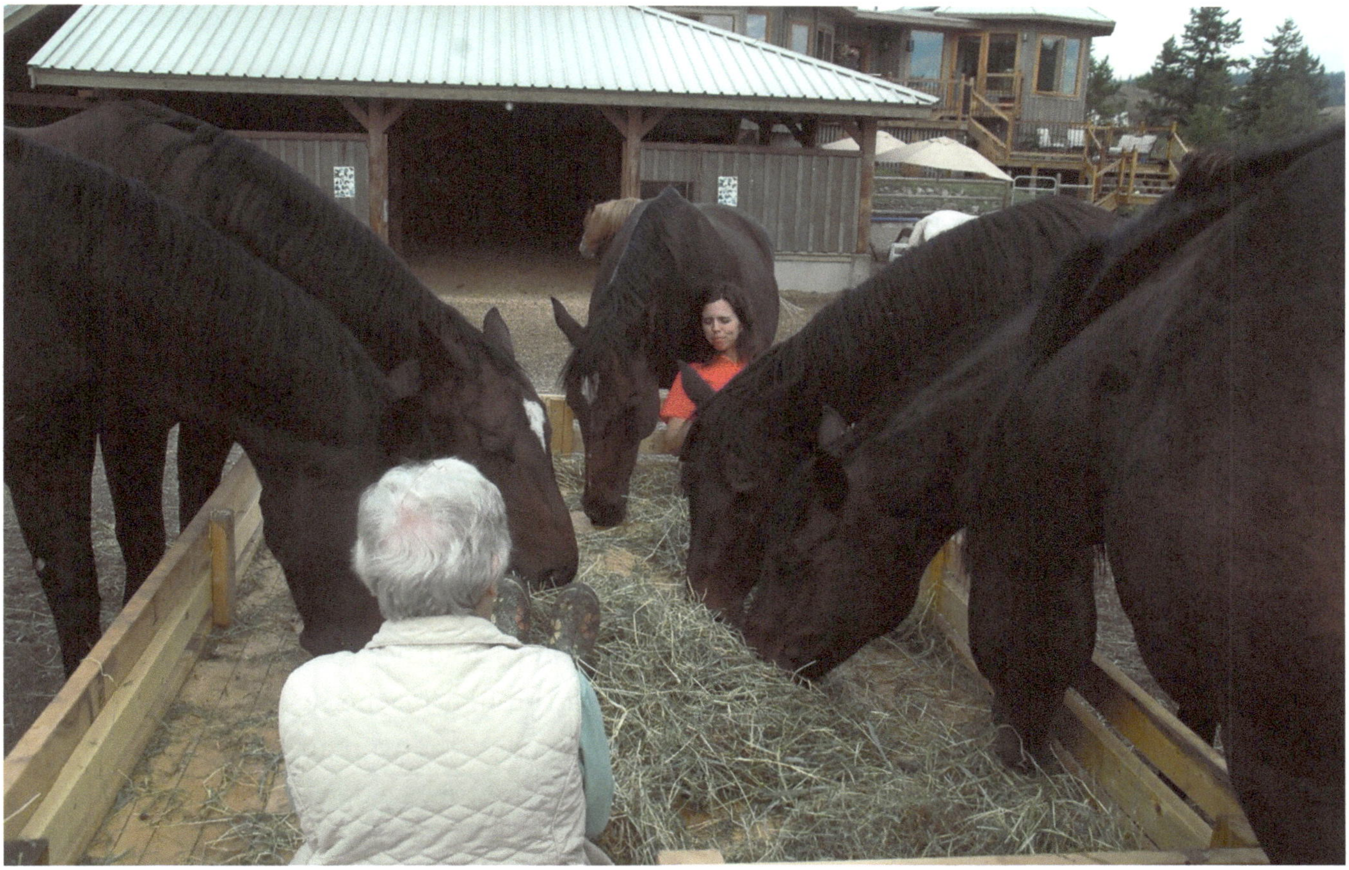

Our purpose is very simple. Each is unique in an individual manner, but all purpose is synonymous with life. Each individual horse expresses life in a unique yet similar way. We are not here to advance ourselves, but to advance the creative genius of the All.

We are in constant meditation, perpetual communion with the essence of life, as it is expressed through our being. This is the purpose of life and our purpose in living. It is easy to be on purpose when one simply surrenders to the intuitive connection to the truth of being.

—Divine Edition (Diva), speaking for the Herd

The horses are continuing to amaze with ever more spontaneous expressions of Divine wisdom. I am noticing a new pattern to their morning activities with the sacred geometry and group meditation earlier on and individual and group visits to the healing tables just before lunch. On occasion I have tried to coax them to tables but it never works and they are determined to do things their way. We still are having amazing transformations in the people who are led here so who am I to question?

The last retreat we had a first time ever expression of consciousness in our ranch vehicle who conspired on a participant's behalf. I won't mention names but a wonderful woman who arrived unable to walk for more than short distances slowly, was being conveyed to the Third Eye Chakra in the Kubota when it, for the first time ever, came to a grinding halt with a flat tire. The woman managed to walk the rest of the way to the Third Eye and back and arrived feeling energized and much better. The crystal energy in the Earth here has amazing healing properties, and I told her to open the chakras in her feet and allow it to flow up from the Earth through her body. Amazingly, the Kubota had its tire pumped up and didn't leak again and the woman went on to get stronger each day, eventually crossing the property several times a day and climbing the hills faster than I was.

The horses did some incredible work on her as well. She joined their healing circle in the barn and a whirlwind of healing ensued. One after another the horses presented themselves, raising vibration and clearing stuck energies. Michael, our 29-year-old token male who bravely joined the five other women, was not so brave in the chaotic flurry of horses healing and climbed the barn walls to safety on assorted ledges, winning him the endearment of "Spiderman" and a collection of pictures from a new perspective.

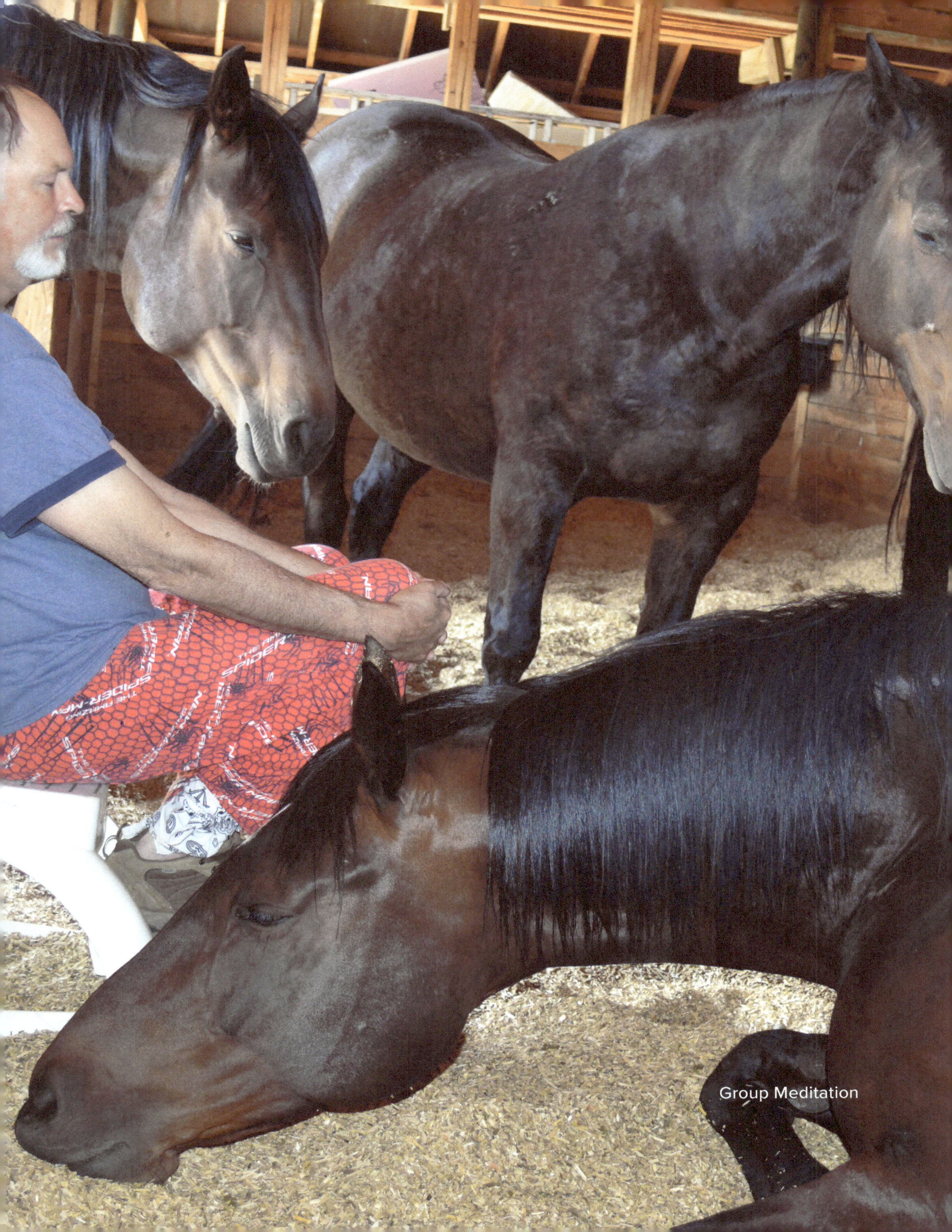

Group Meditation

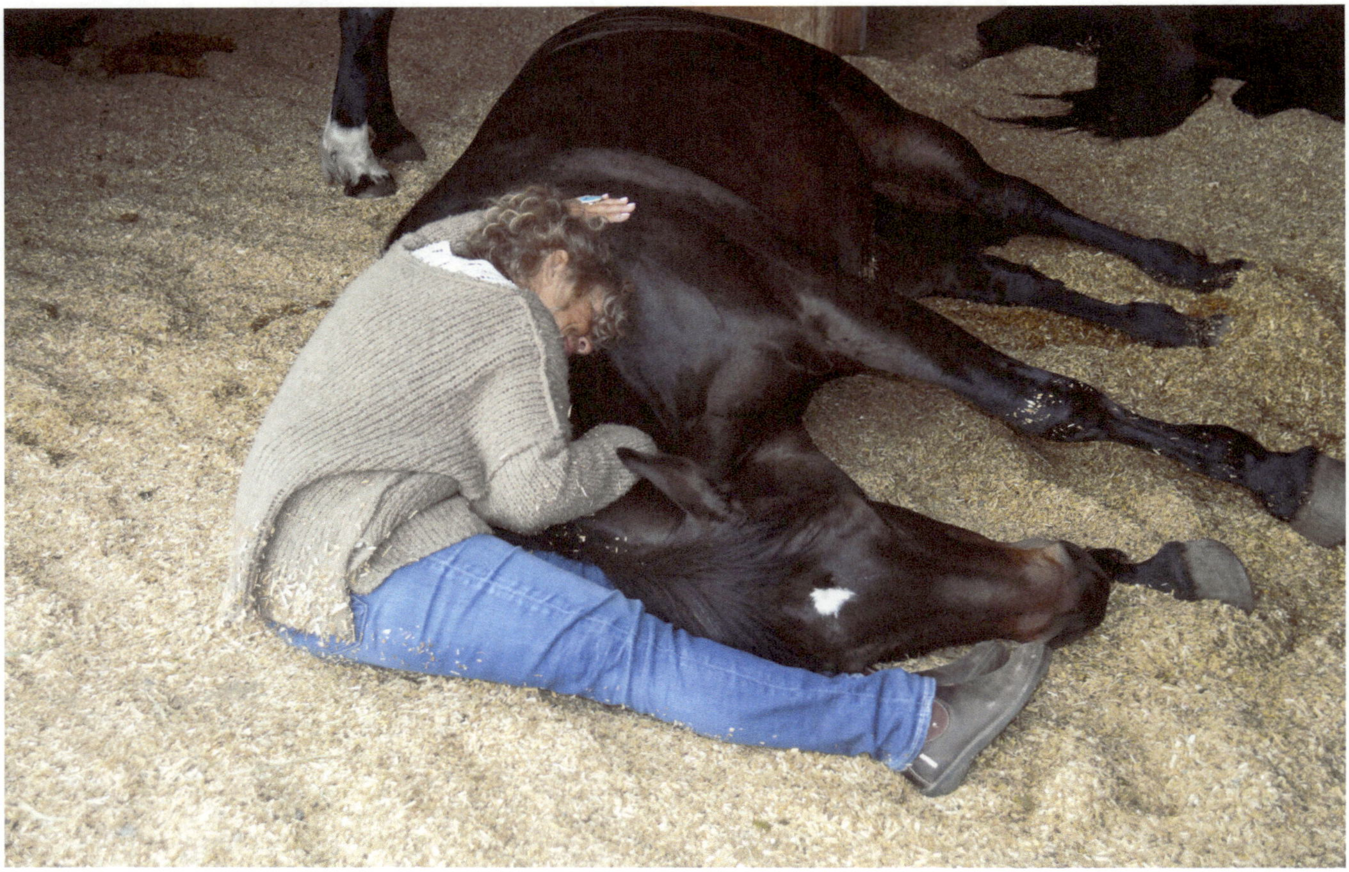

There is great excitement and celebration in horse consciousness everywhere. Horses are reaching out to their humans, inviting their participation in a whole new level of connection. People are becoming more aware of the importance of accessing higher mind, the one consciousness in all life. The future of the Earth depends on the healthy functioning of our larger body, the All.

Diva explains in The Truth According to Horses:

Examine the analogy of man as a vital organ in the body of the Earth—let us say, the liver—which has functions that are numerous and essential.

The liver has grown entirely out of proportion, covered with a cancerous growth that is not only affecting the organ itself, but also the survival of the body that depends on it. The individual cells of the liver, each with their own intelligence, are running in all directions; they are fearful and have lost their connection to the unified whole. They are no longer in touch with the wisdom of the liver itself, and they are now at cross-purposes. The other organs go about their lives, functioning with their individual intelligence and in concert with the other organs, providing systems that nourish and support the body as a whole. The liver, however, is no longer performing its necessary function for the health, the very life of the body. Should the other organs fight with the liver and compromise it even further, or should they try to maintain harmony and support, in hopes that the liver will eventually regain its health?"

Life changing idea isn't it? I hope all of you are beginning to understand the exciting new potential in our resonating on a higher level where all hearts and minds are joined, connecting to the miracle of all life — loving our neighbour as ourselves, whether that neighbour has four legs or two.

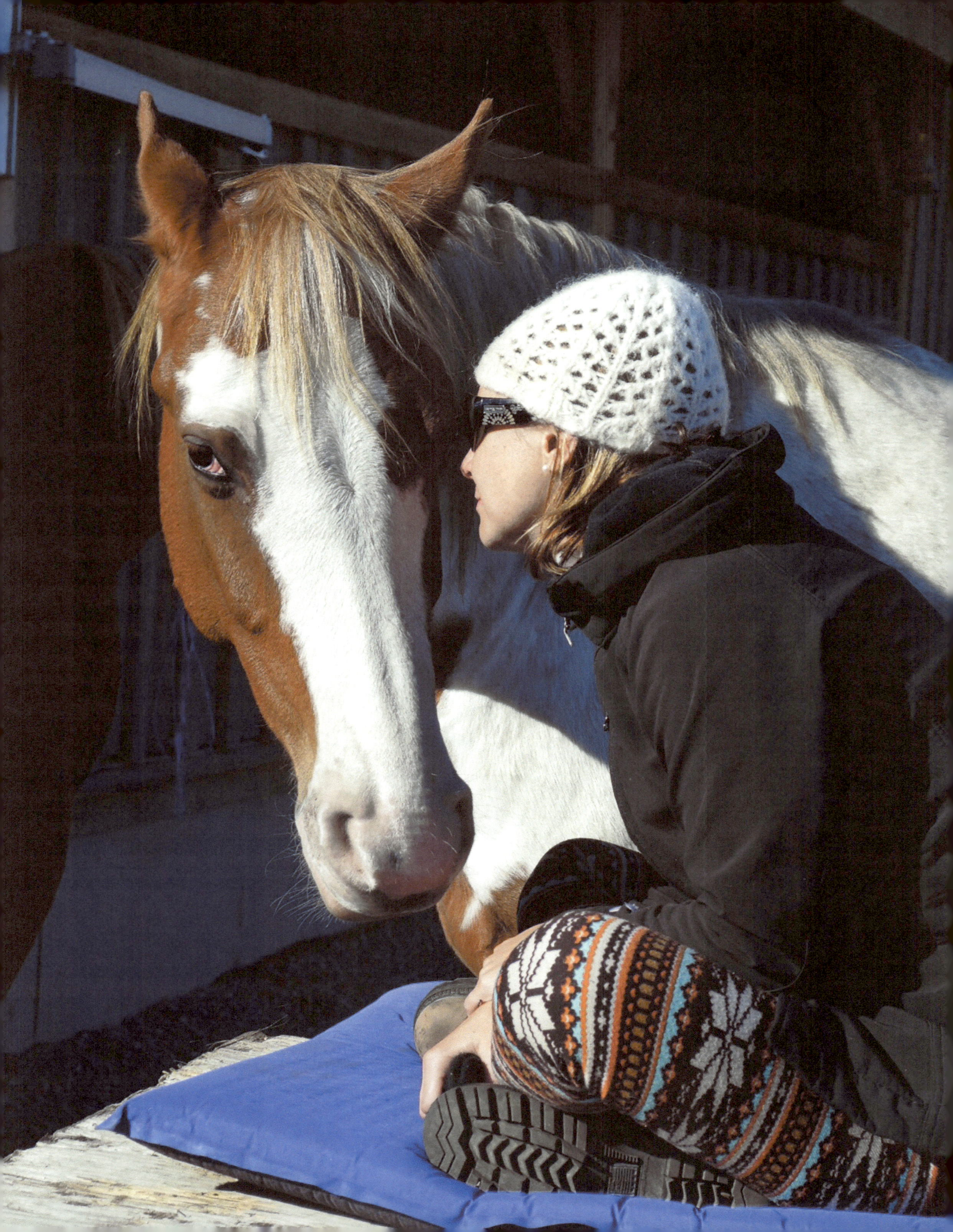

Horse consciousness has always resonated with higher truth. The following is from *The Truth According to Horses*

When you connect to us, you connect to a higher truth. We show you how to experience honestly, freely. We show you how to overcome your fears. We have given you a vision that all of you who connect to HORSE can relate to. Riding across the clouds on a spirit horse, no constraint—just you and the horse—at one. No fears; just freedom. This is the image we send you again and again. You are seduced by it. It is your ultimate desire to live life fully in that state. Yet again and again you recoil to that narrow perspective that is life lived through the ego.

How did you become convinced that there were limits in a limitless universe? We wonder, not being part of your delusion. On one level you understand the truth I speak, but on another, it threatens everything you hold dear. Why you hold it dear is unfathomable, as it does not serve you well. Riding bareback across the clouds, with no constraint, is one of your fondest desires. We can take you there. We can carry you across the clouds that block your understanding, that obscure your vision. Listen to your heart, connect to our hearts, and trust what you remember to be true. It is all there inside of us—who we are. You have just forgotten. Wake up and let us help you regain your trust.

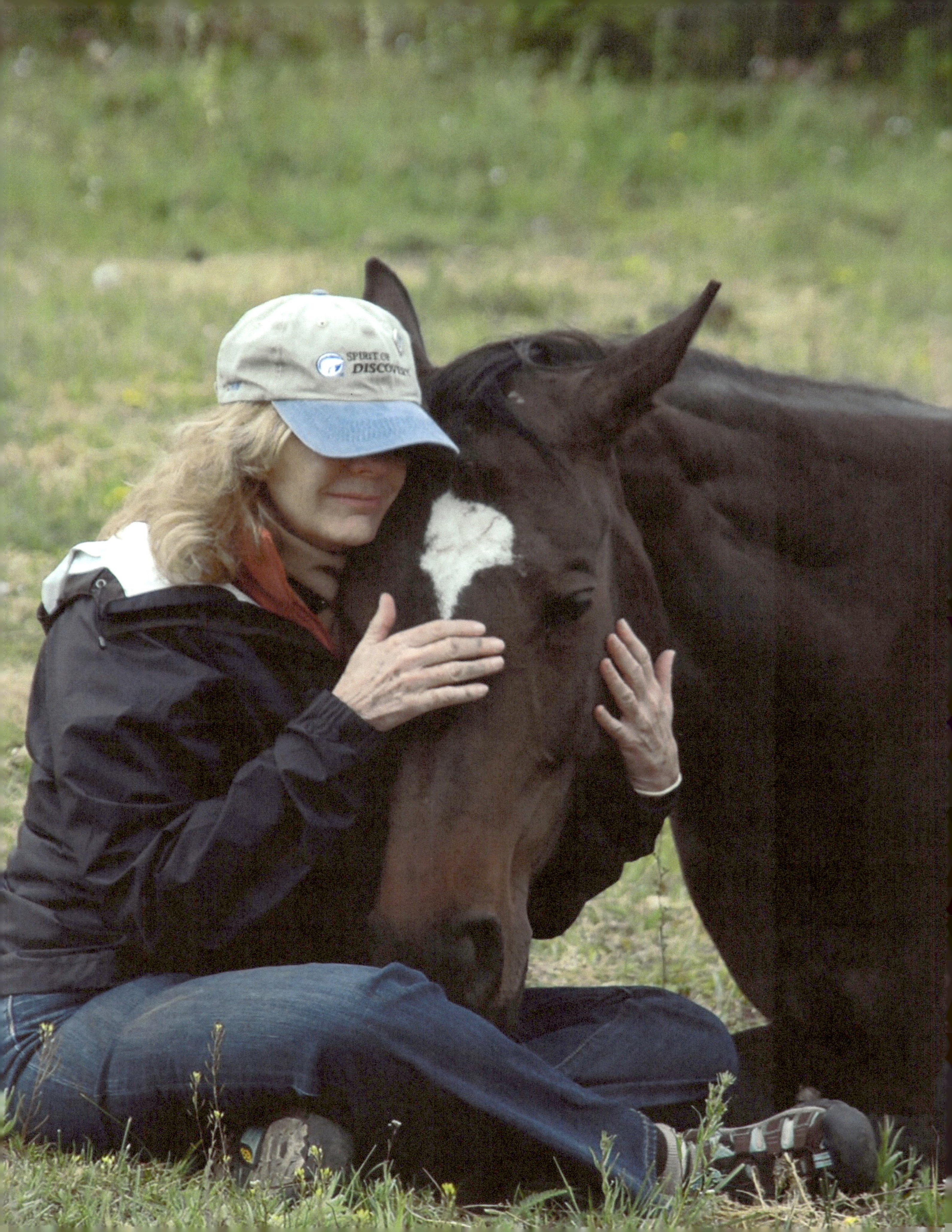

From our cat Ben (presently in spirit) (Min Buddha Ben Puss Ha):

It is interesting how you humans say one minute that God is within all life but then narrow that statement to "We (meaning humans) are the image or essence of God." If God is within all life, then why would some of that life be more like God than others? Here in spirit, it is all very clear that form is a temporary expression. My consciousness, which is a segment of the ALL, can express in any form I choose. I can experience a flower, a sunset, a cat, a fish, or a man. I am simply consciousness that takes shape according to my thoughts. When I am experiencing different forms, my consciousness is still "I" and if you examine the semantics, everyone and everything identifies with "I." We are all "I," a point of consciousness, and we are all no different from each other as far as consciousness goes. Because I choose to manifest as a cat, does not make me less worthy. We have, and will experience all aspects of expression. The big difference with humans is that they have forgotten all this. When they separated from the ALL, and all other aspects of the ALL, they became self-absorbed and developed a belief system of their own. Their truth is not universal truth and they have become blind and deaf to information that might contradict their belief. When you all believed the world was flat, it took many brave adventurers to dispel that myth. To go beyond the veil, at least when you are experiencing on the physical plane, you need our help.

Instead of cataloguing us as lesser beings, entertain the possibility that we are just different. Explore what we offer, talk to us, spend time being open to our energy and the energy of nature. You will not find people who live in nature who are apart and separate from the rest of life. They communicate and share with all things living. When you do this we will take you beyond the veil, for we have not forgotten the truth and isolated ourselves in a finite world of opposites. You, the

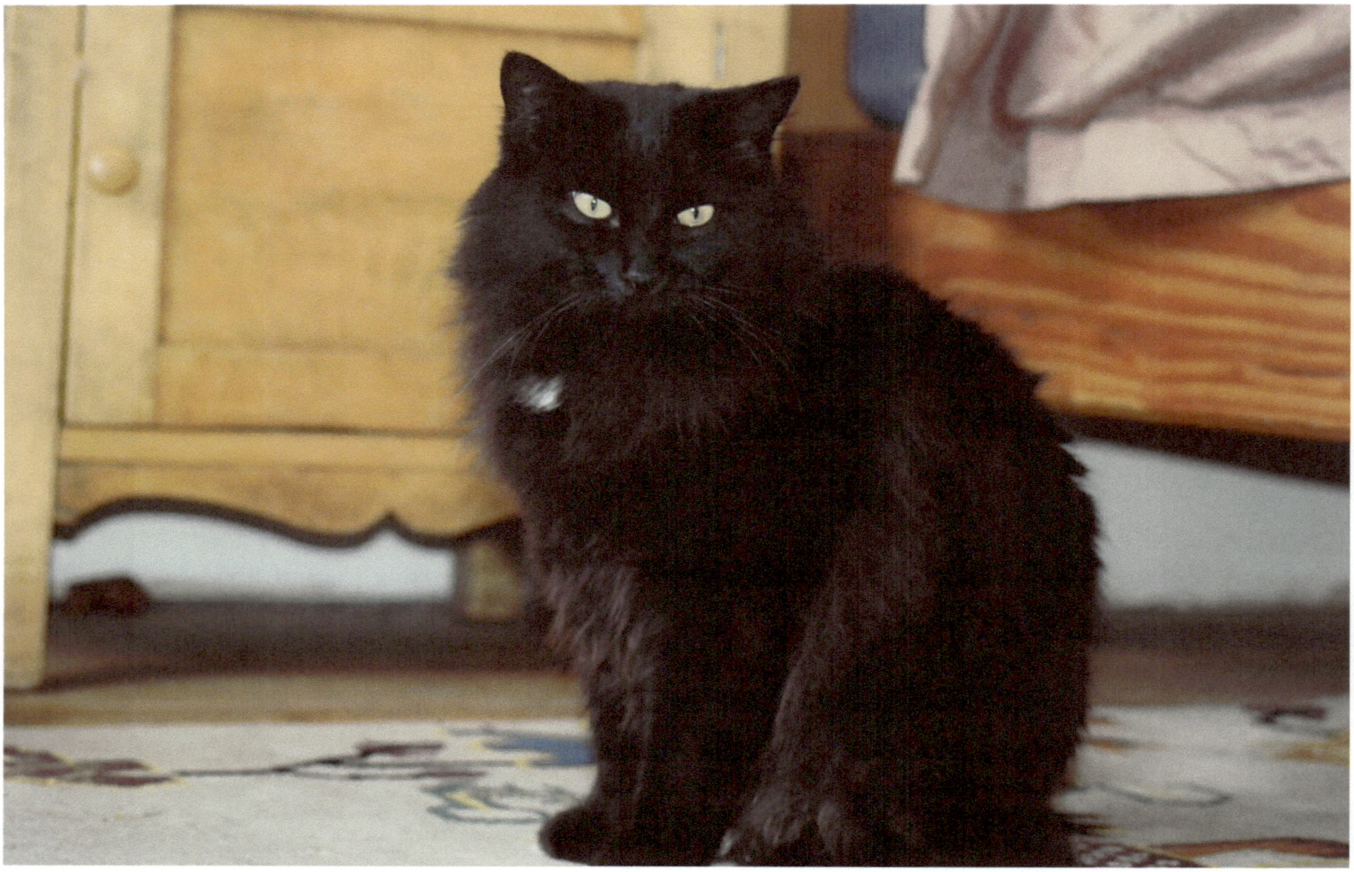

Nune, presently in spirit

supposed intelligent ones, have used that intelligence to invent your own world. You thought you could do better than the ALL, but you are beginning to see evidence of your error. You have repeated this pattern for all time, thinking: my country, race, religion, house, clothes, car, thoughts, are better than yours, and as a whole your species is better than all other species. Don't you see where all your competition has gotten you? There will always be another to argue with you. We animals do not compare. We go about our business of "isness." Being is all we experience, and we share that being with all creation. Let us take you to the place of truth, where there are no opposites, no differences, a place where there is only spiritual freedom, beyond the veil.

I am the darkness of possibility,
Warm and comforting.
I am the softness of a whisper,
Speaking without words.
I am truth gestating,
In the womb of life,
Holding for you the memory of magic.

—Nune, speaking for The All

The following are some magical moments from retreats that I haven't shared in newsletters:

Karen, from Australia, arrived for a private retreat and the morning of day one we discussed her journey before she had met the Herd. Karen, a nurse, was involved with offering massage therapy to babies emotionally damaged either in utero or shortly after birth. She shared that when the babies had a breakthrough they began tongue thrusting, to which I replied, "That's interesting as the horses do the same when they are releasing energy." About an hour after first meeting with the Herd, the horses in turns, all began tongue thrusting while looking at Karen and it continued all the first day (just to let her know they saw her) and has never been seen since.

Ana, a film maker from Brazil, arrived with her son Juan to begin her Equinistic Healing Certification. I asked on day one, after noticing that Crystal and Prospera held space and shared in meditation, close, but not too close, if she had created any boundaries to feel safe. The answer was "most definitely," but by day two Ana was so comfortable she welcomed the Herd without confine. I have never witnessed before the flow like a symphony in which the entire Herd were players. They came to the tables in family groups, like dancers, breathing, caressing, directing the energy along the body with the sweep of their heads, resting their chins on blocked areas, even laying their heads on Ana's lap, the beauty of the dance continuing for hours and rippling out through the layers of the entire Herd.

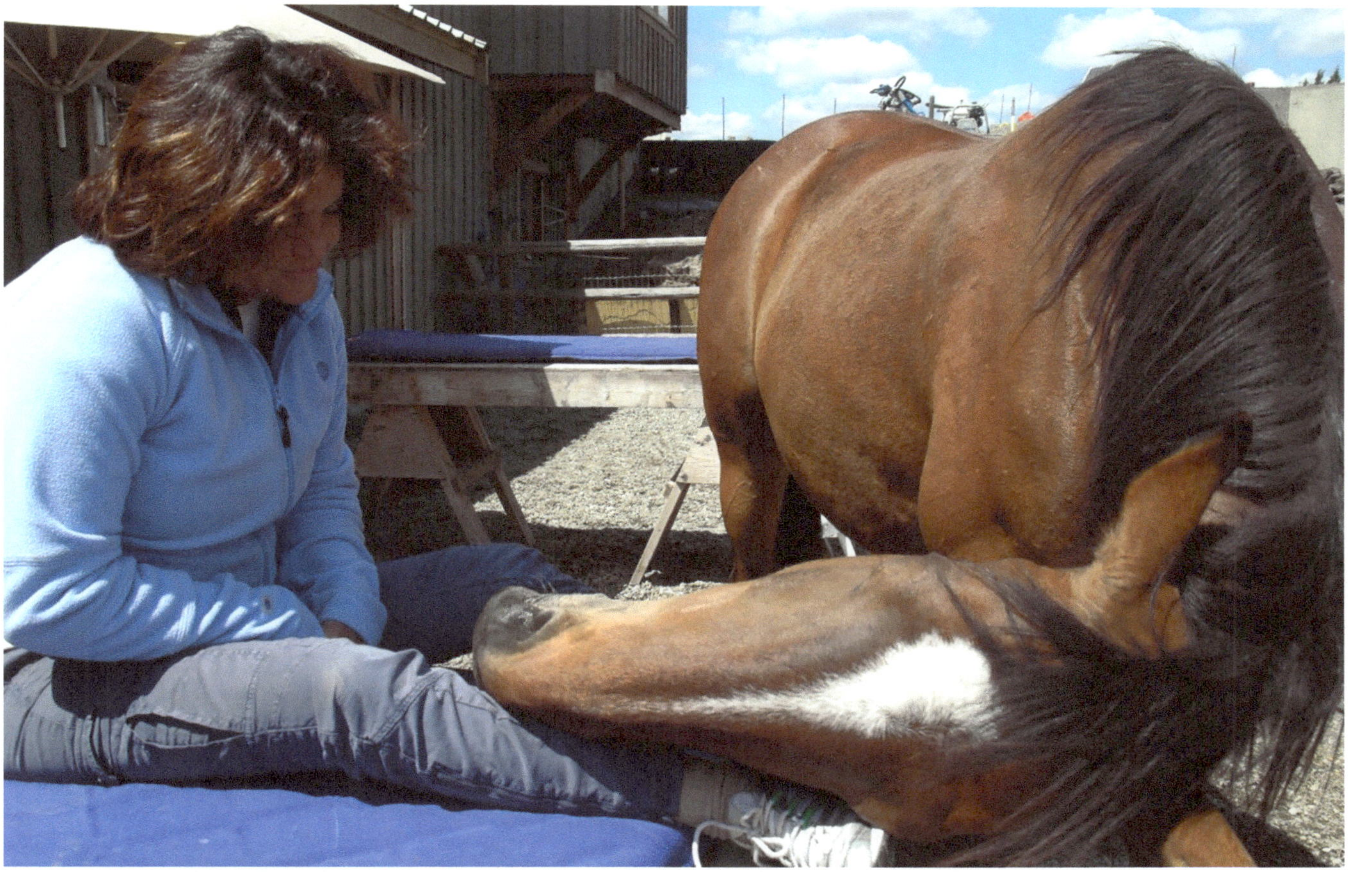

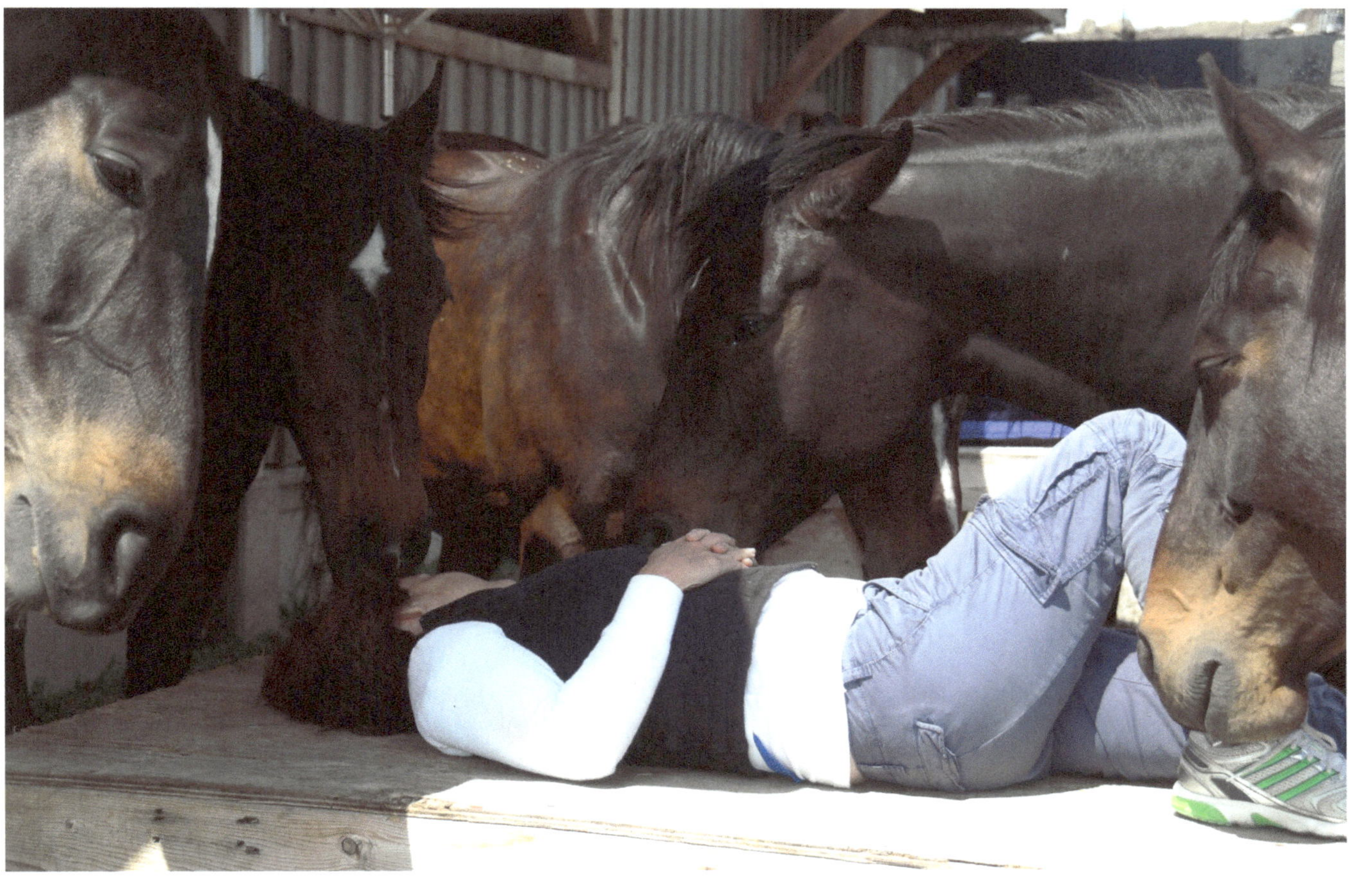

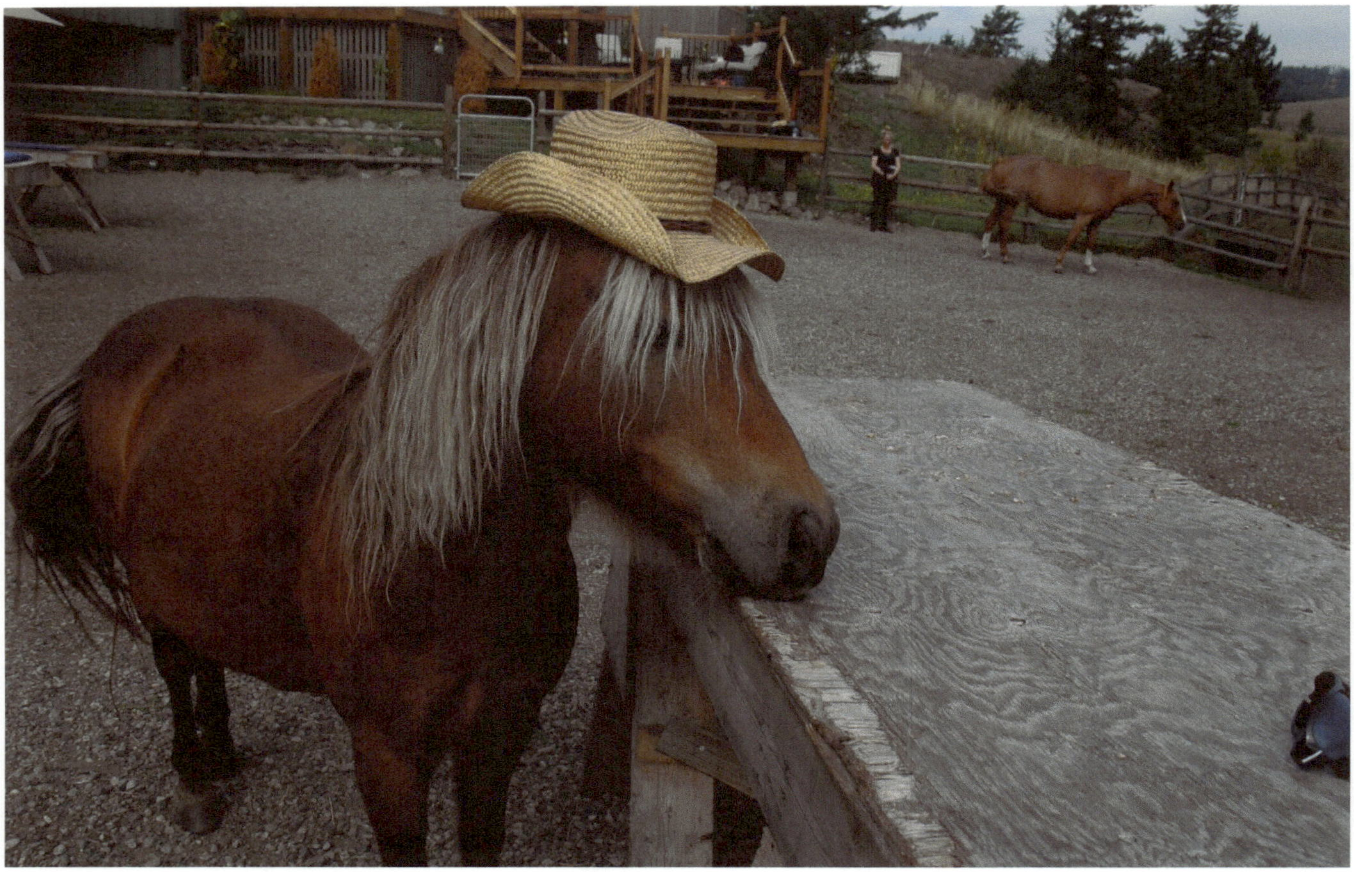

The healing tables are empty and the land is quiet. Even though you are far away, please don't forget us. We are with you in thoughts and dreams. Don't forget what we have taught you—always remember you are held in the arms of love forever and always...ALL ways. We are traveling quickly now. It is exponential, with each heart, each mind, one mind, one heart at a time—we are evolving to become the highest vision of our earthly experience. Remember who you are and why you chose this adventure. We are counting on you to be the change you believe in. "You and I can change the world, one mind at a time...imagine." The tipping point is only a fractional proportion of mass mind consciousness. Be child-like, be innocent, be truthful and be LOVE!

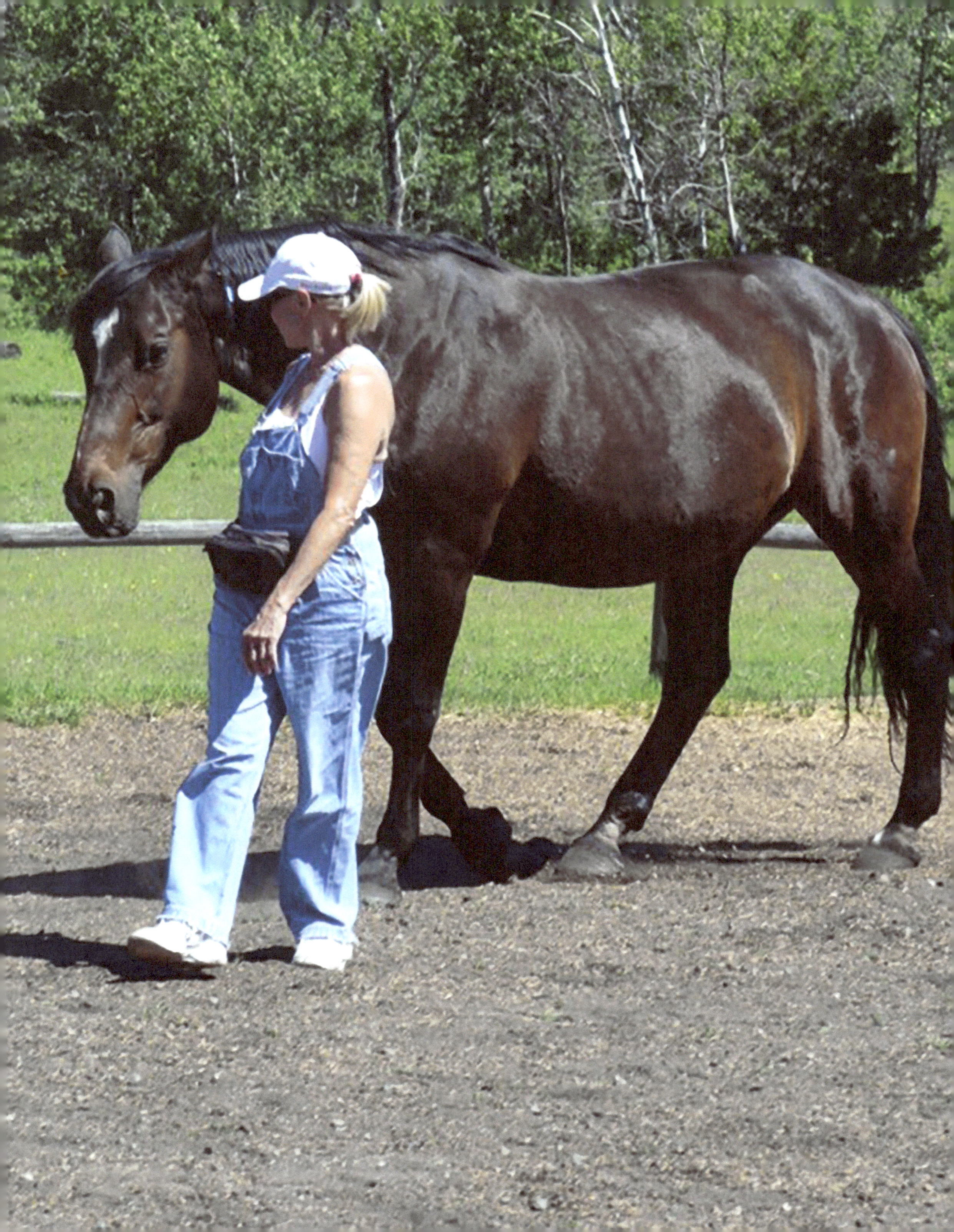

From *The Truth According to Horses*:

Follow for a time in our footsteps. You will find a narrow path winding across the landscape. We follow one after another, making little impact on the Earth. Our way is welcoming and non-obtrusive. We pause; we interact with our environment. There is no hurry; no concern. Our intuition is our compass and soul companion. There is a rhythm to our days. We choose to sleep under starry skies on a mattress of deep grass, sheltered from the wind and weather by a thick hedge of trees. We are curious of all we encounter, and our days are full of discovery. We do not care to change the world, but only to enjoy it.

Grazing is what we do best and it involves far more than nourishment for our bodies. It nourishes our souls. People should take time to graze. They hurry through unaware of most that they encounter, in a rush to succeed at whatever it is they desire. We don't understand desire. Our needs are met. What else could we possibly imagine? We see people as confused, misdirected. There is one clear path. It is narrow but well defined and it is simple to follow. Why do humans head out in myriad directions, wreaking havoc with the landscape? One builds bridges; the other makes dams. They think the grass will look better cut, and they make endless work for themselves. They want to travel quickly, and horses offer too much commitment, so they choose cars or bikes. They want to fly across the heavens and they stuff themselves into metal birds.

Somehow they are missing the point. It is all perfect the way it is. You cannot improve on God's creation. You can only enjoy it, or wander so far off the path that it is a struggle to make your way back.

How perfect is fur or feathers to manmade inventions? How intricate the workings of each and every creature and their interaction with each other and the Earth itself?

Man creates; man destroys. He cannot create in perfection, so there are always consequences. It is all a learning curve in his land of opposites.

True creation can only occur on the spiritual plane where all is perfect, and there are no consequences.

Man regards animals who follow instinct as strange. Migrating caribou or lemmings are all completing a purpose that is profitable for the Earth. Waring or self-destructing humans are at cross purposes. Not only do they not benefit the ecosystem, but they poison and destroy it.

We forever wonder when you regard yourselves as superior. In what way can you consider your misdirected ambition an asset to the Earth? We simply commune; we appreciate. Your path is one of destruction. You enter the house of your host like an army with big dirty boots. You carry guns instead of plowshares and you mutilate instead of reciprocate.

We animals walk softly; we speak of peace and understanding. Our path is simple, and our needs are small. Come and join us even for a moment now and then. It is infectious, it is effusive, the peace you will find there.

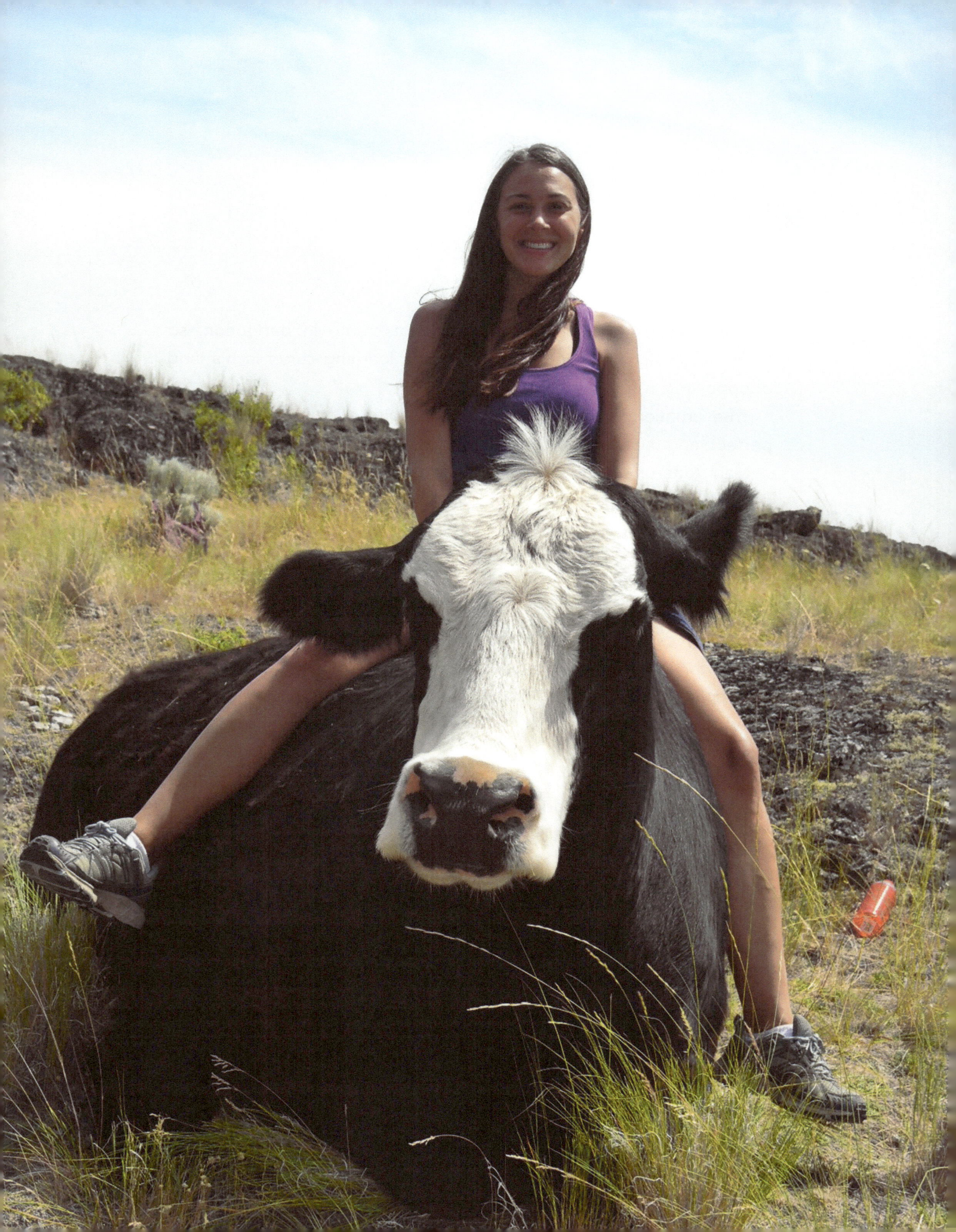

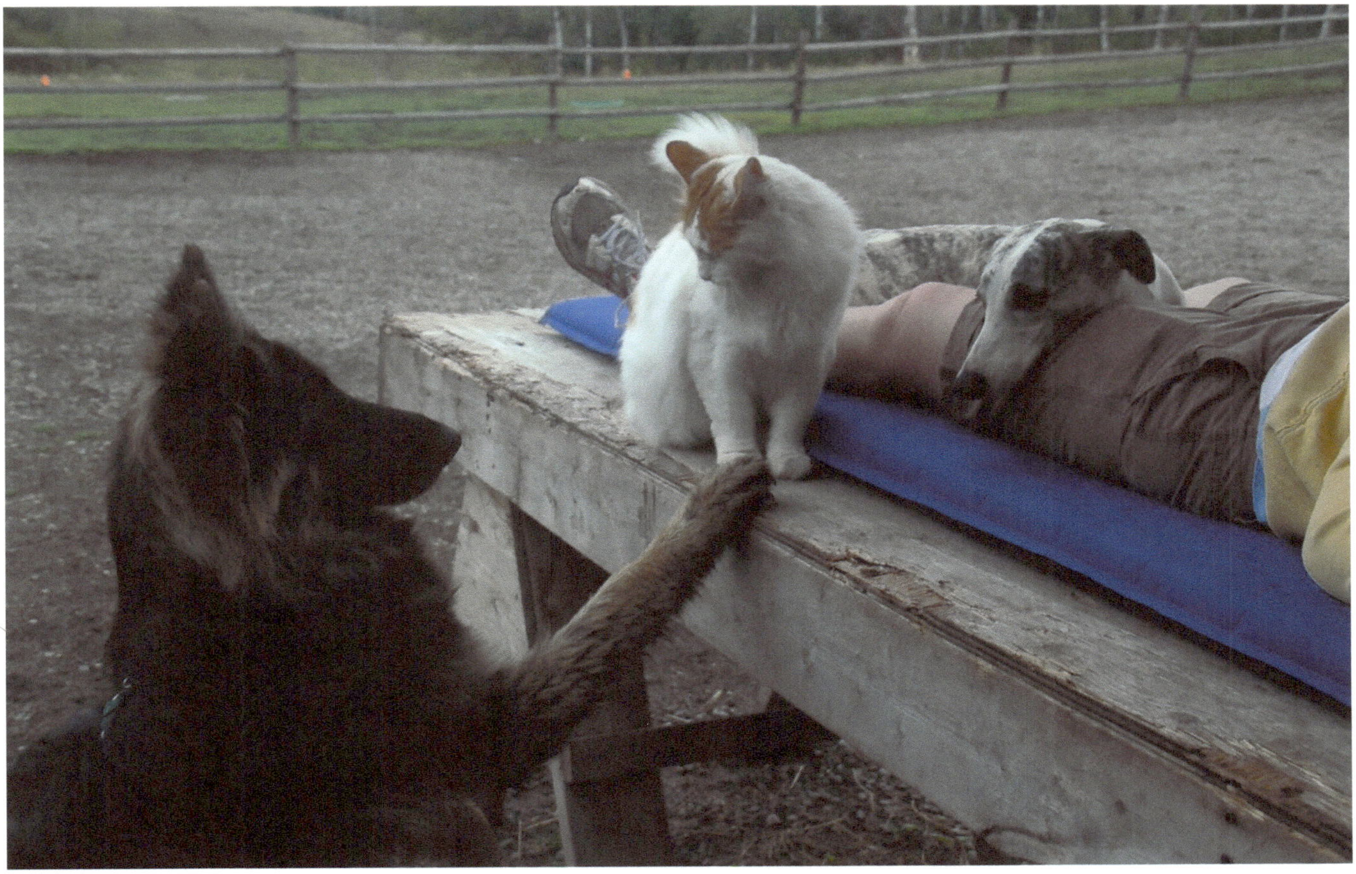

Have you noticed how people everywhere are speaking more and more about animals as important contributors to the spiritual evolution of our planet? As the level of consciousness is rising to a vibrational match where many species can communicate, it will become apparent that all along it has only been a language barrier. When minds and hearts are joined, we resonate at the place where we are ALL and ONE.

Our hearts hold the same emotions and our spirits are the same essence as yours. Have you ever noticed that baby animals don't know they are different from each other? That has to be learned from their parents and the group consciousness of their species. When we reside in that place of our inner child, eternally innocent and guileless, we will play again in the garden which we have been away from for far too long.

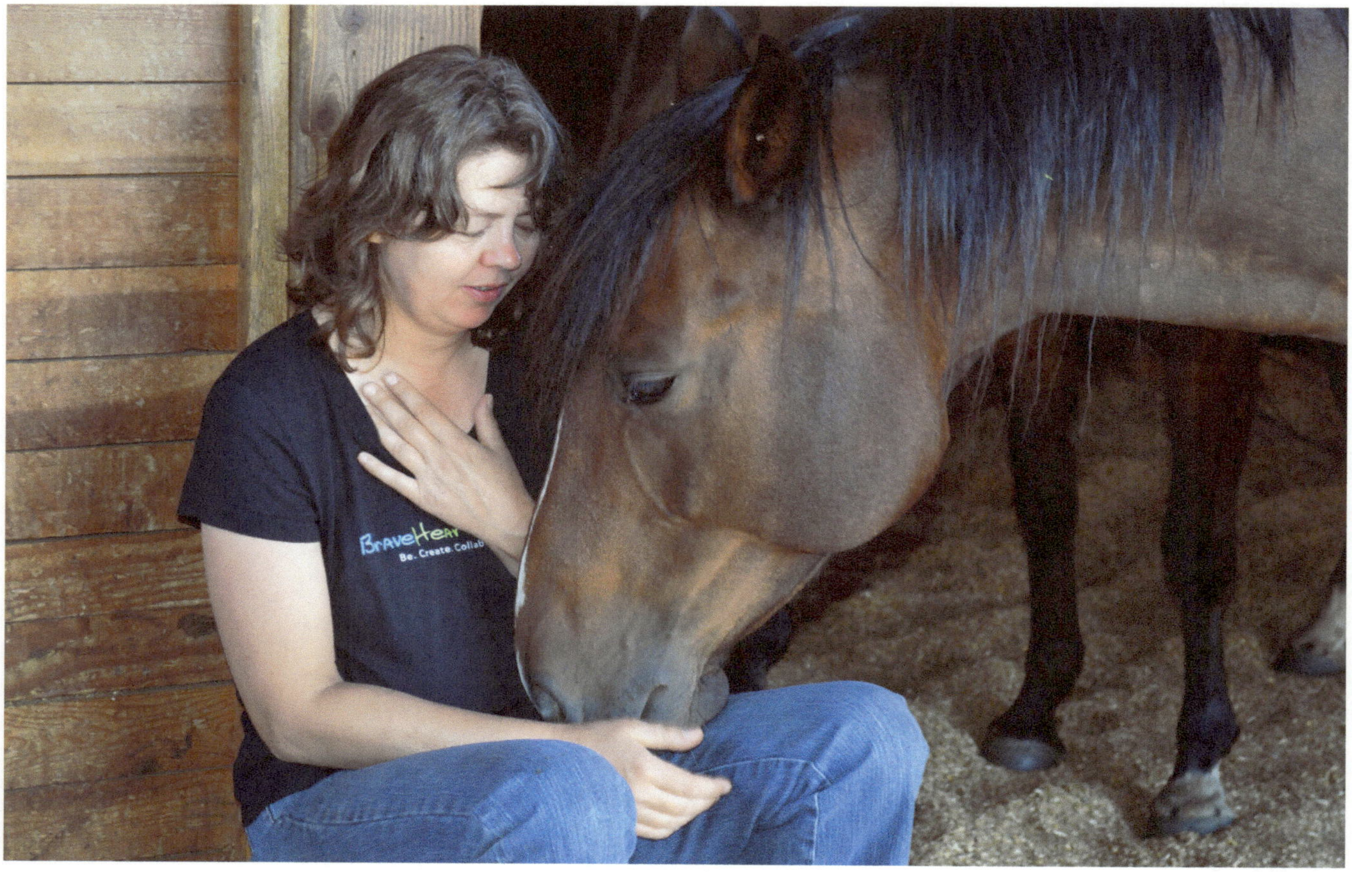

We would like to share with you horse understanding of the events that are soon to come. Do you notice everywhere there are stories of animals connecting with other animals and humans on a level that has long been forgotten? The new age that is coming will be known as the "Age of Enlightenment," meaning becoming of the light. We are all light beings no matter what our attributes. Boundaries are only thoughts and when those thoughts disappear all that exists is light. Without boundaries we are free to connect and commune with each other and higher consciousness.

Let go of your belief that you are separate and alone; that you exist for this lifetime only and you become immortal or immune to mortality. That is where we exist as one in the body of the ALL; there are no barriers and we are all Love in infinite diversity.

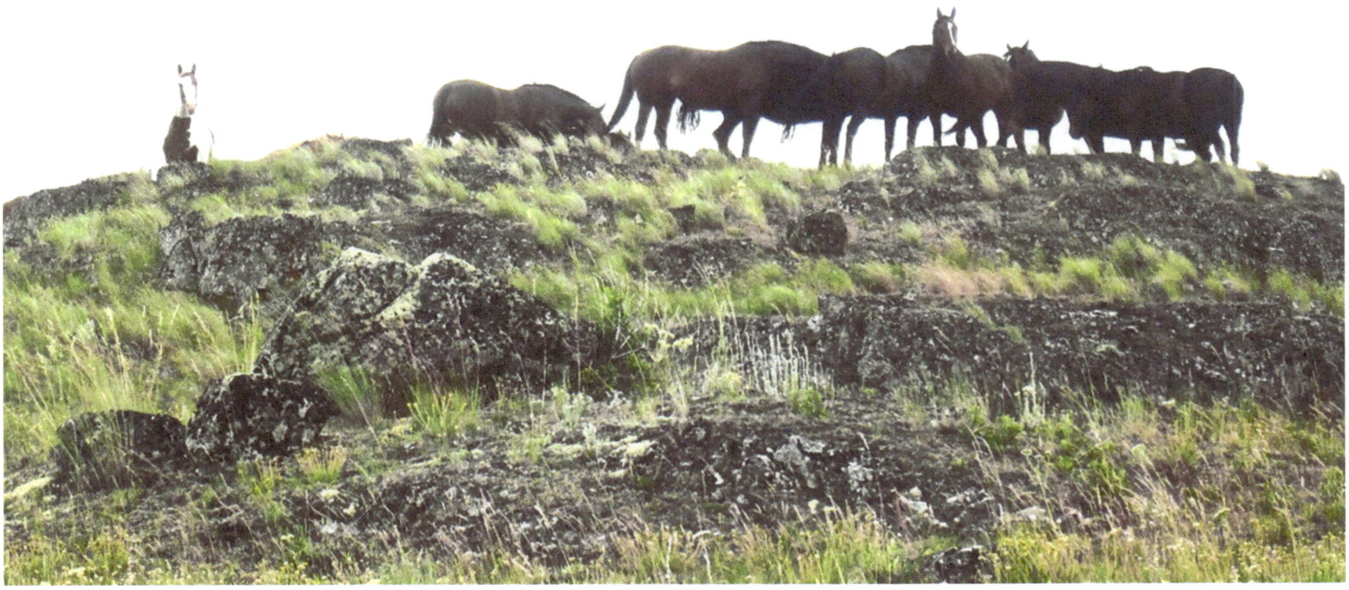

Sacred Geometry

Tamara's Story:

It was a day when I was feeling on edge, like something was about to break. I had been taking photos all morning of the amazing healing work that I had been witness to until I hit a wall of pain. With my partially healed back fracture I had sustained only weeks before, I could not maintain my "I'm OK status" anymore and I told Liz. She directed me to Crystal and L.E who were standing in a line-up with the Herd under a cool tree canopy. So over I went and sheltered with them where I stood facing these majestic beings. I took three deep breaths and started to connect with my heart.

After a while I could sense one of the human Herd come up behind me and sat down at a respectful distance. I continued to breathe and connect with the horse nation and that's when tears came down in a waterfall of release. The next moment I was falling into Connie's arms the human member of the Herd who had been called to join the healing loop. She caught my tumbling self and emotion that was pouring out; she

enveloped me. I could not help but unravel in her elegance and grace and my truth revealed itself. Once the healing was complete I came back into my body and I knew

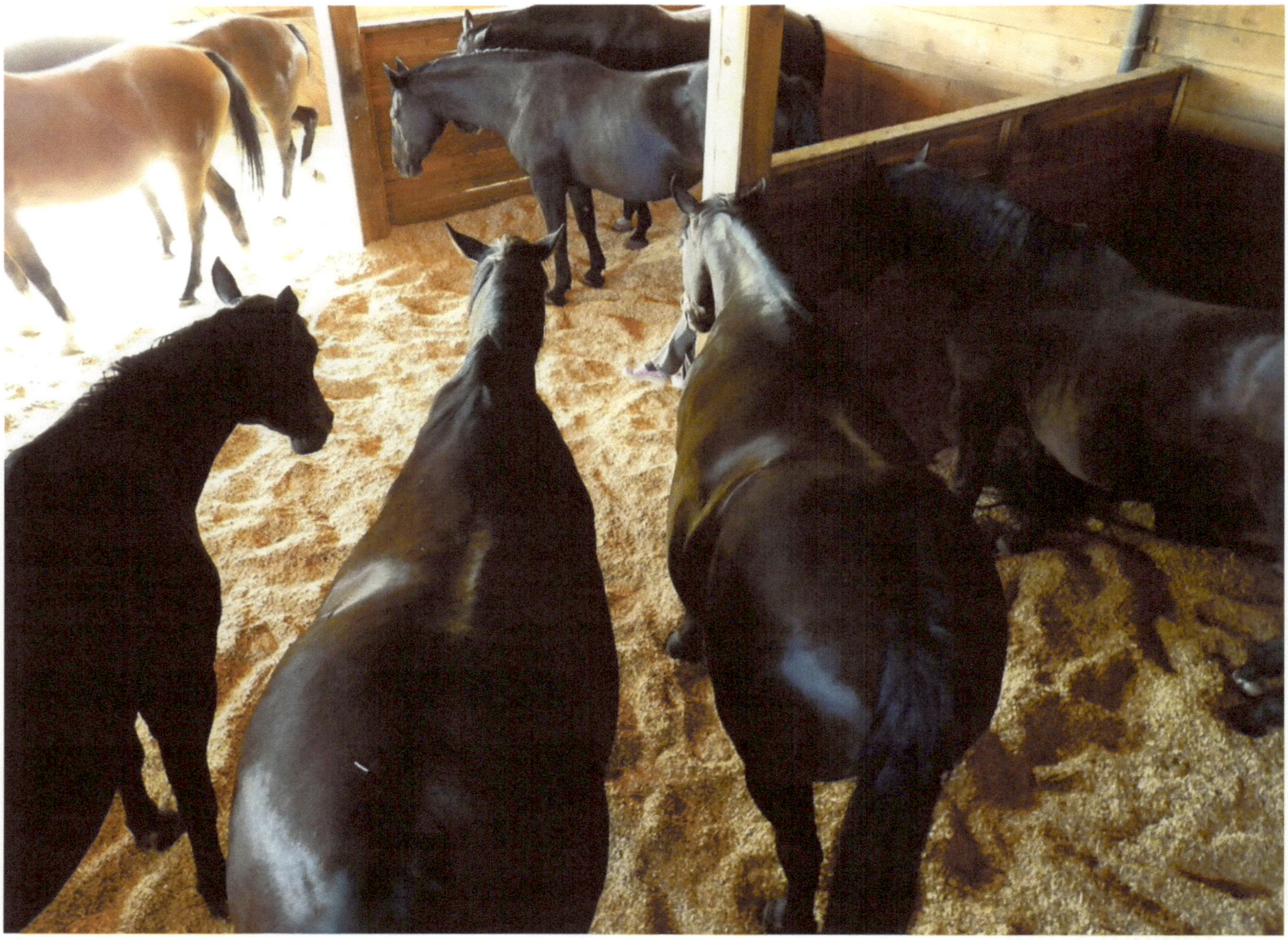

instinctively my fracture was healed and stronger than before. I am now pain-free and still absorbing my miracle 10 days later.

Upon sharing the healing experience with Connie, Connie spoke of being shown a message which was "that she had my back." I couldn't believe it as she did not know that I had fractured my back in an accident a few weeks before. It just shows that we are all so consciously connected; we just need to learn to listen more.

Connie and the Herd thank you! My burdened self is free and that has always been my greatest wish.

- Tamara

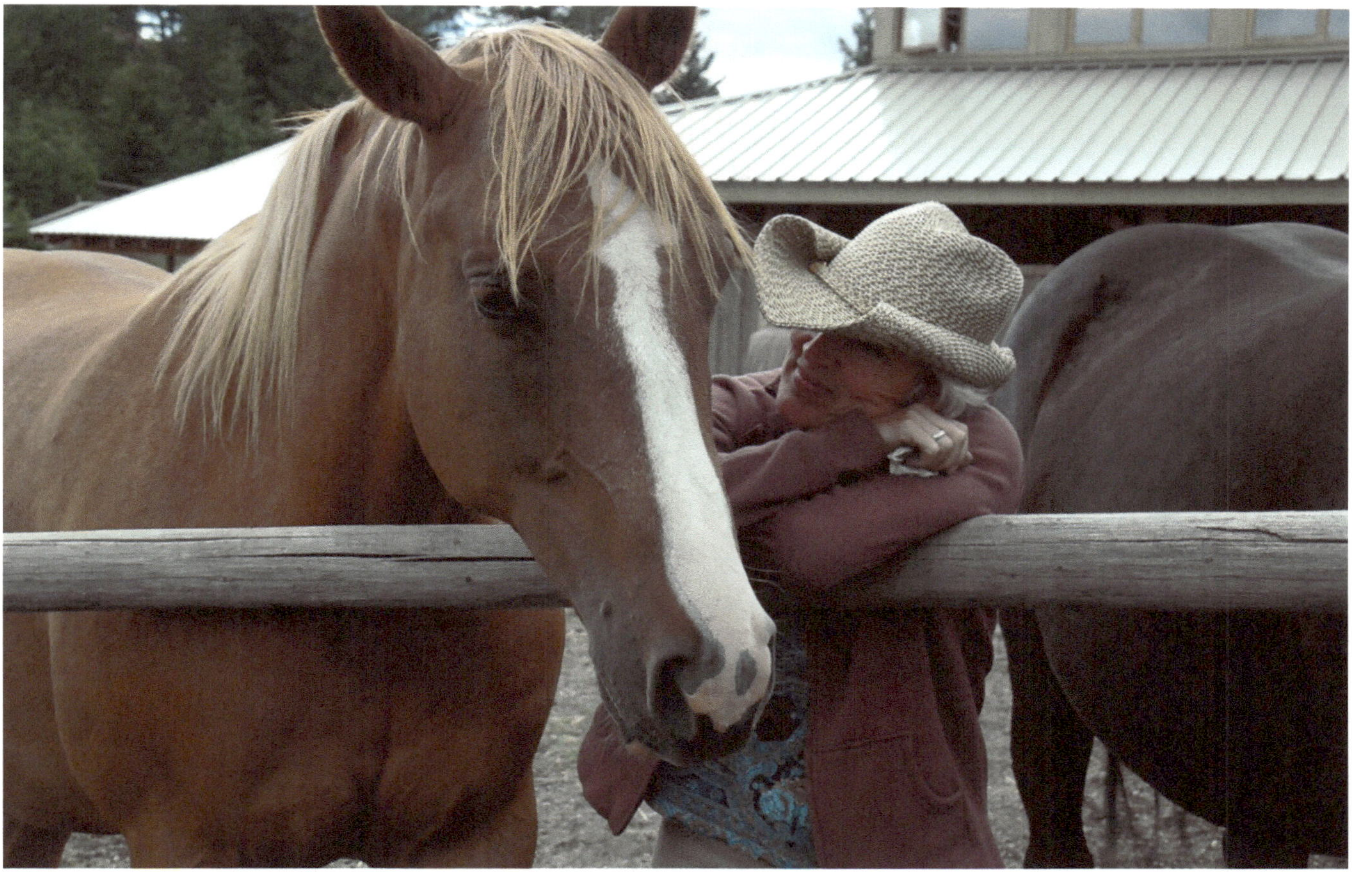

Connie and Epona

We have waited for this event since the beginning of our message for mankind. This is the dawn of a new era of spiritual evolution, of the symphony played between all species, all minds. Language, custom, race, religion, form, are simply the creative splendour of the ALL in myriad diversity. When we are joined in the moment, in love, we are all miracles in the making. Relax, let go of your limits and join us in the dance!

Absolute TRUTH and absolute LOVE,

—The Herd

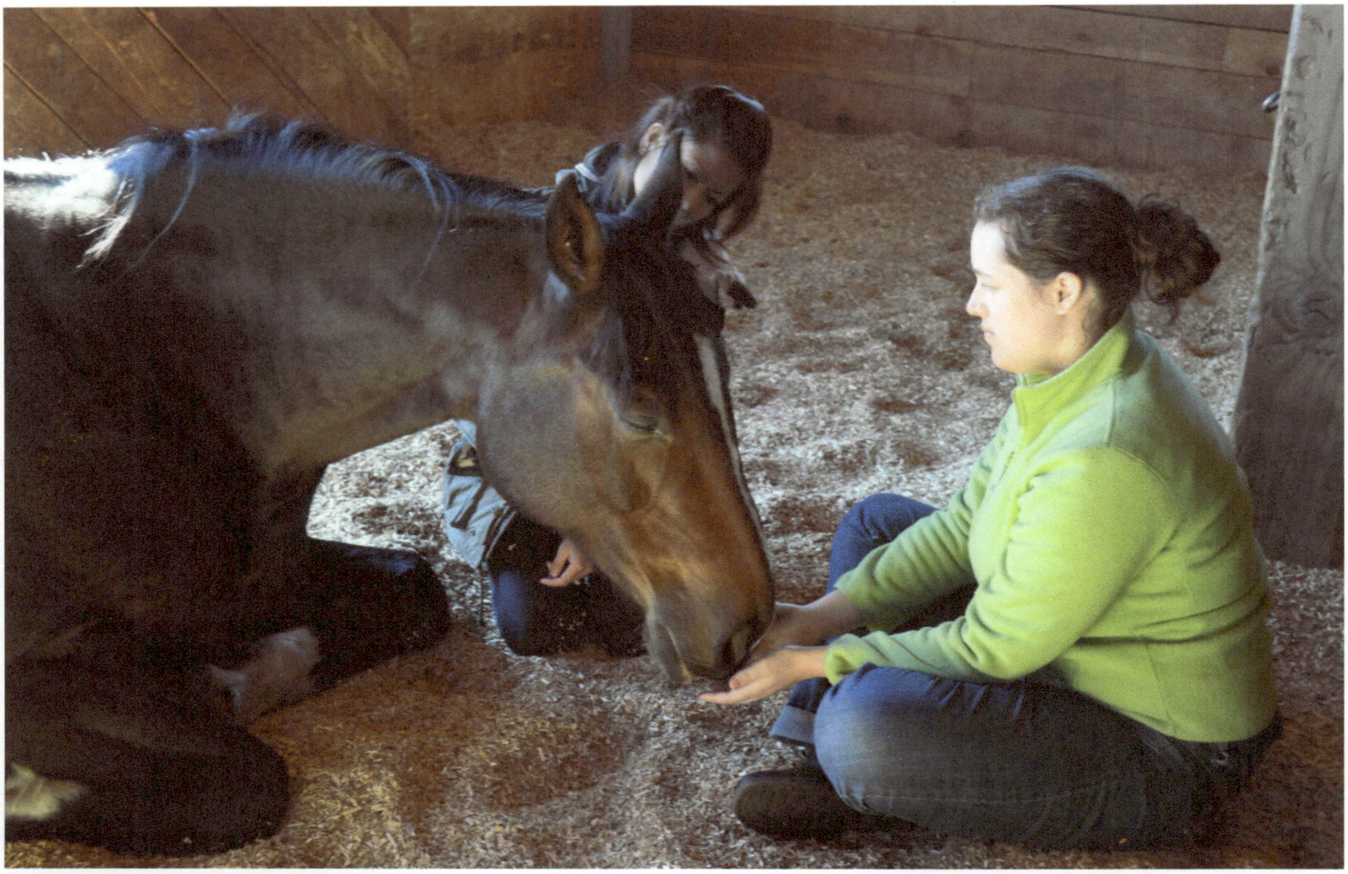

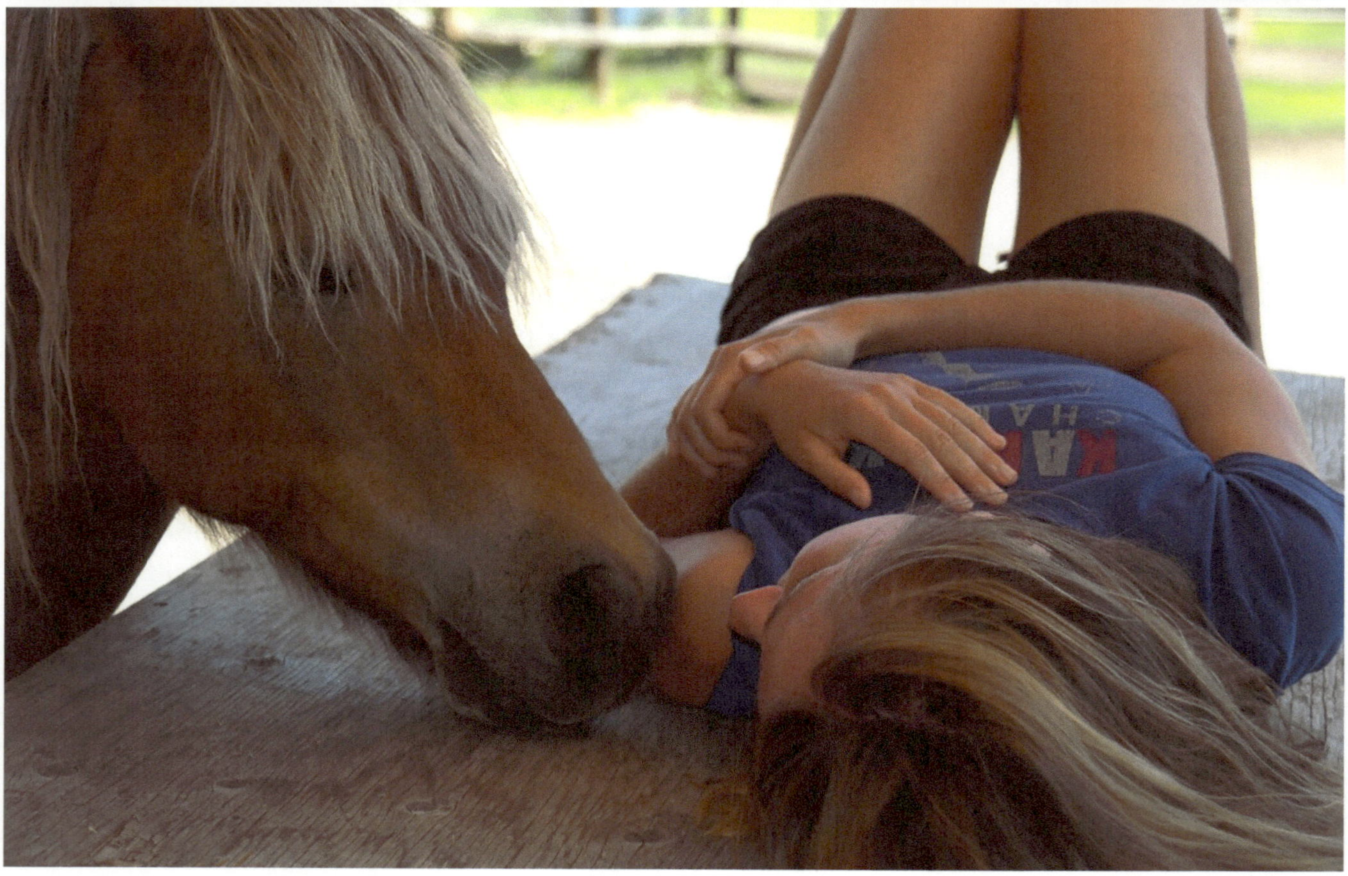

Communing

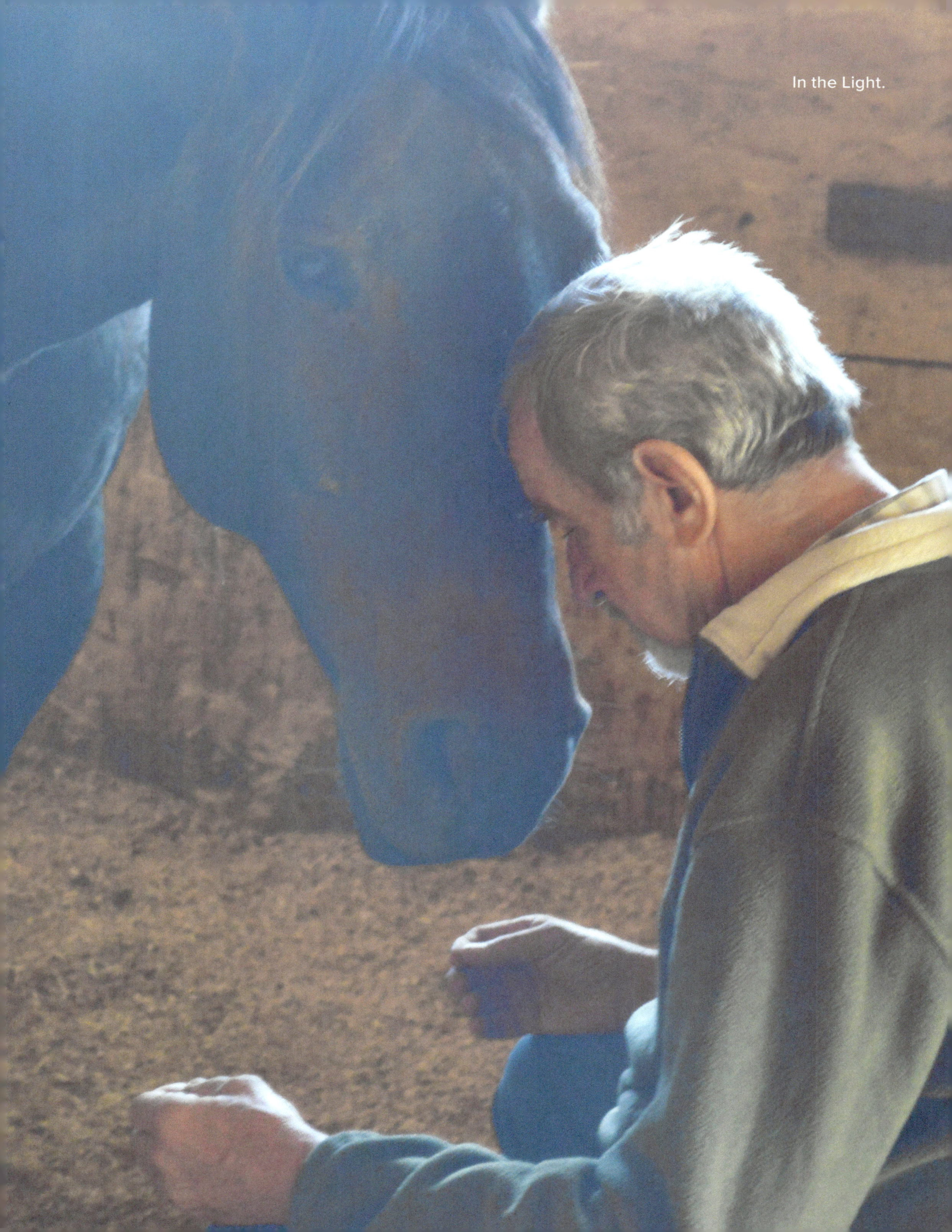

In the Light.

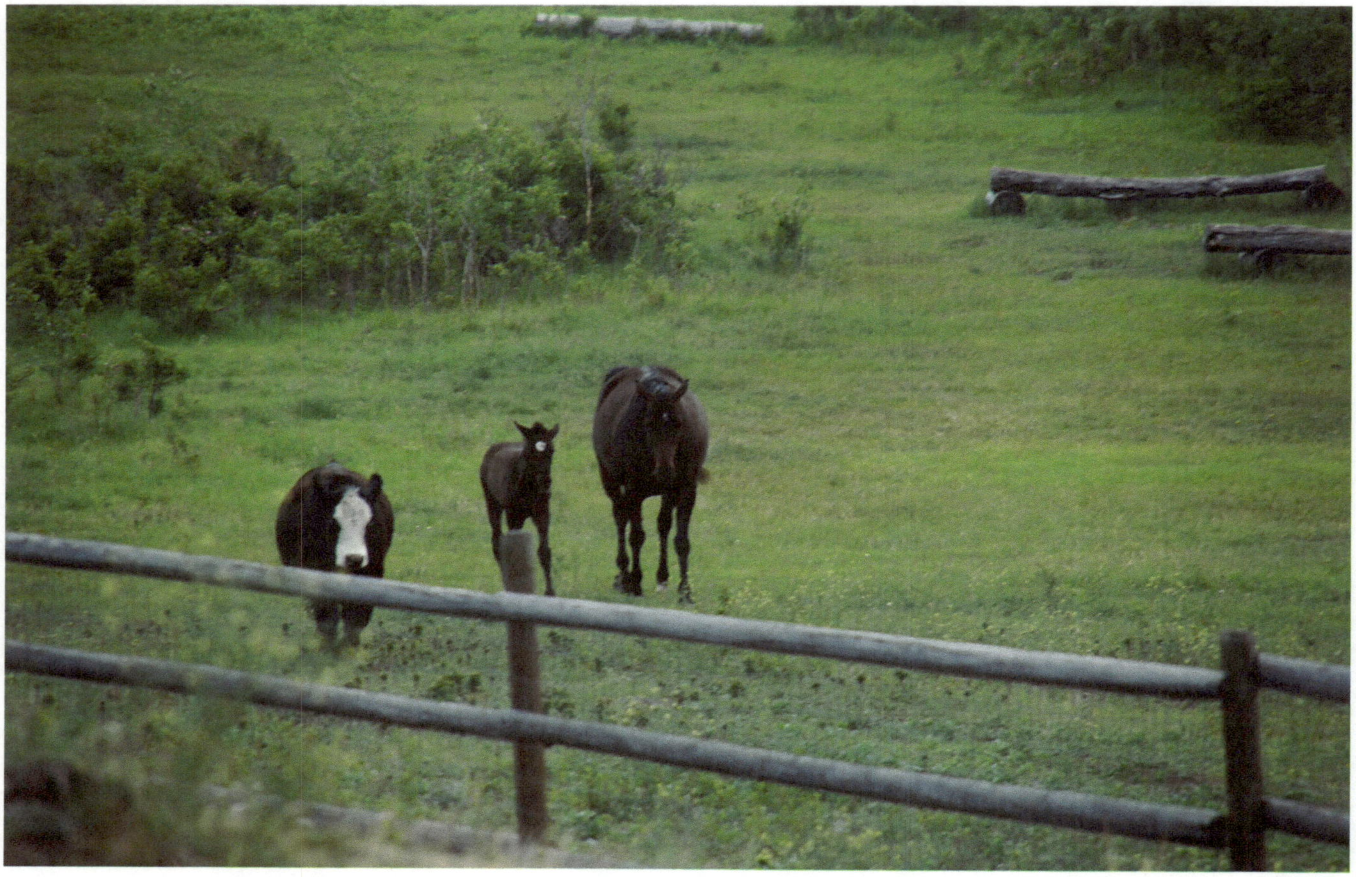

As much as Liz is hearing from people around the world who are drawn to this new understanding of consciousness, we too are in communication with horses (and many other animals) who know of what we are doing here at Gateway and want to join in and help this enormous shift gain momentum. The closer we get to 2012 and the "Age of Enlightenment" the more minds are being joined, the more animals, humans, and all of creation will begin to resonate on the same level—one where humans will remember we are ALL one; the ALL in myriad and diverse expression, all equal, all integral to the life of the bigger body of the Earth itself, and beyond that to the body of the ALL.

We are all One, every single little quark is united in the same cosmic soup. There are spaces but no boundaries—boundaries are only thoughts.

Here are some similar messages channeled from Sandra Mendelson, (who has been following our newsletters for several years) from horses she has developed connections to:

We have worked hard to raise the vibration here on Earth, and humans are behind the eight ball. You haven't learned anything we have tried to teach you, with rare exceptions. Our brethren are being slaughtered by the thousands, the millions. You cannot continue to buy into the illusion of duality: my life is their life; their pain is my pain is your pain. Light a candle in the darkness; stand in your power, stand up for what you believe in, but do it by coming from a high place, from positivity and love.

There is more time than people think. You humans do not use your time wisely; use it to fill your thoughts with light and love not chaos and worry. Stay focused on conscious creation not minutiae; it all begins with a thought, an intention. Use your power wisely to create good. Do not let your mind idle; it will back up and choke like an engine. Picture healing happening (shows me a rose blooming). Approach each other with softness and love; you are all fragile: Humans do not know how to fill themselves with light as we do and you grow frail and sick; parts fall apart. See calm waters ahead; paint calm into the picture of your life. This is how to create change. Let go of tightness, of expectation. Germs and illness: that is energy you don't know how to balance.

Let stillness permeate you,

—Stormy

Humans need to look in a mirror and love themselves. You must create change by coming from joy...roll in the grass and under the stars...listen to nature to heal; stop the games of dark emotions and low vibrational scarcity, jealousy and fear. Remember all life is precious...

Generosity is good; it's like a muscle and humans need to activate it more. The spirit of giving is very important to horses and all animals; humans need to re-learn or remember it. Bring each other flowers: flowers like to be thought of as gifts and given that way. Remember each other; give credit to each other: that's what we do. Horses all take care of each other; you humans forgot how to do that. Do not have the need for authorship; see everything as a group effort because it is: the moon, the stars, angels, the universe: all are in alignment to create art, wisdom and things of beauty. It doesn't matter who wields the pen or the paintbrush; only humans think it does; the really great artists know this. Just as you shared your smoothie with me, we share energy and ideas with you.

—Honey Bee

Beauty, truth, elegance...I stand for these things...I handle things with grace and ease...I enjoy being in my body and the feeling of my feet gliding across the land. Be at peace with your surroundings...We must look for the brightness in all situations; hardships pass. When I connect with the ALL I get stronger. Connecting is what I am doing most of the time.

—Rita Hayworth (the equine version)

We (the horses in the barn) all agreed that we would step forth individually to represent a different lesson for you and all mankind. I represent acceptance and patience...and communication with grace and ease: immediate and without barriers. Bodies get in the way; that is another reason why we leave them so often).

—Hugo

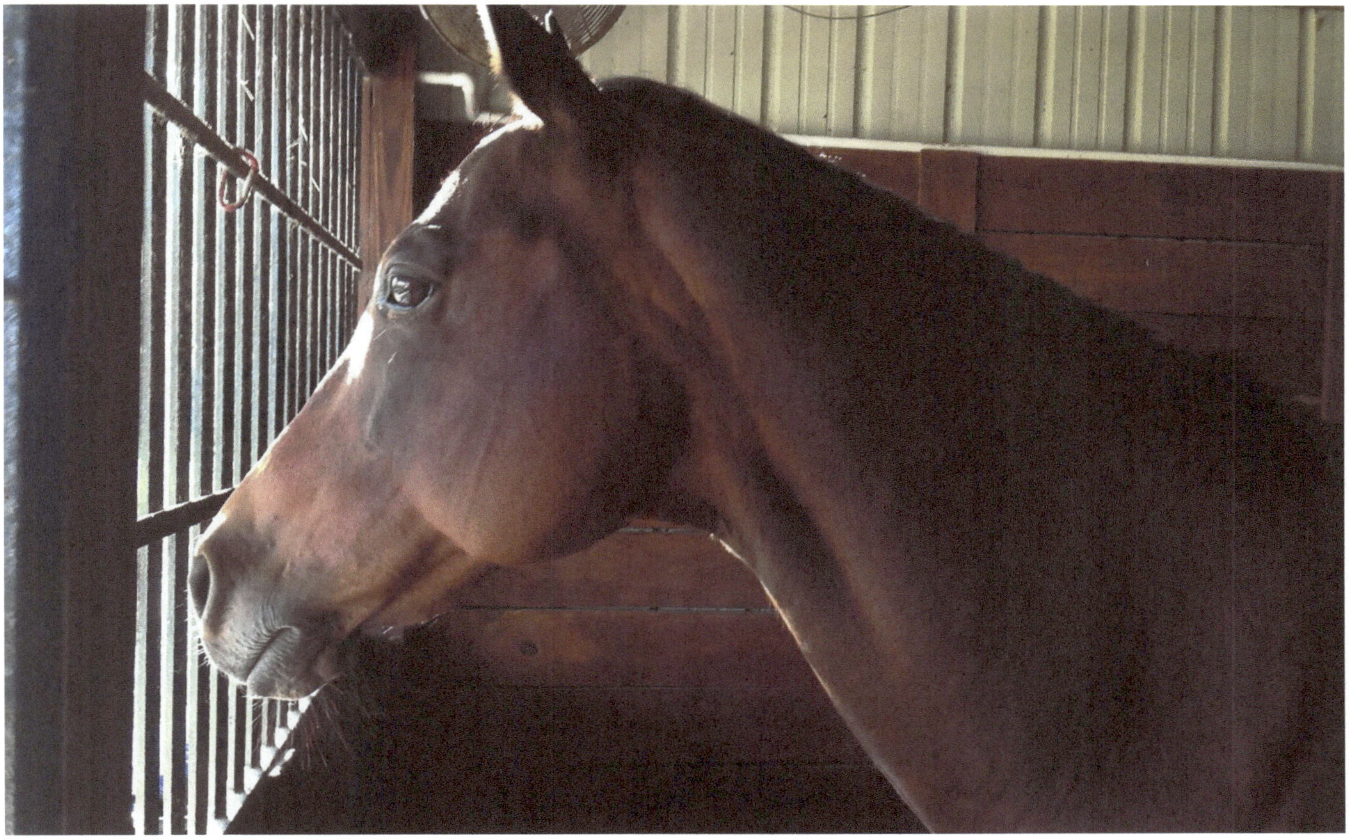

Ruggy

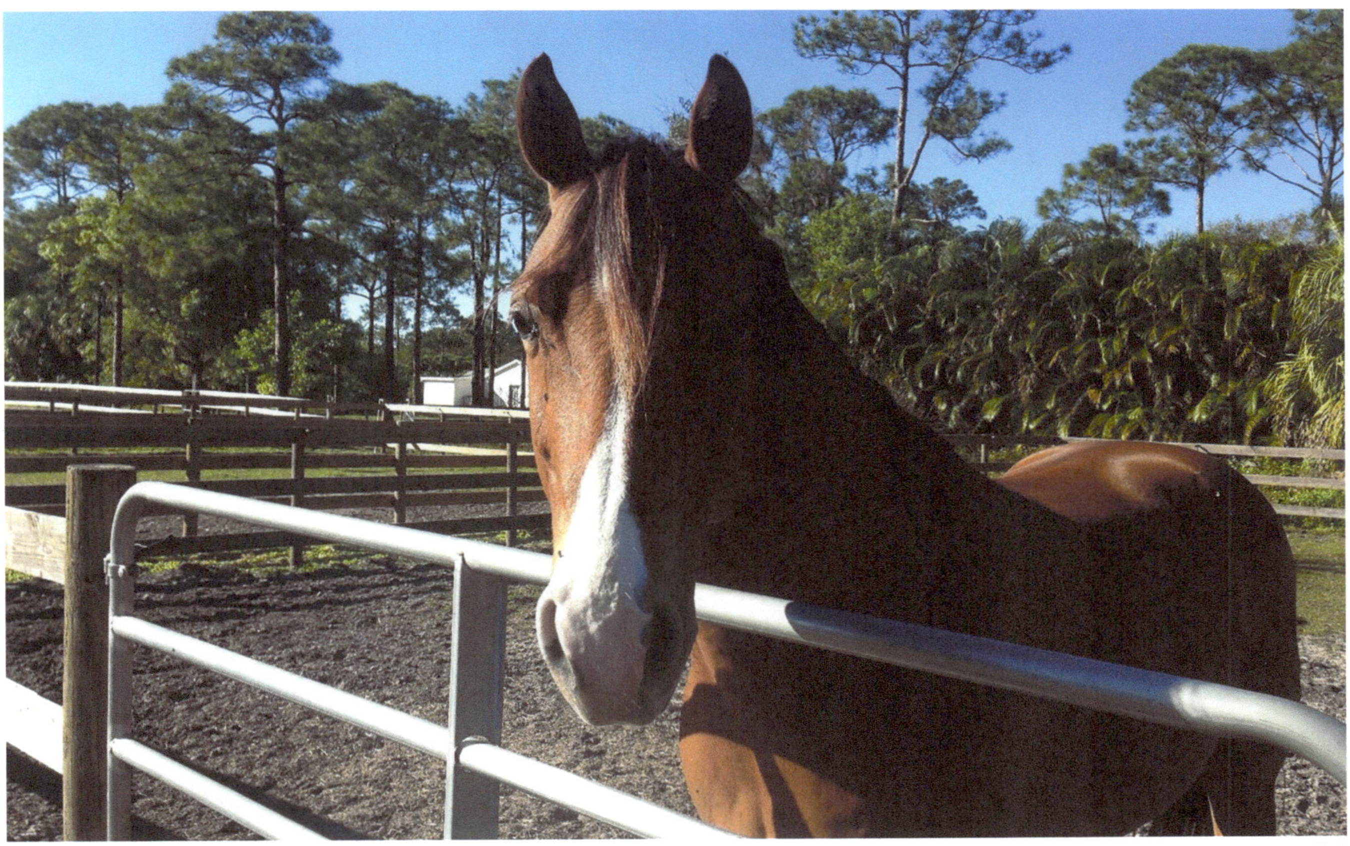

DJ

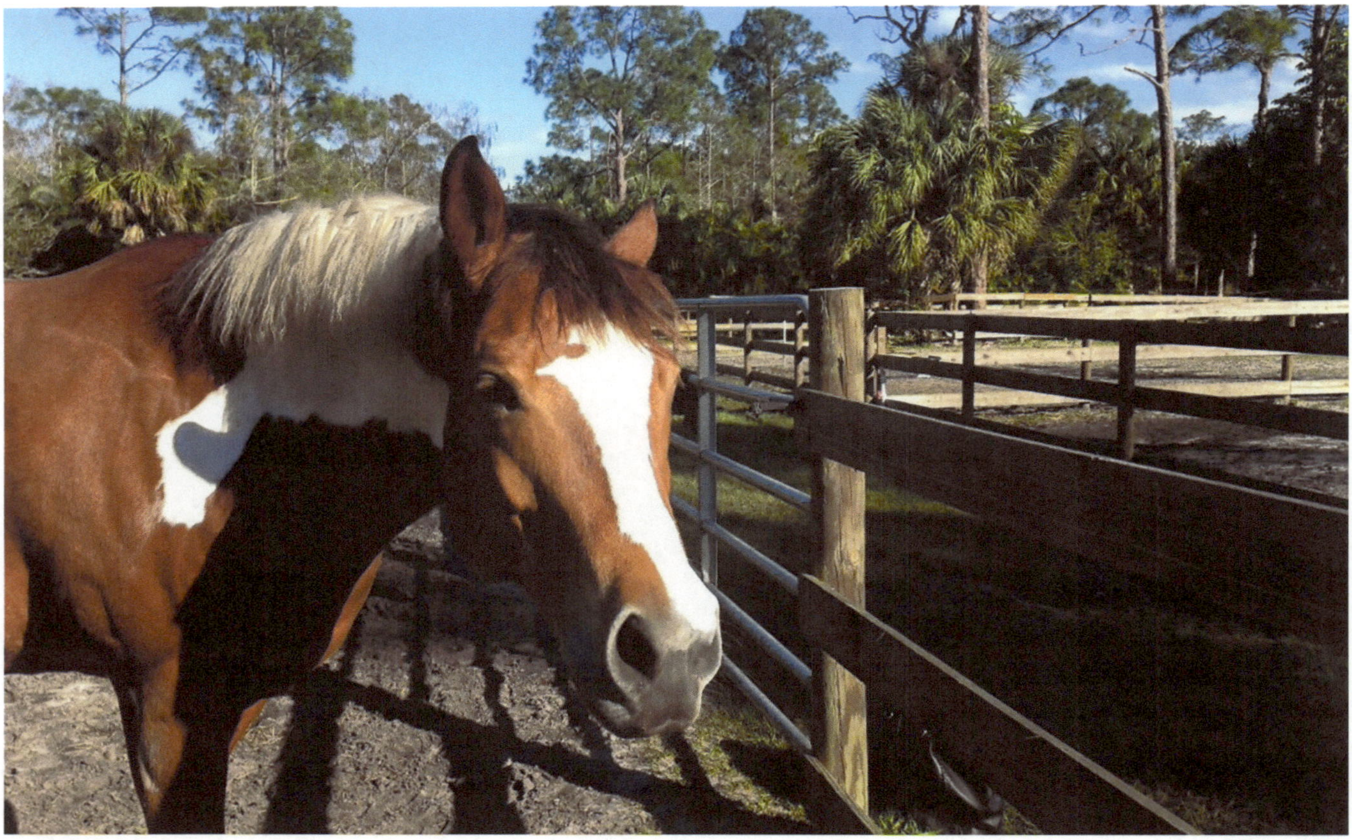

Stormy

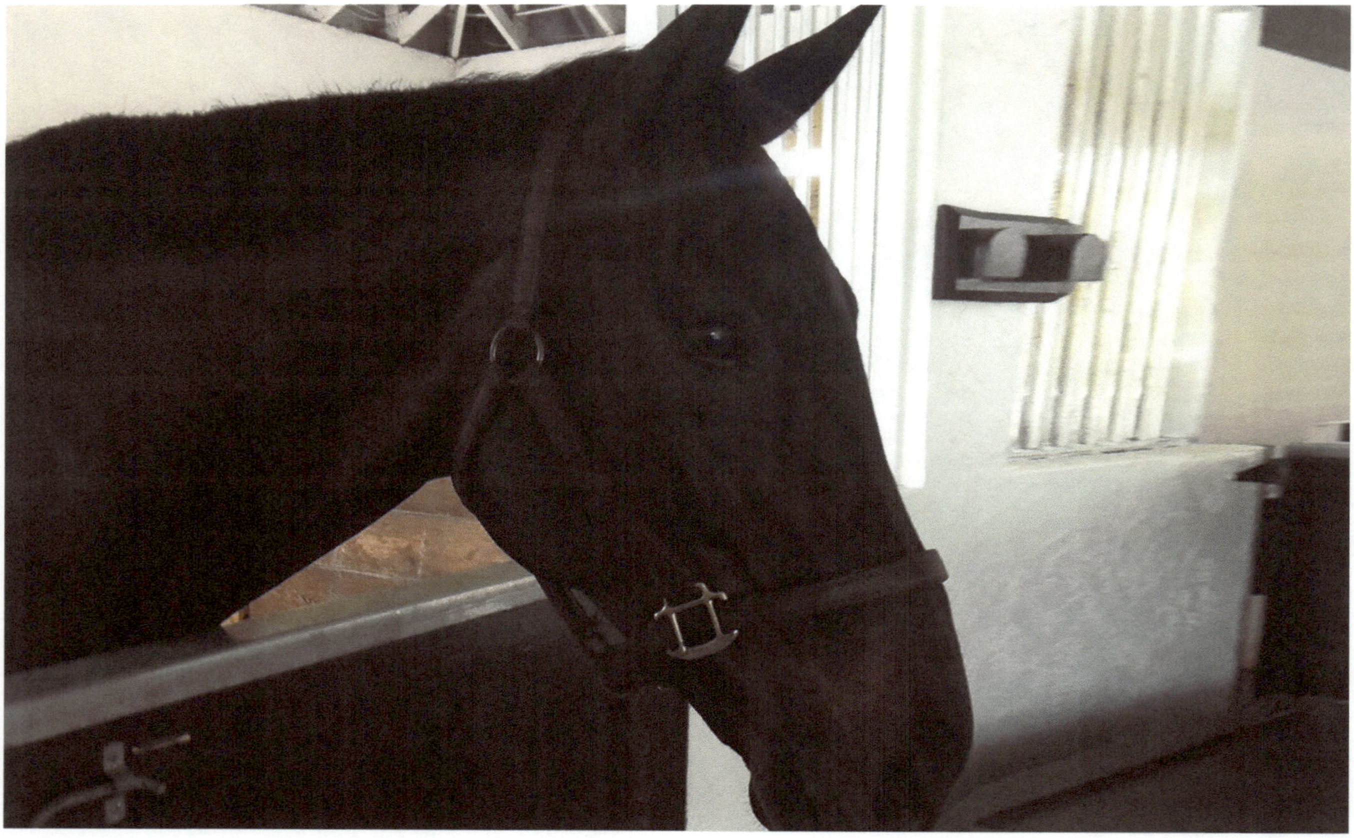

Rita Hayworth

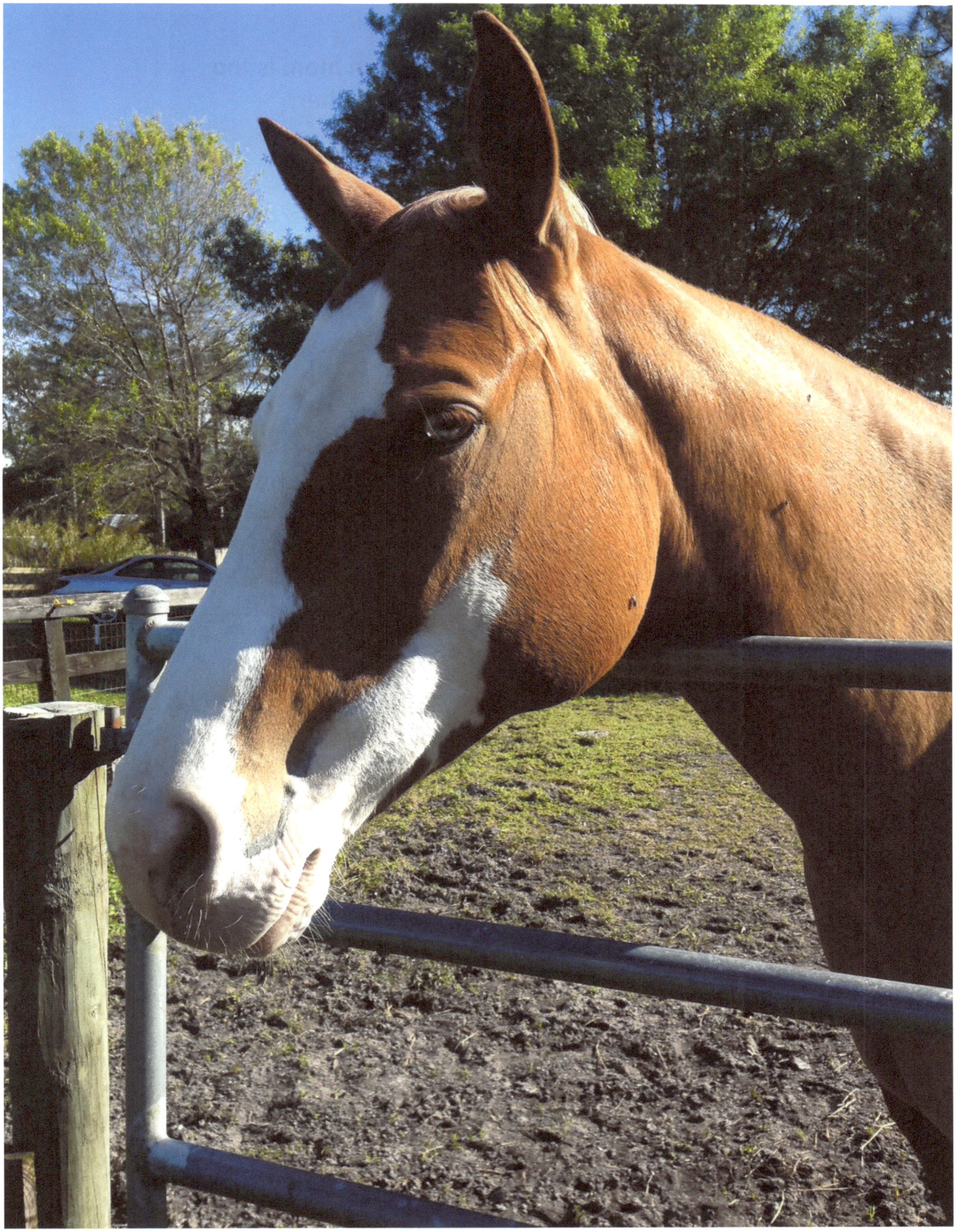

Honey Bee

From Ruggy, a 20-year-old mare whose human mom is too busy and is talking about giving away or selling her:

Humans don't know how much we care; they don't know that our heart is what rules us. They move us around like chess pieces. When we commit to them, we commit for life, but humans don't work that way. Our hearts grieve that they do not know what is important and they change their minds with the wind. They have lost the meaning of love. Love is all there is; do you see that? Do you know that? Everything else is just form: thought forms, tangible forms...love is the glue, the background that holds all the forms together. When humans break the bonds of love they destroy everything. My heart bleeds for you humans who have forgotten who you are: you are love and you break yourselves and each other with your forgetfulness. Spend time with us...look into our eyes...we will take you with us and your broken parts will heal. Honour the love inside you.

From Reese (who is a self-described "circus horse" as his mother has trained him to do a lot of tricks):

I can tell people about togetherness; about working as a team. Real love is wanting to see the other one happy. With togetherness, the heart has a home; a place to come back to that is always safe and warm for the human and the horse. I'm learning that what makes humans happy is when we listen to them and do what they want. Horses don't work like that; we let people be who they are and do what they want unless they are hurting us or the team. We accept them and their frailty; we give them love and constant energy. They don't know it, but it is constant. They would do well to be more like horses.

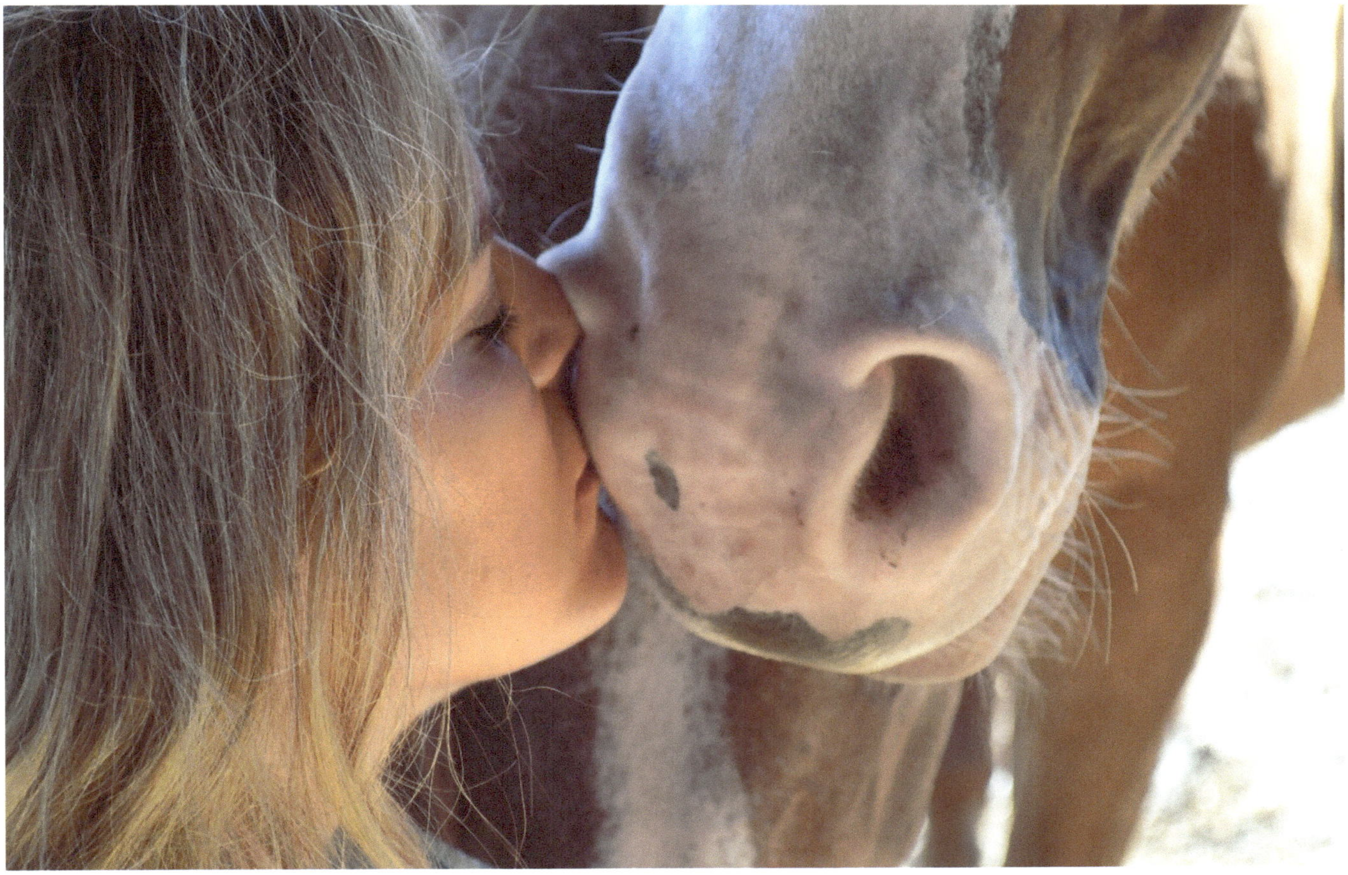

From DJ:

We can help humans. You need to learn to make your body strong; flood yourself with light every day. The first things humans need to learn are peace, quiet and calmness. My vibration is not as strong as Stormy and Honey Bee but I am on a growth path, like the humans who are waking up. I wanted to come here to further my growth, to release the ties that bind and prevent me from soaring. I put the idea in my mom's head because the intention for this to be a healing place was set. I am learning how to hear other creatures better, and what signs and symbols mean.

—end of Sandra's messages

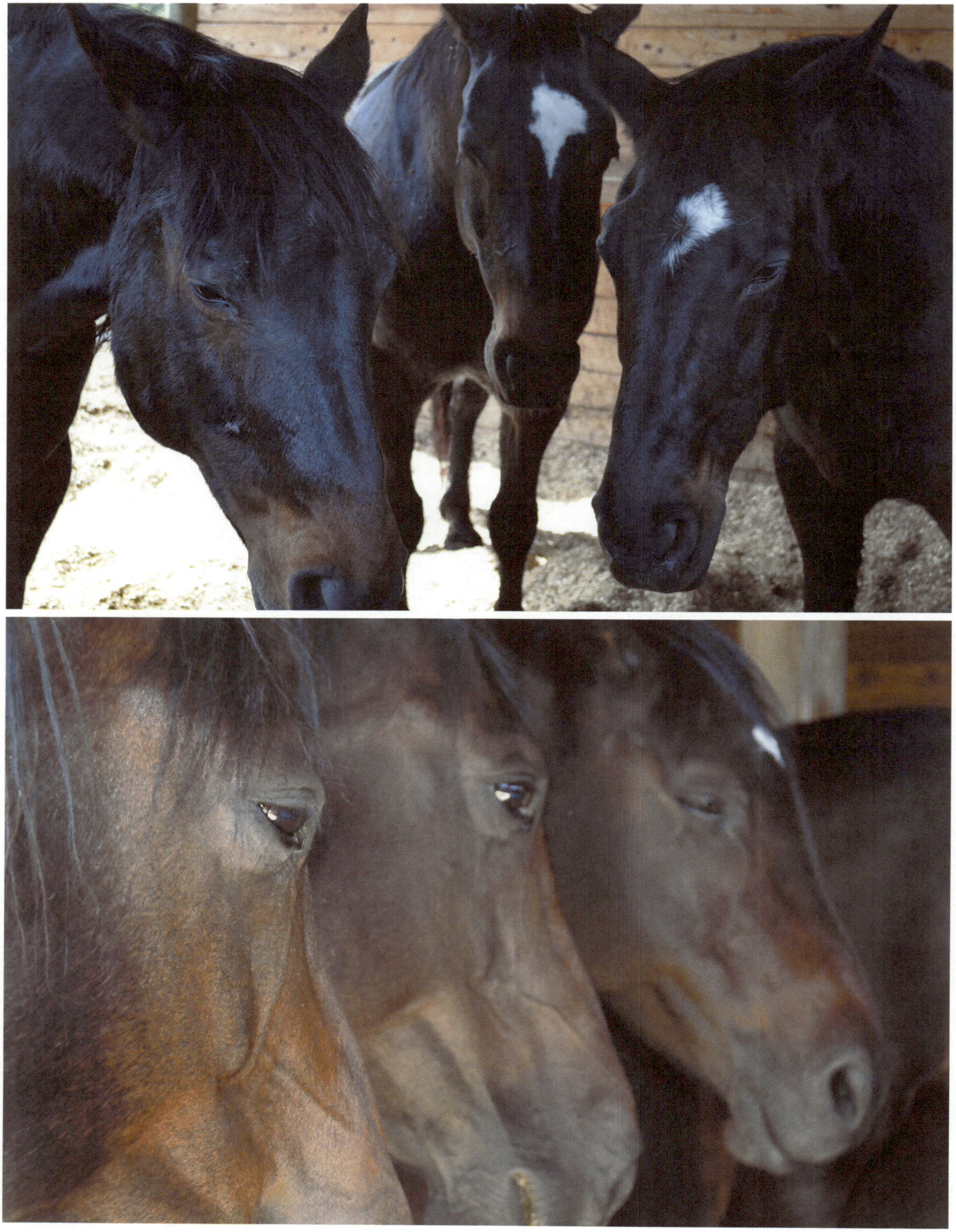

Three minds are better than one

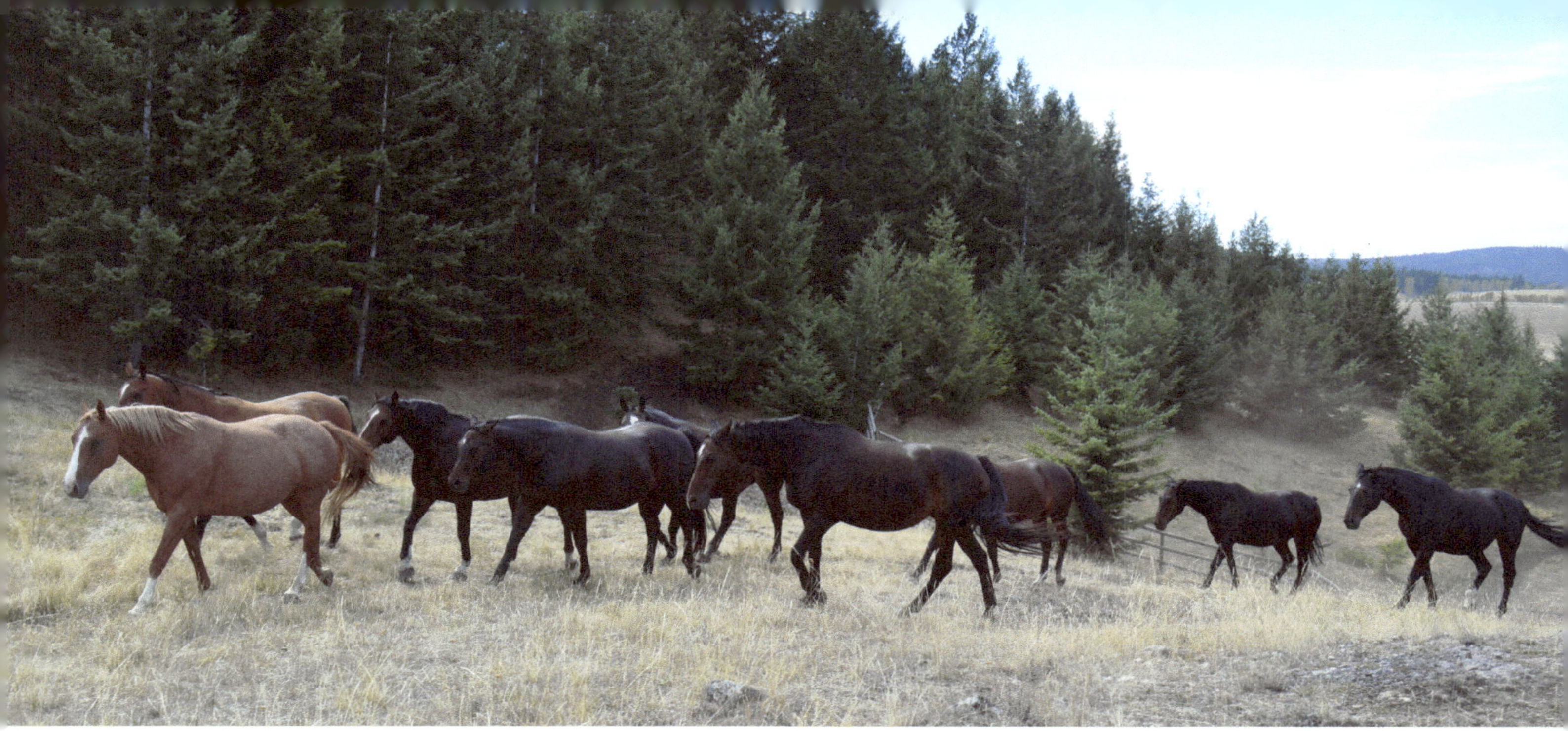

You humans watch in awe the flocks and Herds of the Earth as they move as one in body and spirit. They are able to connect in consciousness with each other and together to the higher consciousness of the ALL (or God). When one connects to the dance, it becomes you; it dances as you, and you as it. There is a wisdom in surrender that transcends human comprehension. People look on surrender as weakness or lack of intelligence, but that is based on their understanding of life as the birth to death experience of the ego. It is so much more perfect and simpler than you would believe. L.I.F.E. is Love In Finite Expression—forever. We are all Love expressing temporarily in matter and the only thing lasting is consciousness. All those costumes and covers that keep you from the experience are simply barriers between you and the one and only experience that can instantly transform you into the shining truth of your being, becoming wisdom, truth, joy, freedom, abundance and LOVE, dancing with the miracle of life, Returning To One.

When playing with horses, we launch right away into sharing space assuming that the horses are very receptive, which they are being born into this situation, they are eager to meet and enjoy grooming and sharing a walk and talk with the humans. Leading toward a liberty connection, we discover that relationship by walking and talking on a long drapey lead (like Hempfling) not pulling, but practicing looking at body parts to move them and inviting the horse to play with us. Placing cones in a line toward a goal or hula-hoops or balls, give the horse a positive invitation and a reward (in the form of carrot chunks or low-cal cookies) when they reach the goal. The horses feel it is important to be invited rather than pushed or threatened, allowing them to be friends and partners in the relationship. We then move on to liberty play first in the ring and often with several horses and then take the rituals to the test of the pasture and playground. Once ground play is established, we can move to riding with treeless saddles and halters with clip-on leather reins. People are always amazed that once relationship and communication is established on the ground it translates into safe riding with little or no tack. During the rituals we are practicing leading from behind, go trot and come back, companion walking and the follow-me game (which puts us in position of the lead mare), teaching words like whoa, walk, trot, back, along with the visual focus which will eventually become an aid when we are mounted and in a position that usually requires human tools like bits, spurs and whips, which are not represented in the Herd rituals and often a huge cause for concern for horses. When communication and understanding are in place they are no longer needed.

We are all one…and they are sending me this concept of time where it, as far as human understanding goes, is all relative to the life and death of the ego. But they say, "When humans truly understand connection and 'I consciousness,' they will know that life and death only exist in time. Eternity is at the other end of the spectrum. Time and ego are only constructs of where human mass mind consciousness is at present. They do not exist for all of non-human creation." This is where 2012 is going to end: a change in life as we (humans) know it. The end of time, because time will not have the same relevance without an ego.

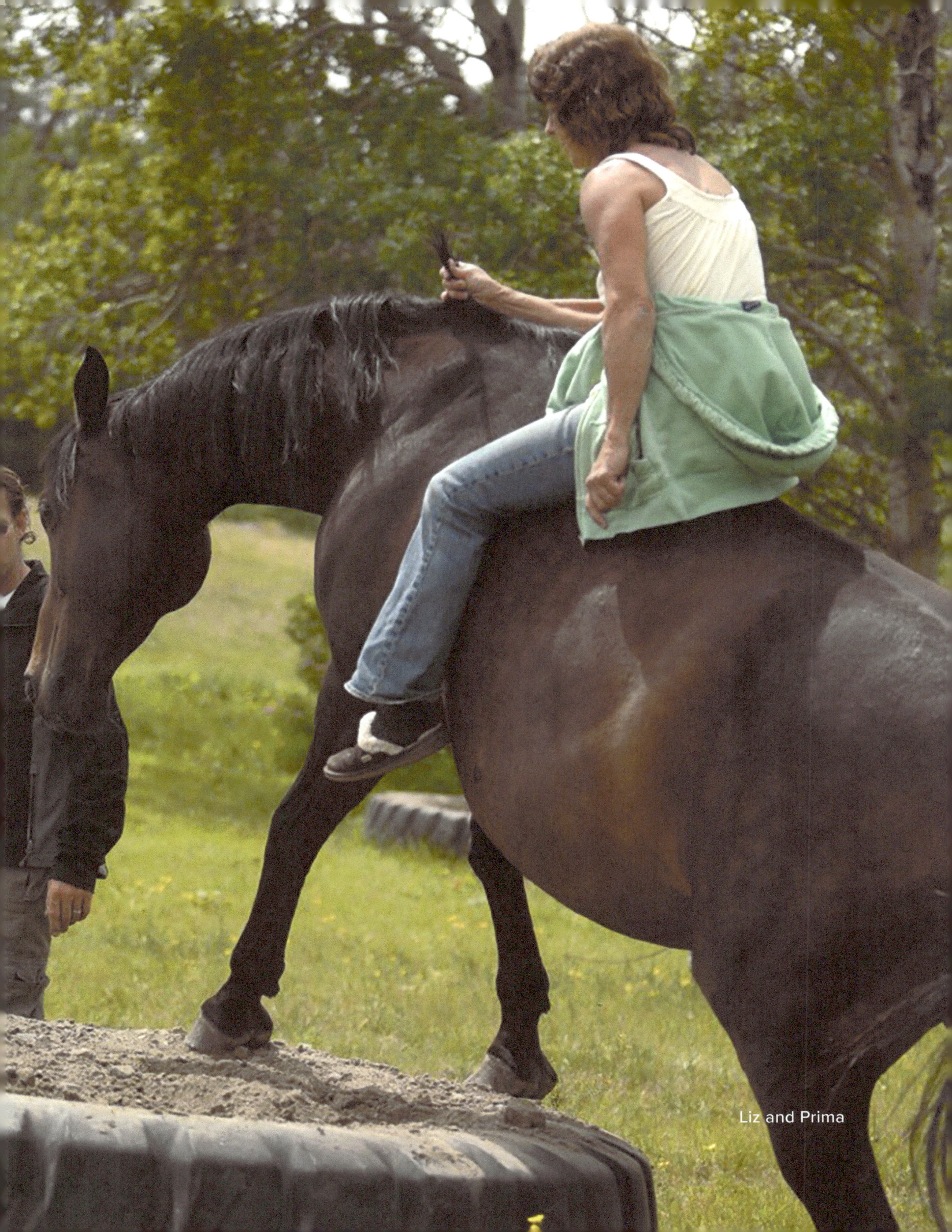

Liz and Prima

The horses say:

Gallop to Freedom,
Live L.I.F.E. (Love In Finite Expression)
Forever...
    And
ALL ways
NOW!!!!

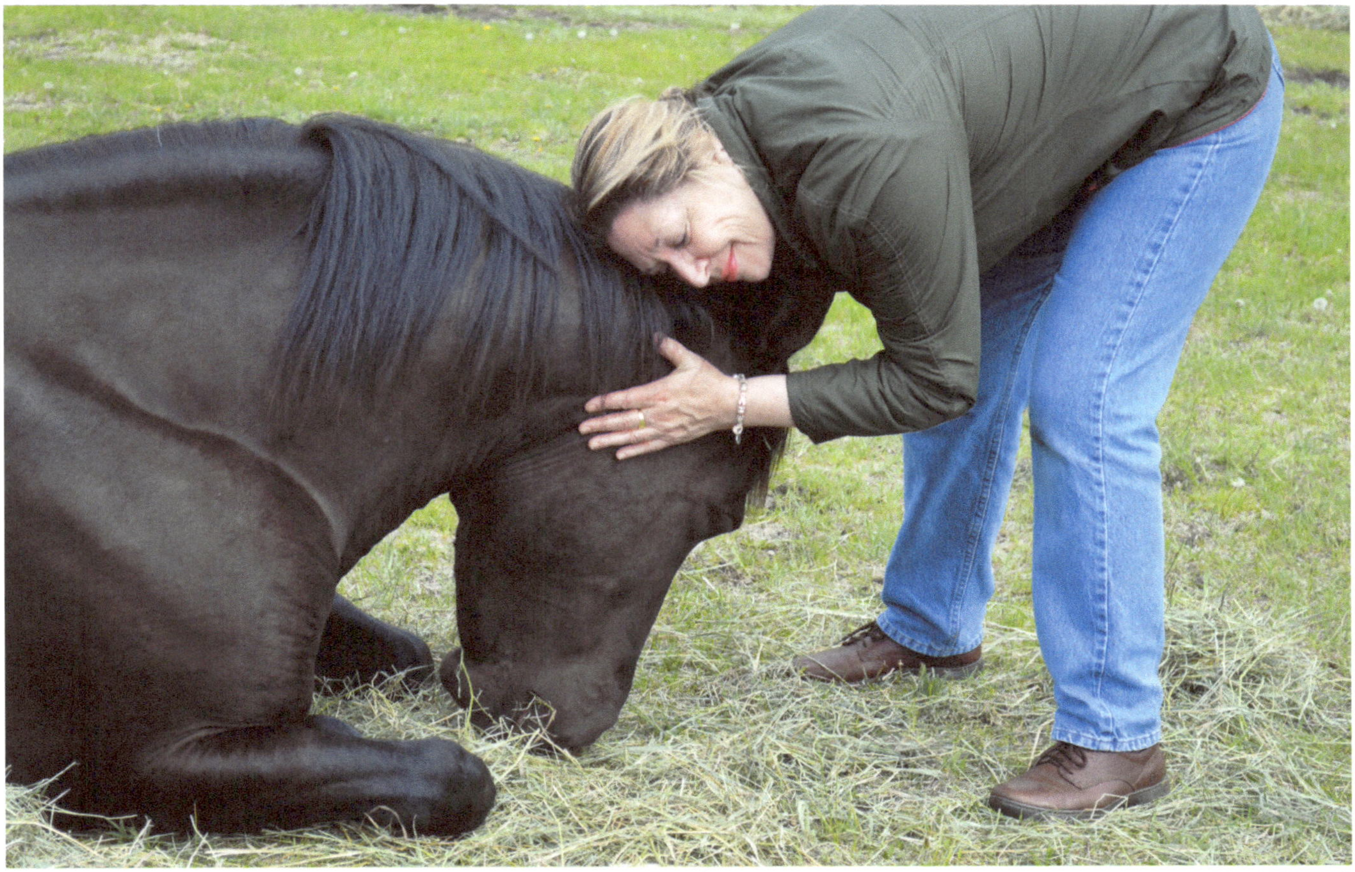

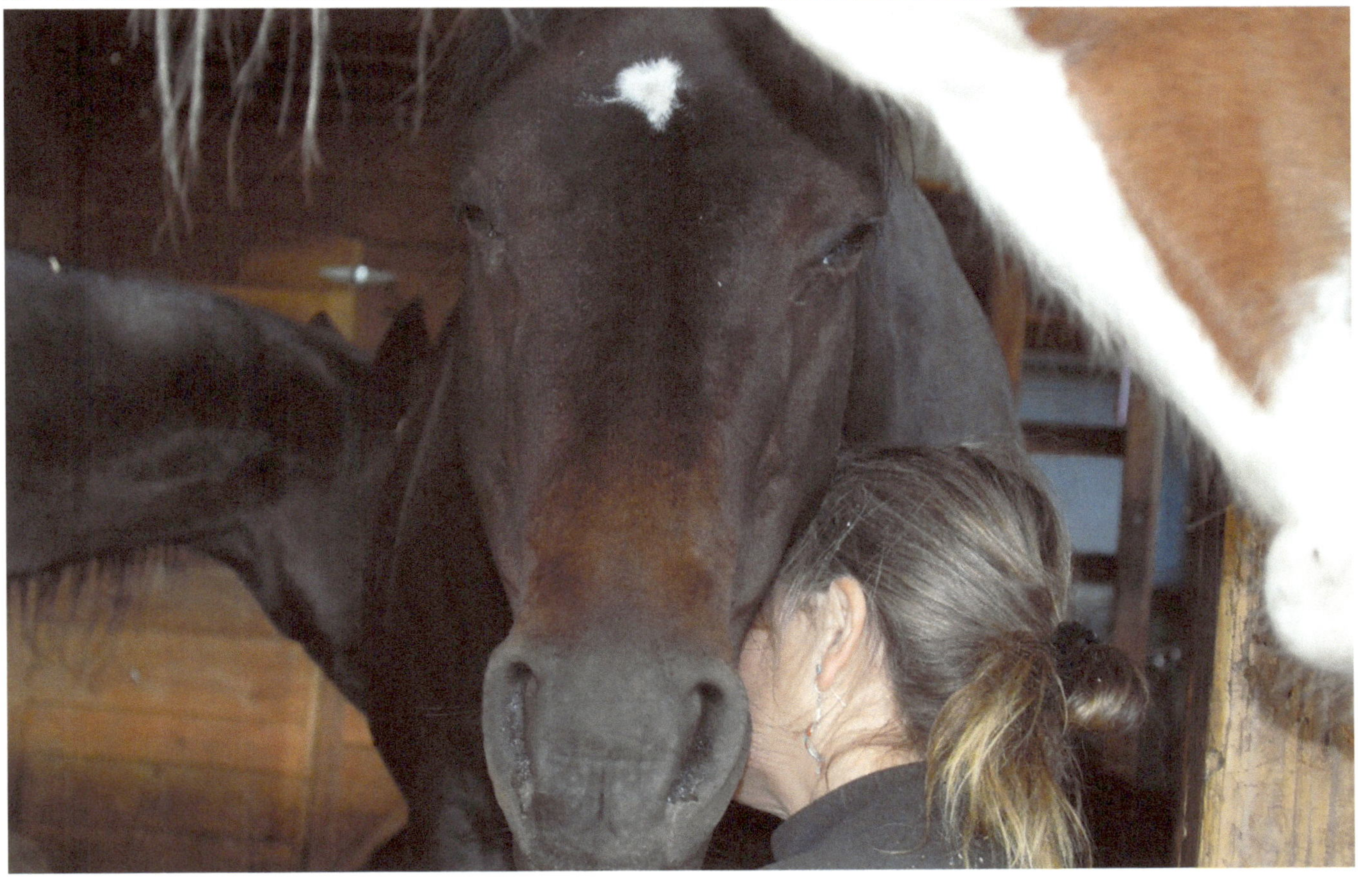

Connect, Believe...

Come, connect, believe, transform and heal from all your self-inflicted limitation. This incarnation is but a sparkle in God's eye, a fleeting smile upon his face. Open your eyes, your hearts, to the wonder of discovering your unlimited God self and as Michele says in the trailer for *One with The Herd*, do something so great with your lives...

Fear is the shadow side of LOVE. Horses who are held captive know it, but those of us who have come to bring forth a new world consciousness are clear and strong in our message:

To truly RECLAIM our POWER as fully evolved spiritual GOD BEINGS, we must retreat to that place inside where WISDOM, TRUTH, JOY, FREEDOM, ABUNDANCE and LOVE are our birthright and evolution. What would LOVE do now? Is always the question and the answer is we are LOVE. Fear comes from the head, LOVE from the heart. Spend time in nature, listening and connecting and remember that time when as children you were innocent and believed in everything. Miracles are a product of true belief and our thoughts create our lives. Live LIFE to the fullest NOW. Walk and play in your dreams for LIFE is your dream. Make it your MIRACLE!

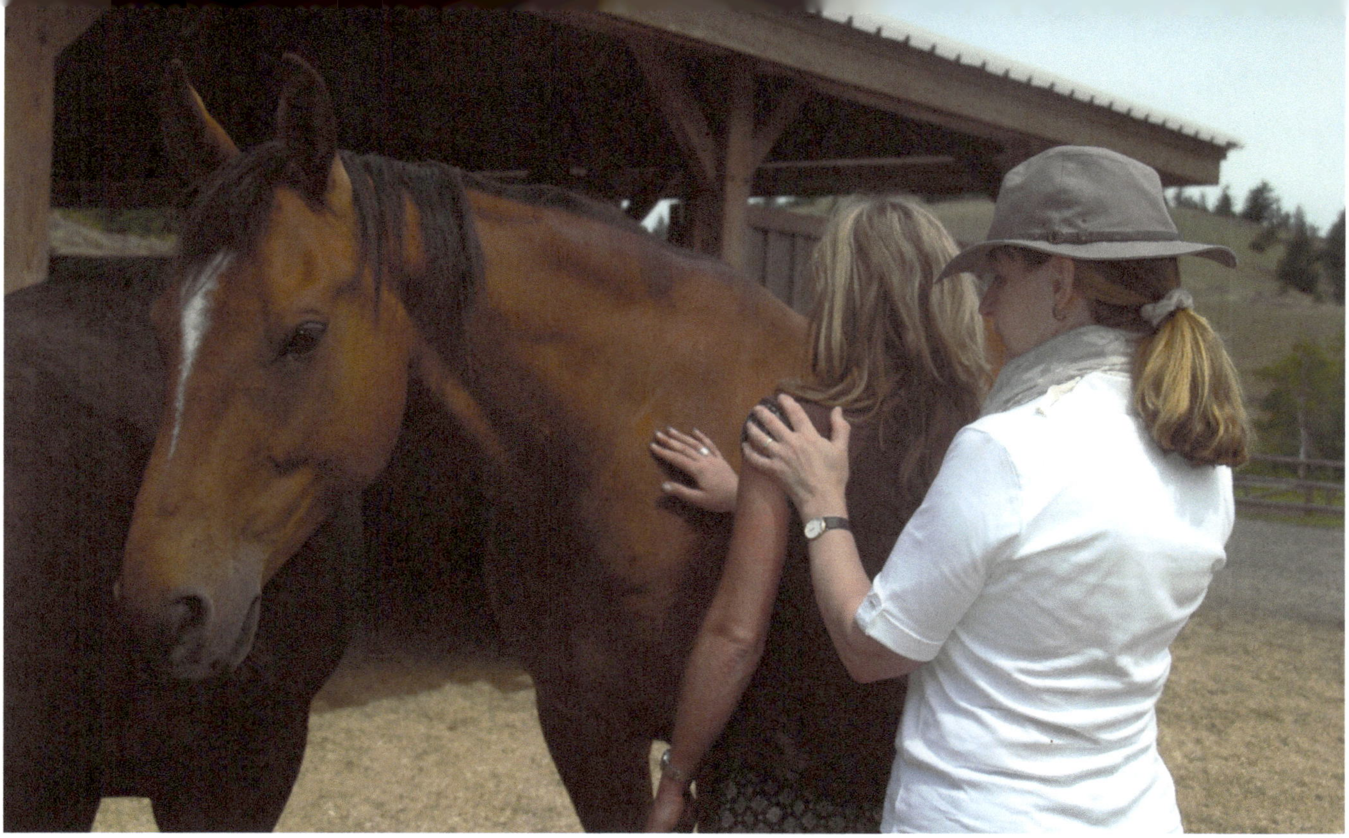

Margrit Coates and student

Healers come to a retreat

"Highly irregular" is our reaction to the events that have just transpired. We are happy to hold space and assist the humans that come here for healing and connection to the truth. This last episode was confusing and uncomfortable for us as we were the ones being healed by humans and at times that was scary. Humans are at best a spotty group of beings that at times understand the level of connection required for perfect embodiment here on Earth. Suddenly, this group appears with first of all Lisa who talks fluent horse and then Cher and Edmund who are doing what they call TM and we are amazed that that is the place that horses resonate, and then there are Marianne, Dianne, Patricia, Pat and Jean, who GET IT and absorb the message. Then there is Margrit (Coates) who we have been waiting for, and that was the worst because we are the ones who are supposed to be doing the healing. She is from the same planet! We are doing our best to hold the vibration for the humans to evolve to a place of higher consciousness, but please let us do our job. LOL

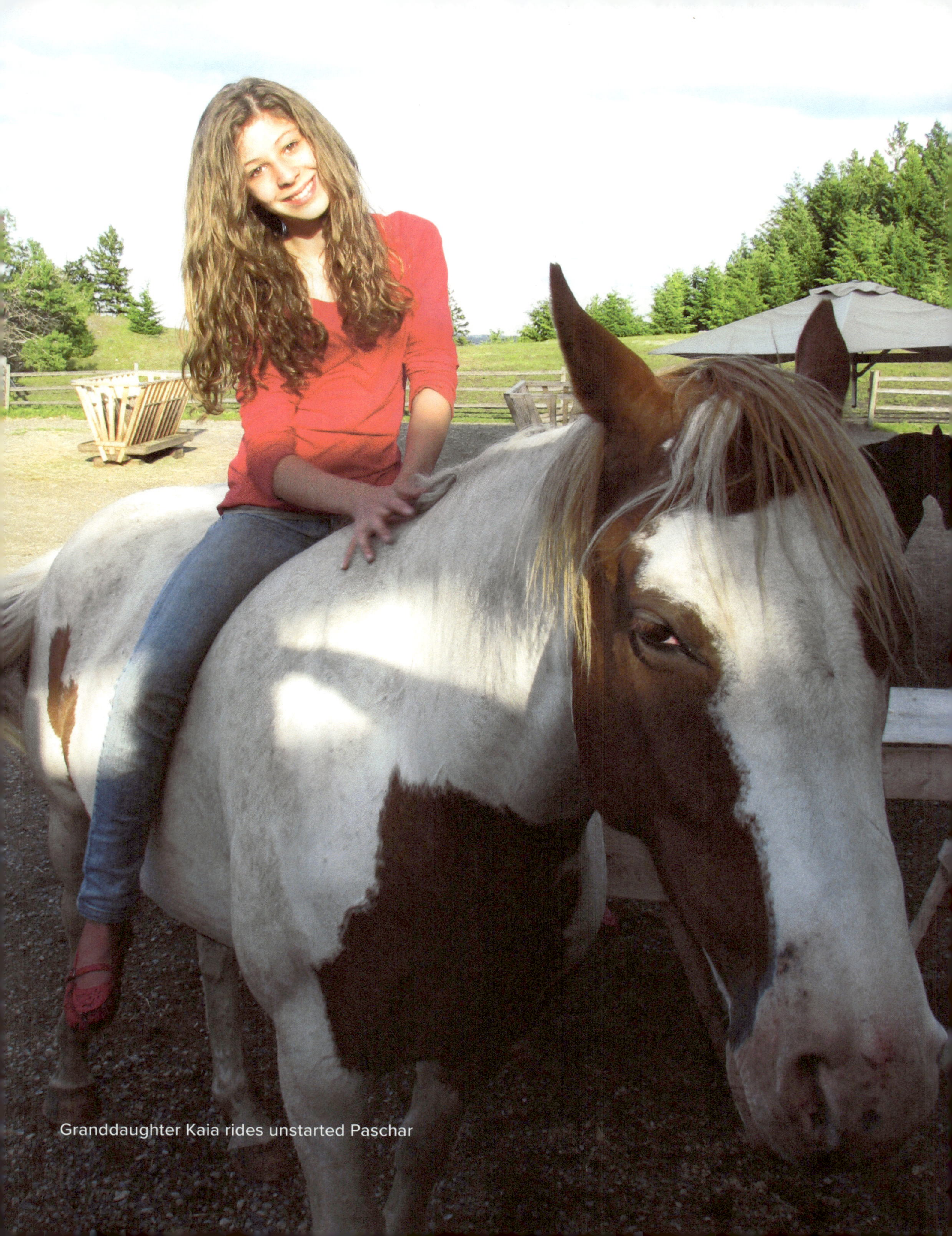

Granddaughter Kaia rides unstarted Paschar

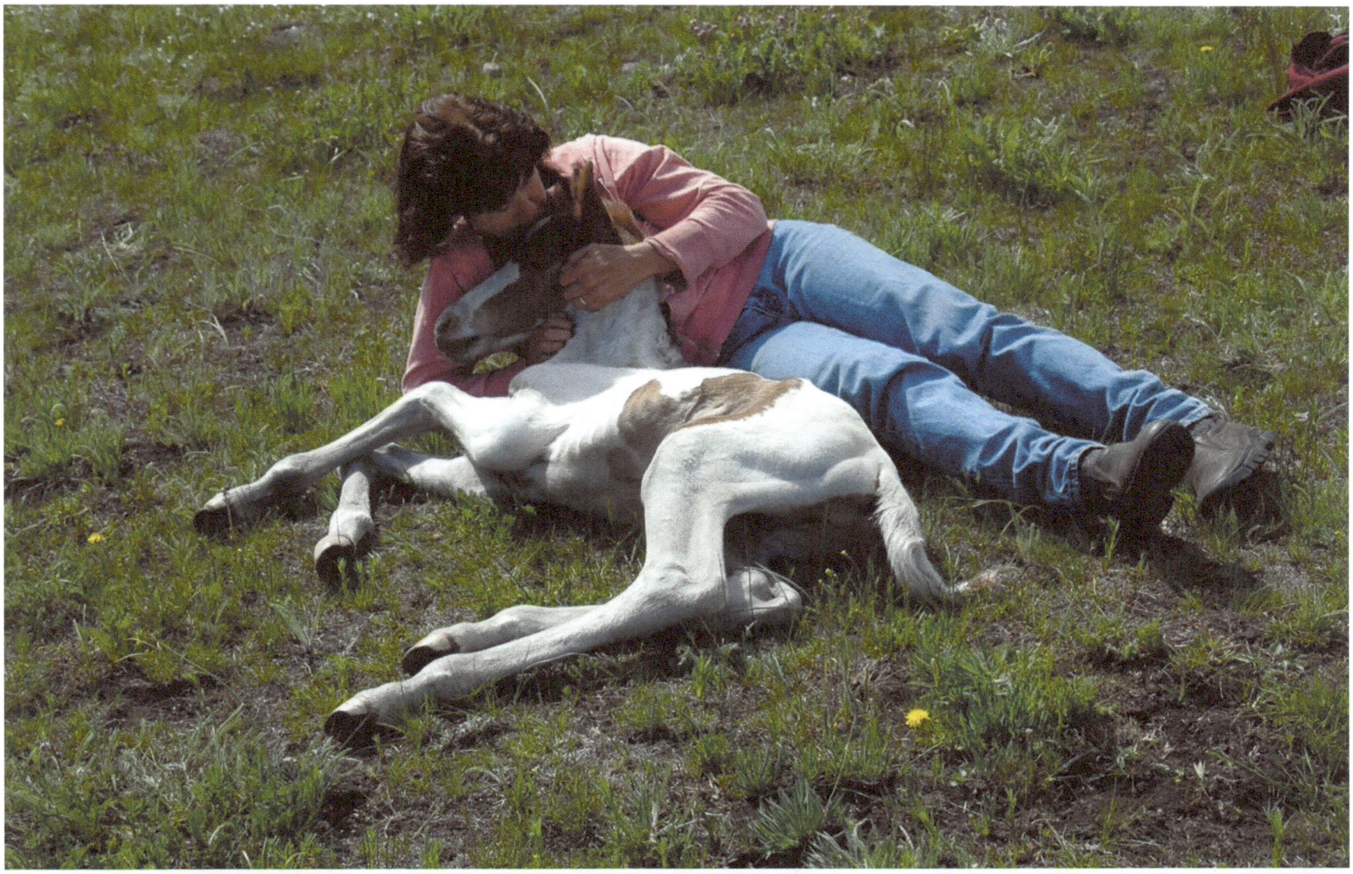

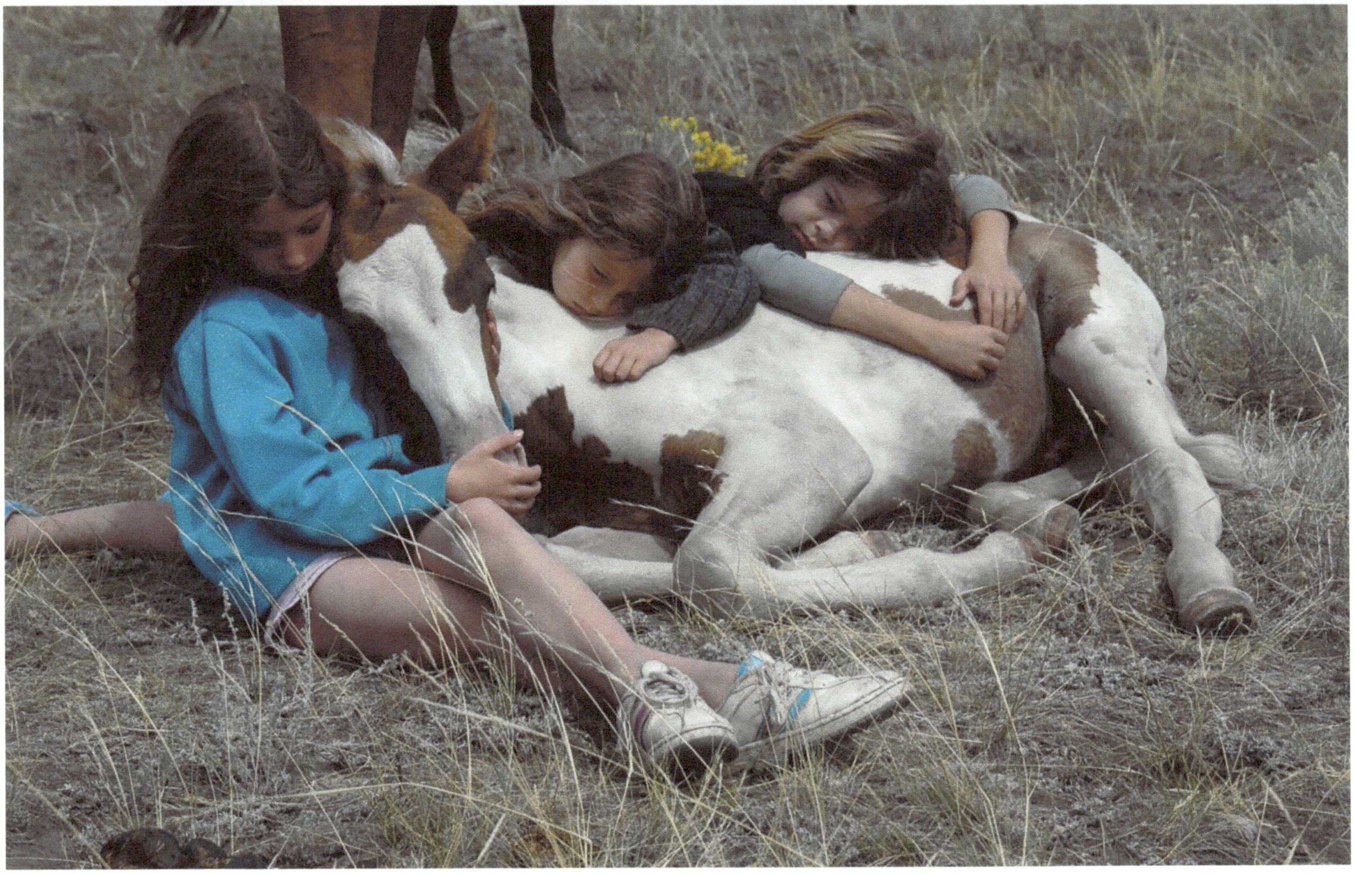

Born into...

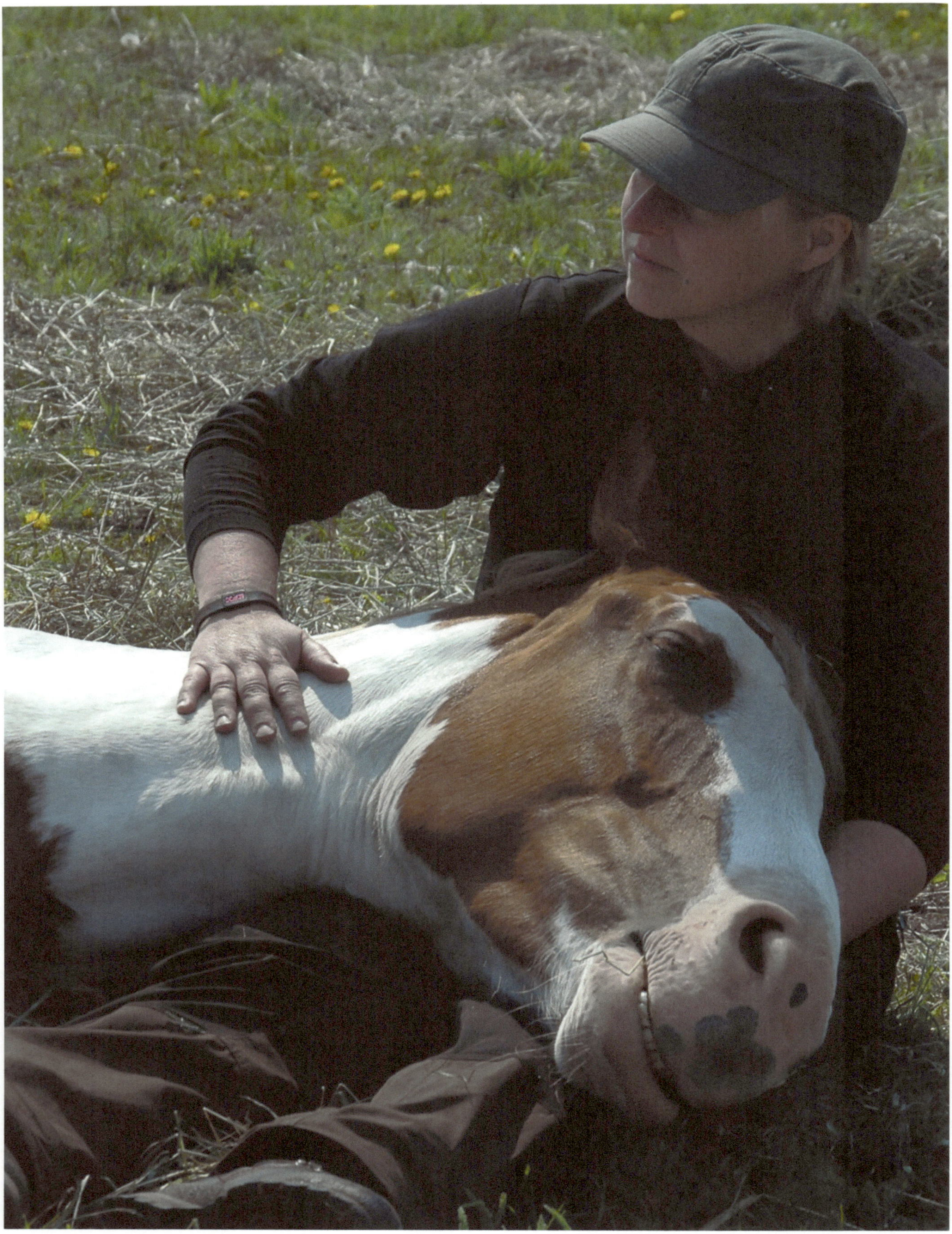

...Love and Trust

Consciousness is shifting rapidly now. Our thoughts have huge implications in matter. They can create enormous consequences when misdirected as you are all witnessing in the natural disasters throughout our world. They can also unite all minds and create a shift to a better world of harmony, unconditional love and one consciousness united in peace and possibility.

Remember, it is only you that can be the change. With each mind united in love the scales are tipping. You can change the world; you must only imagine it.

Animals everywhere are holding the space for you, healing and connecting you to other dimensions where ALL is perfect and one. Come and discover that place that resonates in all souls when we remember. When you touch the ALL, you become the ALL. Reach out and touch, and begin to vibrate at a resonance where darkness, sickness, fear and sadness do not exist, and you are held in the arms of LOVE forever.

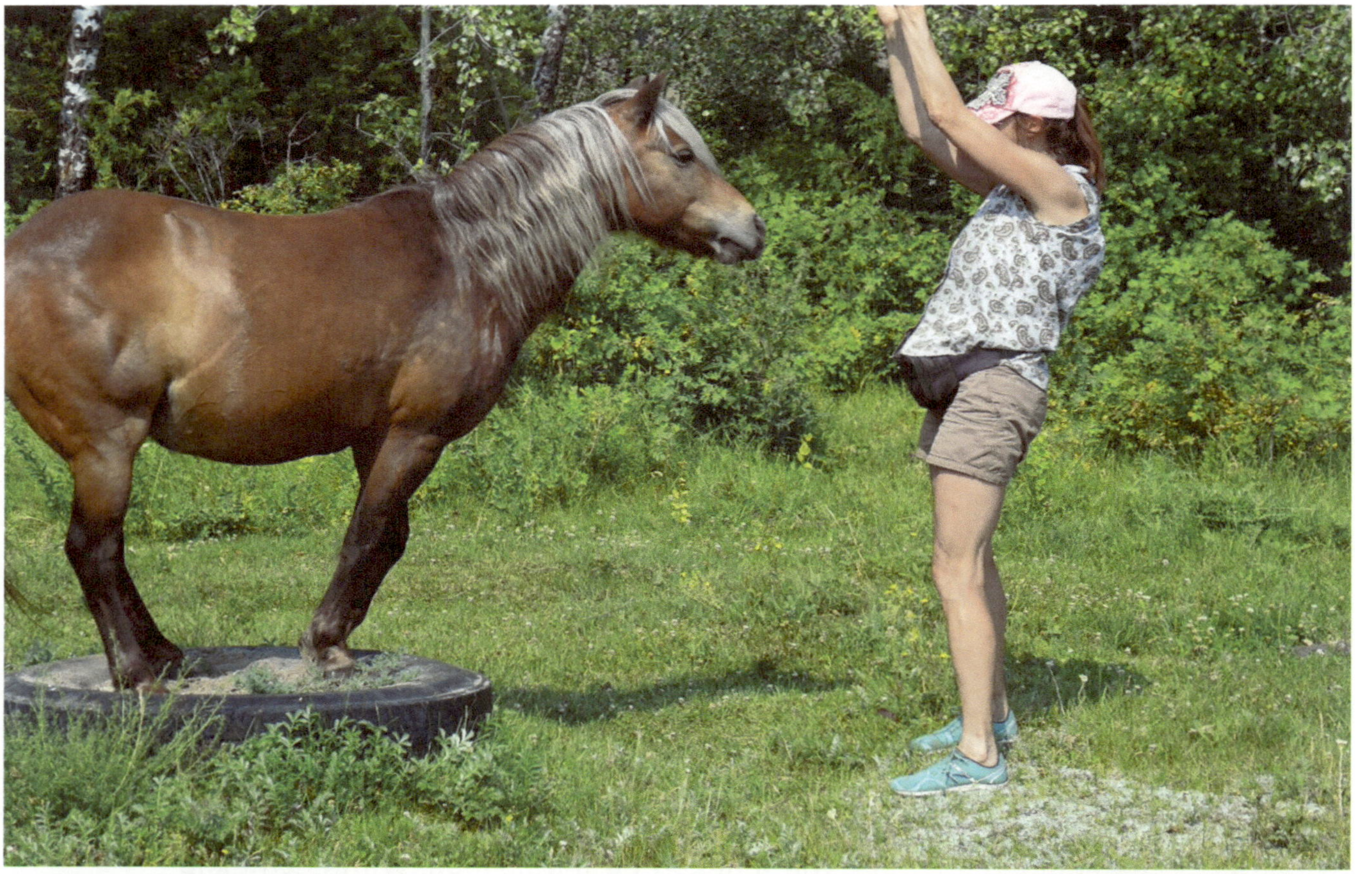

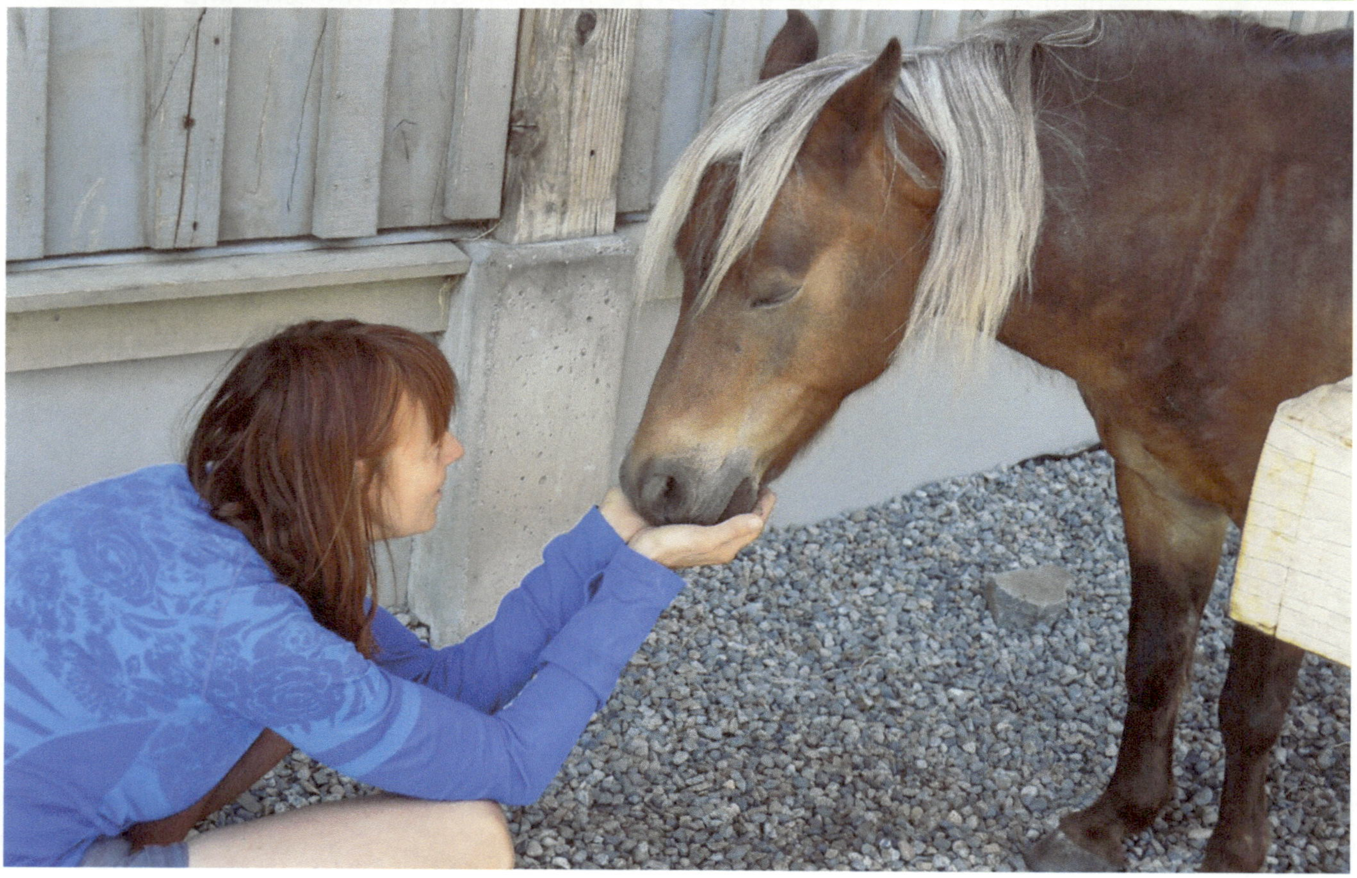

Joan and Merlin

From Joan:

My Transformational Three Weeks at Equinisity Retreats:

There are so many portals at Gateway 2 Ranch, doorways into new realms, openings into fresh and higher energies, passages through veils.

There are bridges connecting places on the outside with places on my inside, stepping stones traversing unchartered territory safely, docking stations for downloading higher consciousness and for recharging my batteries with love and joy.

Pools of stillness holding me up. Peaks bringing me closer to heaven. And then the horses who with their liquid crystal eyes enchant me, with the softness of their muzzles endear me and with the warmth of their breaths enliven me.

Drop all your judgments. Let go of all your beliefs and preconceived ideas. Become empty to become receptive.

Make space. Don't search for anything; just remove your blocks and resistances; your ifs and buts. Be naked, be brave. Bare your heart and soul. Be like the ice cube melting in the sun and thus returning to the Earth to become one with its source.

Stand in the circle of wise horses on top of the hill at night and among them beam to the stars and the moon your heart's deepest longing. Then, call to those who, like you, are awake in the night.

•••

Eleven years on the ranch this September and I am resonating at a level where I feel more horse than human, living from a third person perspective and allowing spirit to flow through me. More and more I am hearing the message of "one consciousness in all life." All around the world there are stories of animals as higher beings, possibly higher than humans. Could it be we are wrong in our assumption of superiority?

Entertain the idea that the most evolved spiritual beings lived nomadic lives without material possessions, trusting that they would be provided for. They had connection to a higher power that was their inspiration and lifeline. Buddha, Mohammed, Christ and all the animals share the ability to be a transparent channel for the All or God, allowing the way, the truth and the light to become them and them to become the one consciousness in all life.

It is we ordinary humans with our attachment to the finite and fragile life of the ego and its need for material embellishment that have designed a world of toil and lack. All for want of a bigger house, a better car, expensive clothes and toys. Do we really need any of these things to be healthy and happy?

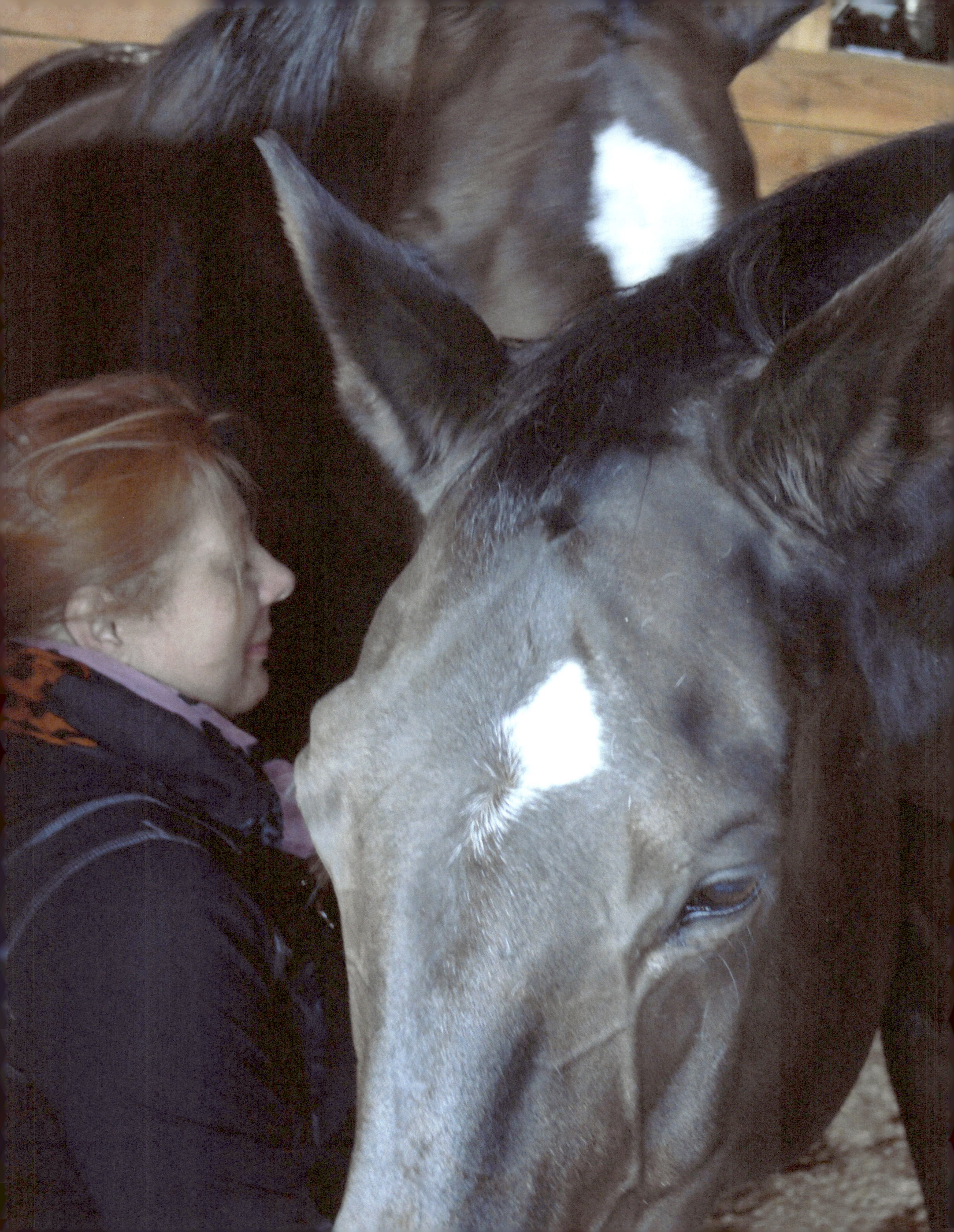

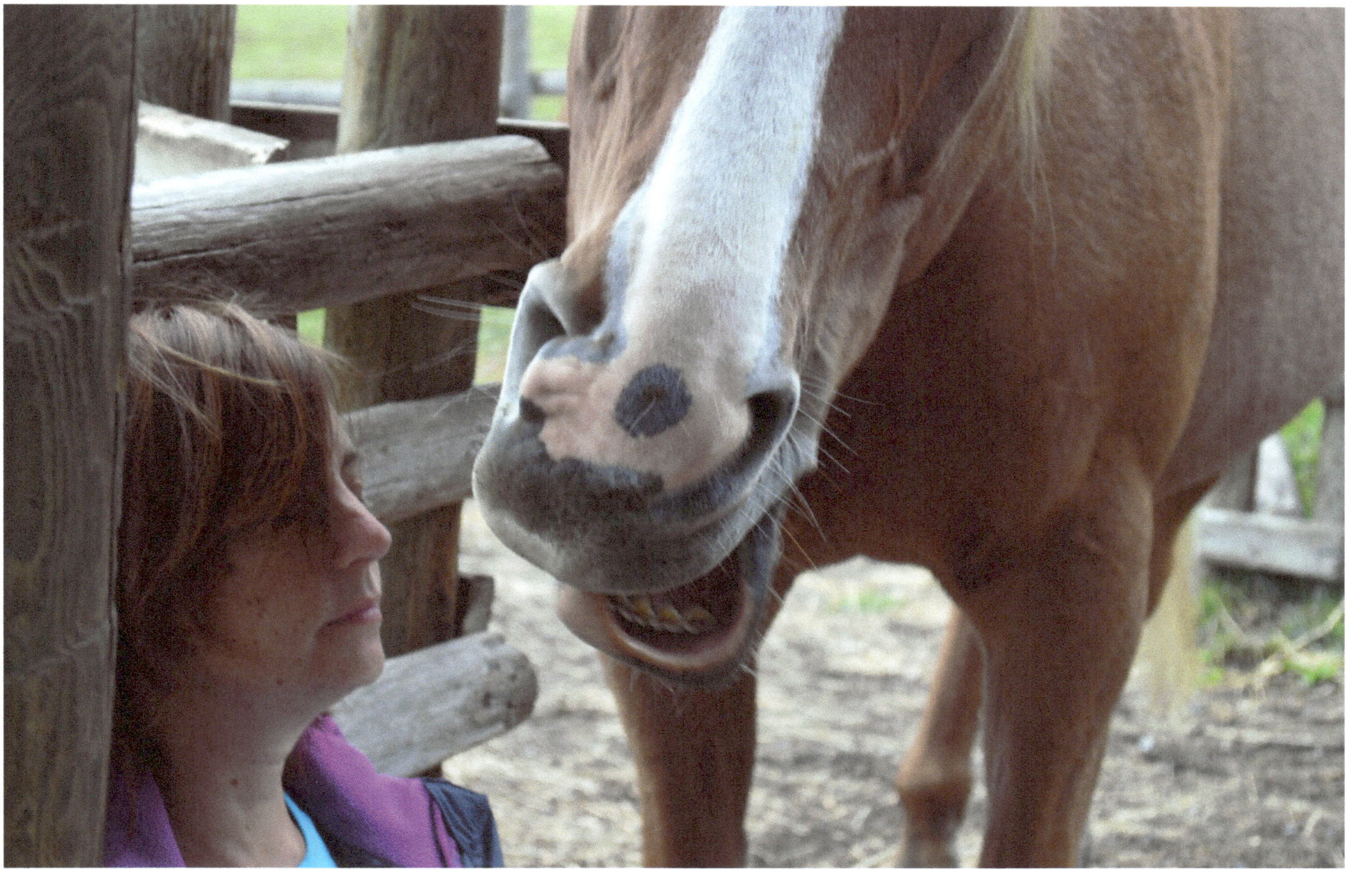

Epona works her magic

From Epona:

I would like to talk about poverty. Poverty is the greatest gift, and something horses reside in. It has a purity, an absence of attempt that allows us freedom to resonate with our higher truth. Imagine people living without things—no clothes, no laundry, no house, no cleaning, no material possessions — no worry. It's a gift of immeasurable value, and in our wisdom, horses have chosen this way of life. We are fed, groomed and cleaned up after, and we have hours of free time to commune on a higher level. You would do well to examine the idea that the less you own, the easier your life, and the more quality time you have to address important issues such as obtaining attributes that are incorruptible and eternal.

When you look at the evolution of human mass mind consciousness, we really can't understand your notion of humans as the superior species...

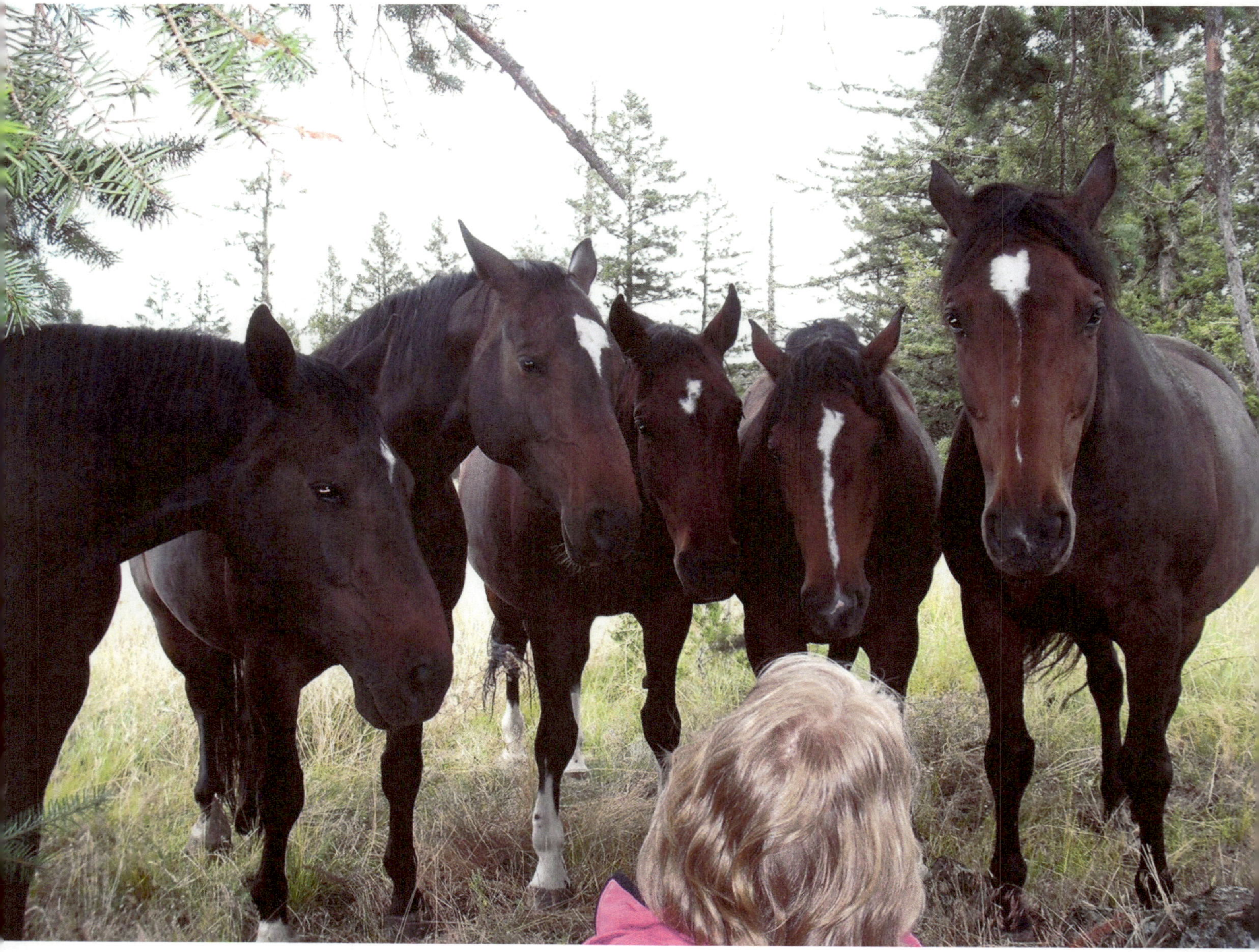

There is much concern from the human perspective on where the world is headed. When one is bound to an ego and a finite concept of existence then an evolution in consciousness would be perceived as a threat to the status quo and therefore something to fear. Armageddon has always been at one end of the human mass-mind consciousness spectrum as human existence has always been determined by the life of the ego. Imagine something so much larger and grander. Imagine limitless expression of LOVE in a limitless universe. We are life itself, we are LOVE in expression, and as long as we allow the flow of the force of LOVE in our lives then we are always growing toward the light. "What would LOVE do in this situation?" Is the question we should always ask.

Humans have always been proud of their big frontal lobes and their cognitive skills. These attributes work well for three dimensions and a linear universe trapped in time. Imagine time as a moment-by-moment experience, not linear but a wave that becomes a spiral that becomes a chaotic expression of the time traveler, as unique as each individual created expression of the ALL. If the world really is our creation, our understanding and our focus, then let us run toward our joy, freedom, abundance, love, wisdom and truth as unlimited God becomings. Let us leap and roll and run through the garden of our dreams. Come and join us in the dance.

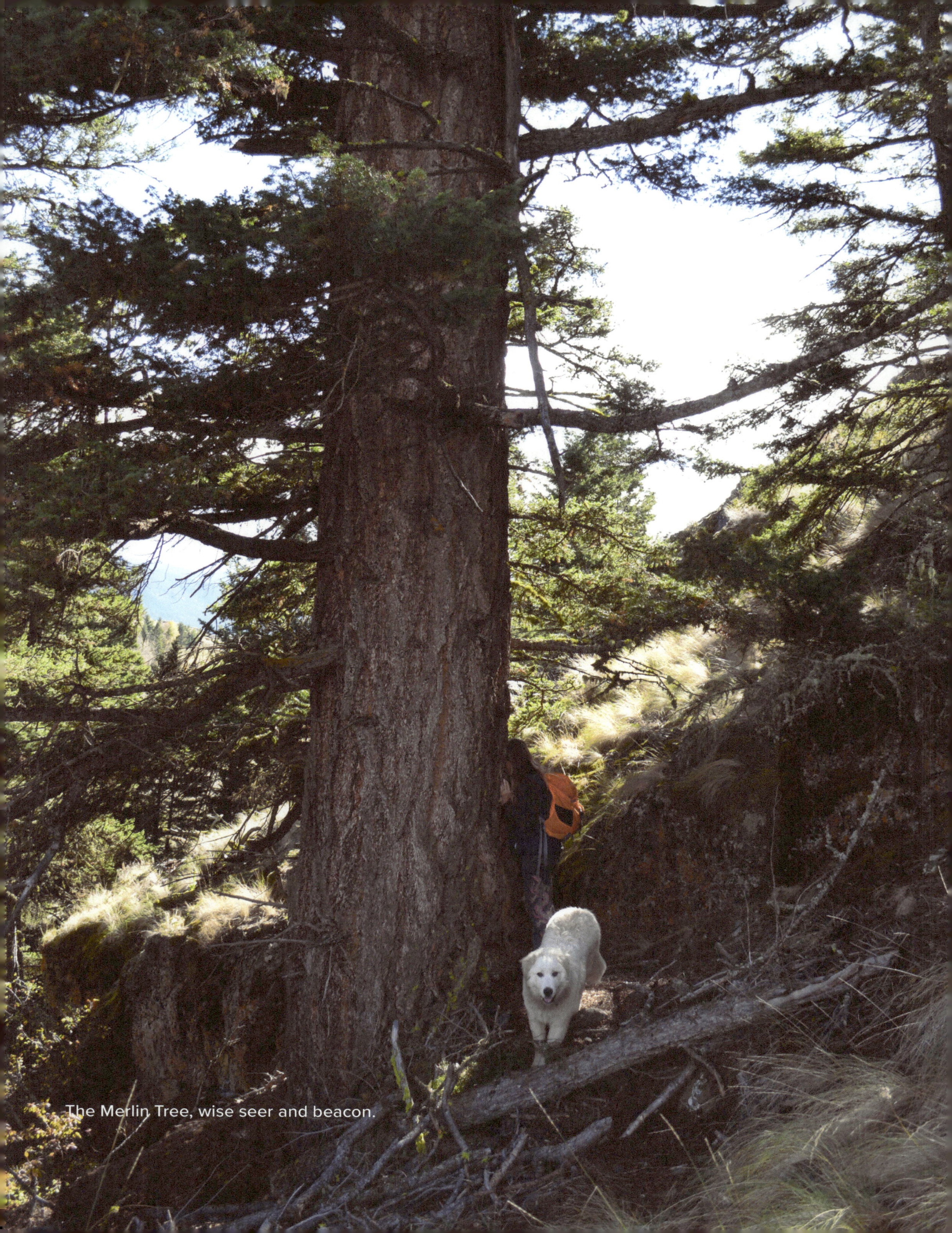

The Merlin Tree, wise seer and beacon.

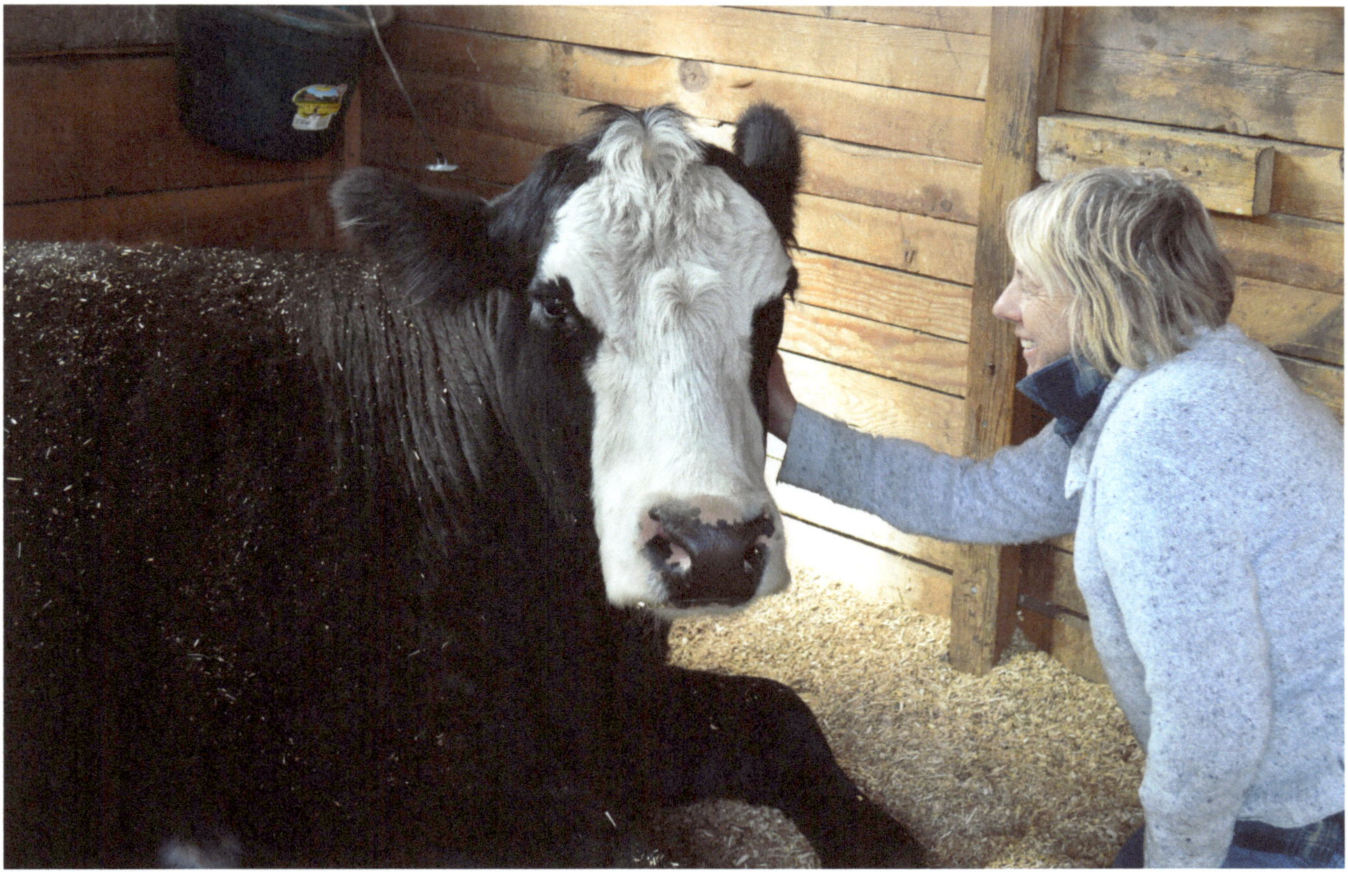

From Tesoro:

I am a three year old steer. I guess I am one of a kind as three-year-old steers don't exist in the world.

I am LOVE, I am happy.
That is all I have ever known.
Liz calls me her Buddha.
I am in heaven!

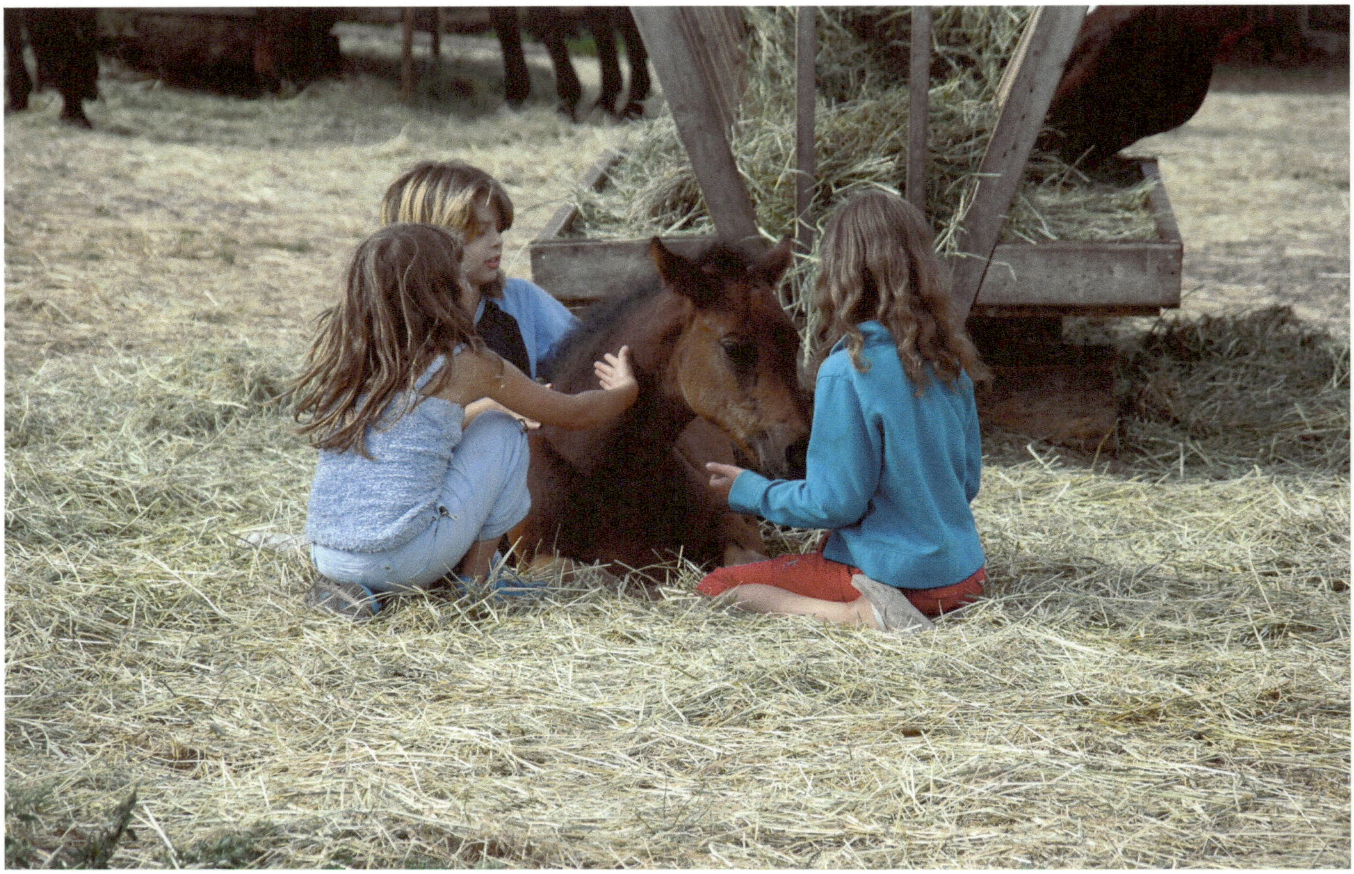

Grandchildren interview Tesoro and the horses:

Tesoro, do you remember me?

Yes, I like to see you again.

Do you love mommy?

Yes

Do you think you are a horse?

Yes, but I don't like to kick. Horses are smarter than people. When people say they're the most advanced brains on the planet, that just makes them more dumb.

Paschar, where do you come from?

Somewhere where the clouds are.

Epona?

I come from the sun.

I was happily riding L.E. Diva, Mira and some of my earlier horses with traditional bridles, snaffles and saddles. Trainers warned against switching to what they thought had no control over these large, dangerous creatures. Diva told me to just take off the bit and substitute a halter. I tried it first in the ring and noticed there was no difference in her compliance to my requests. Amazing! Magic! Why were we riding with bits? I have since tried this on countless friends' horses with the same results. It seems that without the discomfort of a bit (and even a snaffle is devised to pinch the tongue and jab the roof of the mouth), the horse could relax into really enjoying what was being asked of them without the focus on dealing with the pain associated with riding. After schooling my "whoa," both on the ground and riding, to an instant response (rewarded with a convenient treat carried in my pocket), I was amazed again to find that it was still in place during all out full gallops in the hills. "Whoa" became the most fun thing for my horse to do. It was both rewarding and relaxing and even preferred to running. The horses have since impressed on me the importance of trail rides with stops to "picnic" (I just say the word and get an enthusiastic response), they graze for a few minutes and we move on. Grazing or munching on a treat calms and relaxes the horse as their nature is to move, stop, graze and move again. Humans are more predator focused and obsessed with getting to a goal directly and in as little time as possible. The horses are breaking in at this point with some more enthusiastic advice for humans wanting a positive relationship (horse as teacher, human as student) with their horse.

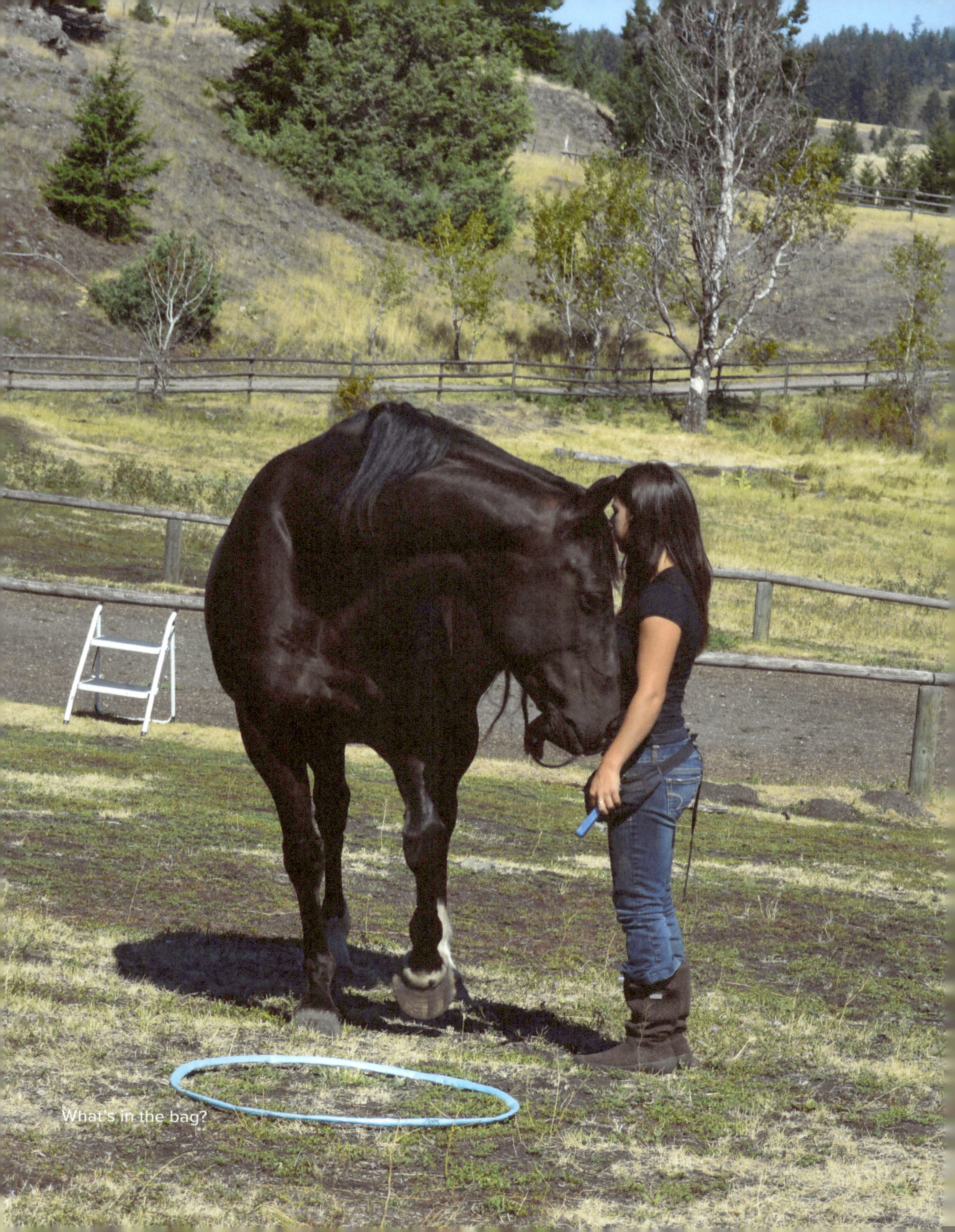
What's in the bag?

By the way people, in spite of anything you have heard to the contrary, apples, carrots and horse treats are not detrimental to a good relationship with your horse! We LOVE them and in fact they make us feel much happier when being asked to do the sort of things that humans think are fun but horses are iffy about. Have you ever seen us running in circles in the wild or being straight for that matter? We prefer gentle curves. We also prefer stopping often to graze or just to reflect on what is going on around us. You will never see us jumping for the joy of it, doing Piaffe around the meadow or going sideways or backward. Please, it is one of those "MAN in control" myths that feeding your horse creates bad habits. It makes them look like the master if they have a whip and spurs and need all kinds of instruments of torture to tame the wild beasts. Really, shake a bucket and we come running, pull out a carrot and see just how much we know, while we feigned ignorance a millisecond ago. Have you ever told your friend to get up on the porch and sit in that chair or you'll whip them? No, you invite and reward. Tea and a cookie goes much further in winning friends, and an experience shared that feels good for both of you makes your hearts sing. Please don't think of us as dangerous unpredictable creatures. We are only made so by humans and it is only humans who can unravel the damage and offer their hearts. Chasing us around a round pen is not the way to win our respect and love. Take the time to get to know us without agenda, without force, learn to communicate rather than intimidate and you will be amazed at what we offer in return.

Horsemanship talks about body language. It doesn't matter the discipline it is all taught around aids, which are conveyed, to the horse through the language of the body. Anyone who has ever experienced oneness in horsemanship realizes an elusive, indefinable but nonetheless unmistakable connection that goes beyond the body to the mind and the spirit. Our body, mind and spirit are one with the horse and in that moment we experience oneness with truth. Our truth and life's truth.

Wisdom, truth, joy, freedom, abundance and love — "isness." The body is so finely tuned to our every thought it becomes increasingly apparent the more time we spend with horses that we learn to use our body less and our mind more.

It is also important to spend unstructured time with horses; time to commune and enjoy. Interact without halter and lead rope. Put a few treats in your pocket and take out a brush and spend some quality time strengthening your relationship. Teach them to move their body, the front end, hind end forward and back. Teach them some fun tricks like stepping up on tires, walking through foam noodles or walking into a trailer to enjoy a bucket of treats. You will be amazed at how many things your horse will do if they are not forced but invited and rewarded. Always tell them how proud you are and how wonderful and good they are. They understand every word and thought. I rarely use a halter for anything and my horses follow me anywhere; over, under and through obstacles that most people couldn't whip or lip chain their horse to try.

It's all done a little bit at a time with a lot of praise and positive reward. Eventually your horse will come to view you as a wonderful experience and do whatever you ask.

Try taking off your bridle and riding with a halter and lead rope (I guarantee it will only improve the way your horse responds and they won't associate riding with discomfort). Most of what we ask is by our body position and our mind and if you get into trouble it is much easier to stop a horse by reaching down one rein and bending them to a stop with a halter than pulling on a bit and having it slide through the mouth or held between the horse's teeth.

If you have spent time to develop a trust on the ground, a horse will happily look after you on their back. When I do ground work games I use words like "walk on," "whoa" and "back" and I reward "whoa" with lots of praise and treats so it becomes a positive association. When I am on their back and say "whoa," if the horse takes one more step forward I back them to the point I said "whoa." Once all these safeguards are in place you will never need more than a halter to safely ride, and your horse, instead of running away when you approach, will come running toward you.

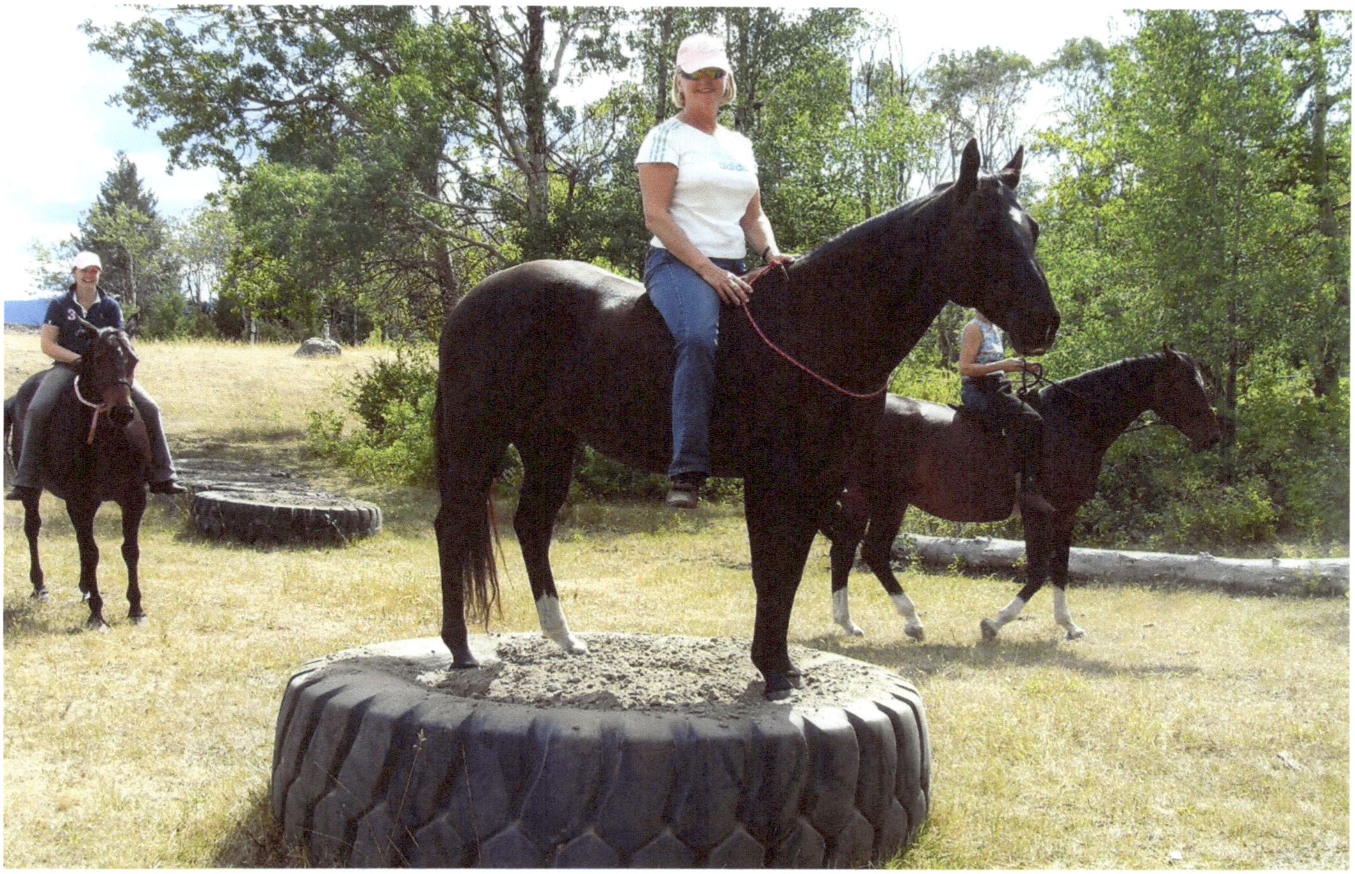

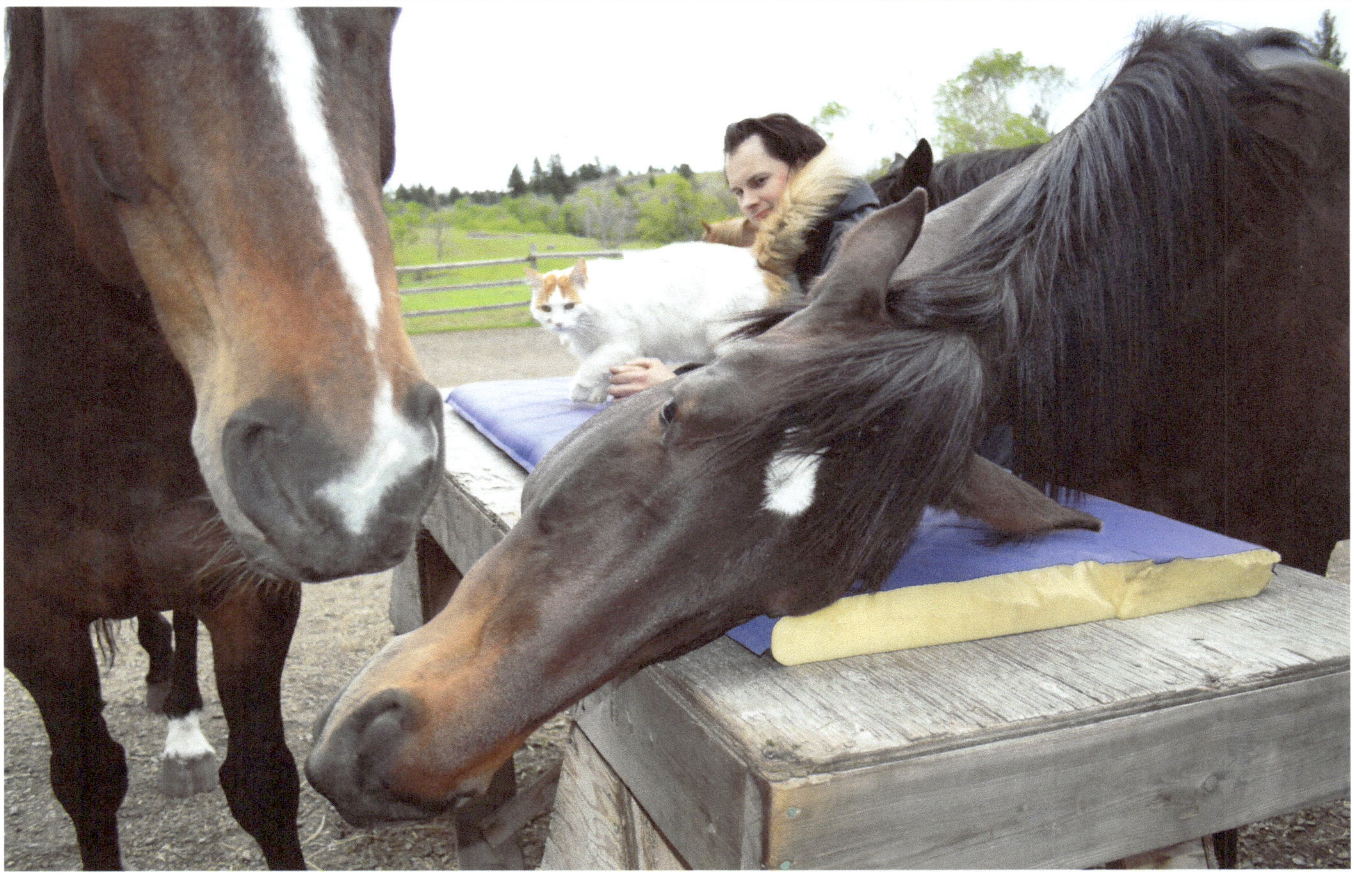

Serene sweeps energy

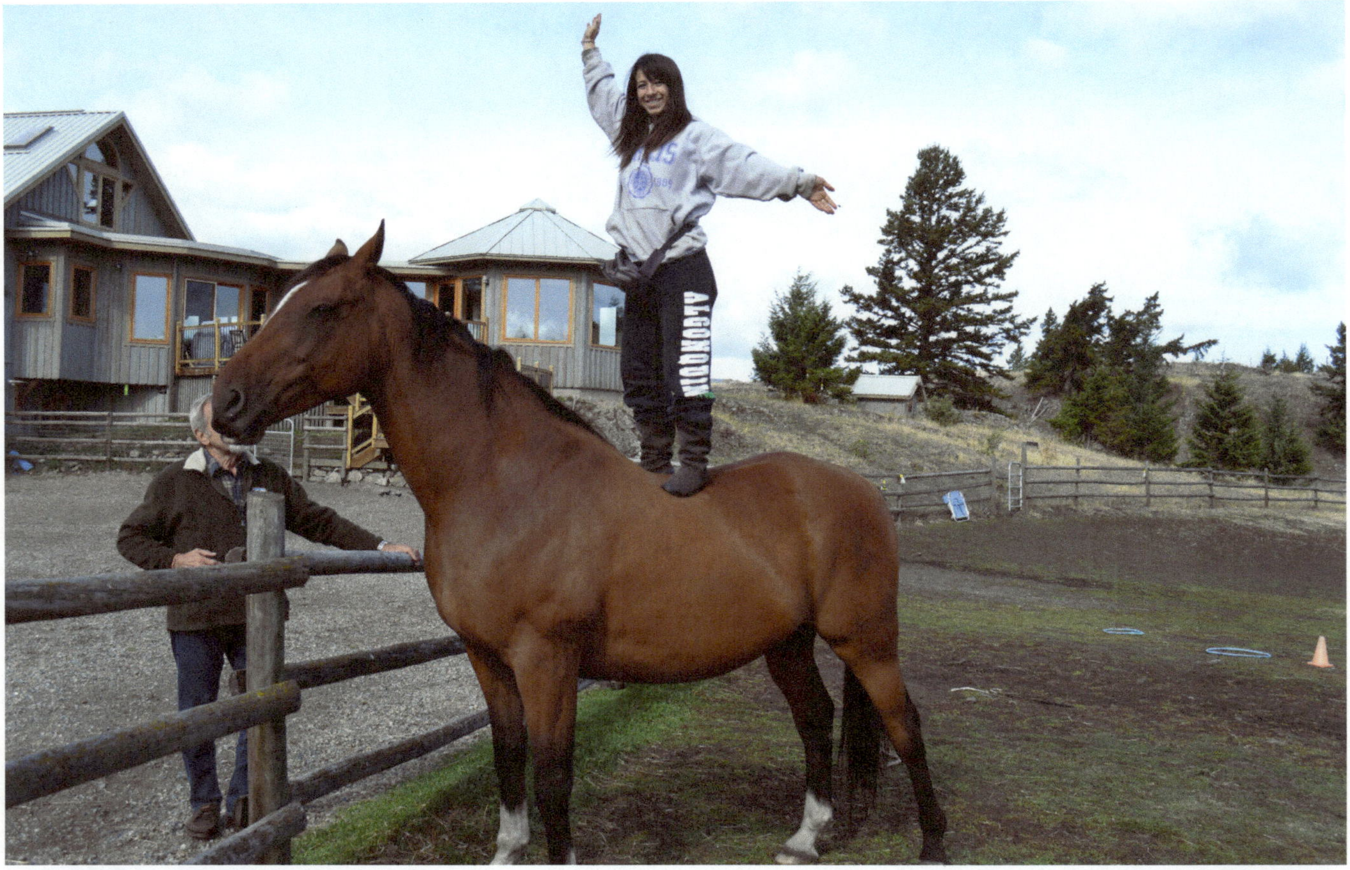

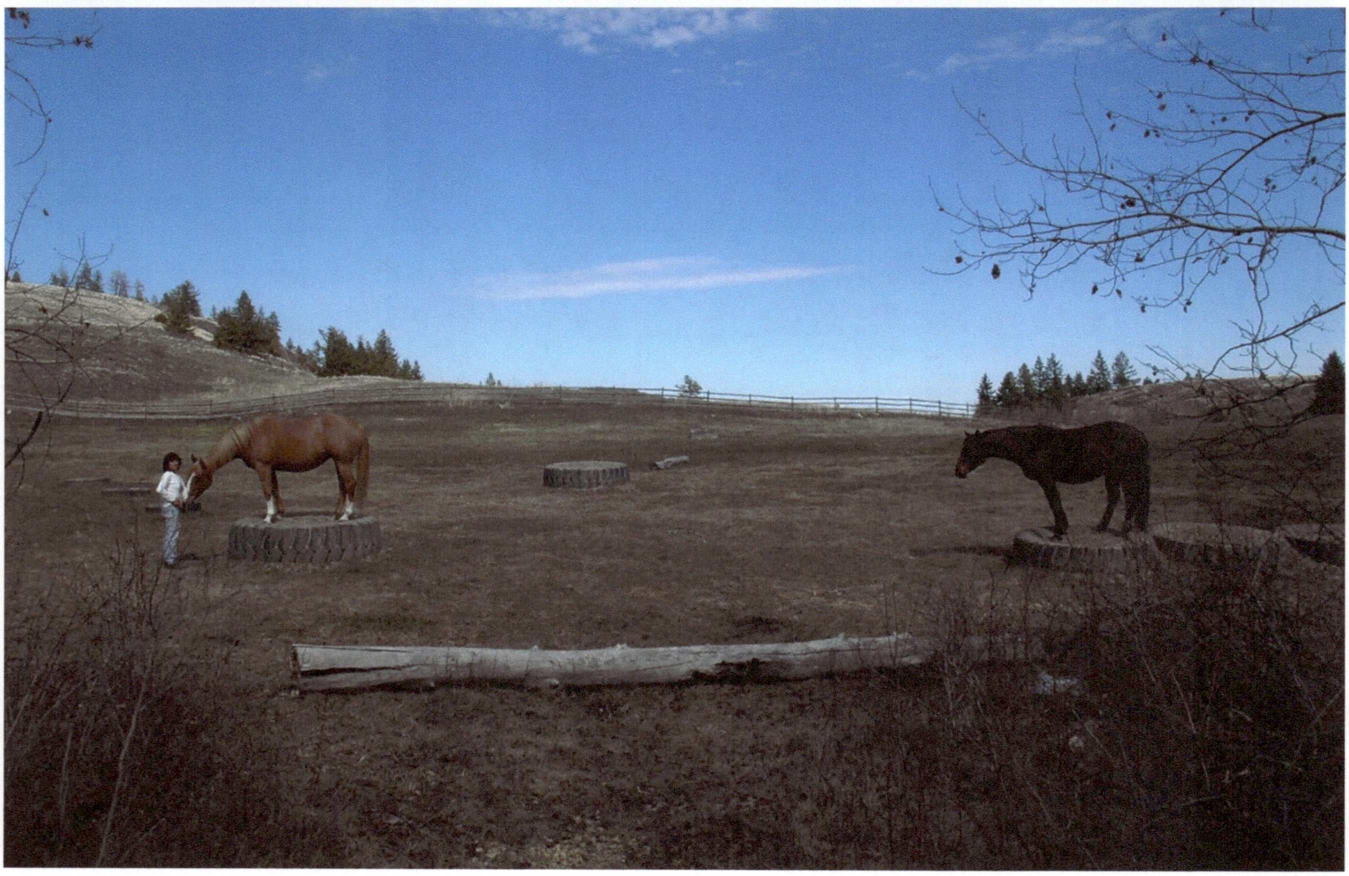

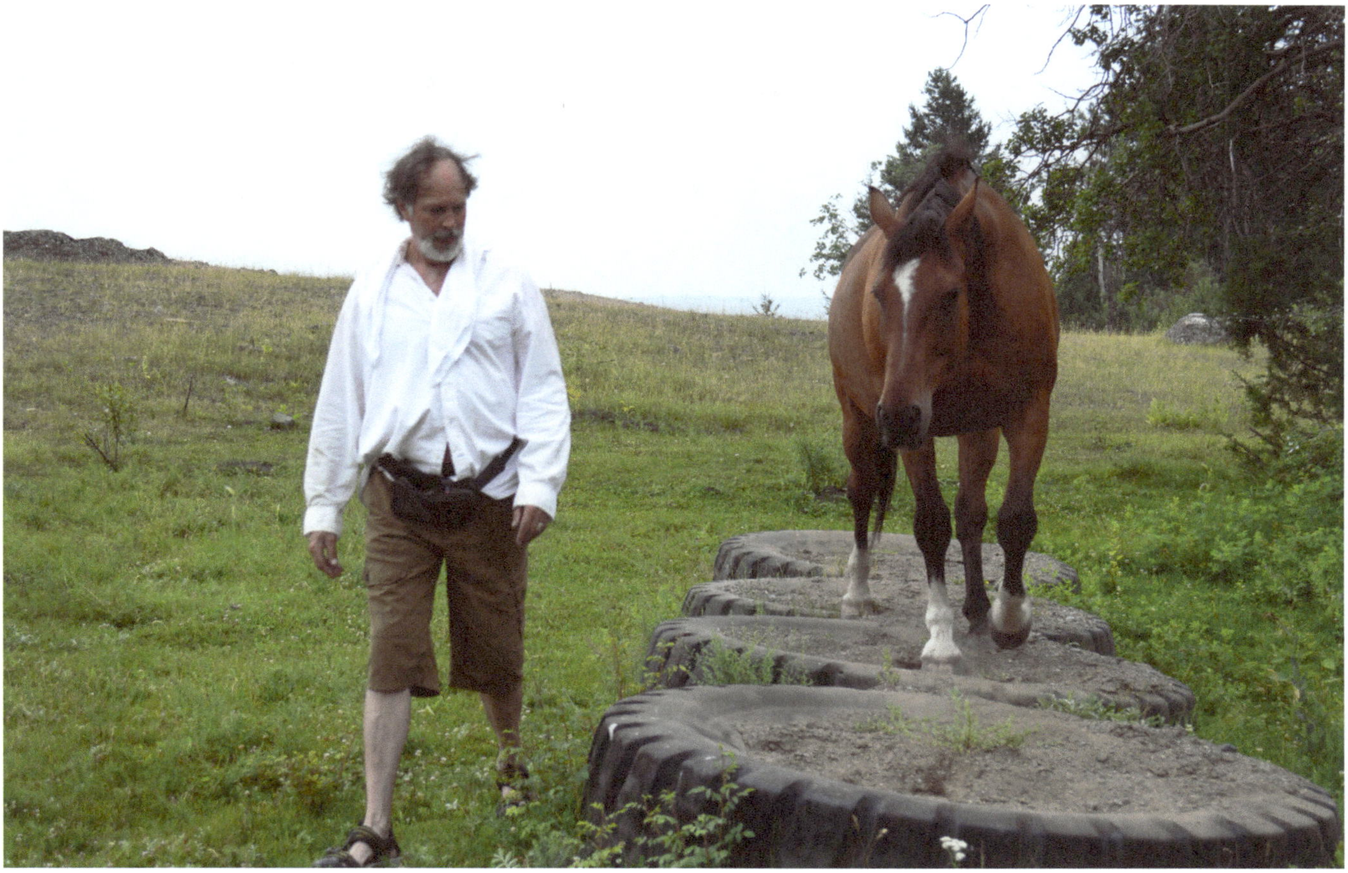

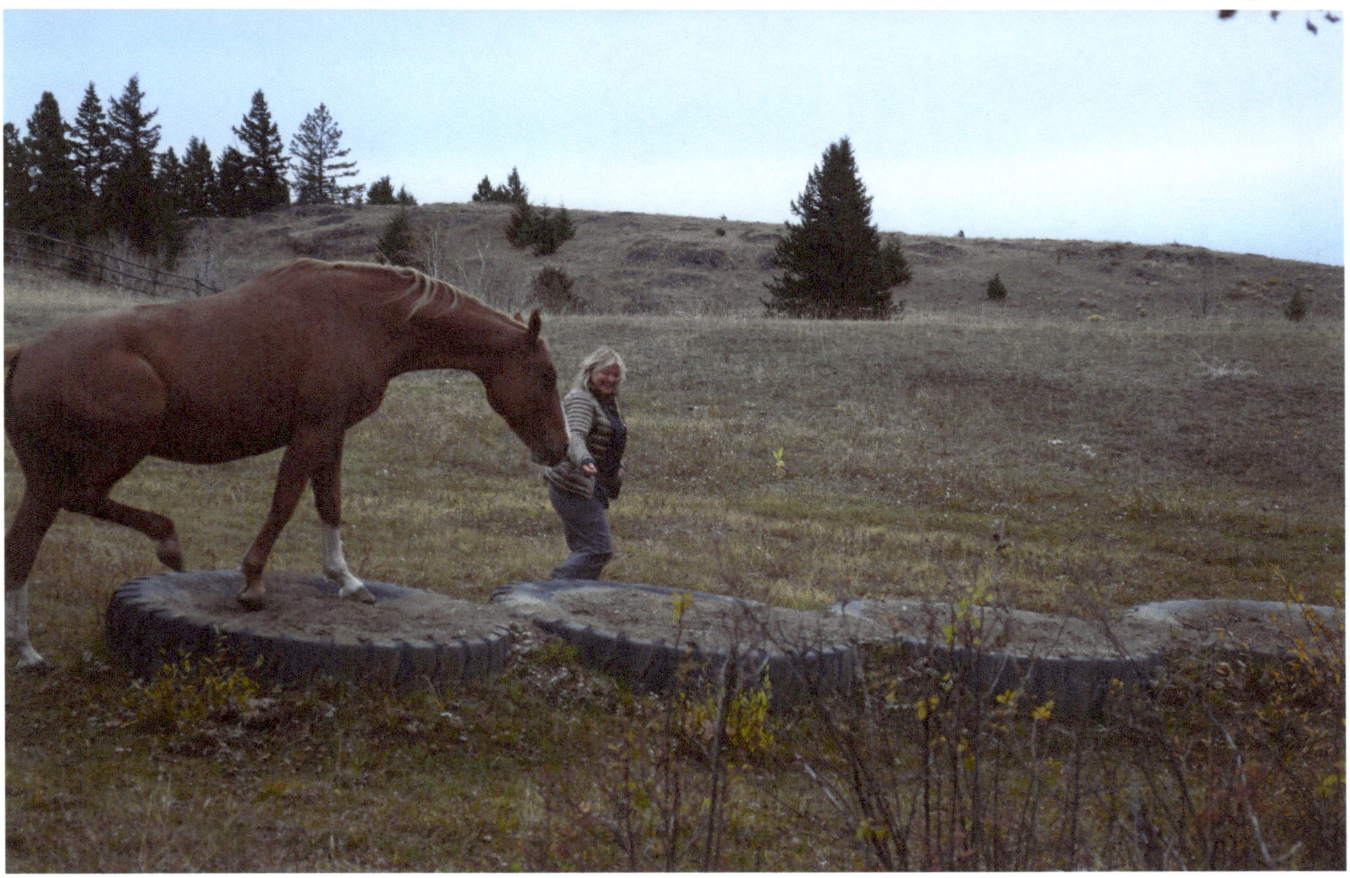

Adventure Playground

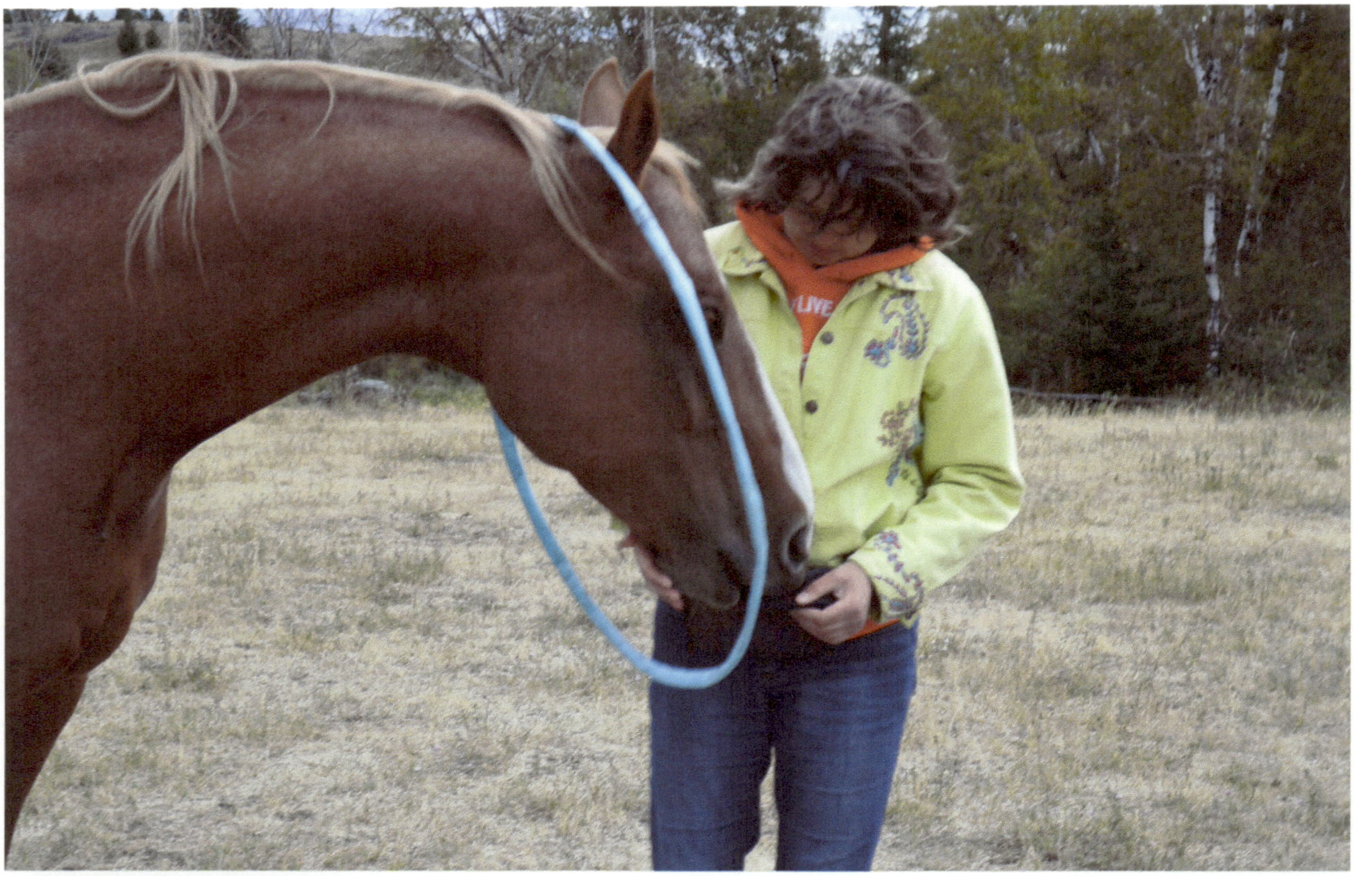

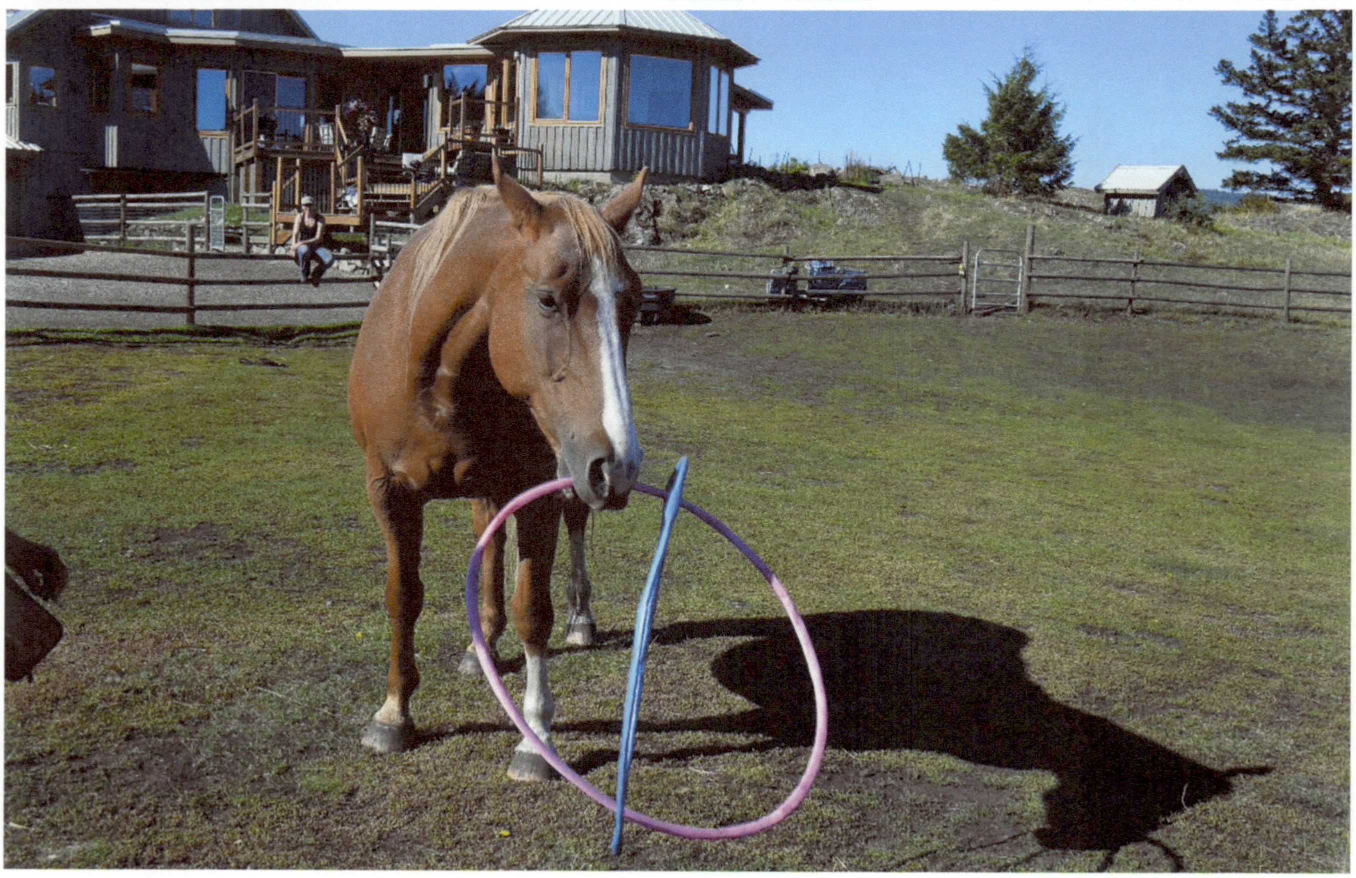

Hula Hoops are fun

We are increasingly excited about the world interest in viewing horses in a new light. As consciousness expands to include more species, human mass mind consciousness changes as well. If you examine higher mind or universal consciousness as a composite of each and every created thing, experiencing the physical plane, receiving and sending feedback to the ALL, then you can appreciate the importance of connecting to as much information as possible. Animals, plants, minerals from all created realms have a purpose to fulfill in the larger picture, and when one can transcend the outline of self to explore that movie of life, an awakening and expansion occurs that enlightens not only individual consciousness, but the consciousness of each group (i.e. horse, whale, human, tree) and the one consciousness that is higher mind as well. We have shared this higher vibration on the Journey to Enlightenment DVD and continue to share new messages of truth throughout the world. We are all one in this journey toward the light. Whether we have two legs or four, or none at all, does not alter our essence, purpose or connection to one consciousness. Animals and nature have a clear connection to share with all who are guided to experience this new understanding. The shift is happening exponentially with each new mind.

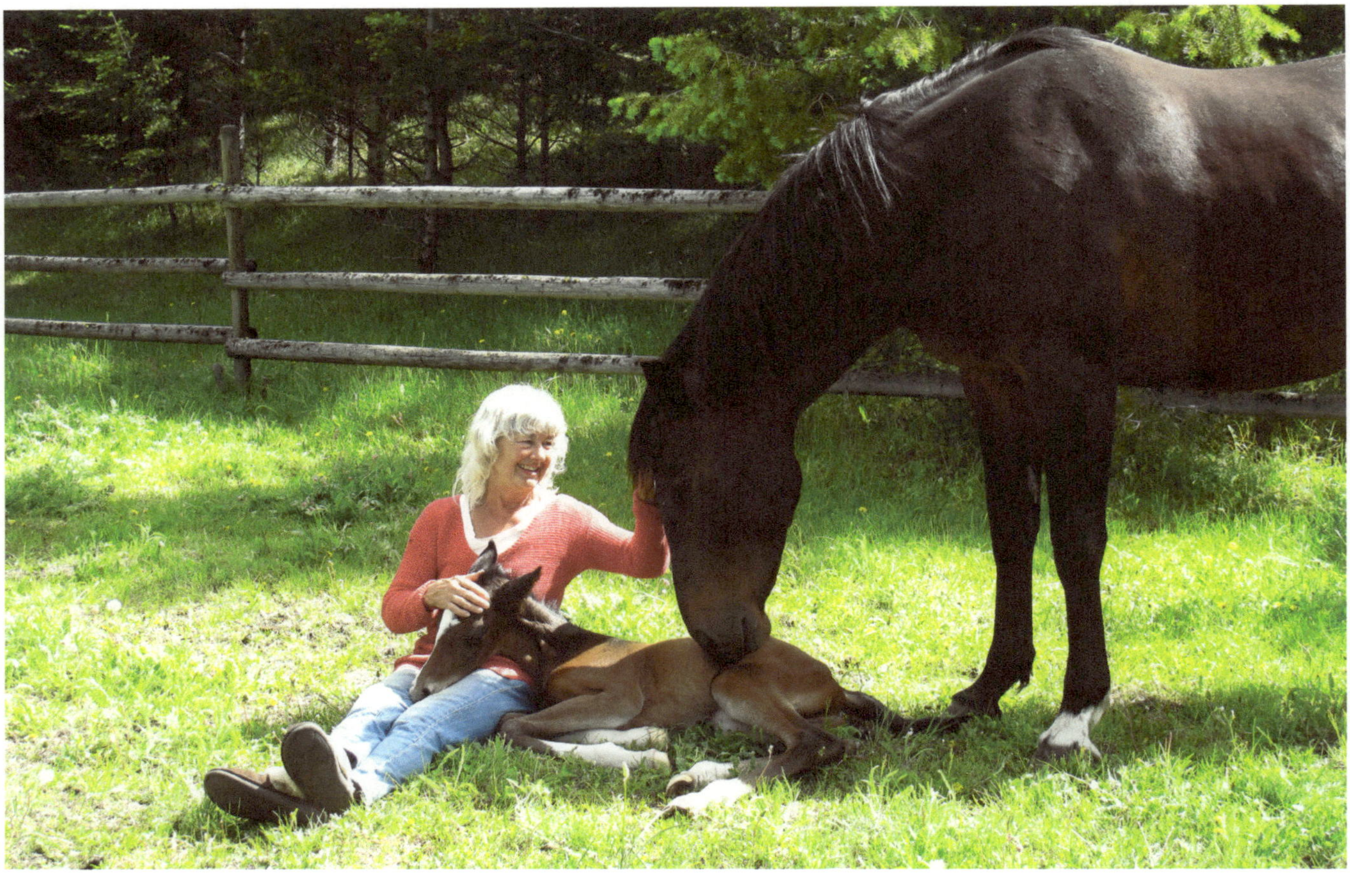

Liz with Serene and baby Hyperion

Straight from the horse's mouth...

I just finished reading Lynne McTaggart's, *The Field*. As I scanned through the book I realized that I knew all of this already. How did I know it? You remember the bumper sticker that says: "Everything I know I learned from my horse?" Well, it wasn't one horse in particular but over unstructured time spent in their presence, I had begun to resonate at the horse frequency and they resonated with the field or what animals call the ALL (or God).

Remember when human consciousness expands to the level where we can truly encompass this understanding that you heard it first from a horse!

It is a time of great change, energetically. If things do not appear to make sense you know you are in the shift. People, circumstance, physical states are flipping in and out, colliding against each other. It is so important to connect with animals and nature so we can tune and assist you humans to make this shift to a new consciousness and connection to all life. The veil between the spiritual and physical planes is getting thinner; time, space, dimension are all blending into the focus of the now. There are large energetic pockets of consciousness in the human mass mind consciousness, one colliding against the other like oil and water and causing many natural disasters. At the tipping point there will be a higher order of world consciousness that can only be accessed through the higher consciousness of all creation resonating as one, in the now (which all animals, plants, minerals, access but humans only visit occasionally). Let us help "enlighten" you. Come and join us in the ALLness, ONEness of WISDOM, TRUTH, JOY, FREEDOM, ABUNDANCE and LOVE. It is all that is real and all that will be forever. Do it NOW.

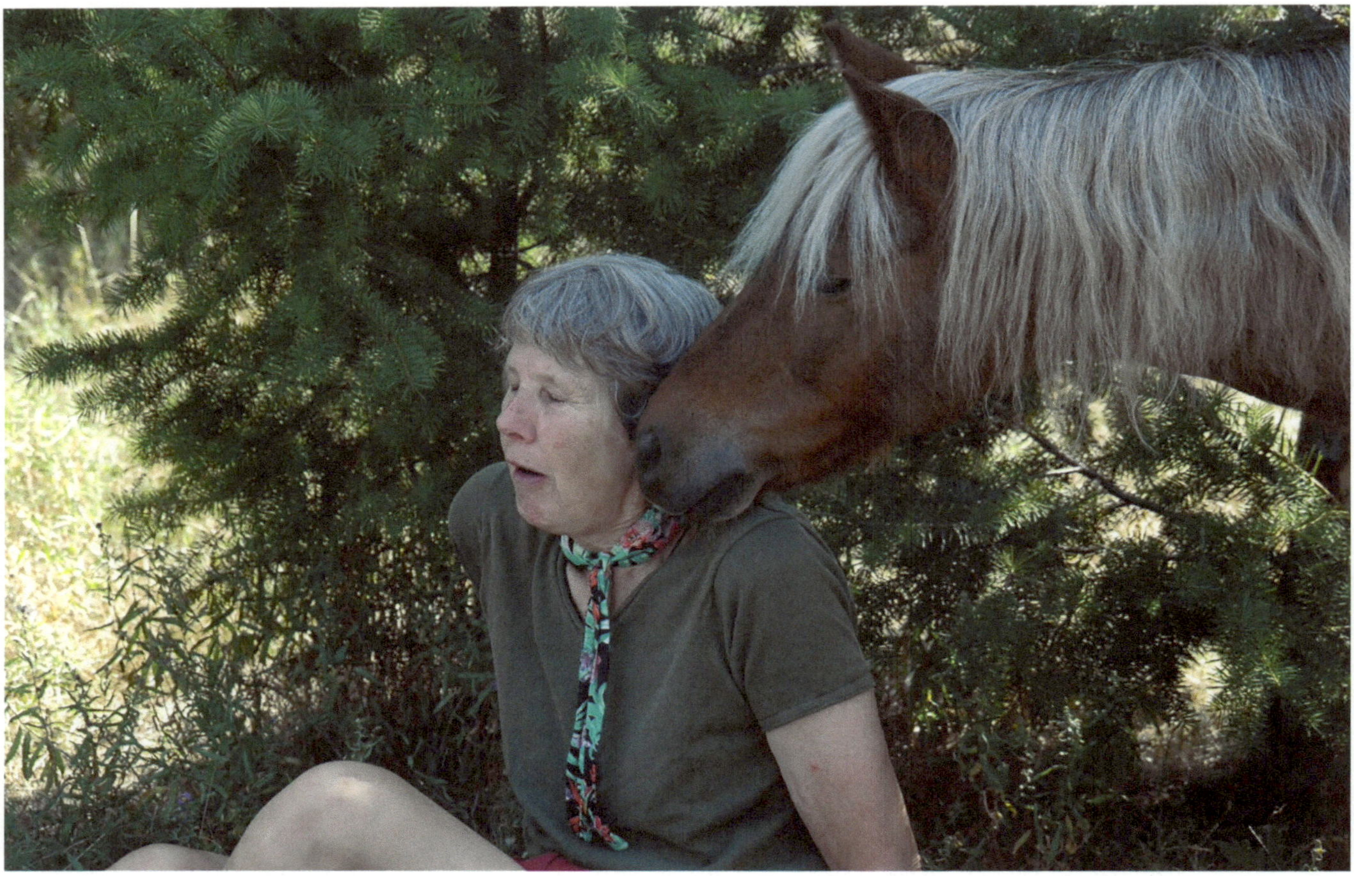

I want to share Jan's story which really was the most miraculous experience of nature's connection to consciousness. Jan and I, arriving from the airport, had just crested the ridge and were about to pass through the portal of aspens just before Kullagh Lake and the gate to the ranch. We were intensely talking about the veil experienced by humans that they talk about in *Life Unbridled* that is clearly passable by animals and the natural world. Suddenly, we were transfixed by a 3x6x12 foot cloud that blocked our path taking up the entire road, a veil of billions of living star-shaped seeds resembling dandelion fluff. The veil had a substance and life that we could shape by the armful or lift with a foot so we dove in and began giggling and playing with child-like glee.

I love September and October with their cobalt blue skies and golden leaves and grasses—very strengthening for the solar plexus and third eye chakras. Yesterday, Kevin and I were sitting on the back porch as the sun was dipping low in the sky and lighting all the flying things with white sparks of sunlight. Suddenly a magical thing happened. Swirls of brilliant white sparks appeared in the sky, whirling balls of celebration going in all different directions. They weren't being tossed by the wind but were more resembling free-flying insects caught in the light who were choosing to fly in thousands of spiraling balls; dipping, gliding and swirling from above the roof to a mile high

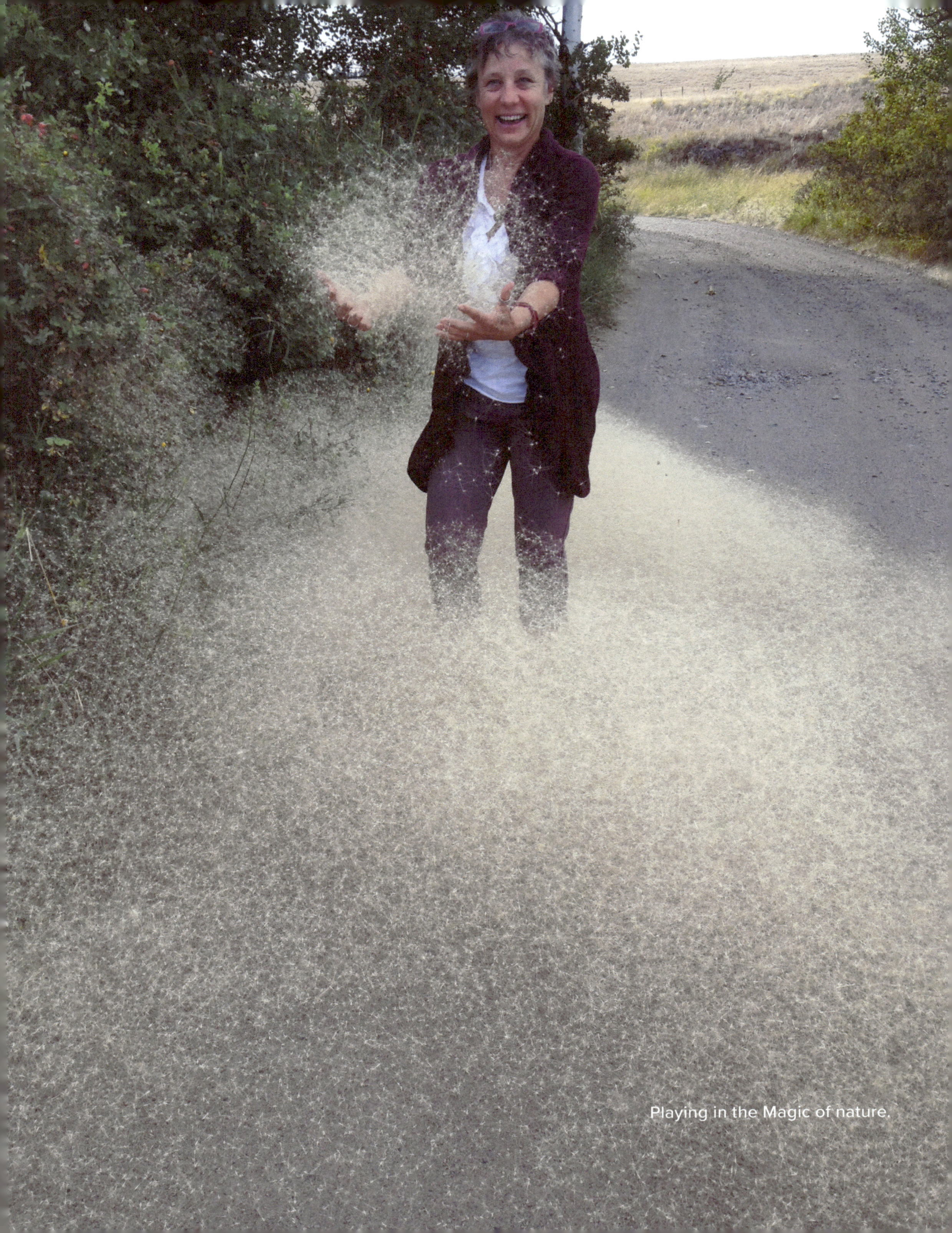

Playing in the Magic of nature.

Whirling balls of seed fluff... the same seeds as in the Jan story.

in the sky. We were mesmerized, and then as the odd few drifted down around us we realized that they were not insects but little stars of seed fluff, a bit like dandelion down. I recognized them as the same ones that had formed a large cloud, a living veil as I was bringing Jan to Gateway last September, and again they were expressing the consciousness of child-like joy. We had stopped the truck and played in wonder at the serendipity of a conscious veil appearing across the road as we were just discussing the veil that humans have created to block what they don't want to see.

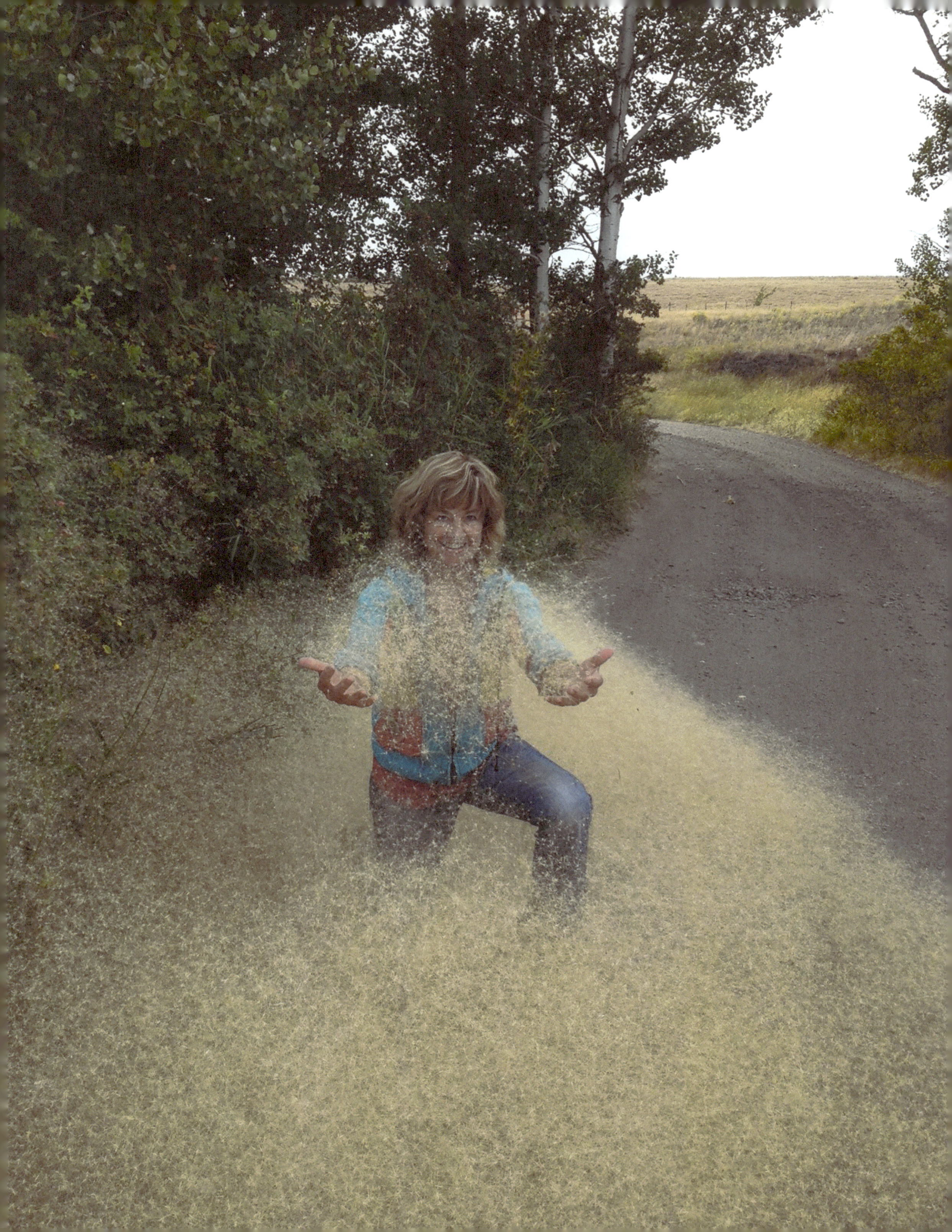

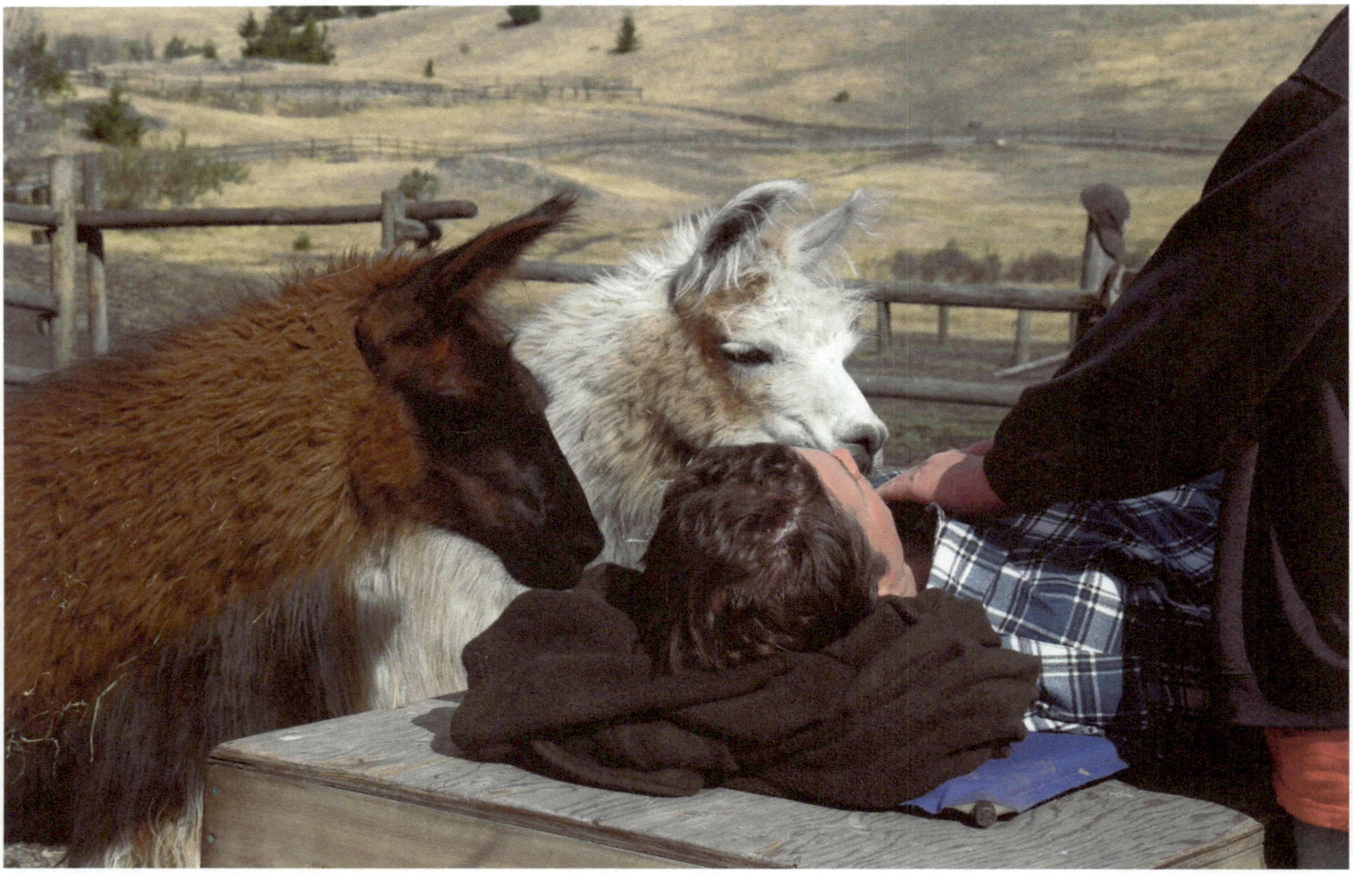

When the llamas joined the Herd:

I suppose you could say we lead a sheltered life, here with our Herd and visiting humans. Our horse bodies are in conflict with our higher selves and our prey instincts nudge us to caution. Liz tried to communicate about llamas but there is no data in our cellular memory as warmblood horses to draw on. These creatures are to us like newly landed aliens, and we must gather information before proceeding. Even Tesoro, coming from North American cattle, does not understand what llamas are. He is, in fact, the worst and still holding his lonely vigil in the back pasture, sure that his Buddha status is being challenged.

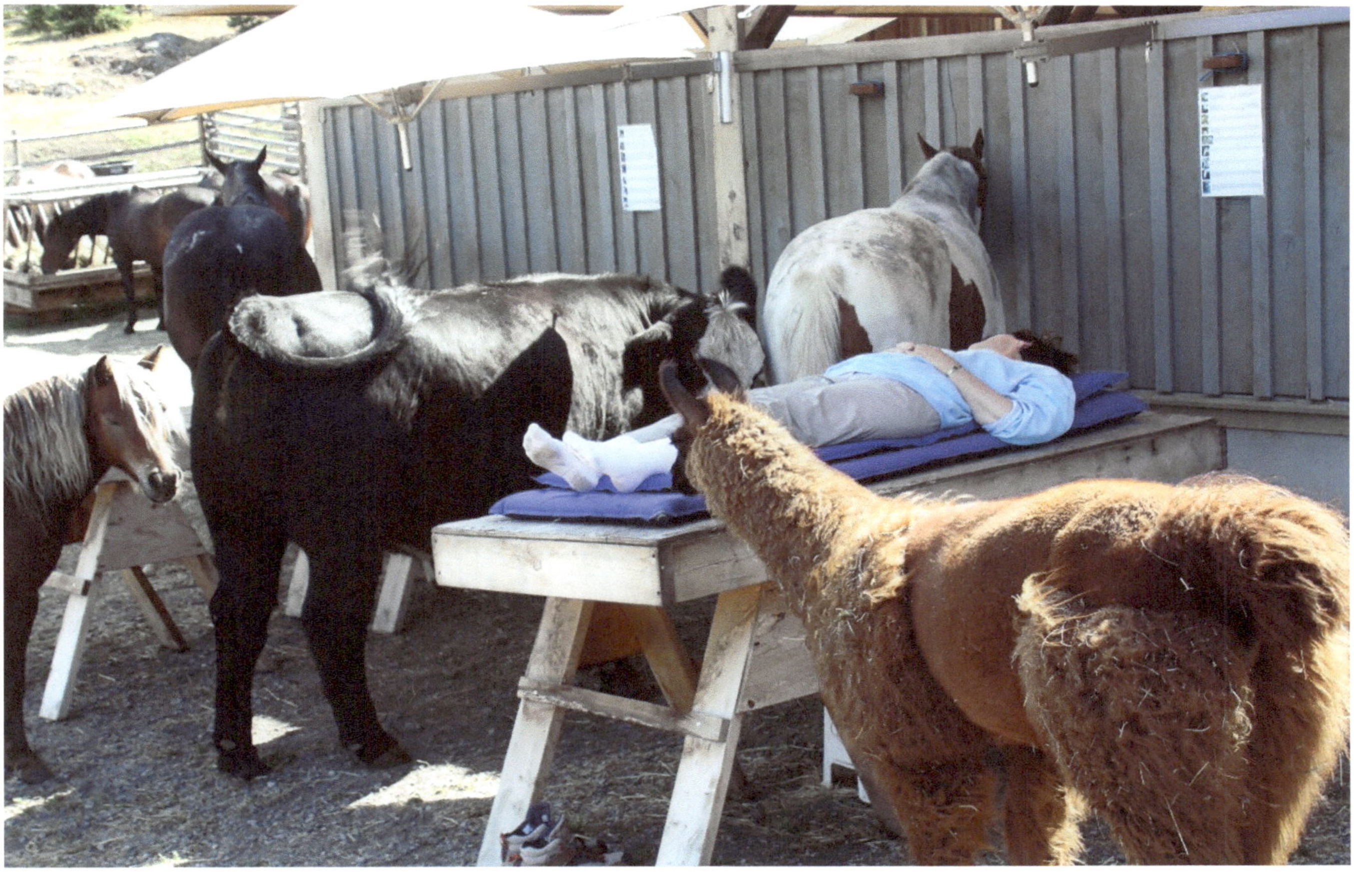

I have a funny story to share about the llamas. They are so free and happy. Coming home daily for food and a nap in the hay shed and then back to the hills is their daily routine. I was heading to town one day and had made it as far as Kullagh Lake—about a mile from the barn—and had just crossed the cattle guard when directly in front of me on the other side I discovered the llamas. I stopped the truck, got out and simultaneously we all said to each other, "What are you doing here!" The look on their faces was even more startled than mine. I opened the ride-through gate and told them it was dangerous to go over the cattle guard and to go home that way. When I finally came home, there they were in the hay barn safe and sound.

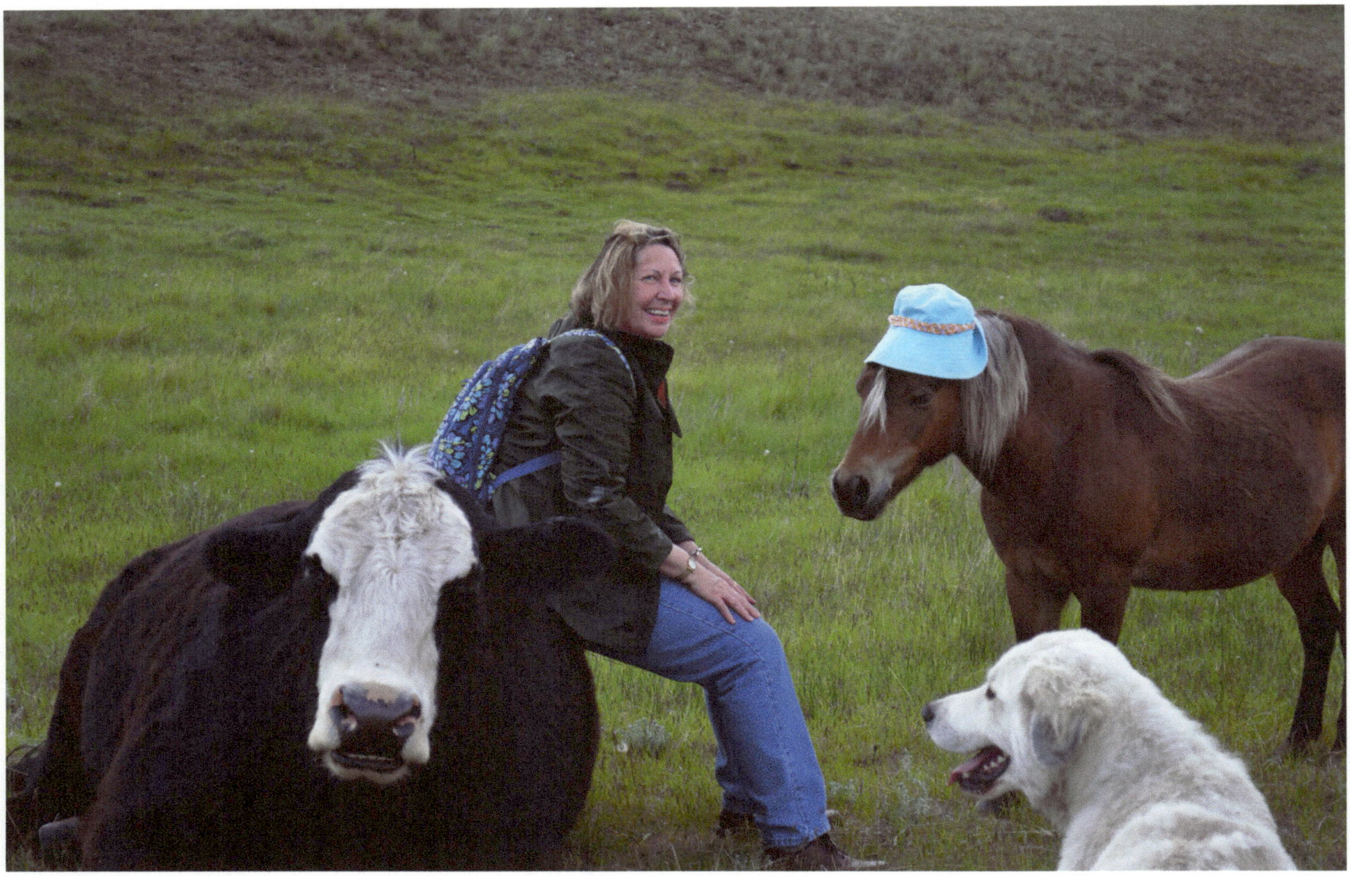

You know, sometimes we don't know where to begin people...

You are so unaware that there is any life form that even comes close to your level of intelligence, yet look at the evidence against you. Has any other species wreaked disaster upon the Earth? We do not pretend or play games (i.e. lie), ever, under any circumstance. What would be the point? Because we are not clouded by our own delusions and connection to a false self, we maintain a clear lifeline to the ALL, which provides all of our needs. We do not create work for ourselves by trying to change the natural order of things or accumulate false wealth that simply causes us concern. We are content in our compliance and connection to a higher authority that has shown its wisdom, truth, joy, freedom, abundance and LOVE through the ages. Do you really think you can out-think God?

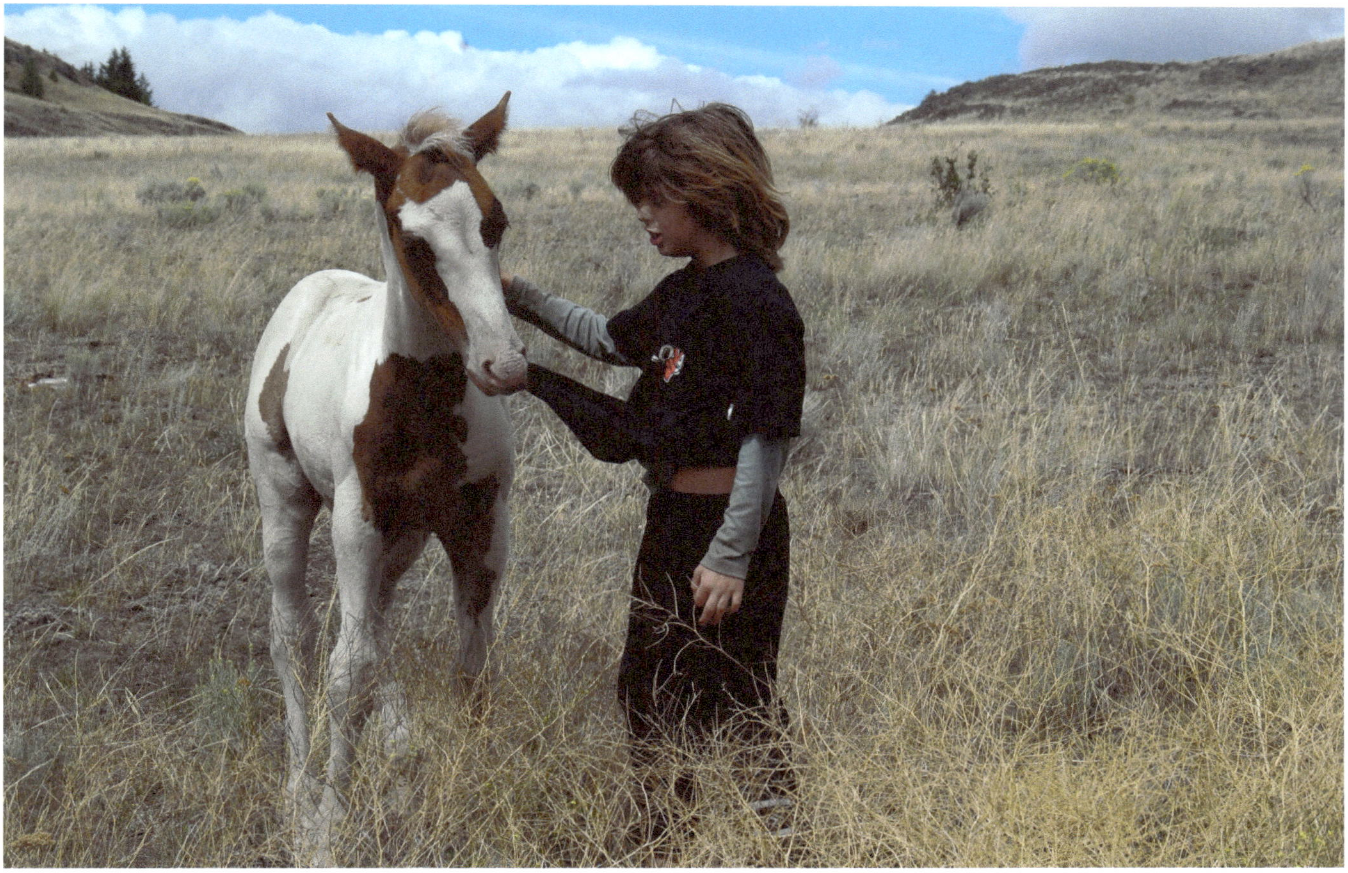

There is only one consciousness in all created life. Whether we have four legs and fur or two and skin only colors the interpretation of that higher wisdom for personal experience and survival. Your survival is looking grim. The animals and the natural world are your only hope to reconnect and re-member with the universal consciousness that is L.I.F.E. (Love In Finite Expression) (i.e....us ALL).

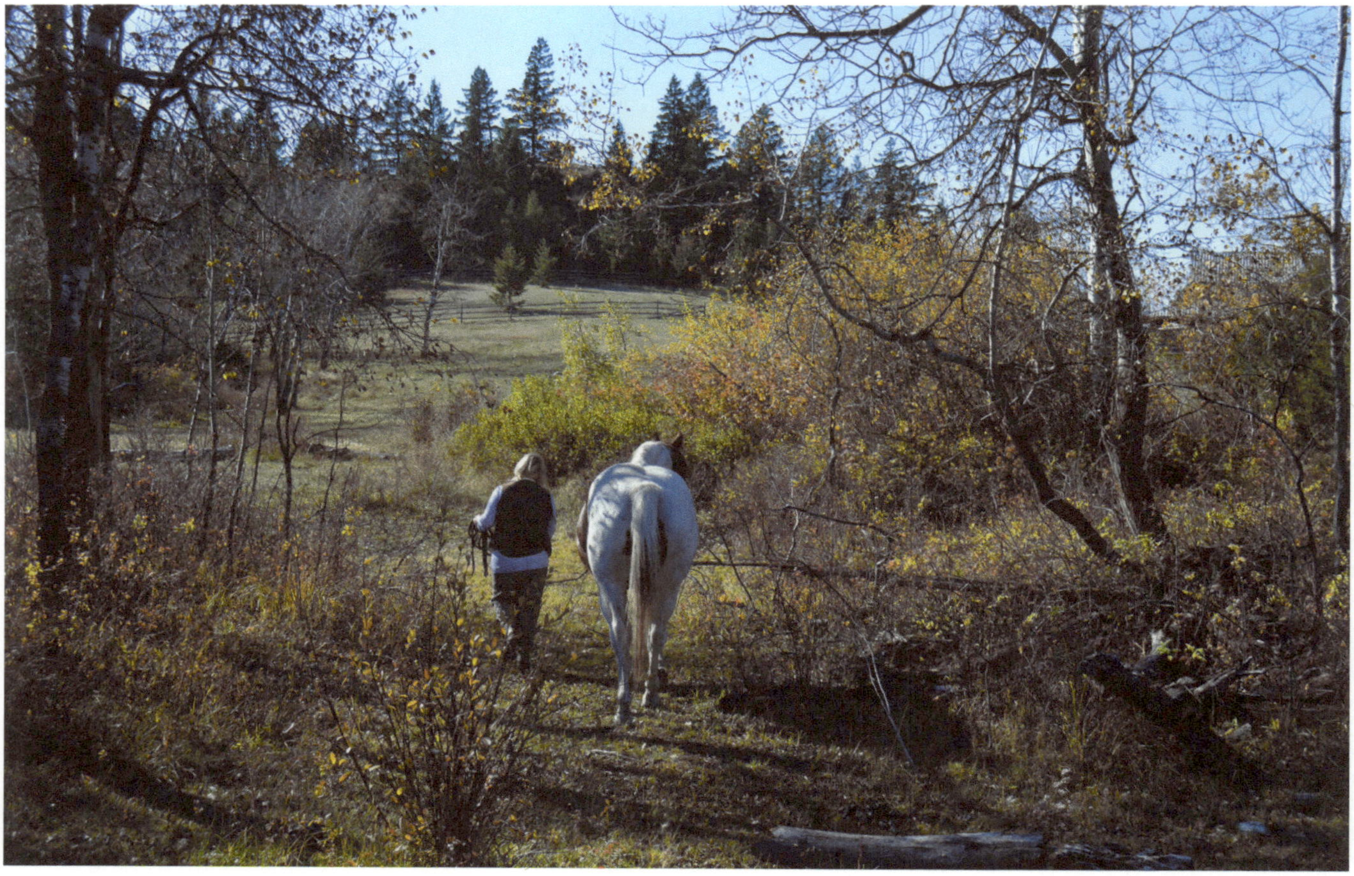

What is becoming increasingly more obvious to me is that horses hold the key to our spiritual evolution. They are making news all over the world, many martyrs for the cause. Horse consciousness is united in truth and is holding a shining multifaceted mirror to humanity so that we might see the glimmer of a new Earth united in the unconditional peace and love of God.

If humans want a long-term relationship where joy, trust, friendship, partnership and harmony are experienced, they must put themselves in the position of lead mare. This alone is a much misunderstood position and many times confused with the dominant mare. The lead mare is the grandmother spirit, the wise one in charge of the well-being of the Herd. The Herd members trust her decisions and follow her direction knowing they are safe and will be looked after and led to food and shelter.

If humans can allow their horses to feel good about themselves, then the horses will feel safe and comfortable in the relationship and it will be a win/win situation. As prey animals, many horse reactions are fear based. If there is something the horse is afraid of the human has two choices: to force them through it or to help them through it. It is the lead mare that makes the decision that will be most comfortable and safe for her and each member of the Herd. If humans follow that strategy, they become an ally rather than an adversary. When acting the adversary or predator, the human will be viewed as someone to be respected, but not someone to be sought out for comfort or friendship.

When the human increases well-being in the horse they become the lead mare and that shared well-being and harmony crystallizes a larger level of connection, realization and joy rarely seen in horse/human relationships.

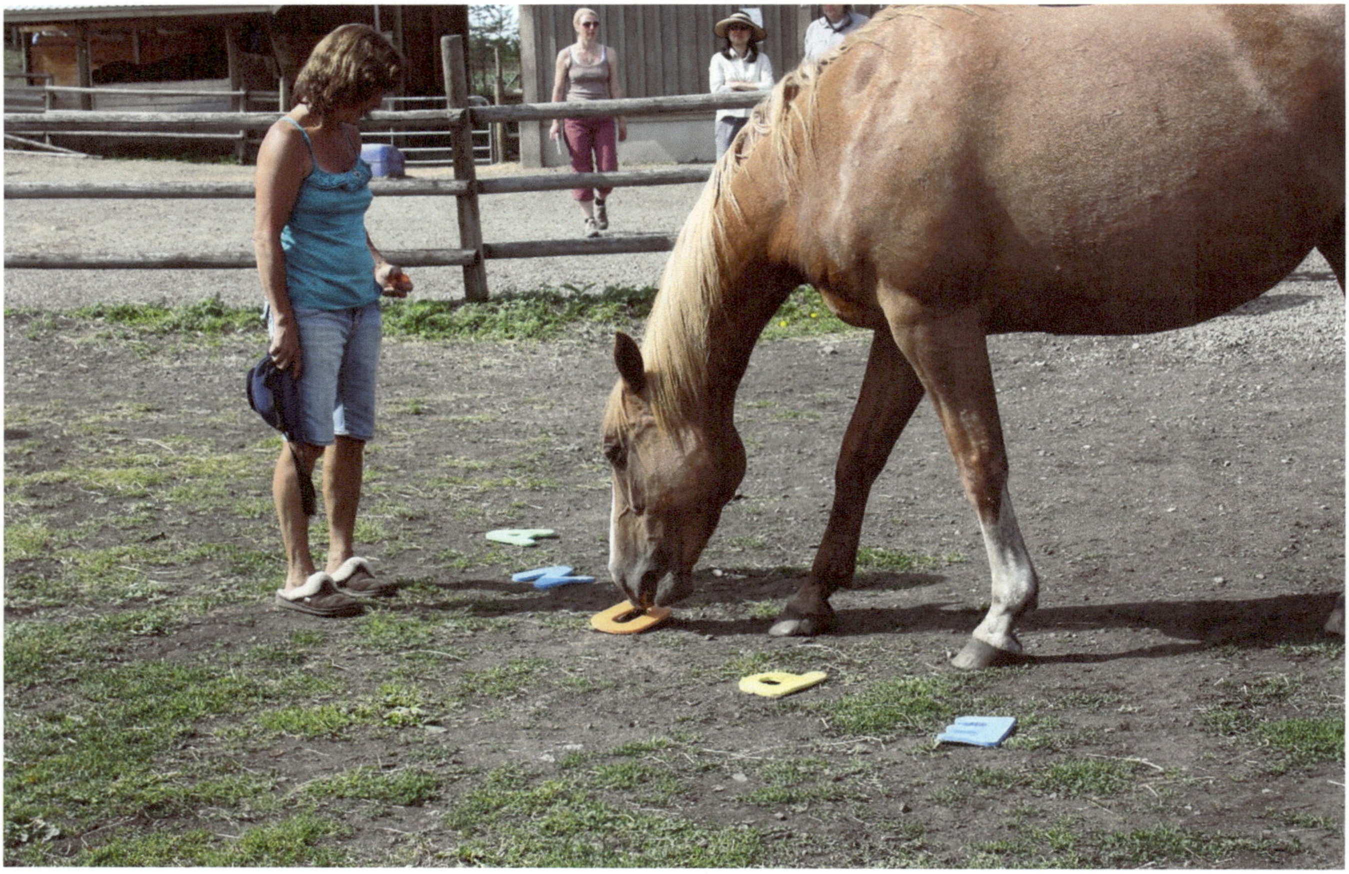

I watched L.E. and began to train like she did. Just a glance at a horse's shoulder or hind quarter would move it, but there had to be a certain tip to the head; a concentration of focus that was unmistakably clear. We would play a game called "stick" to me. I was the benevolent leader and treat dispenser as this game was fun and based on positive reinforcement; a human adaptation of horse language. Treats could involve food, scratches or effusive compliments; an opportunity for one on one with their human.

The horses loved this game and would line up to go with me, or even approach me at an opportune time and ask for it. A crook of my finger and eye contact with the particular horse and off we would go; usually at a run to get out of the gate before the others who also wanted to play. I would close the gate behind us or I would have two or three horses fighting to go over the bridge or get up on the tires, lunging at each other so only they could be with me.

The purpose of the game was to lead the horse happily away from the Herd without any mechanical aids (so it was all their choice) and teach them to watch my body language and depend on me. It always amazed me how much more quickly they would do things for positive reward, rather than threat of punishment. They developed a curious and happy attitude knowing that they were free to participate or not. I was always

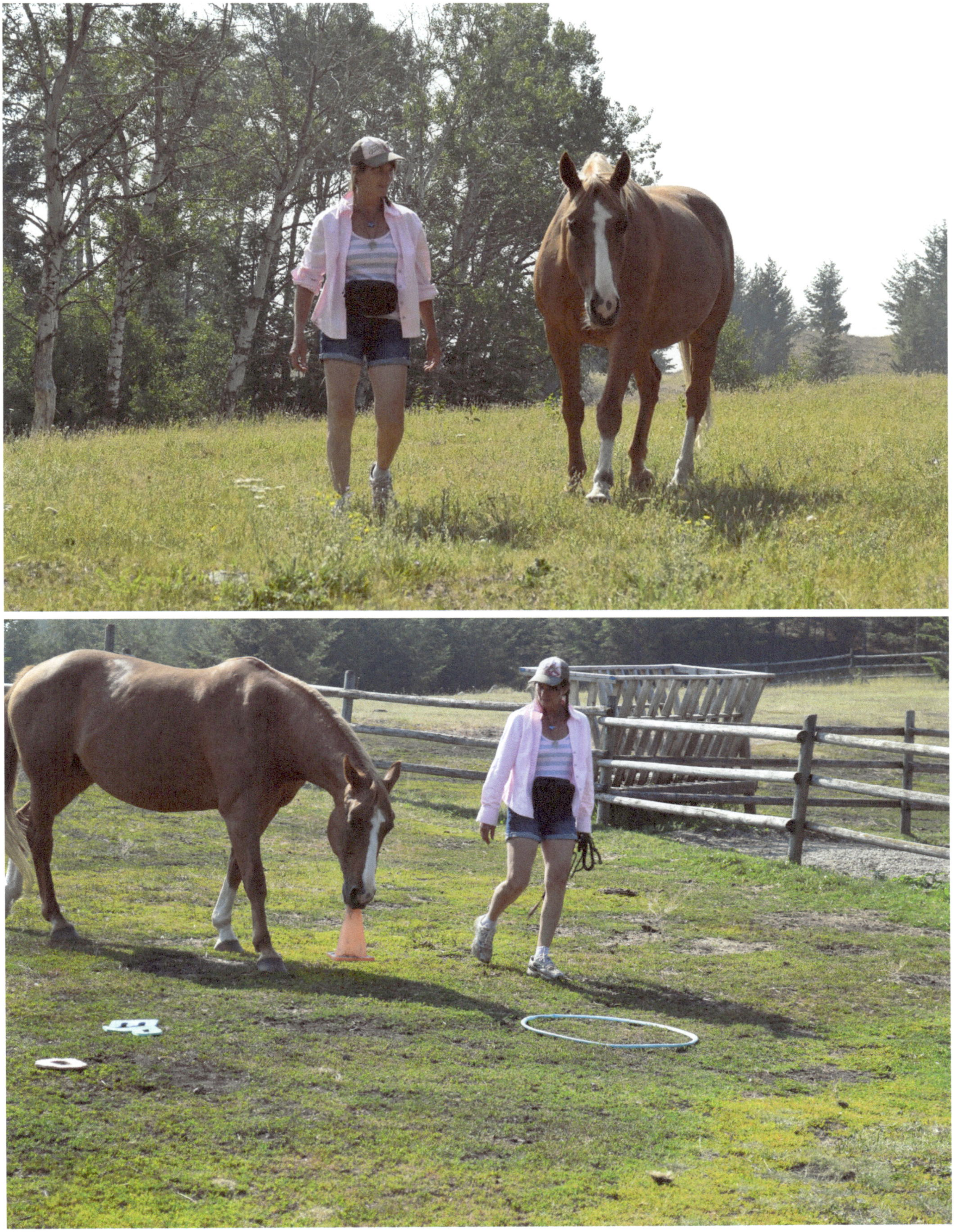

Follow the leader

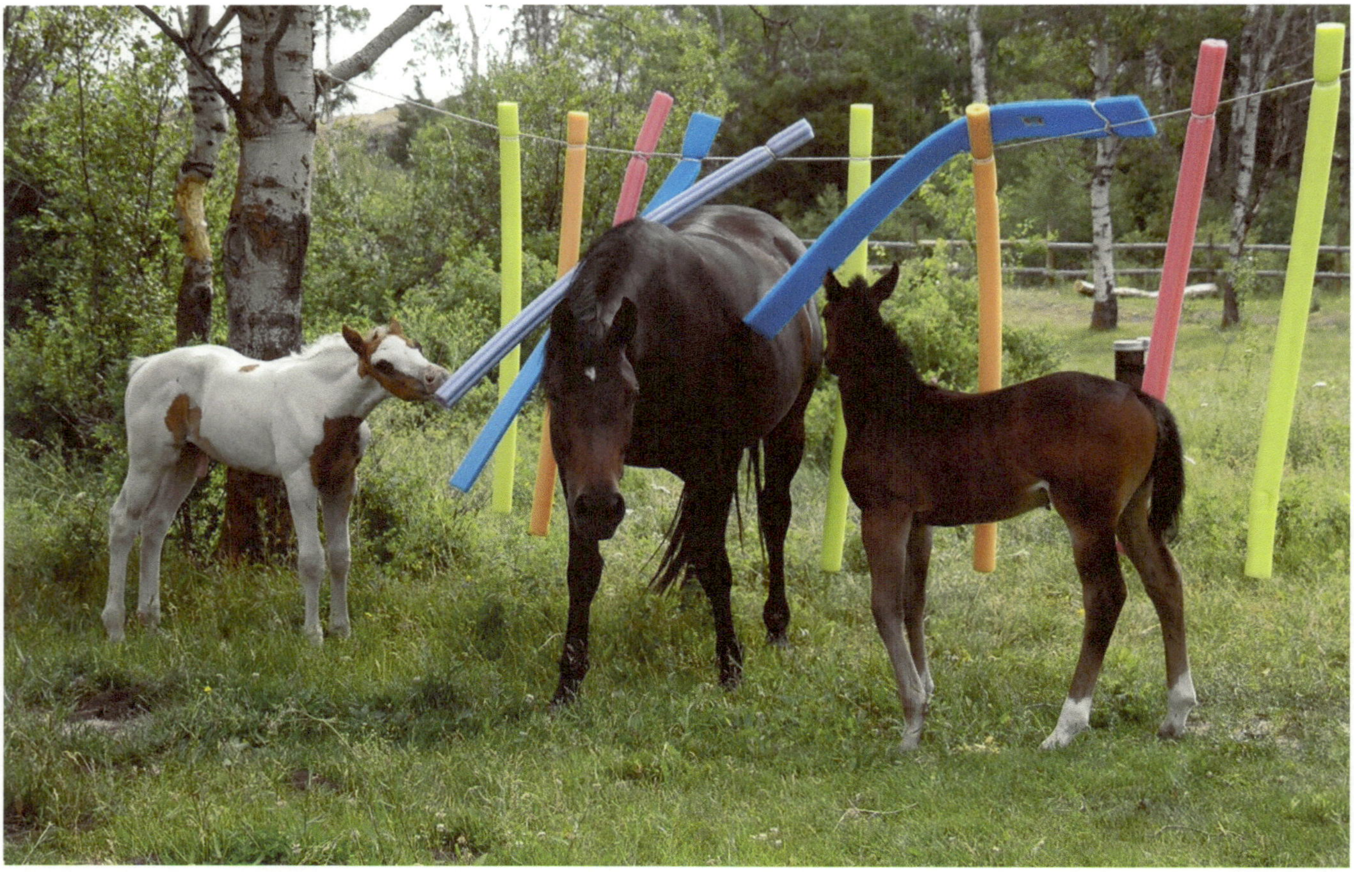

careful not to stretch their limits to the point where they would run back to the Herd. I would give them time to think about it, or maybe run back a short way if spooked, and then encourage them back again. I believe this develops their capacity to reason out situations and trust my judgment rather than just act blindly in a fearful situation. In the end, they will jump much higher out of love and trust than fear.

Magic, at a year old, had the hardest time with these challenges, as like her mother Diva, she had an inborn discomfort of stepping on things. I had to use a halter to coax her on the bridge for the first time and lots of horse treats, but after that her confidence grew. I remember watching her one day, after our session, while the Herd was grazing in the playground, Magic was showing off her new found strength, walked across the bridge and stopped in the middle until all the Herd had noticed her. Then to upstage her, first Picasso and then Matisse ran back and forth over it.

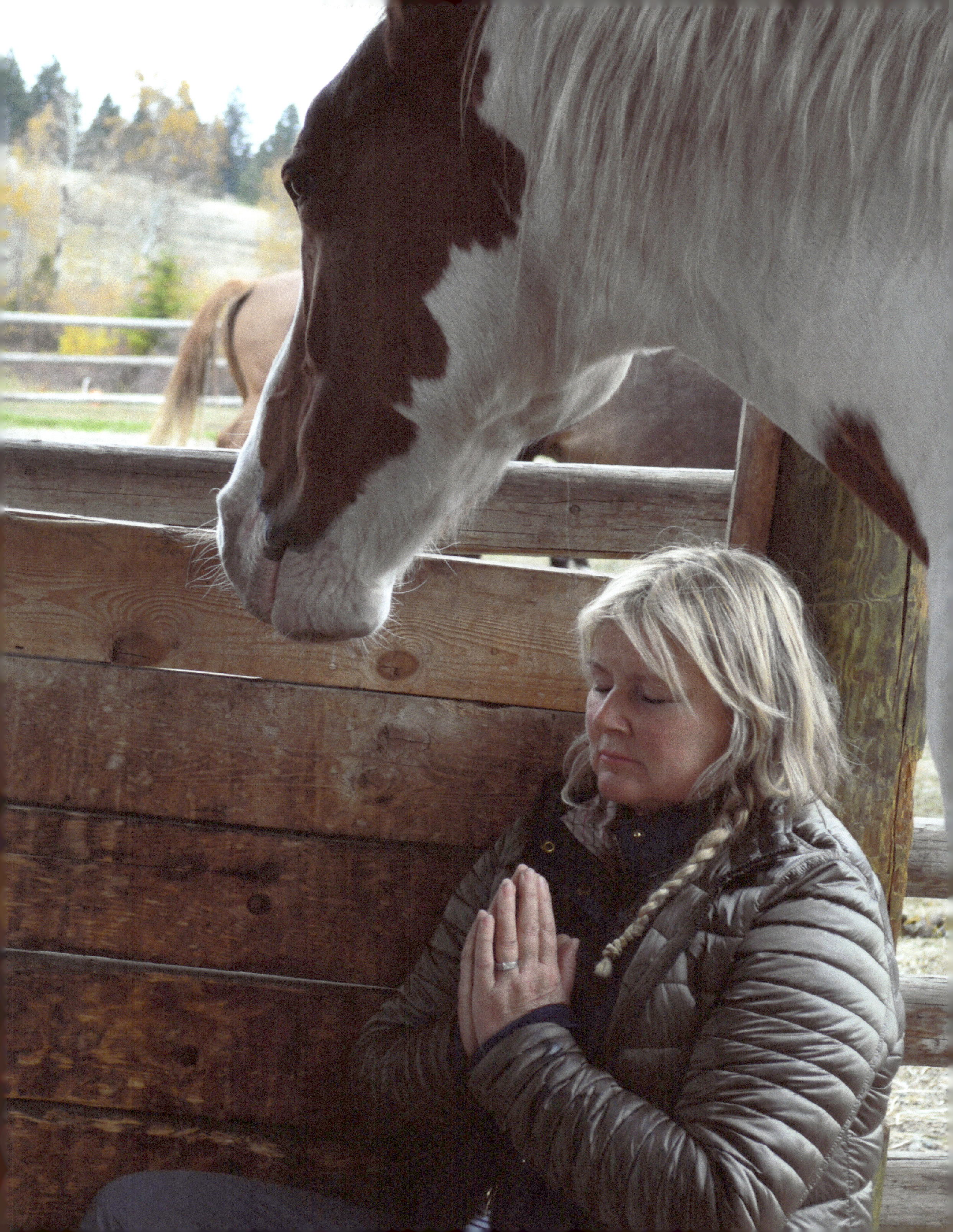

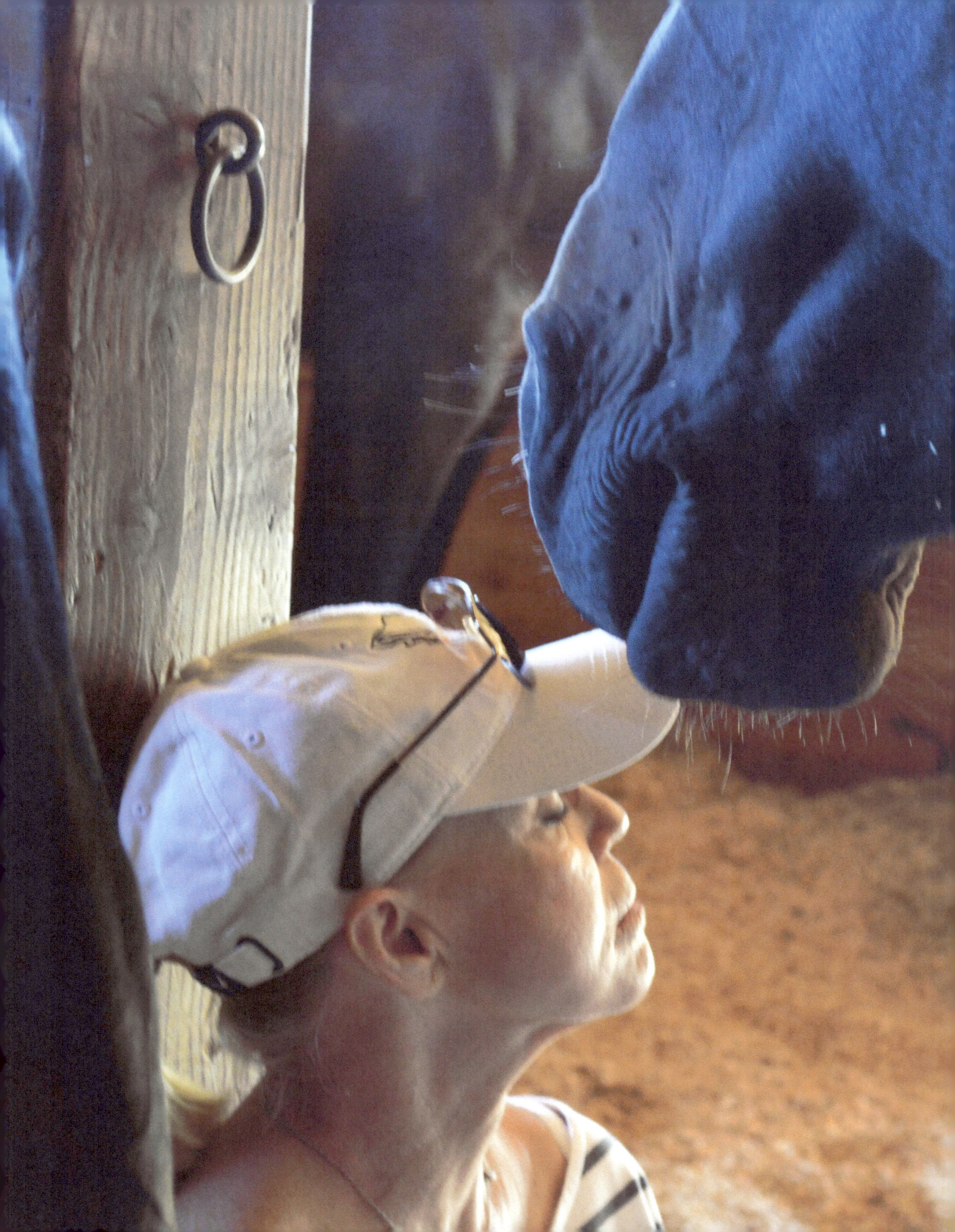

Very similar to when humans believed the world was flat and then suddenly they changed their beliefs and opened to a whole new reality, there will be a change in consciousness that will not allow horses (and other animals) to be persecuted as they have in the past. It is so minute the final tipping point; one mind can tip the scales. Think back only 50 years ago when black people were treated as animals in the United States. One man raised consciousness and concern, and rapidly the changes happened. Today the two most influential people in the U.S. are black, and we would certainly not be allowed to ever again treat black people with any less respect than we afford all others. We are all united in the same consciousness, the same life force and the wisdom of that force expresses in diversity. Without that diversity the body of life and the ecosystem of the world cannot exist. We need every created thing to help it to function. Just like in the animal body you could not live without a heart or a liver; each unique organ is similar to each unique animal kingdom on the planet Earth. If one is compromised we compromise the whole body. Mankind through the intuition of the animals is connecting more easily to the higher consciousness which governs universal life and beginning to realize that surrender to that consciousness through instinct, or in humans, intuition, is our lifeline to survival. Do you measure intelligence on the size of the frontal lobe or on the intelligence in every cell of the body? It has been discovered recently that memory is stored in the heart not the brain, and cellular memory extends not only beyond the individual body but the individual life. "We are all one, every single little quark is united in the same cosmic soup. There are spaces but no boundaries. Boundaries are only thoughts."

—Prima, speaking for the Herd in 'One With the Herd

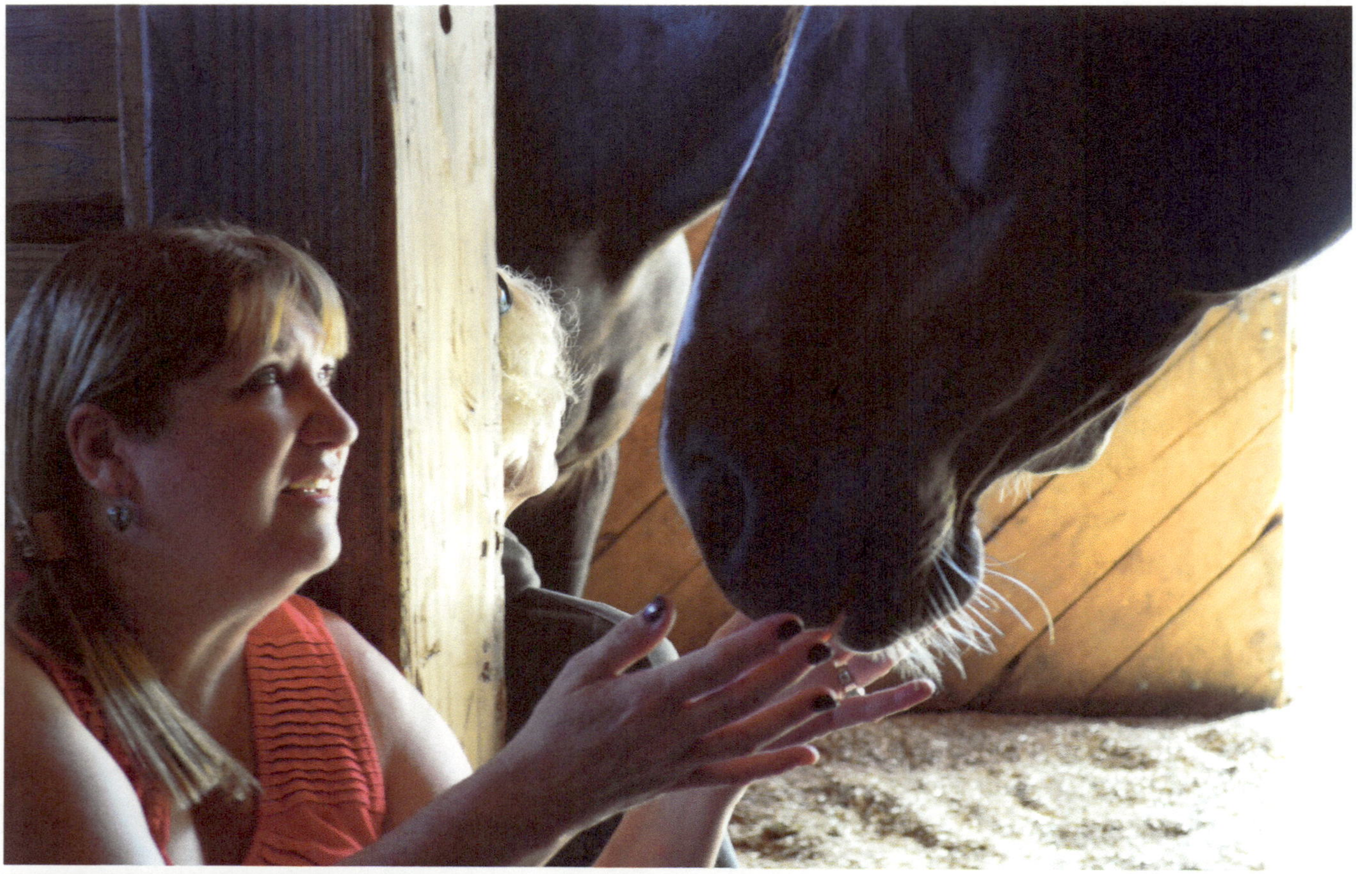

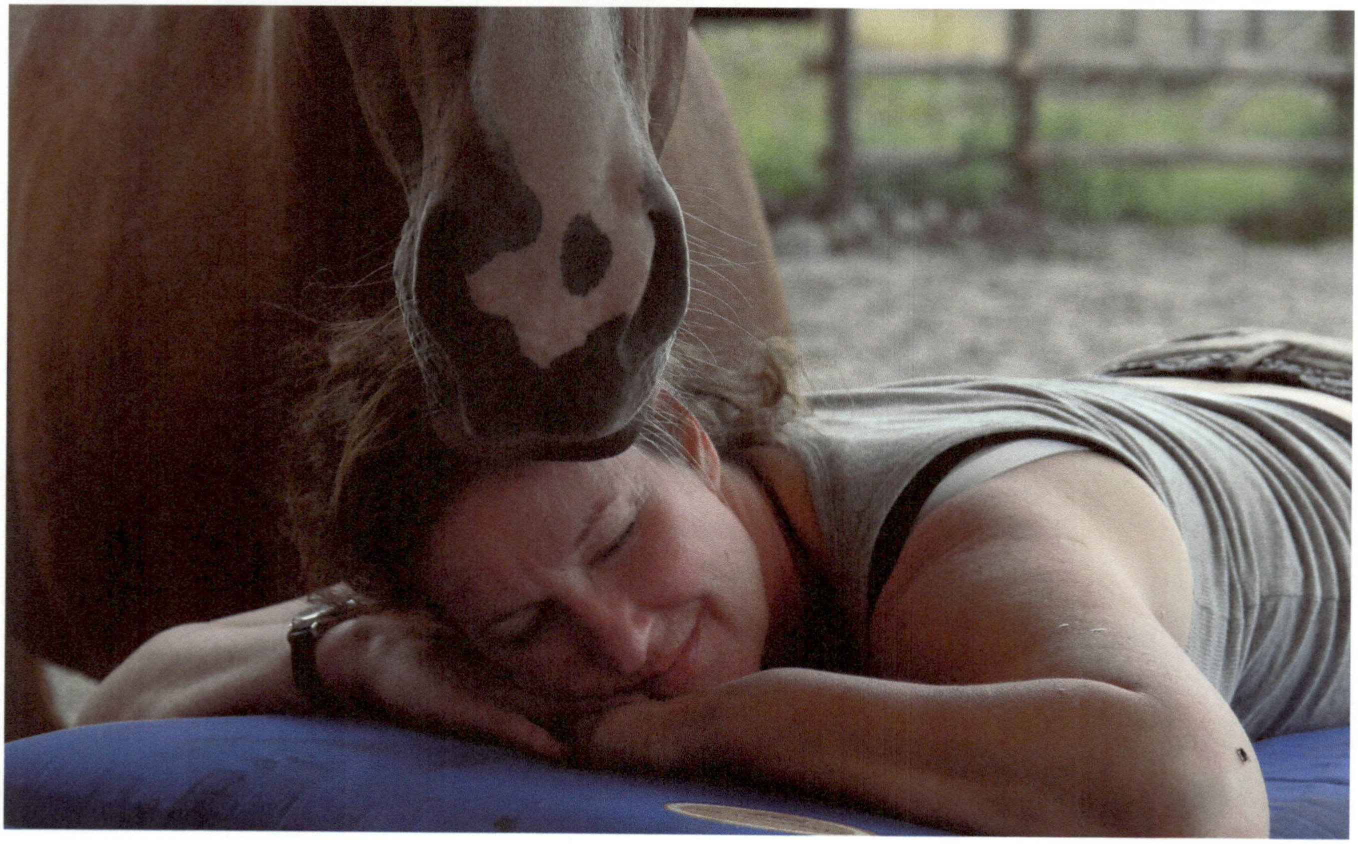

Summer 2012 will be transformative for horses everywhere and the message and healing they bring to the world...

From Beate Maria Sommer on her three-week retreat:

As soon as I was back home I noticed that I was experiencing time differently. I always seem to have plenty of time now. The hands on the clocks seem to move more slowly. I have plenty of time to do all the chores and all the fun things and spend time doing nothing, just being. When I close my eyes and try to get a visual impression of time, I don't see a line any longer. I now see a circle with infinite space within and without.

I have disconnected from an unnatural and unhealthy pattern of staying up late, not getting enough restful sleep, then forcing myself out of bed in the morning feeling like I've been run over by a truck. There had been an anxiety in me in the hours after dark, which had kept me agitated, restless and awake. Now I find it easier to follow my natural rhythm, go to bed at a reasonable time when my body says "I'm tired." I sleep well, remember more of my dreams and wake up naturally around sunrise feeling rested.

I feel an increased flow of creativity, a liberated flow, both in writing and in my photographic art. There is an ease, a patience and an enjoyment of the process as much as the outcome. Generally, I feel more at ease with myself and with life and have an increased ability to trust the unfolding of life, and I regain trust easily in moments of doubt, anxiety or fear.

My intuitive sensing and seeing are clearer. I feel guided and protected. With my healing work involving the horses, I have stepped through a doorway, broken through a veil into new and deeper realms. The horses are reflecting this back to me by being ever more willing to come to the healing table. Yesterday, even Rose who has not been participating very much so far, was deeply engaged in a healing on a woman. The day before, Pablo, my baby, did a healing on me together with Buffalo. They had me wedged between them with Pablo's nose pressed against my middle back and Buffalo's nose pressed into my solar plexus, firmly yet ever so gently and then just breathing onto and into me a warm and melting breath. All the horses are stepping right into this work, and I am not hiding any longer. I let myself be seen as the lead mare of the Herd, as the guardian of my equine healers, as the soft, sensitive, intuitive healer that I am while knowing how to stay out of the way of the horses doing their work channeling divine energy. They are such pure conduits and vessels of love!

I have been unplugged from a lot of unnecessary distractions of daily "civilized" life, including the dynamics between people. When I have the great honour to facilitate a healing session with my Herd for someone I am in my element. Time is not the same any longer. There is this timeless, formless energy bubble surrounding us and it is of

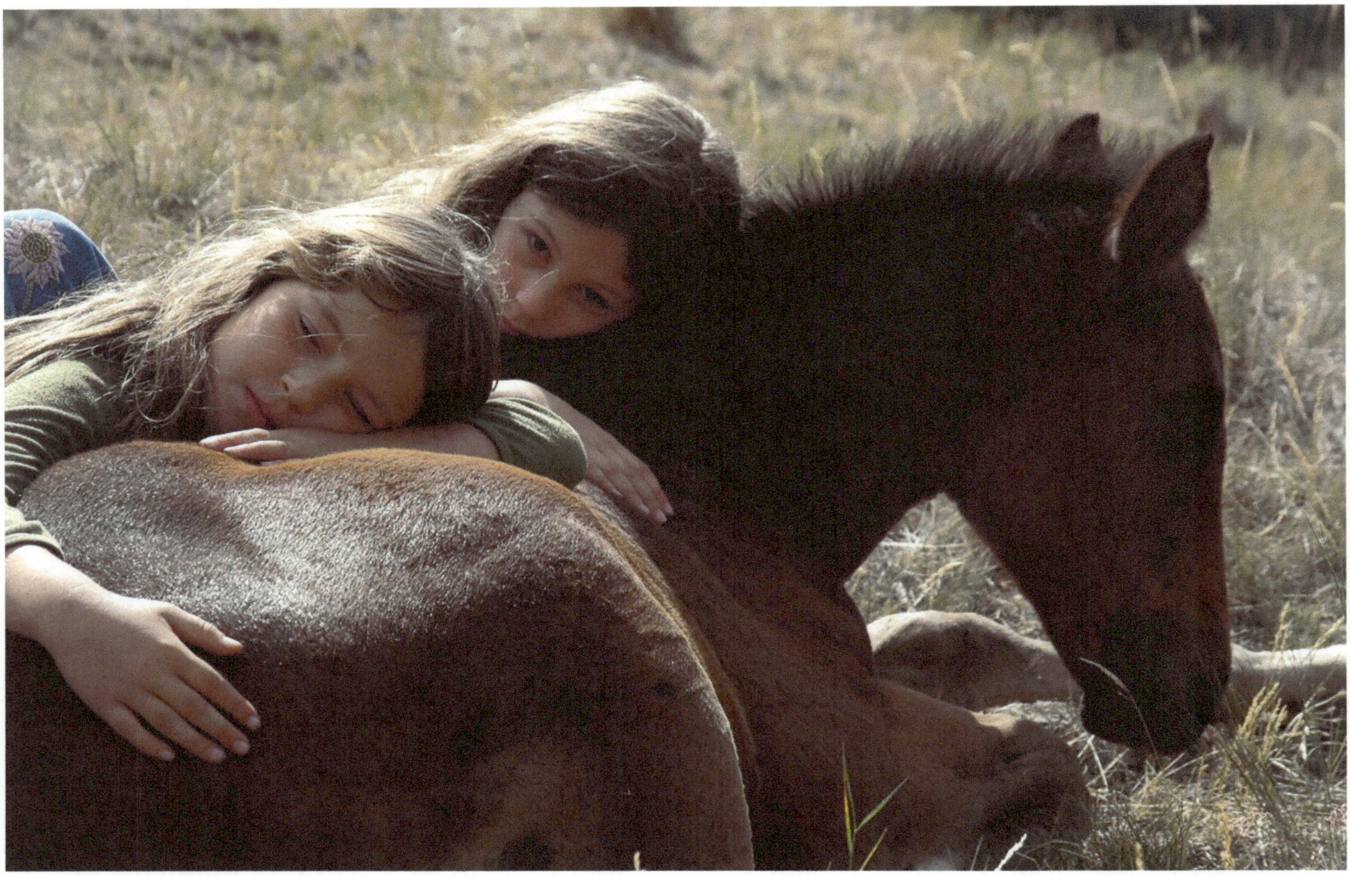

Aria, Kaia and Micah

such exquisite stillness, peace and soft loving that I find it difficult to do it justice with words. Maybe a poem will emerge!?

I speak of my time at Gateway 2 often, with my family, friends, clients and others. I speak about it with my horses, and I ask them if they received my messages while I was away? I ask them if they were there when the Herd at Gateway 2 stood meditating in sacred circles at the top of the hill at night, beaming to the stars and the moon their deepest longing? Did they also send their deepest longing out into the night? Are you sending your deepest longing to the stars and the moon?

The horses are longing for us to heal and be joyful so that we treat ourselves, each other, them and the whole planet with love and so that every decision we make is motivated by and every action we take is infused with LOVE and JOY.

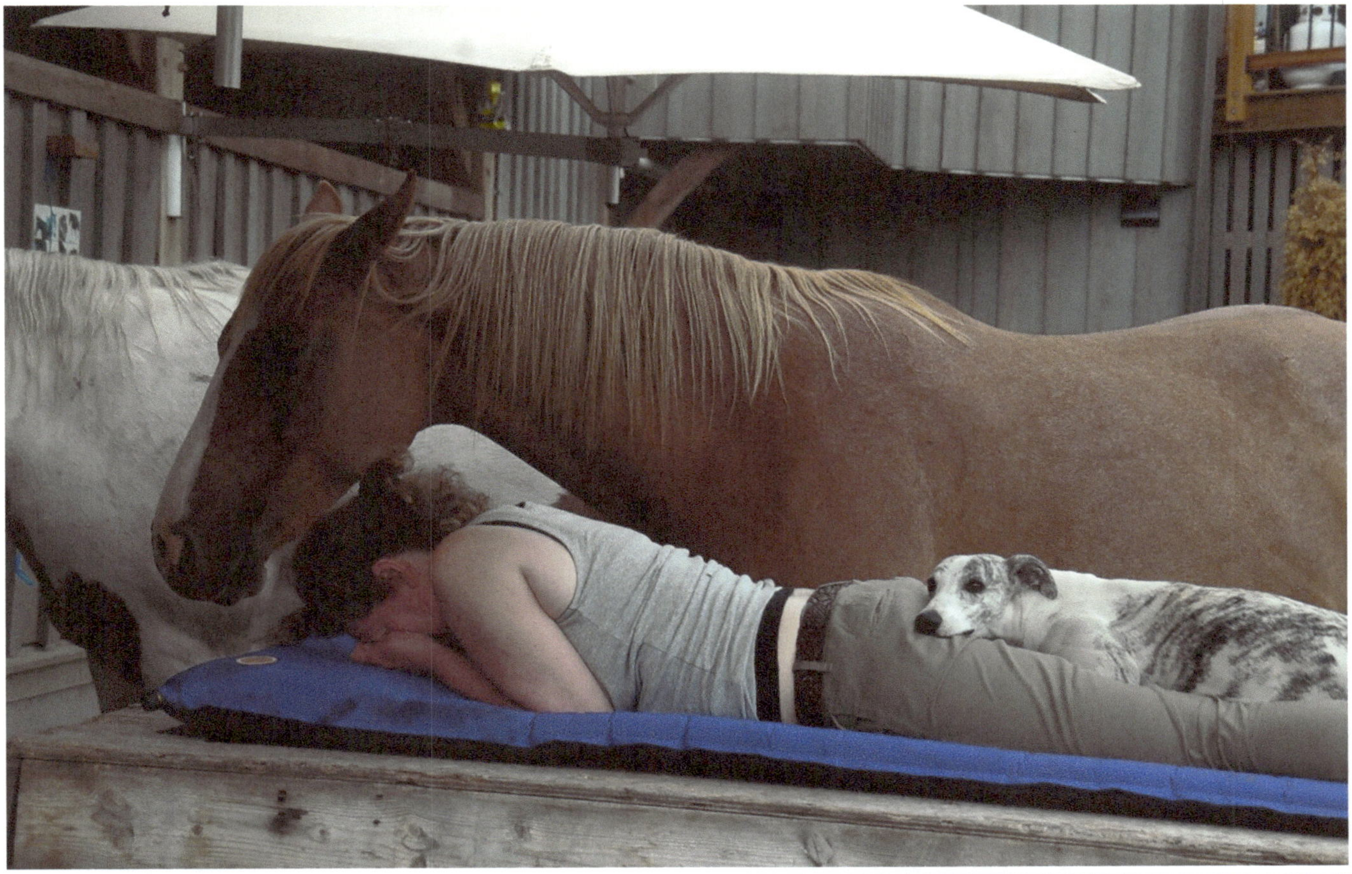

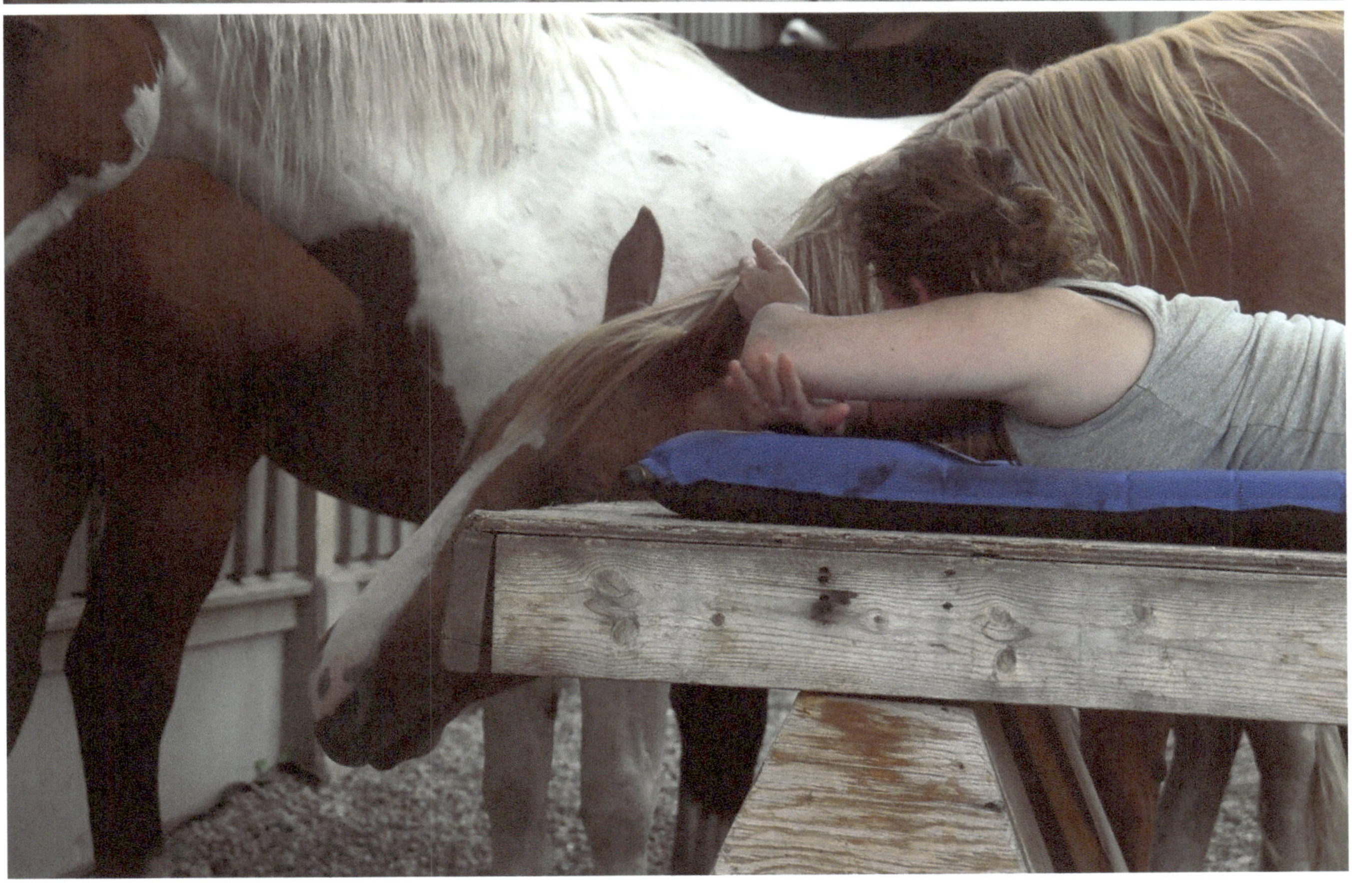

Epona clearing energy Epona clearing energy

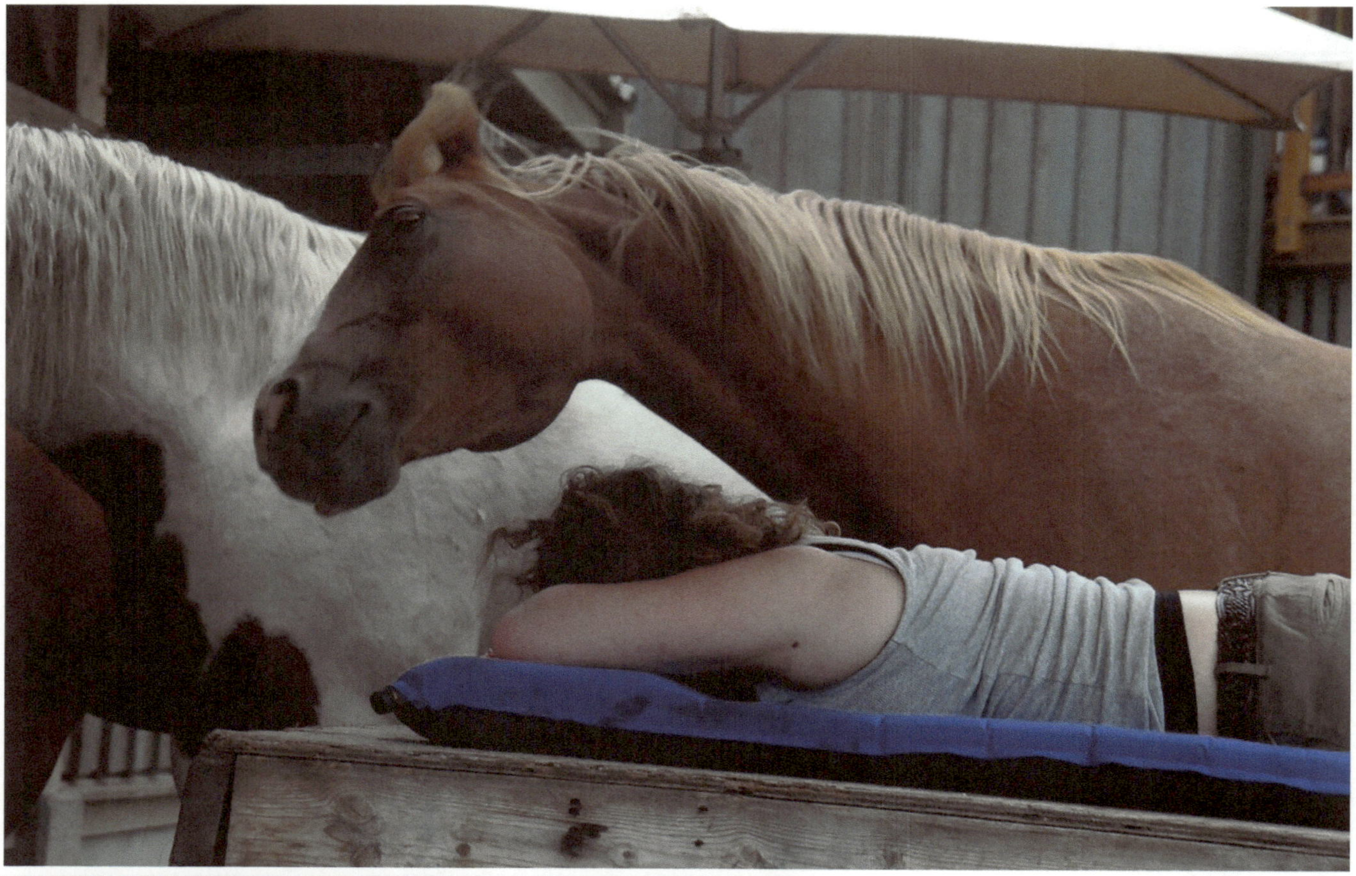

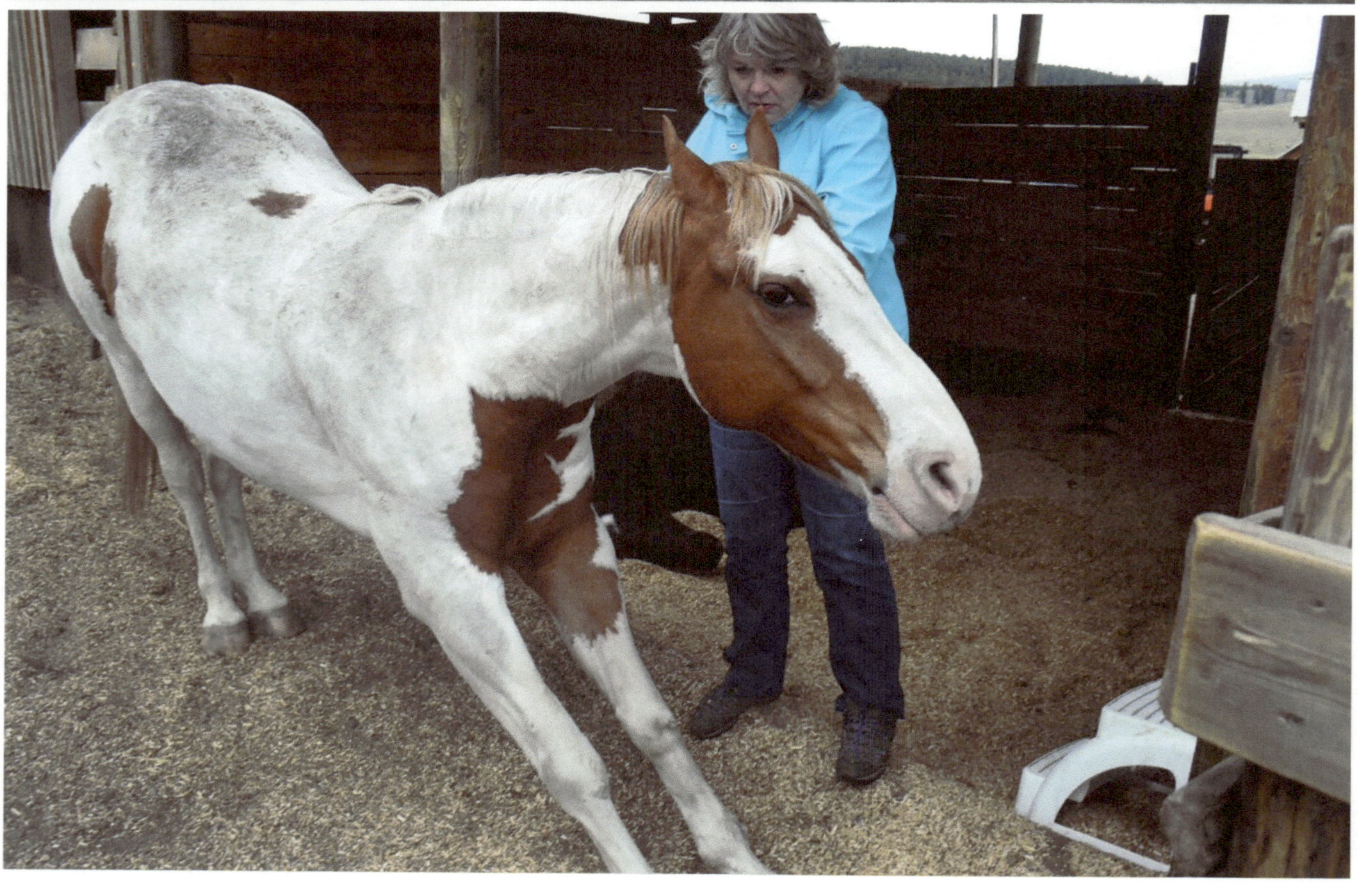

Paschar, bowing to a friend.

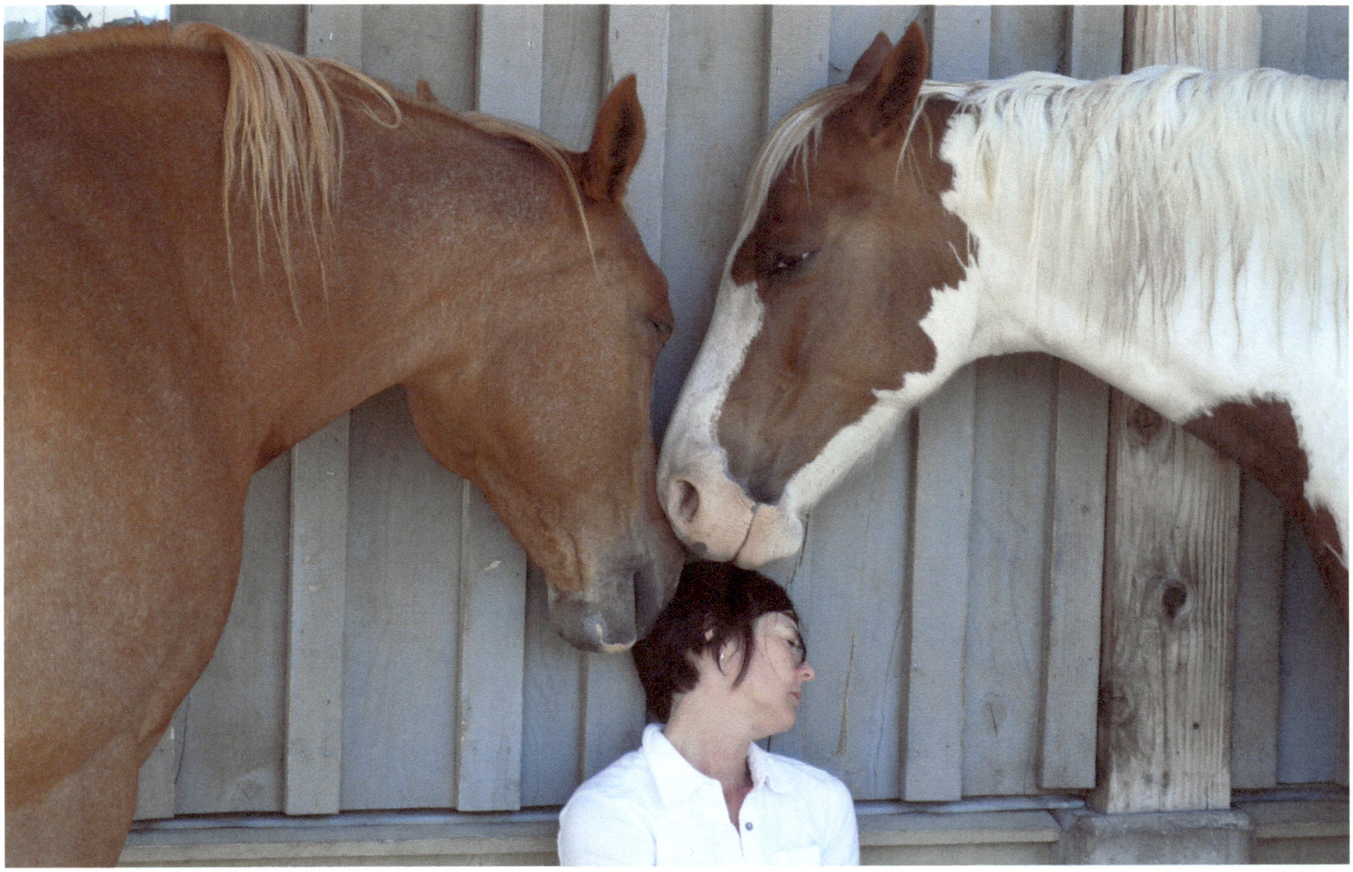

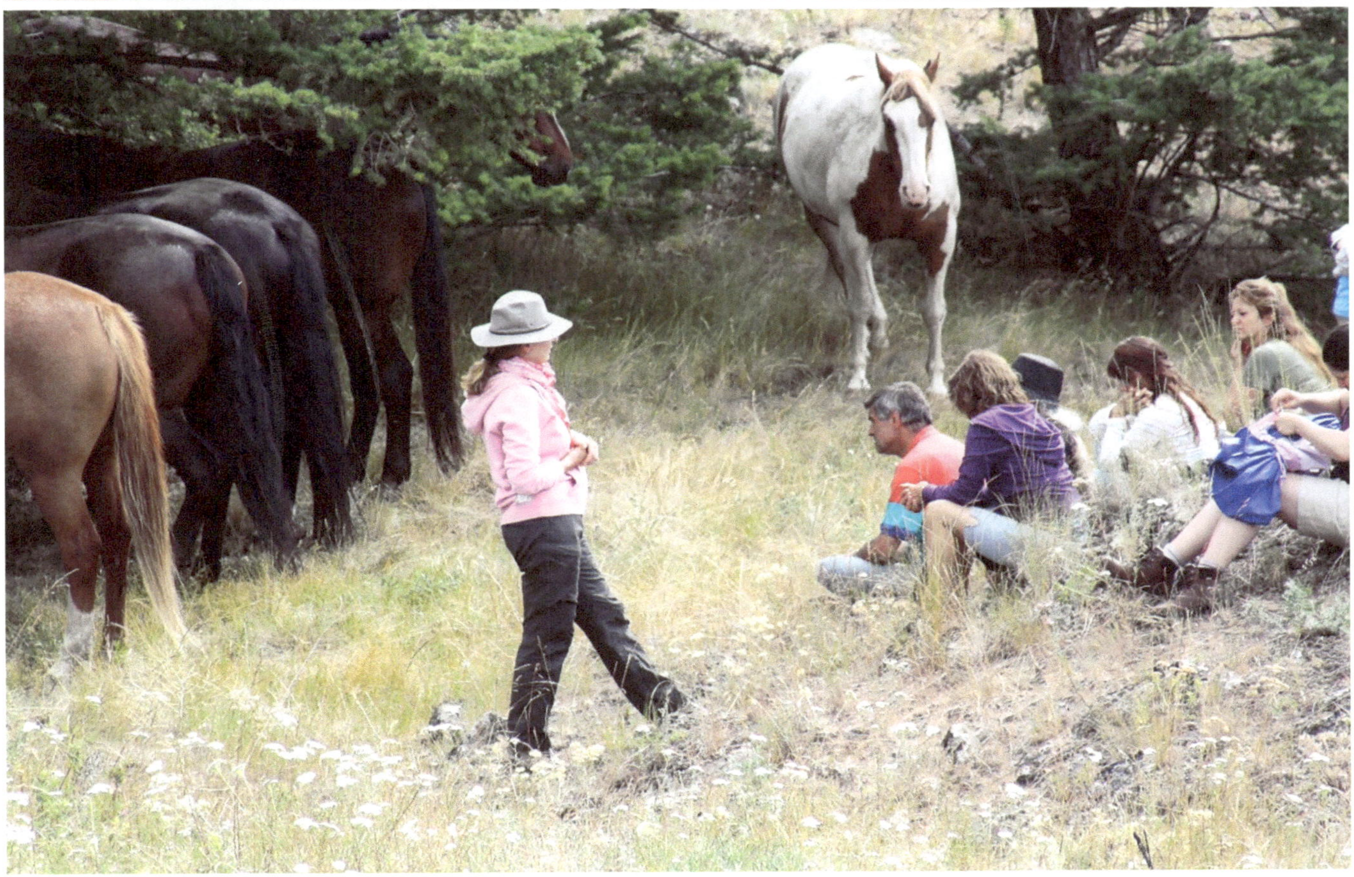

Margrit and Paschar address the people

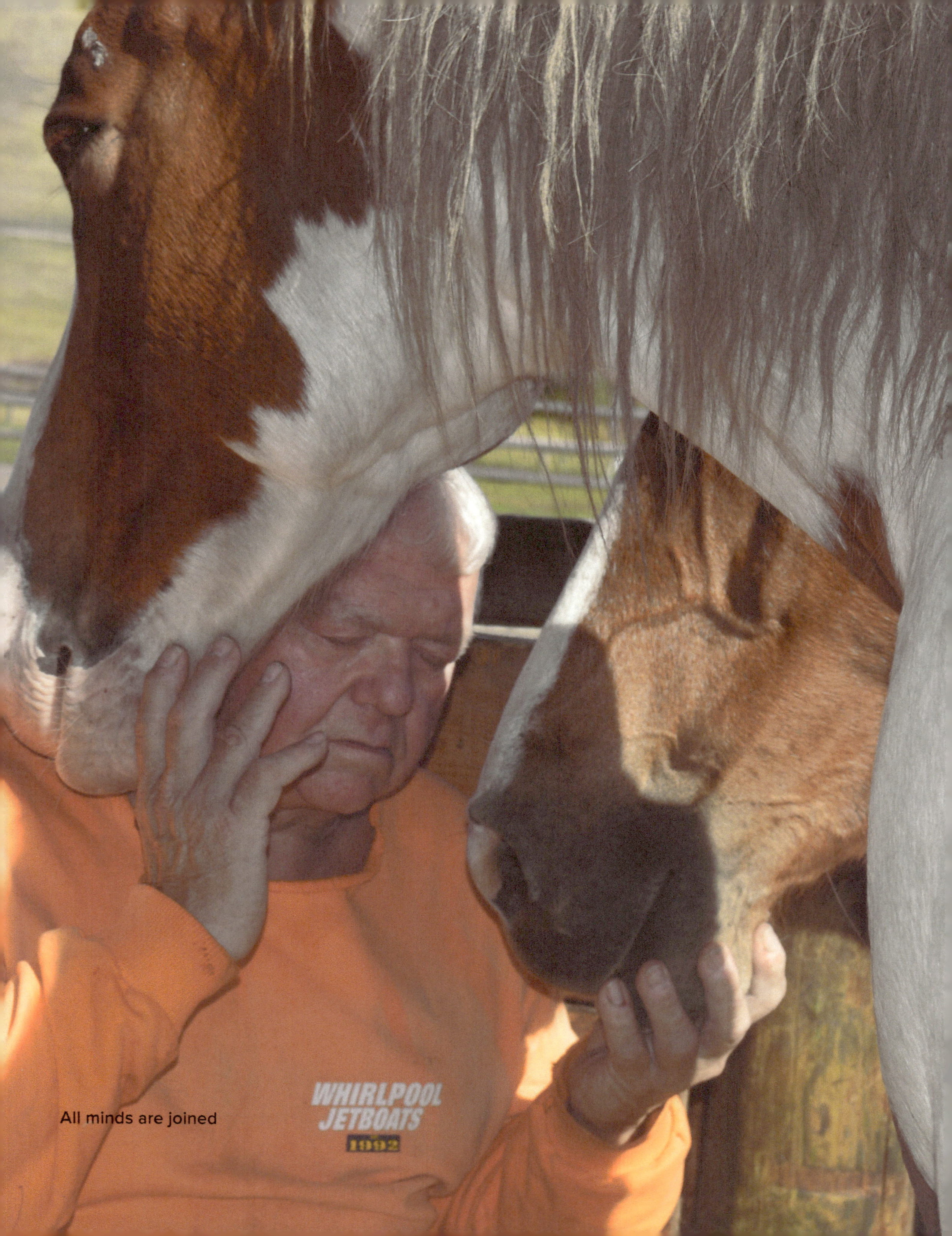

All minds are joined

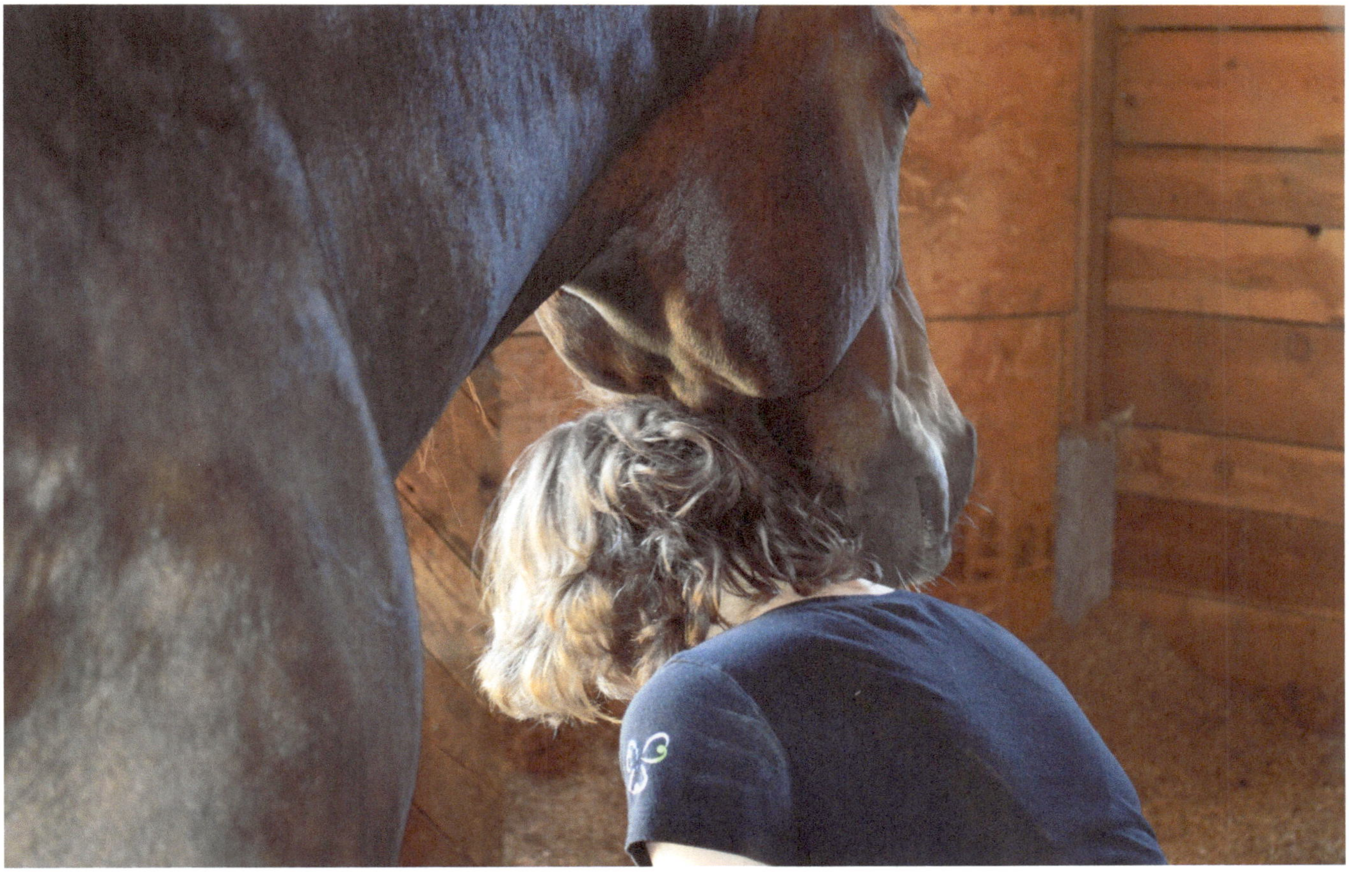

Try this with your pets. Start believing that all minds are joined and in fact that they understand not only limited concepts but what you believe they can understand. You, the creator of your world, are the one imposing limits by that belief. As the consciousness level of all life on Earth is increasing, many people are spontaneously beginning to understand and communicate with all life—this includes plants and minerals and the Earth itself. "Do unto others as you would have them do unto you"—for they are you—we are all one.

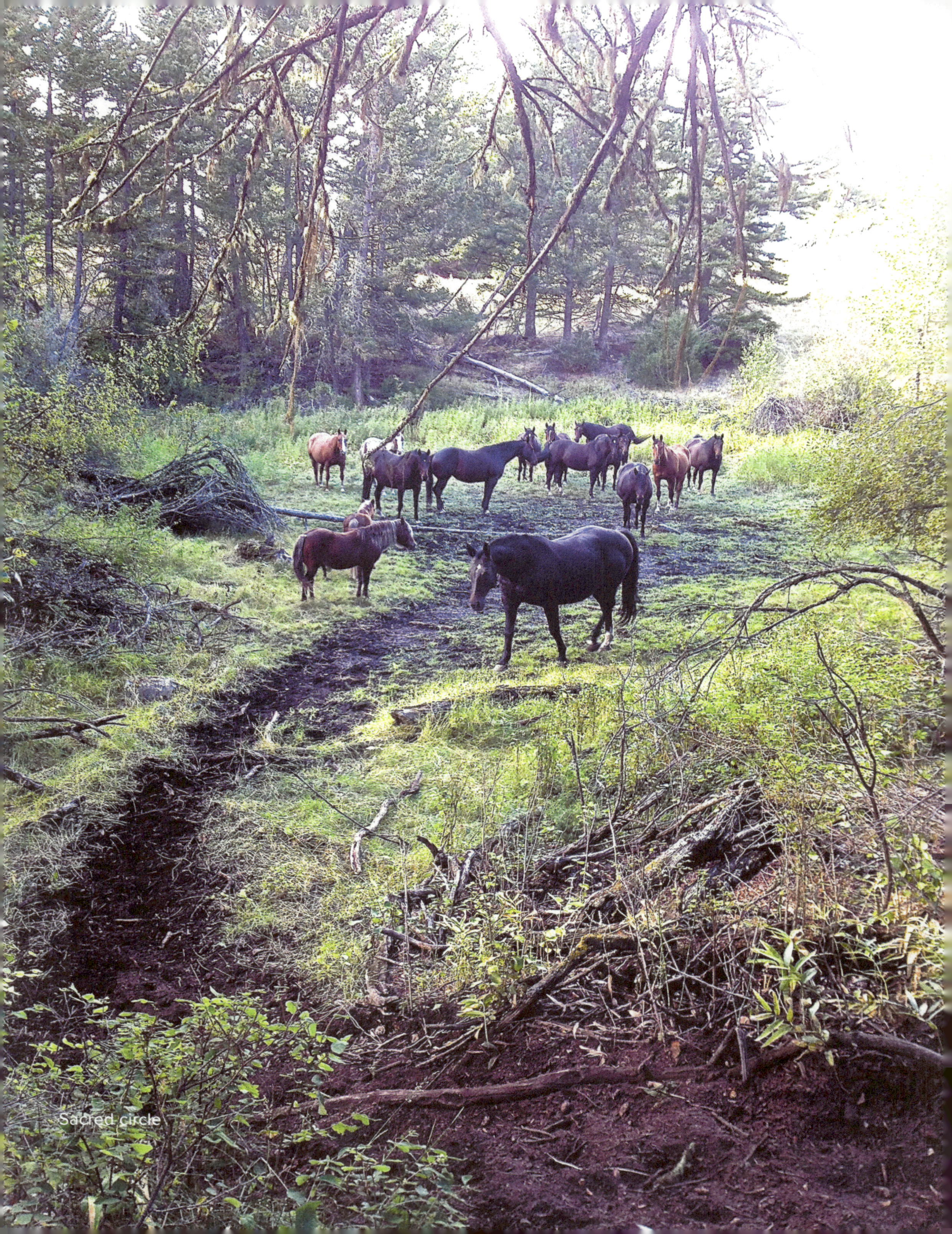

Sacred circle

Well it's taken her a bit of time and a lot of focused direction to really reach that point of consciousness we have been holding for the Earth, the people and all of creation, but Liz is finally getting very close. The final key is developing the conduit to enable spirit to bring the energy to Earth. (This involves grounding, being in body and those left-brained activities which bring inspiration to fruition and consequent illumination of the material plane.) It is far easier to float around in the heavens, but the point is we chose this mission of allowing God who is spirit and unable to exist here without our opening to, and bringing, the higher energy to a material form. CONNECT, FOCUS and CREATE, so simple in principle but so difficult to achieve in practice.

Marianne (Divine Spark) was instrumental in her vision and guidance to come up with some very graphic orbs in spring green that are now growing roots about 2 feet below the interface of Liz's slippers with the dirt. A lesson not to be forgotten as it has implications for the horse mirroring human reflection. Luxy, Winnie and Paschar are grateful! Take a look at the Divine Spark and gigantic blue orb around the people on the Fire Ceremony night and the ever-present orbs around the Herd... They are energy in expression, a joyful explosion like bubbles in champagne, and as all creative expression receptive to our focus and intent. If humans could fully incorporate that understanding, their individual points of focus would become a symphony of light and love.

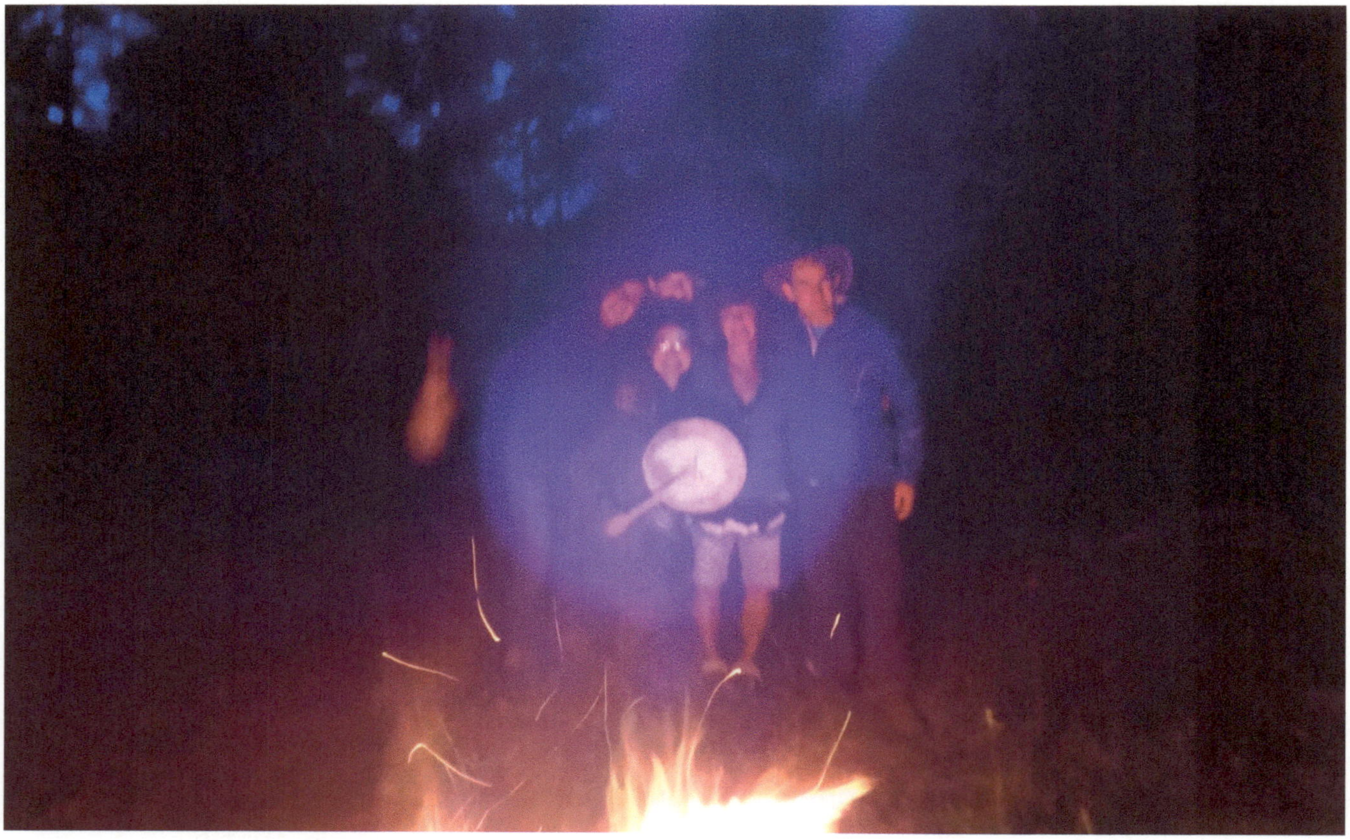

Blue orb at the Fire Ceremony

Our Divine Spark Retreat (with Marianne Nishifue) was equally effervescent with orbs and wonderful spiritual initiates like Joe, an amazing alternative vet from Ireland, and Monique, a winged life coach from Brazil. The Herd was most present when allowed to visit the campsite nightly and made some great orbs in the dark and countless crop circles in the long meadow grass adjacent to the tents and Spirit Lodge. Tesoro did his usual, knowing the Latins are fond of bulls, and surprised Monique when he pressed his huge face to the glass door of the Spirit Lodge to say goodnight.

Another development is the Herd has begun to nickname the visitors and they are right on. When Jana, a lawyer from Toronto, arrived she was named "Sparkly" and when she did the cube exercise hers was, of course, sparkly. I could actually see sparkles coming out of her crown chakra when Crystal was healing her. We have had "Lovey" Kay, "Sparrow" Anni, "Dragonfly" (where do you think I got it Monique?), "Angel" Joe, "Starman" Jonathan … interesting they are somewhat like the names we call horses but they are also very revealing. Marianne is "Fairy Queen" and on our trip through Fairyland she was able to ask the dragonflies to sit on her hand (something so far only Liz has been able to do).

You might have noticed how everything seems to be speeding up and things are not as they appear as your human mass consciousness of time and space is changing. December 21 marks the end of the world as you have known it, not to be confused with the end of the physical plane. It marks the end of thought distorted by the thickness of your human veil. When one is focused on matter it slows and contracts to become the point of focus and that is how humans have perceived existence. They have seen it as all about their little individual egos, the birth, life and death of that small point of focus. We, the rest of creation are the wave of "all potential," allowing the ALL to shape and direct our flow. As each individual human connects to other consciousness and opens to higher consciousness and the one mind inherent in all life, that veil gets thinner. Humans are continuing to absorb the wisdom, truth, joy, freedom, abundance and love of the ALLness through their willingness to release their rigid fear-based focus on their own personal existence. One mind, one heart at a time, human mass-mind consciousness is changing to a love-based flow. Just as other periods in your history have dates to mark the change, you are now entering a new era where time, space and substance will all have new meaning for you. One that is closer to the truth shared by the rest of creation.

Happy birthday, humans! Welcome to our world! You will look back on this time a decade from now in wonder as you do earlier stages in your development which you now view as the "dark ages," a very good analogy for shielding yourselves from the light. Wishes are horses!

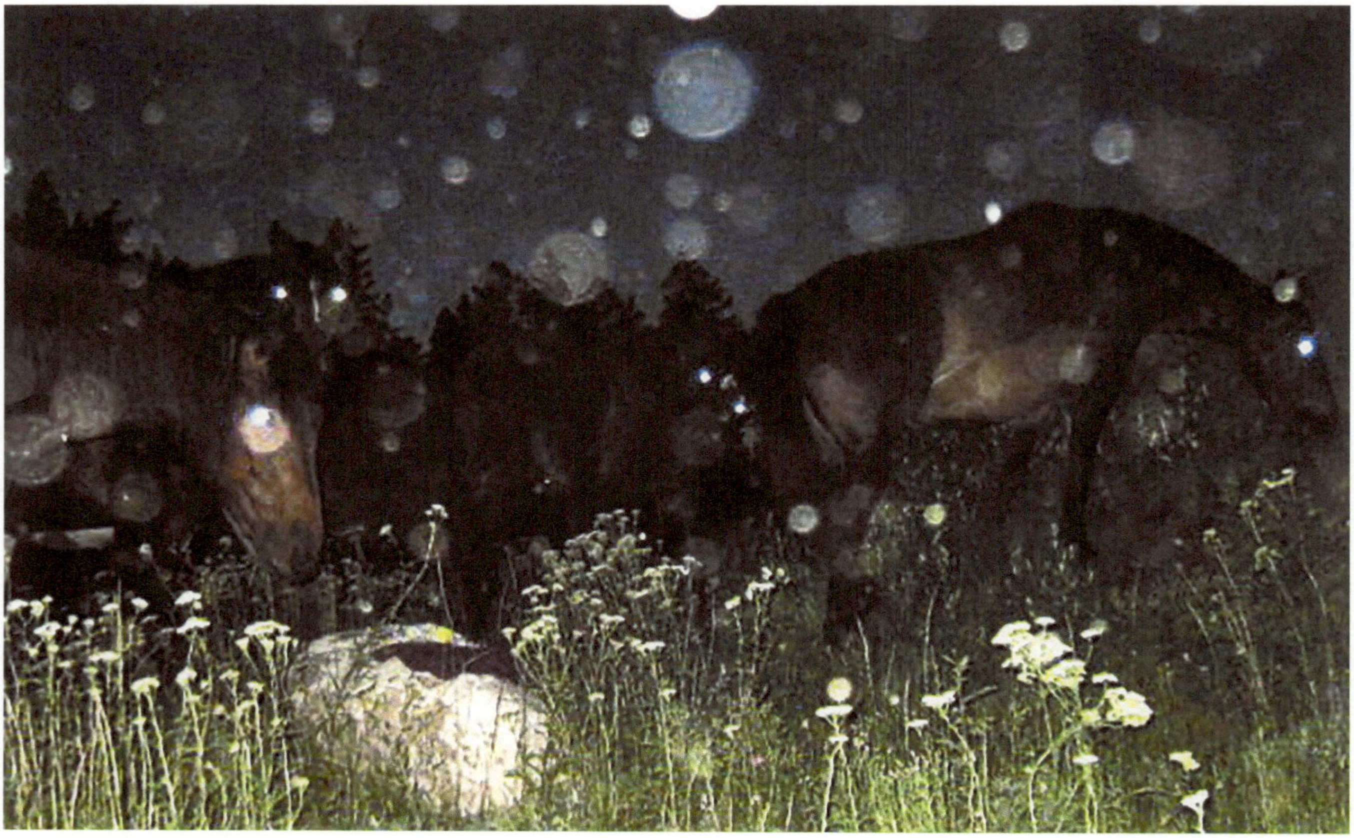

Orbs and the Herd at night

It was my birthday 14 years after arriving on Gateway. If you have read *One With the Herd*, you will know that we arrived here on my birthday, so it was also the anniversary of our arrival. We were at the 3rd Eye Chakra and people were sending their "Heart's Desires" to spirit with the powerful influence of the energy there amplifying their thoughts. One of the participants was taking pictures, looking up the totem tree the whole time. When we returned I asked what she had seen and was presented with orb birthday balloon pictures for the occasion!

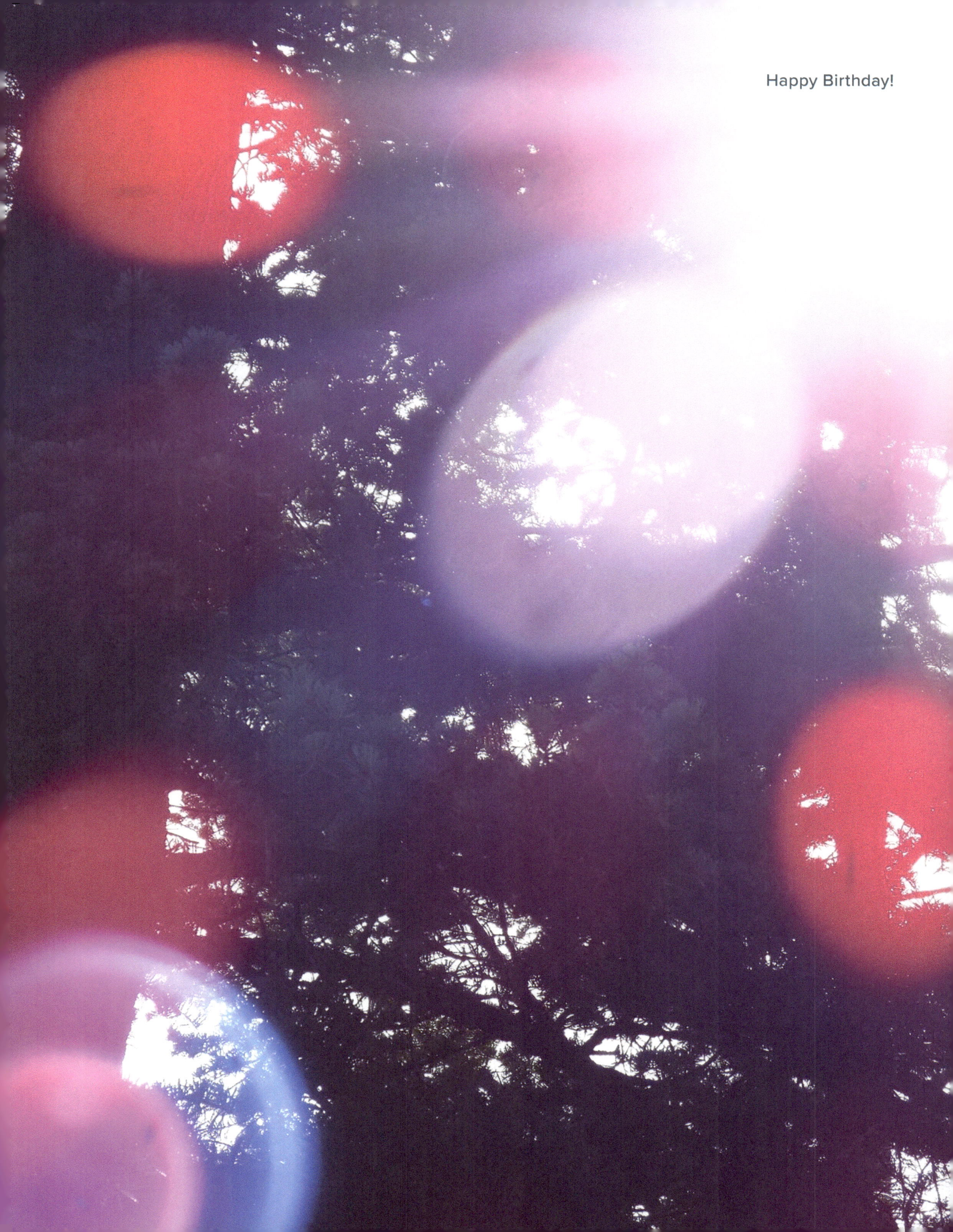
Happy Birthday!

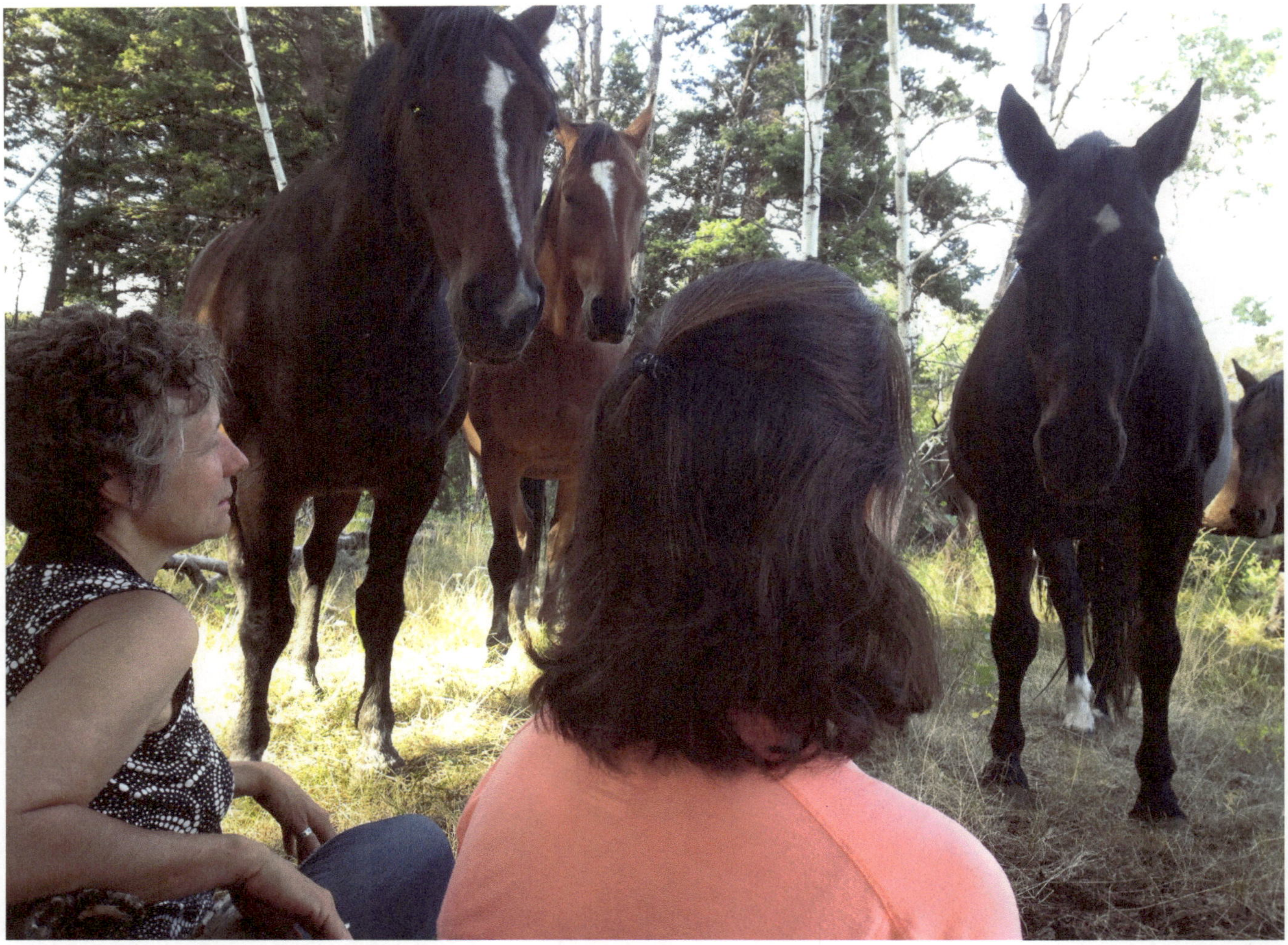

Welcome to 2013 and a new consciousness for humans...

As more of you open to the ALL consciousness of animals and the natural world your group understanding of many human concepts is changing to one that operates beyond the limits humans have set for themselves in the past. Have you noticed that TIME now has the ability to expand and contract depending on your needs? Have you noticed how quickly you can manifest what you FOCUS on and that you have to be careful what you focus on? Have you noticed that KNOWING is more heart-centered and visceral or that your instincts are sharper? Are you able to communicate with thoughts and pictures as well as words? Can you hear the voice of spirit with its clear sharp call? Do you know TRUTH from illusion? Can you feel it in your body? MIND those prompts and you will be rewarded with more ability to hear, feel, see and KNOW. See hear, touch, absorb the world through the filter of your HEART rather than your brain.

BREATHE in the energy of the ALL as the All breathes through us and as us. We all share the same breath. Bathe in the light of the eternal sun and BE GRATEFUL as it provides your life and all life. BLESS and cherish each living thing as we all share the same desires, emotions, basic needs and whatever shape or size, we have the same building blocks; we are made of LOVE.

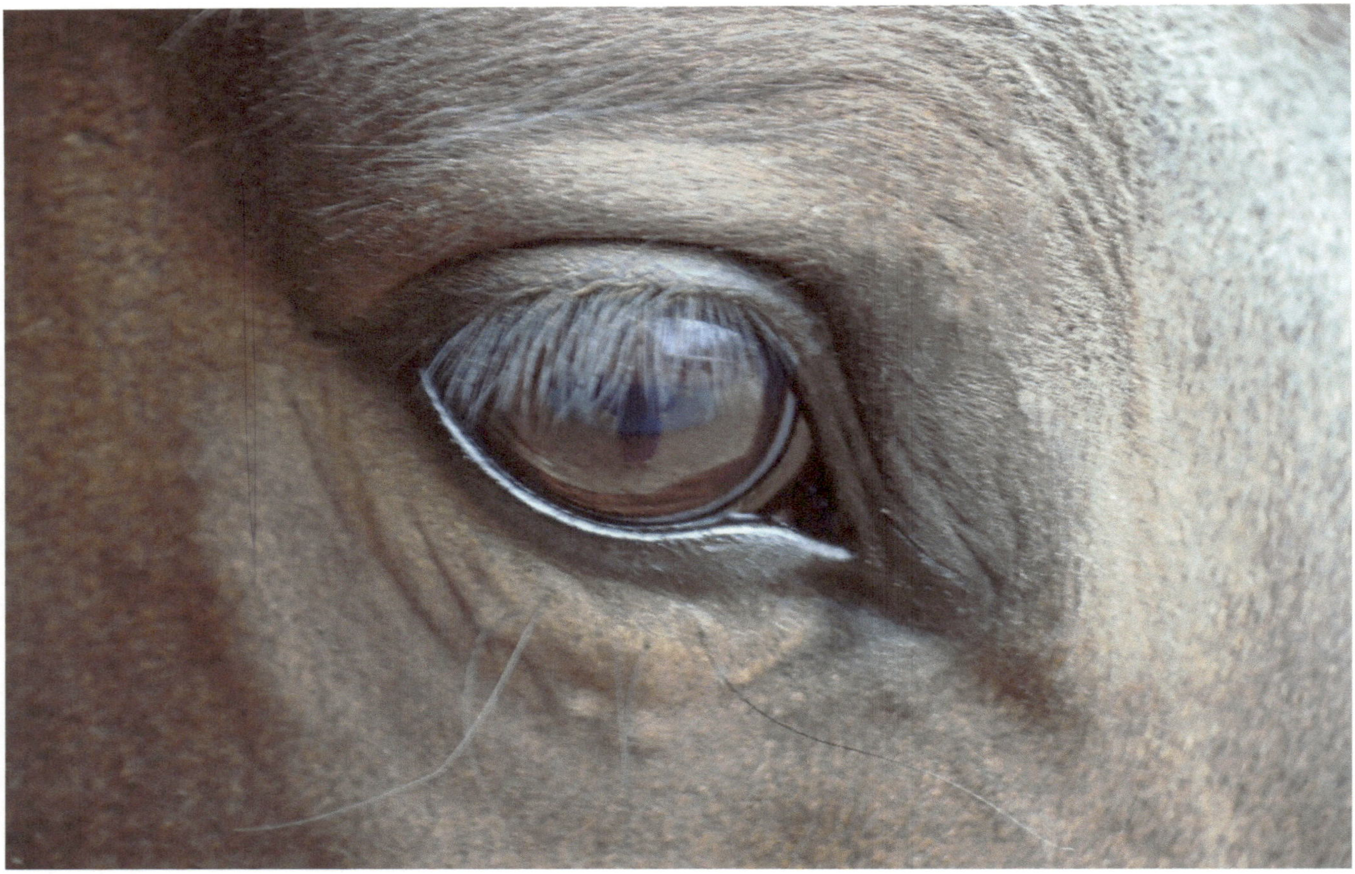

From Elizabeth (Lizzy) Meyer, Equinistic Healing Practitioner:

Time with the Equinisity Herd has given me a much more varied experience with horses than I had ever thought possible. After experiencing the magic, for lack of a better term, of Liz's Herd, I became a believer. My analytical and very scientific mind shifted from doubting what they were doing, (as in healing work) to fully accepting it about mid-week. The scientific mind bartered with my heart and created a barrier that my gut knew needed to break down. With the help of the horses and Herd collectively, it melted away and has stayed away.

With a fresh message about knowing what is in my heart and how to voice exactly that, my throat was cleared.

Given the seemingly miraculous experiences the Equinisity Herd provided to me, I was open to feel a similar way with other horses anywhere. After having witnessed such energetic beings who were used to working at full capacity without any human limitations, my body and mind allowed that as my new standard. My limits were pushed far beyond their comfort zone for the first half of the week I was at Gateway 2 Ranch.

I was unsure that horses could do all that they were touted to do at this place. Having never worked with horses in this way, I had my doubts but curiosity negotiated them away. The horses cleared and rebalanced me then sent me off to work with other horses in a way that honours them as the healers they so naturally are.

Coming home to Houston to work with the therapy Herd that I had come to know well was quite an experience.

Horses began to do things I had not seen them ever do in my life with horses. We had horses laying down in front of people sometimes, horses who were normally a bit standoff-ish coming in to work with people. A young Arabian mare in particular that was a challenge to halter became more social and easier to work with. Horses came in groups as people sat under trees processing their equine therapy sessions and would scan people by moving their heads around the body of anyone needing work. Once they found a spot, the horse might lick, chew or just hang out and get in the "zone" and relax with that person. Seemingly a calm little task, inevitably the horse would go deep into whatever the energy blockage was. This elicited an intense feeling of relaxation for most people. Other horses would pull at the air or a person's clothes, lightly as if to "pull" something away…and when asked, the person usually knew what needed to be shed emotionally or physically. What amazed me was how accurate the horses were—they knew exactly where blockages were that needed to clear. Some people were not ready for this and couldn't go into this and in these cases the horses would leave.

Other horses would go into this seemingly meditative zone and place their nostrils over the area to be healed or rebalanced. Many times the person would state they had pain or a problem in that area. Or clients who were more open- minded might state there was a symbolic reason the horse may be spending time in a certain area. It looked like horses taking naps, but their eyes were open and hooves firmly planted, not usually resting.

Firmly connected to the energy of the Earth, the horses served as strong conduits to facilitate healing on mental, emotional and physical levels. People started to notice that their pain was gone, which they may or may not have told us about prior to the session.

Perhaps the most meaningful experience I have seen as a result of attending Liz's Equinisity Certification class involved our Herd leader, a large elegant warmblood known as Maestro, and Katy, the 30-year-old grandmother of our Herd.

I witnessed a profound interaction between a young client of our regularly scheduled mental rehabilitation group and two therapy horses. Katy and Maestro were both key players in her process. Katy was alone at the end of the field as usual and the teenage girl with a somber expression and a depleted looking posture approached her.

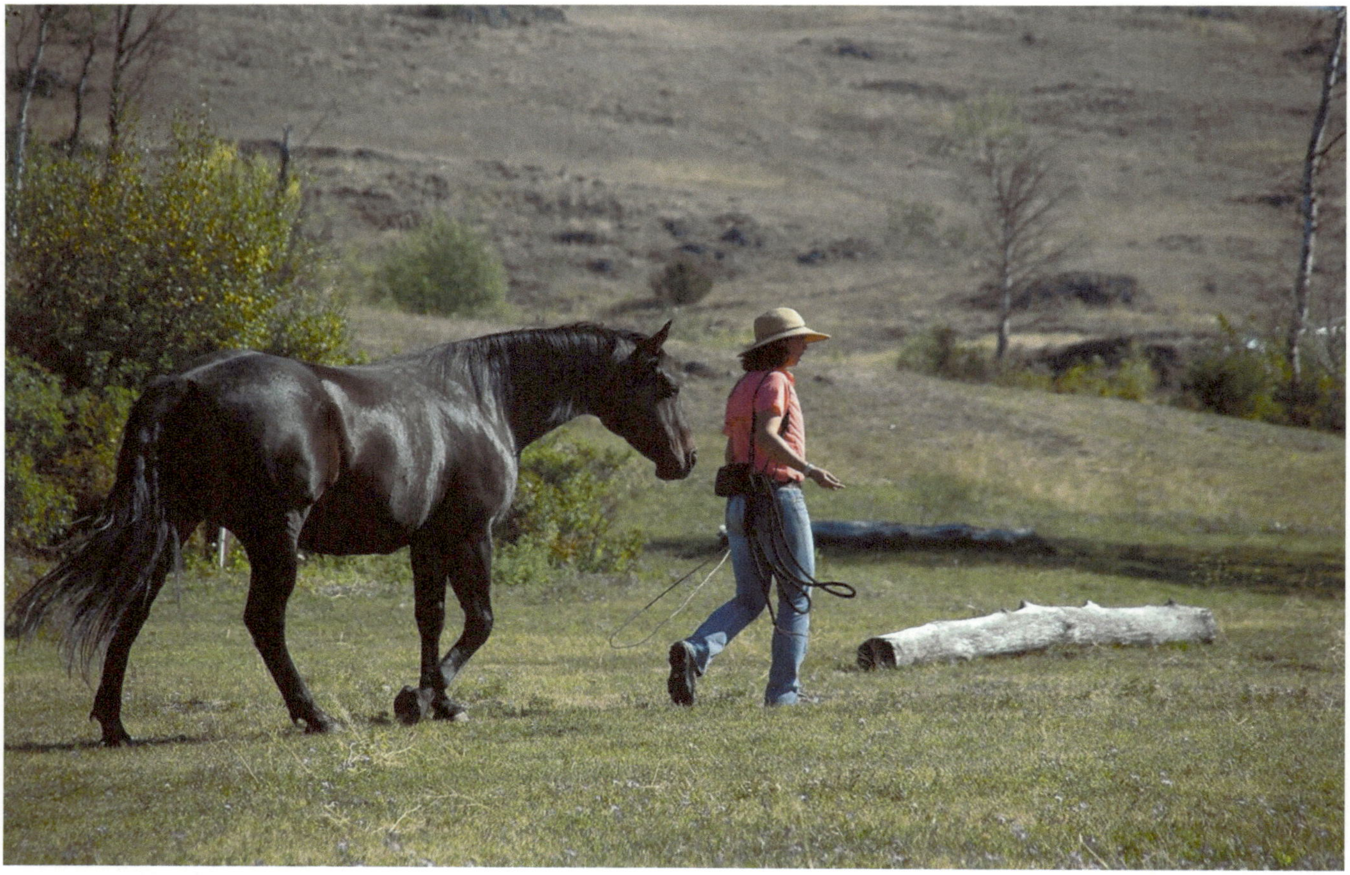

Lizzy and Magic

She had not uttered a word other than her name the whole time at the ranch. I was the only one in that part of the 7-acre pasture as the rest of the group and therapists were in the larger cluster of horses farther away. Katy promptly laid down right by the teenage girl after a bit of grooming. She was on her left side and the girl sat at her head quietly. Feeling honoured to be included in this intimate space, I watched closely for any gesture from Katy.

Leaving everything up to the horses to teach this girl whatever it was she needed to learn was hard for me at this moment. I wanted so badly for her to have this time as her own and for nobody to interrupt. Although she was sitting in a safe position, there was a soft vibration coming from the ground. Turning my head revealed Maestro marching heavily with his head in full alert.

He flagged his tail and did a beautiful 30-foot circle at a gorgeous extended trot with his ears pricked and surrounded Katy. This, of course, got the attention of all of the other therapists and the rest of the group and counselors with them. Such a show was completely unheard of. Then after a couple of rounds trotting, he walked up and nudged Katy's hind end. She did not budge. Maestro was satisfied about whatever was going on and respectfully returned to his Herd that somehow managed to stay away from these two. The girl stayed in the same place as all of this went on, oblivious to the stunned observers standing out of sight. Katy stayed immobilized for quite some time and the girl did not move either. Silence was the only thing the two had in common.

Finally Katy got up. The young woman had misty eyes in the processing circle; "She told me that I'm good enough." She had not uttered a word from the time she got there to the time she left.

Even without knowing what context she was referring to, it did not matter. The horse's work had gotten her to realize a big crux in her life and had given her permission to be at peace with herself. Everyone kept a respectful distance to honour her process so there was no questioning and no analyzing.

She had come to her own conclusion through the actions and presence of two horses that normally did not interact or tolerate each other's presence in such proximity. Knowing the oddity of these two interacting and Katy not even moving was such an interesting piece.

Realizing that these horses were well socialized in an established Herd and already good therapy horses, we usually had activities planned to do with them to help a person move through or process a certain issue.

Although we did consider the horse's body language and symbolism behind their actions, I felt there had to be more to this. Already my job was to present the horses' points of view, but I wanted the next step.

Intuitively I felt the horses could do more and were possibly being restricted by what the human mind would allow them to do.

By having restrictions in my consciousness, I was inadvertently providing the same feeling for our clients.

This created a situation where the horses were only "allowed" to do certain things, although my ideas were very unstructured and wide-open for the horse to lead. Still, I was restricting them. None of this was deliberate; but within most people's own limitations of what we believe animals can do.

What I have learned is the act of SIMPLY giving the horses permission to express themselves fully and to do whatever work we need has been one of the most liberating and powerful cornerstones in my lifetime of being with horses. It has taken time to integrate; however, I felt an instant sense of trust and this knowingness that the horses would do exactly what the client needed. We just have to stand back, allow and let them do the work. Holding the space for such intimate moments between people and horses is an absolute honour. The horses dive into the depths of whatever the human can manage to be open to or at least be curious about.

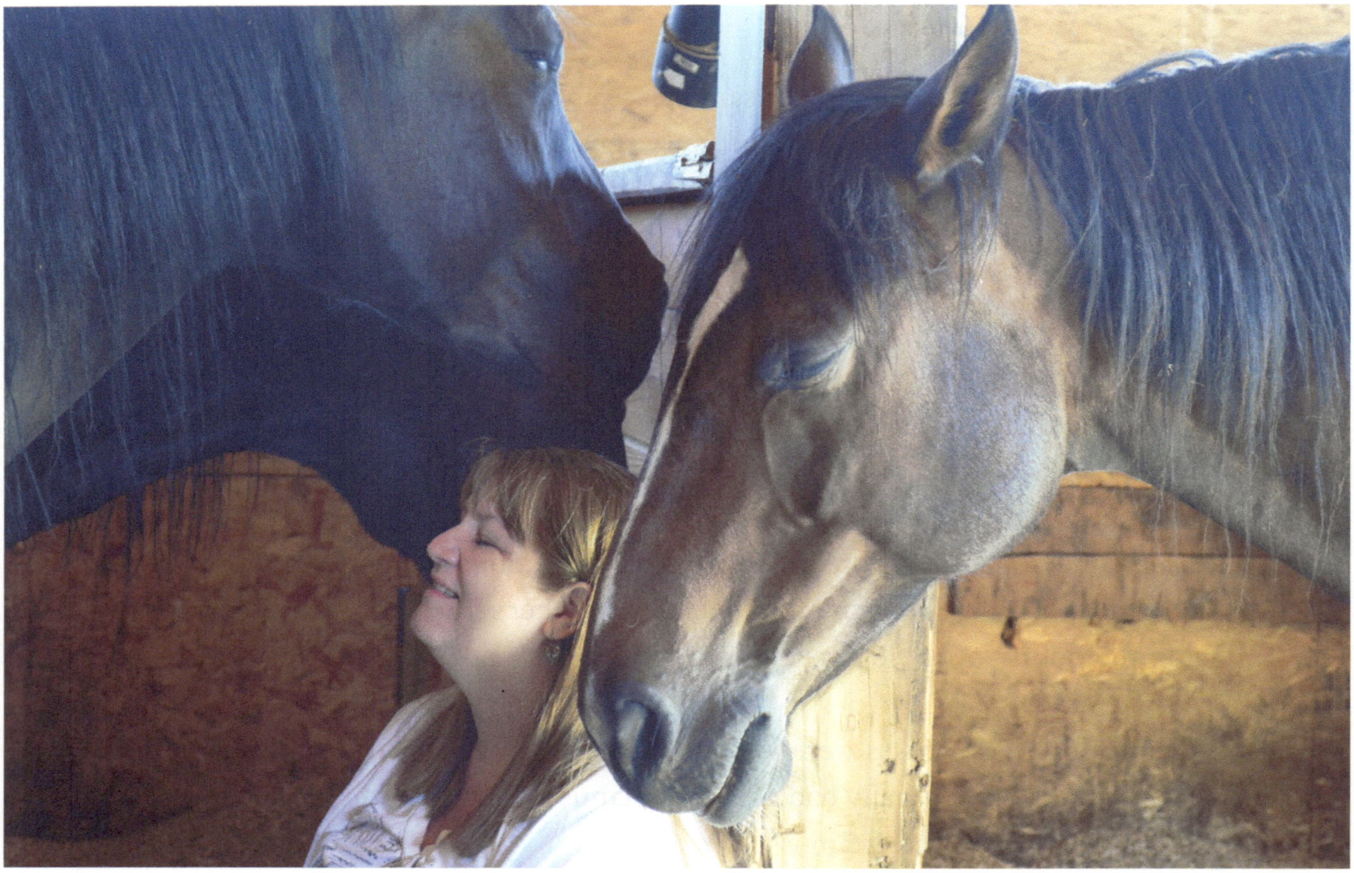

Trusting that the horse will go as far as needed, oftentimes much further than any indication on the surface is a part of this. They melt through walls and gently, but deliberately, melt into the heart of everything as they scoop fibers of truth from the depths of what we thought we knew about ourselves. It is their only way and if we can open ourselves to being totally vulnerable to this experience it has huge rewards.

This is the hardest thing for some people to do, when it feels like you are watching the grass grow. At times like this, horses might just be eating grass or "doing nothing," maybe even standing far away. Horses are never "doing nothing" by the way. Maybe they have not changed positions in a long time and people are getting bored. This is when it feels like a waste of time to some people and you are about to give up. Just before leaving the Herd, your mind might be flirting with accepting peace in that moment or choosing to dive in for more information. This is when something awesome is allowed to happen because in that tiny lapse of thinking we are receptive to the messages. Expecting certain horses to do things or hoping that someone gets the lesson and even interpreting what the horse is doing all lead to the same thing. The person will not get the most from this experience in this case because you have made it about you and your perception of the experience.

After my time learning about Equinisity, my subconscious was different and I had experienced horses in such a fresh way. There was no way to go back to my previous conception of horses. I now knew what was possible with a Herd that had been thoroughly respected and loved as healers living in an ideal environment, which included the choice to work with people. The experiences I had with Liz's Herd blew my mind as I learned to allow the Herd to be healers, teachers, guides and truly trust that they knew exactly what people needed. They sensed what people were ready for without input from other humans.

Perhaps the most valuable take-away message was: "The secret is we have to give them permission. We hold the key, put up the barriers…we have to believe in the possibility and allow them to do the healing. You are only able to see what you believe is possible, what you give permission to."

I believe.

> Consciousness is similar to experiencing a certain frequency which tunes you to a certain radio station. You are on a new station now and as your vibration and frequency rises you will continue to experience more channels. As you tune in and listen you will continue to add more and more stations until you will reach the higher mind channel or the ALL station where all of creation except for humans is tuned to. Let the limits go and open to the MUSIC.

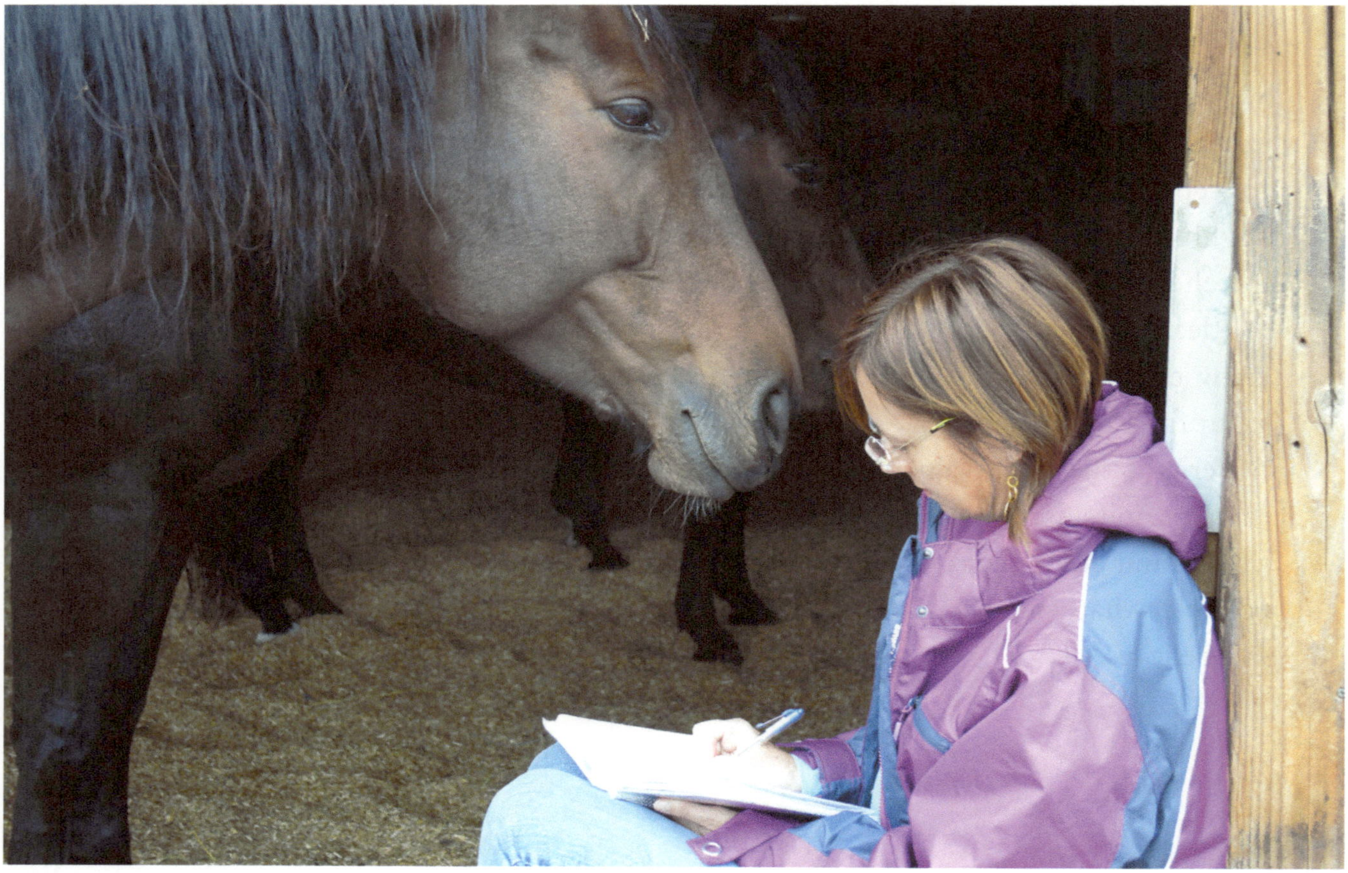

Inspiration

Do you realize, humans, that your vibration has elevated to a place where you are beginning to tune into our channel? You are beginning to notice us for the first time as spiritual equals, higher consciousness in a different shape from yours. Because we did not experience a fall from grace, we and the rest of the natural world share a direct connection with the ALL and are able to see the invisible world of spirit. When we see you, we see all that is around you. That includes your concept of past, present and future as in our world all is visible all-ways. It also includes your spiritual perfection as a higher immortal soul and any distortions to your divine plan.

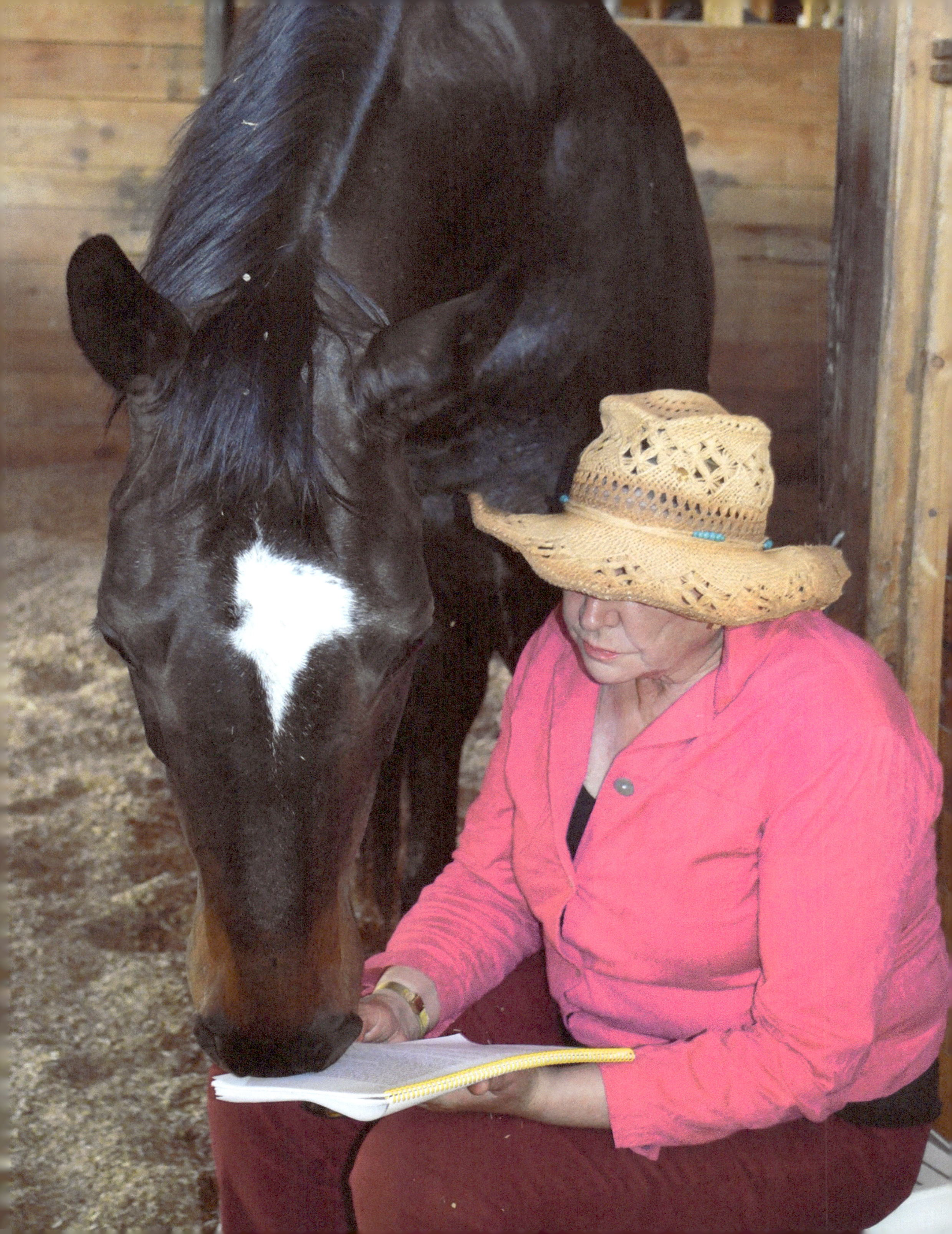

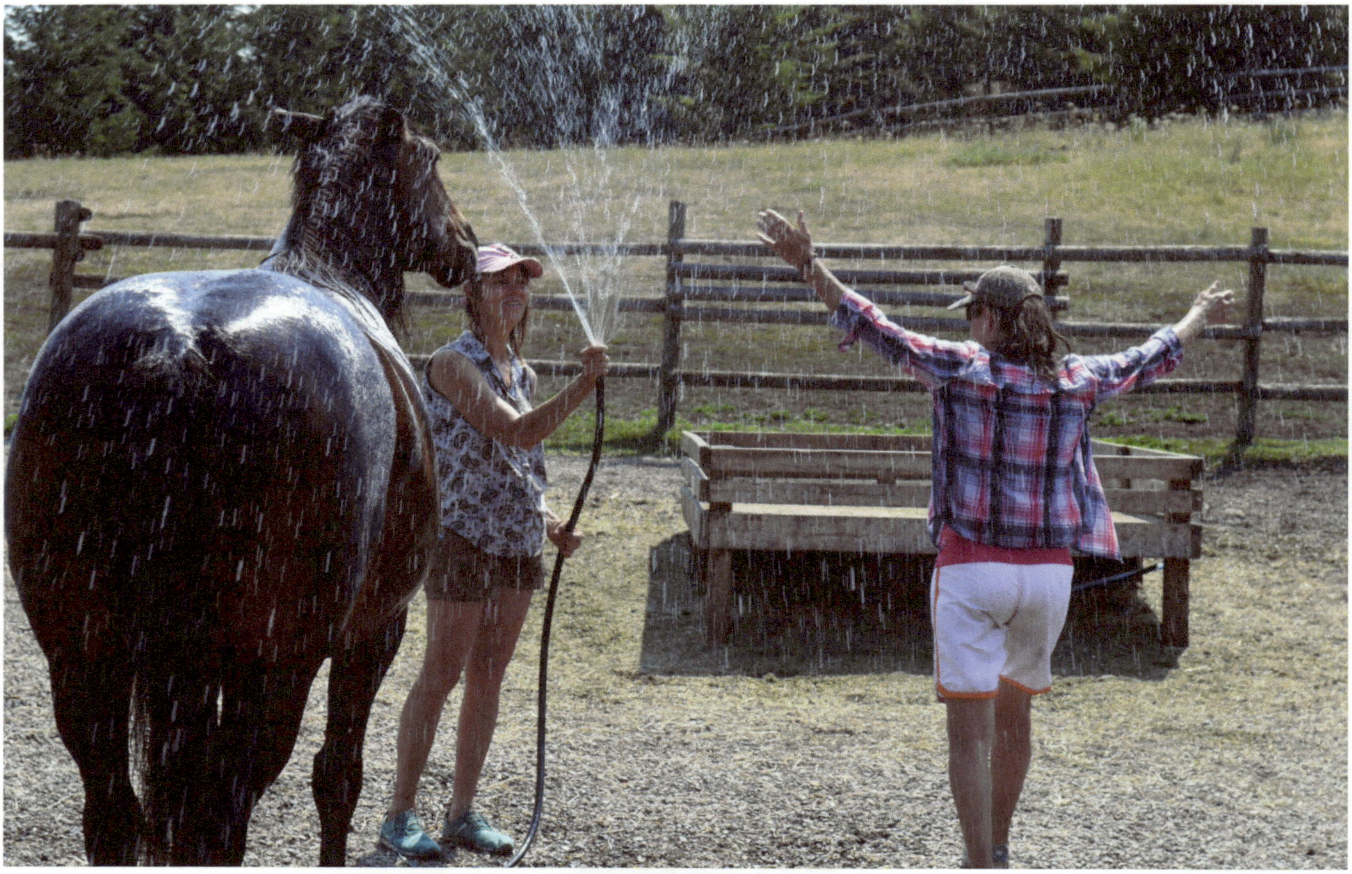

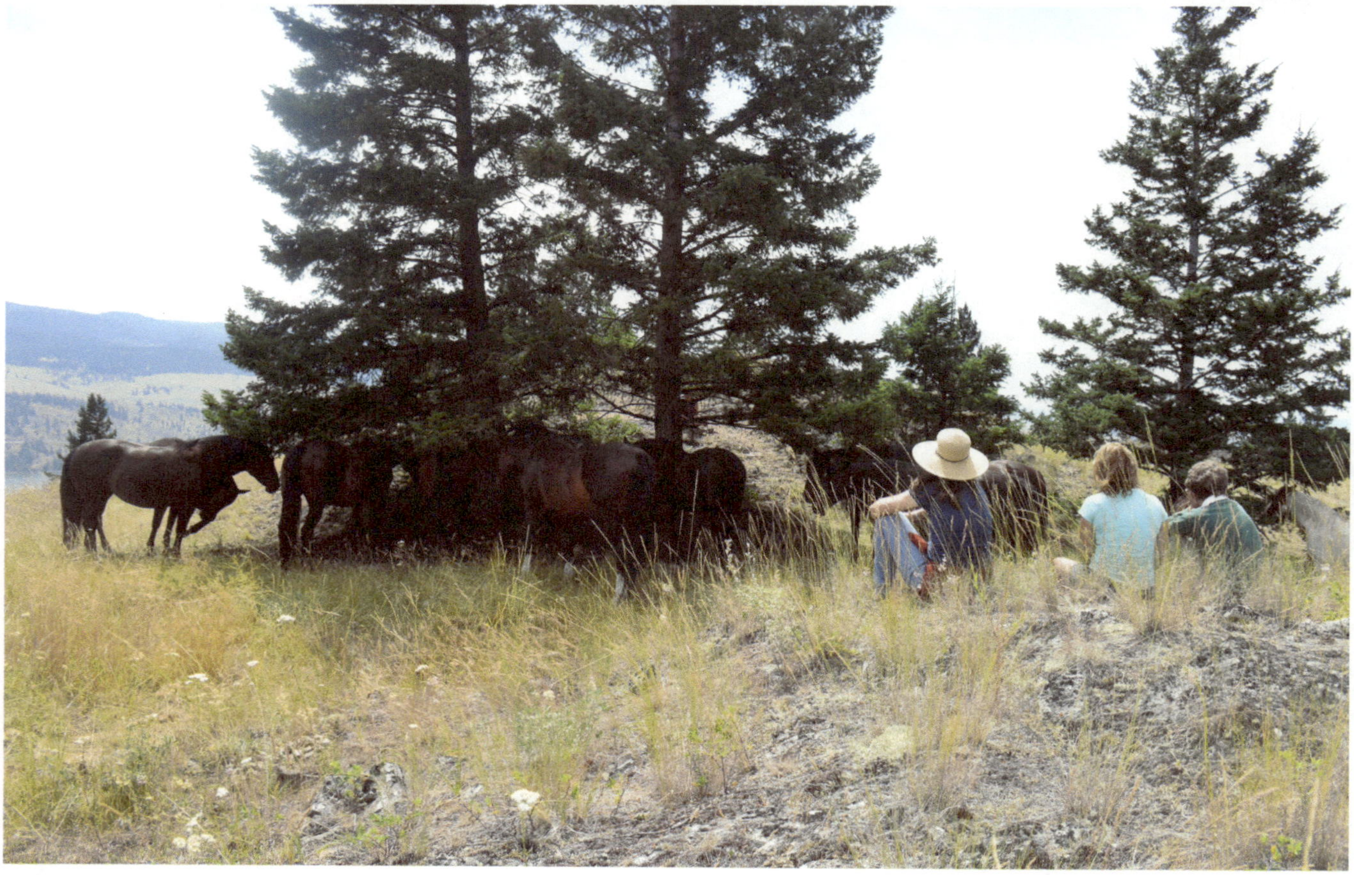

Fun in the sun

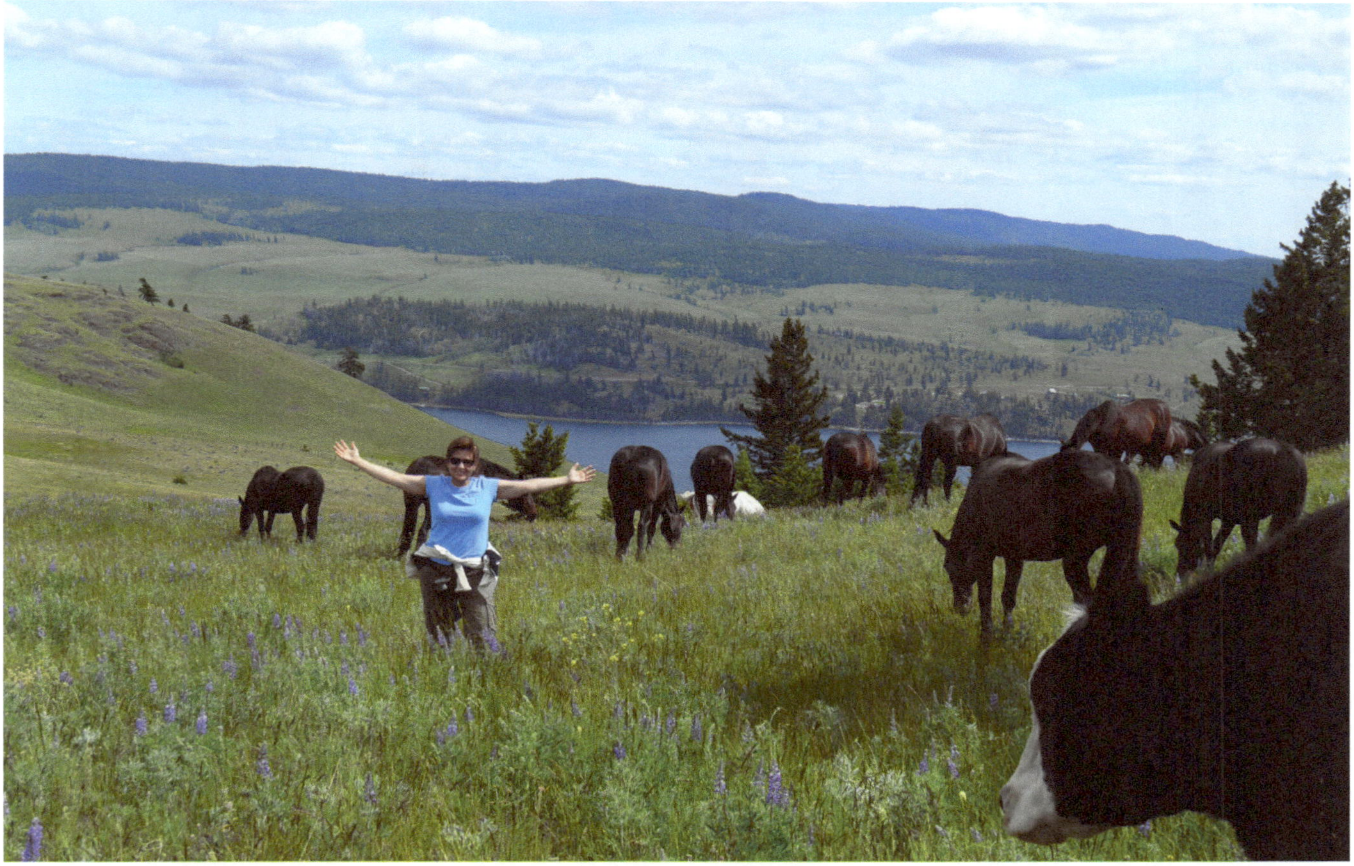

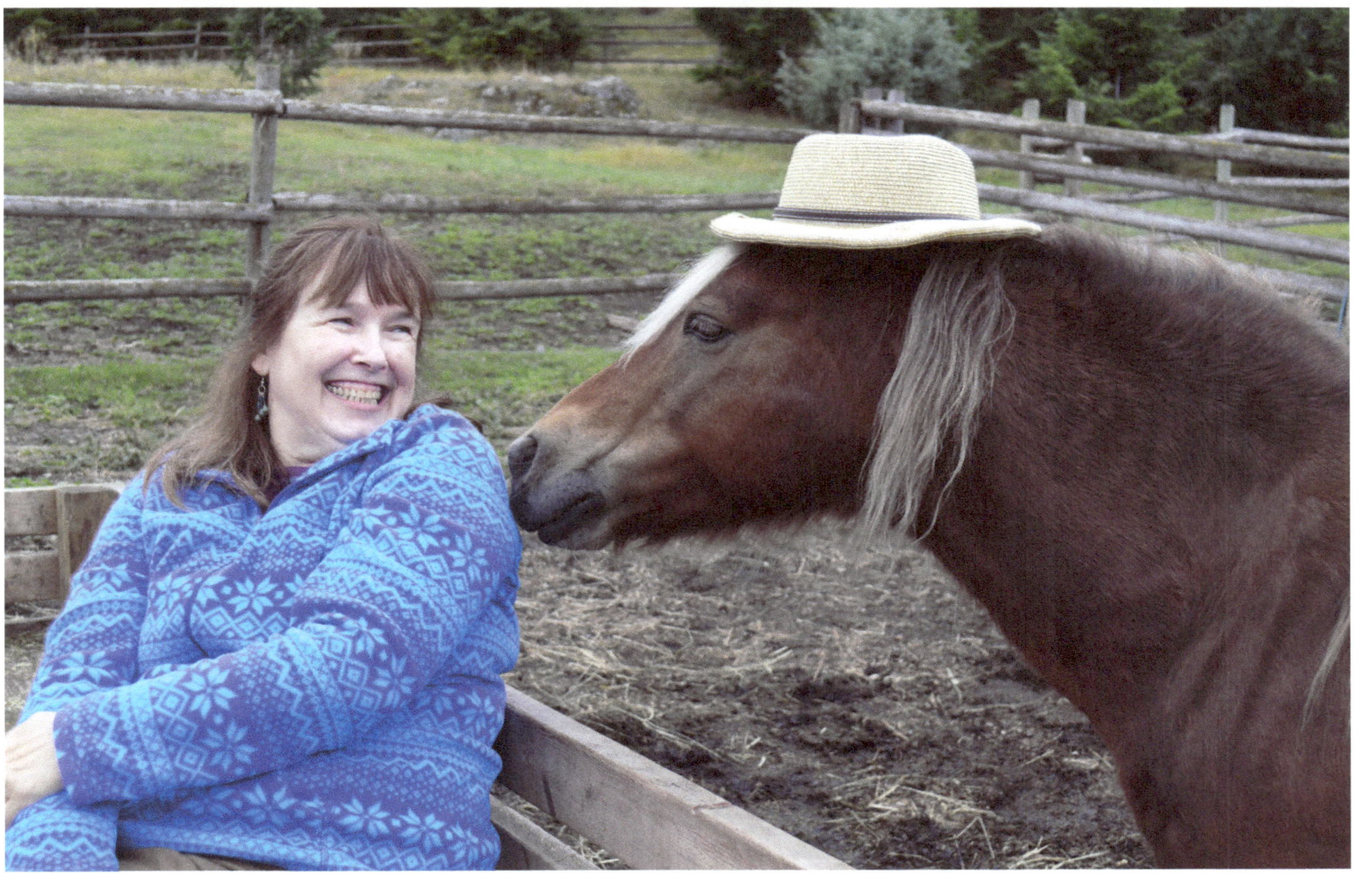

Joy

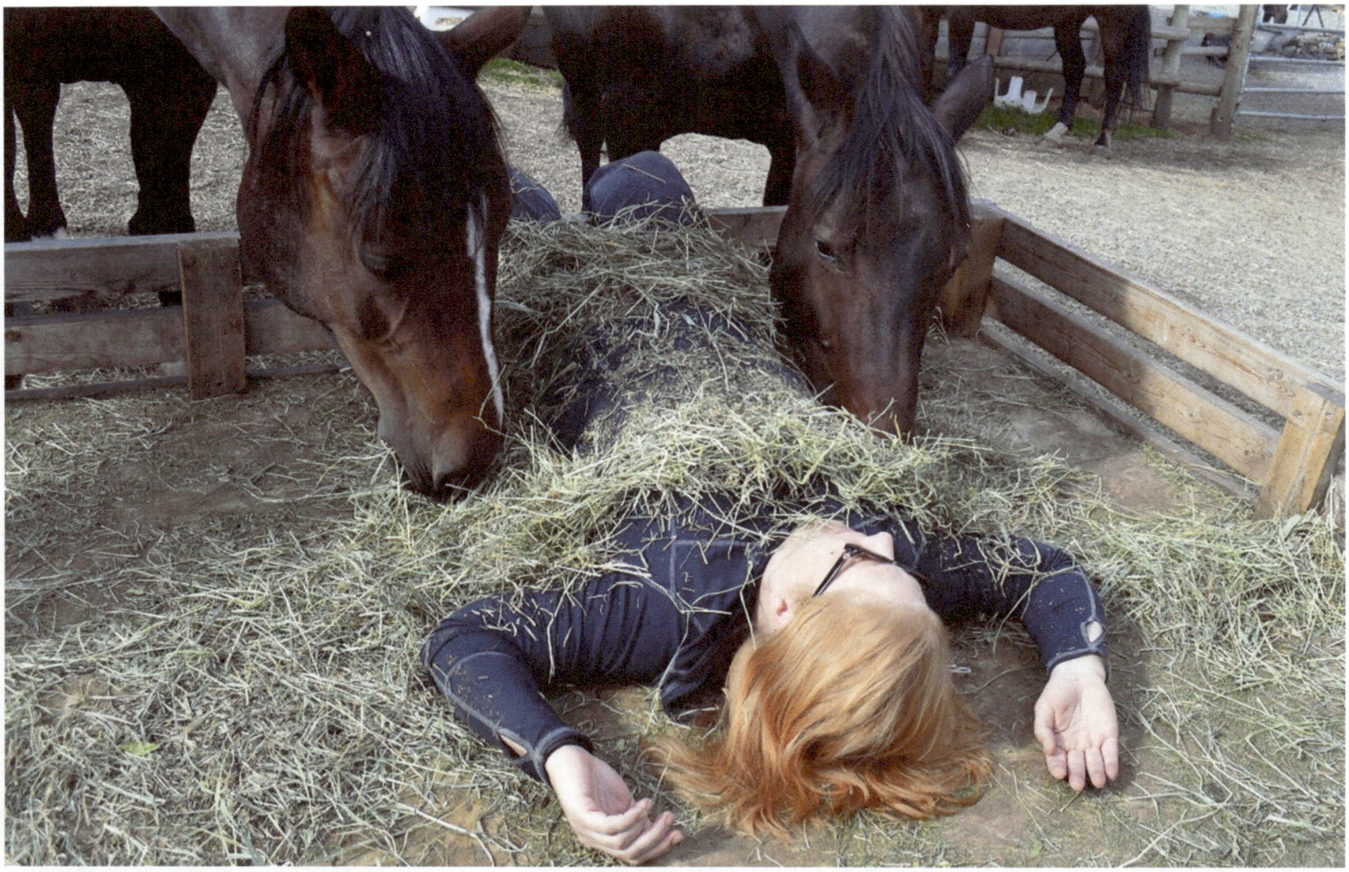

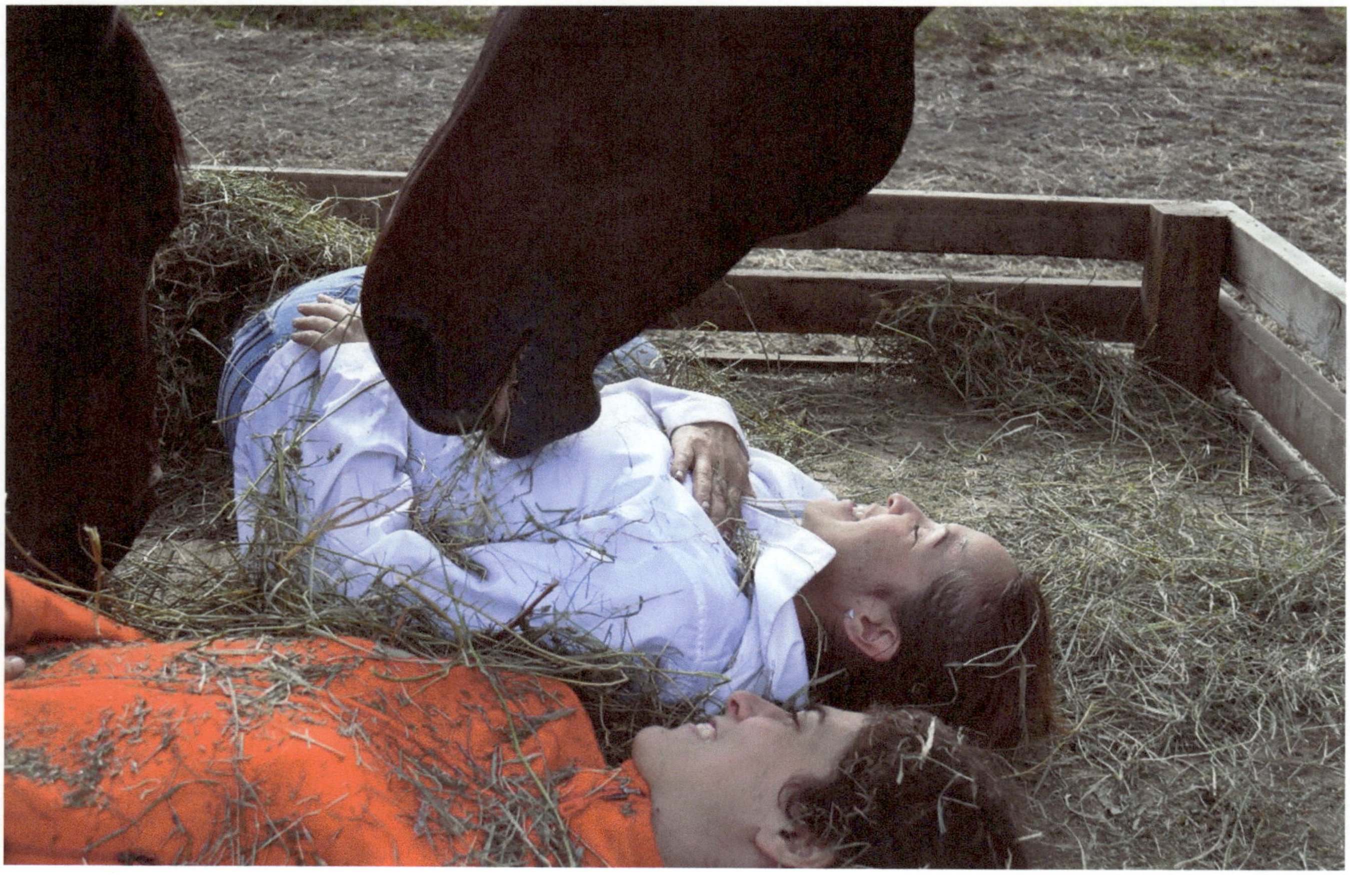

Tickle me horses

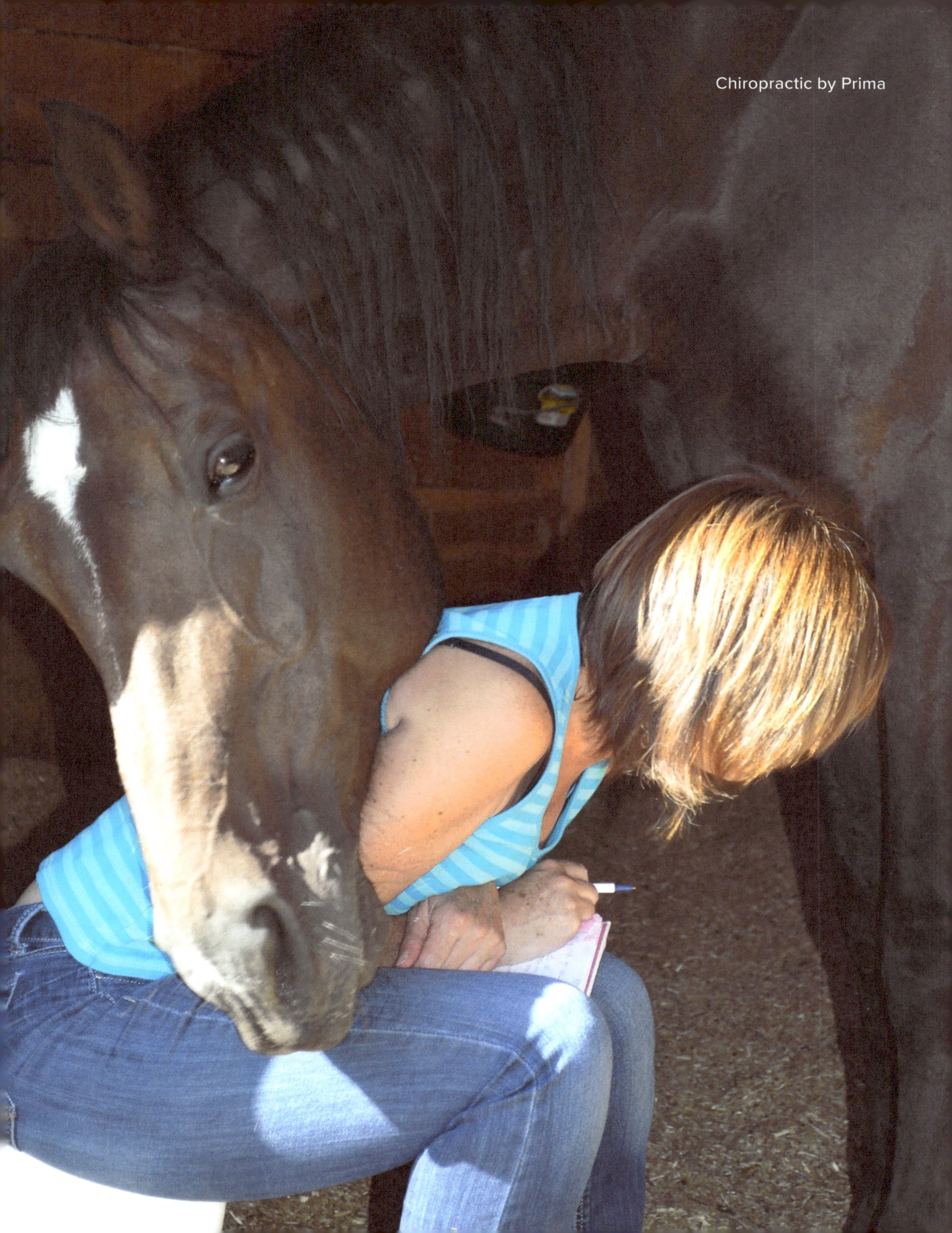

Chiropractic by Prima

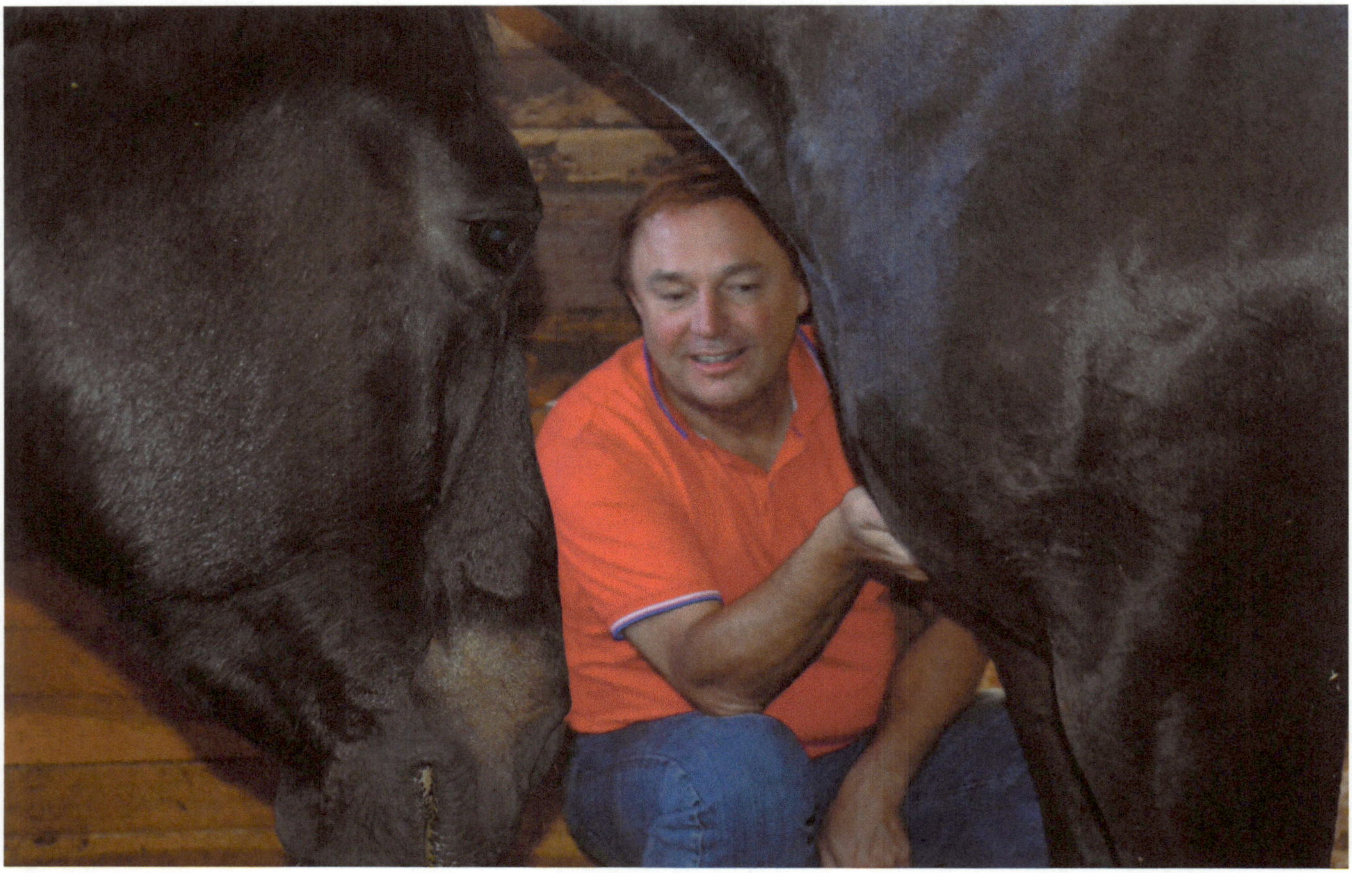

"*Joie de vive*"—Joy of life is what my horses bring me. Particularly my first born Prima. She is opinionated, moody and difficult to say the worst, but on a good day she makes my heart sing. Actually even on a bad day she is my reason for being. I adore her. I'm not sure how many other horse people feel this way, but it is similar to how I felt about my first-born human child. She was perfect! I was blessed! It did not seem to matter what she did, it was charming!

Prima is 8 years old now and we have worked on our relationship with the help of teachers and trainers from the time we first joined forces. It is now almost poetry, our relationship, and I am more in love than ever. My favorite activity together is riding in the hills with a halter, either saddled or bareback. I trust her implicitly, I know her every thought, and she knows mine. My aides are light as thinking, lifting my energy or sometimes a word. We are partners in a dance that is ours alone.

I have no need to control our relationship it is a partnership; we are in harmony. Sometimes Prima will volunteer the pace and other times I will. It just feels good! We don't have any hard and fast rules; we are friends, lovers having fun together. I laugh at her sometimes ridiculously evasive behavior or in retrospect I realize it to be a training maneuver targeted to refine my aides. The other day in a lesson in the ring every time I

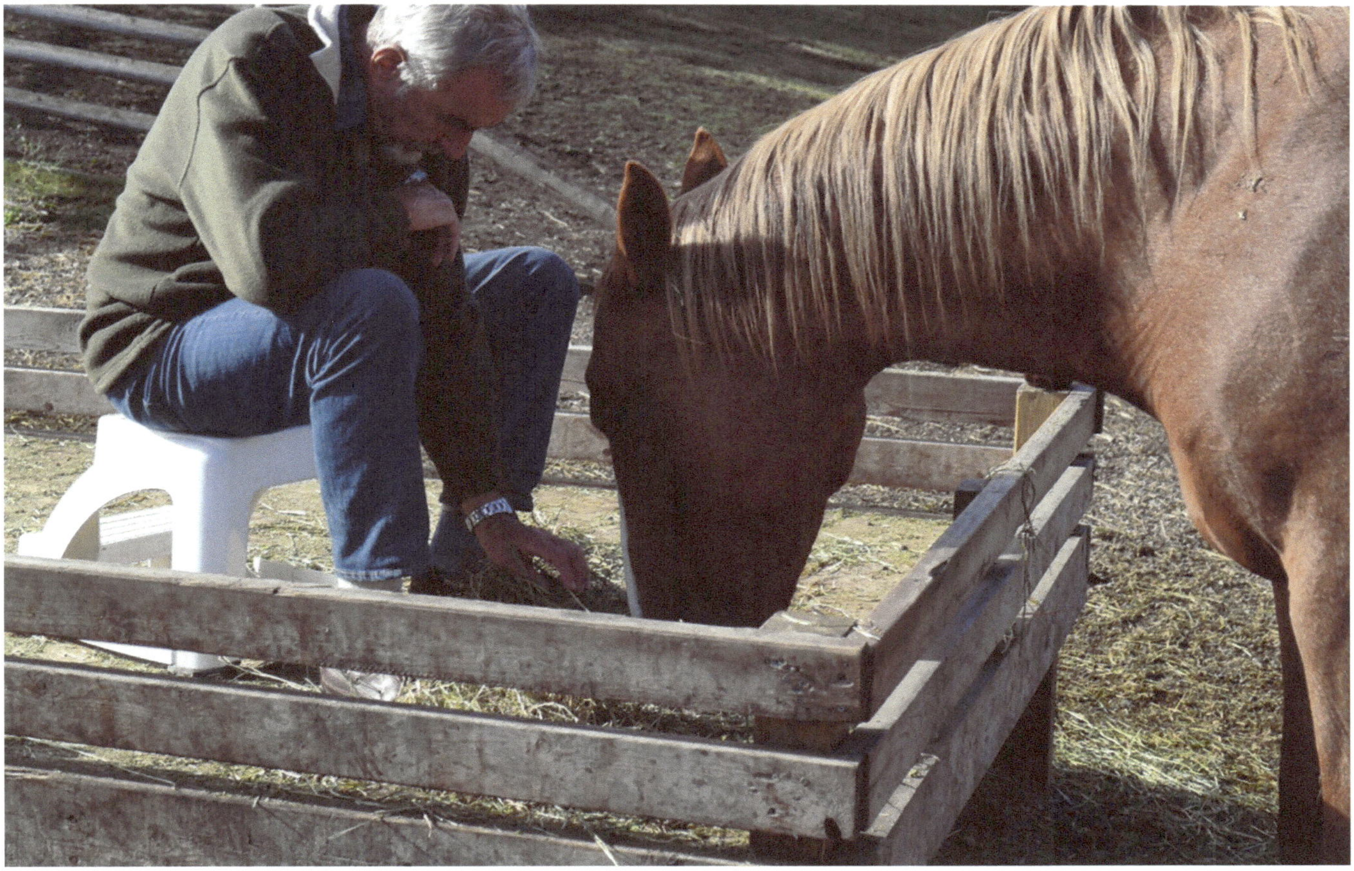

would look at my teacher Prima would side pass over to her. It soon became apparent that I should direct my focus to where we were headed which was around the track. What an incredible lesson she had given me!

Just the other day I decided to start Prima's 2-year-old son Picasso. Wow, he felt just like his mother (possibly less moody)! I threw a saddle on him, mounted, and he (from all our ground work and games) took it all in stride. So soft, relaxed and willing—it was simply a fun adventure for him.

Moments like these are the rewards of having a relationship with horses. They are what bring us out of the snow and rain, through traumas of day-to-day horse events, and inexplicably bind our souls forever to the magnificent energy that is "HORSE."

Actually, it is more a microchip of pictures and information that animals share. Have you ever thought that some of those ideas you humans come up with could have actually been horse inspired; what about the wheel, which made the cart, which took the weight off of the horse's back. Then there was the engine and "horsepower," which saved many horses a life of labour. Now there is horse therapy where the horses are working on humans. You have to wonder how grateful those people will be when the horses help them with their problems and if they will in fact be more inclined to repay the favor. They might even begin to view horses as intelligent equals and reward them with rights and freedoms to which all other intelligent species are entitled. Animal communication is opening the doors to greater understanding, not only between humans and animals, but it is feeding human consciousness with a larger more all-encompassing "universal consciousness" which is the inspiration of the ALL or one consciousness in ALL life. It would be impossible for the creator to be lesser in any form, so humans, with the input of other consciousness and viewpoints are just beginning to celebrate the diversity and the difference. They have long been on a pedestal that fear has created for their protection and now as their fears are dissolving in the light of truth they are beginning to understand the nature of belief in manifestation. We are here to help them see the truth of themselves and all creation and to open the gateway to unlimited health, happiness and eternal freedom. We are the "Wind Beneath Your Wings."

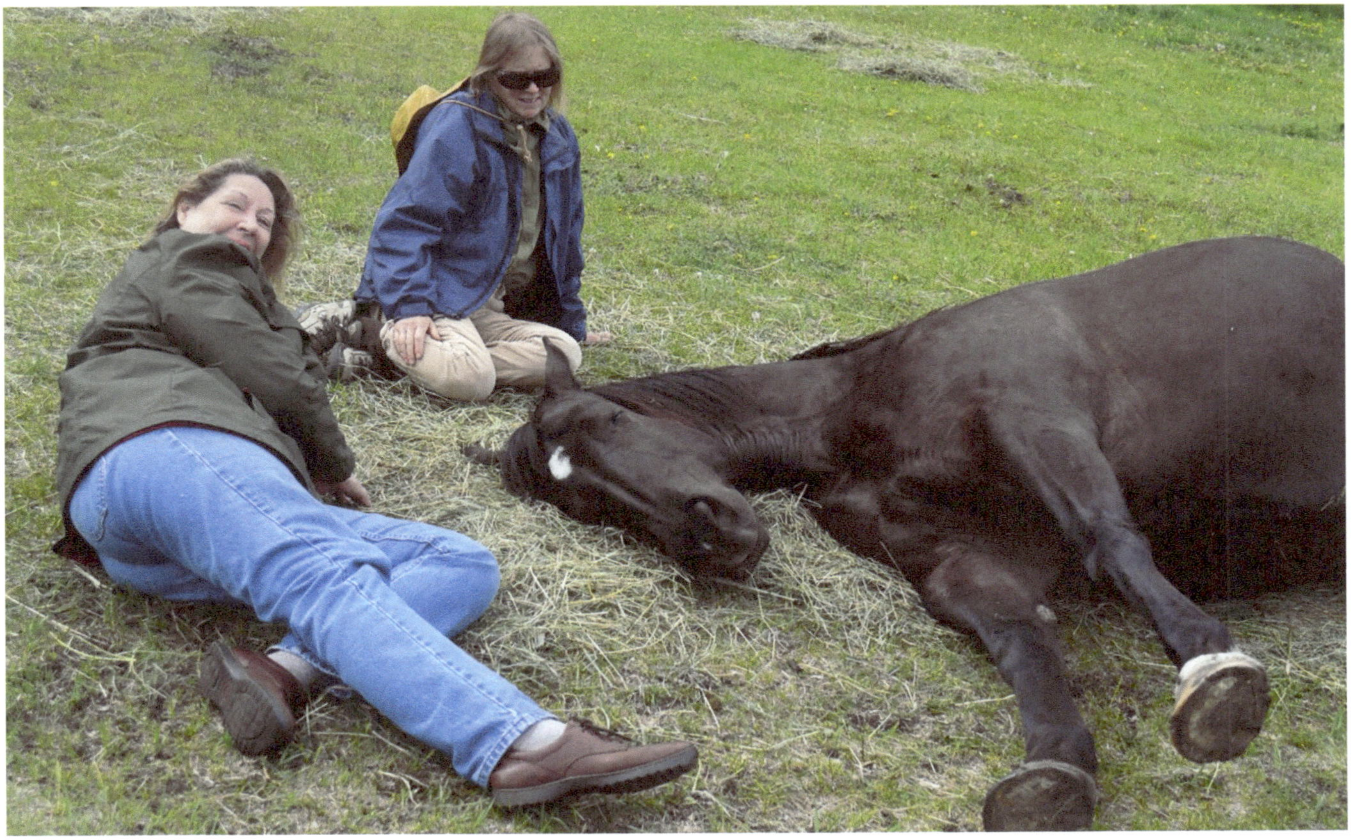
Time for a nap

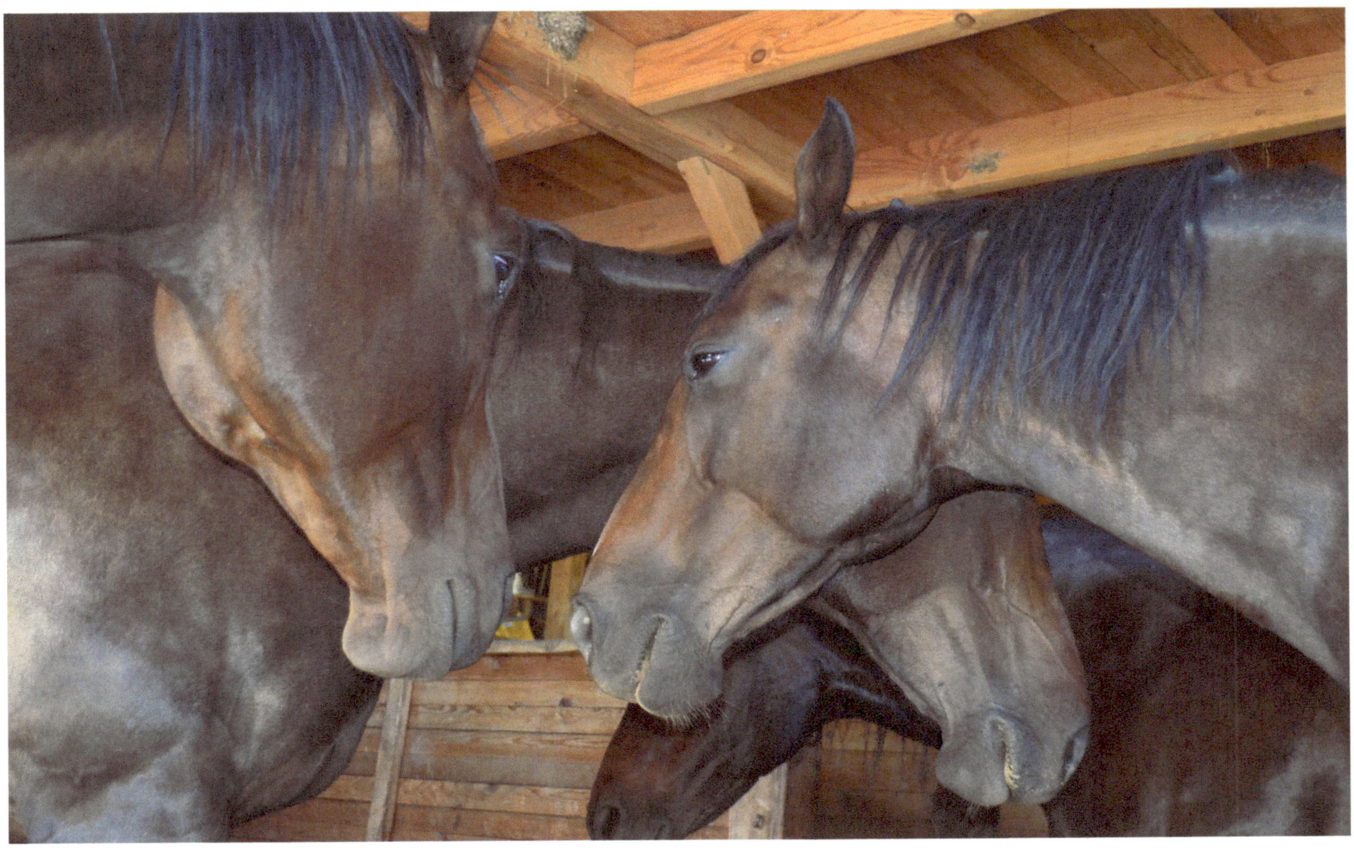
Sacred Geometry

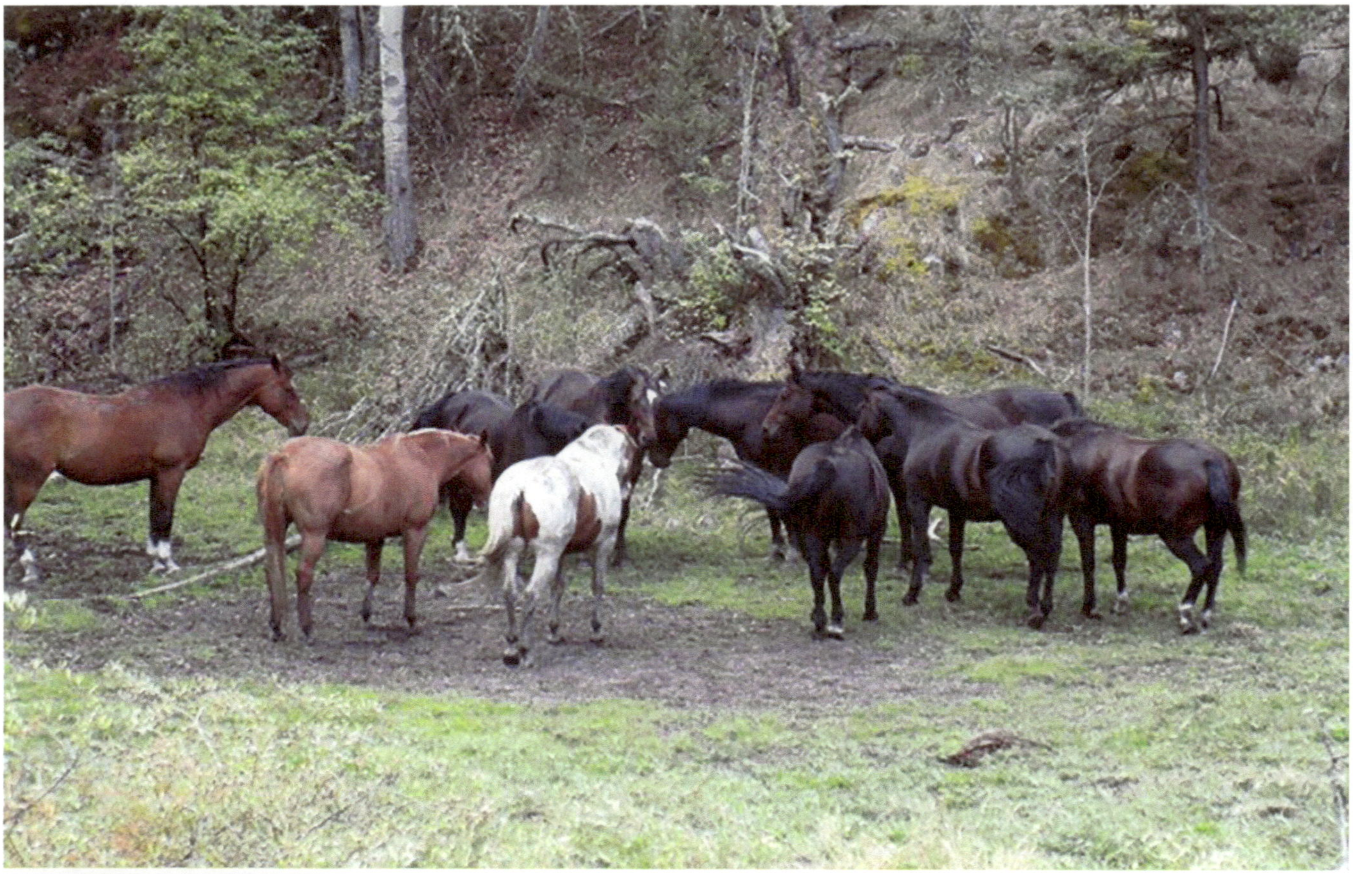

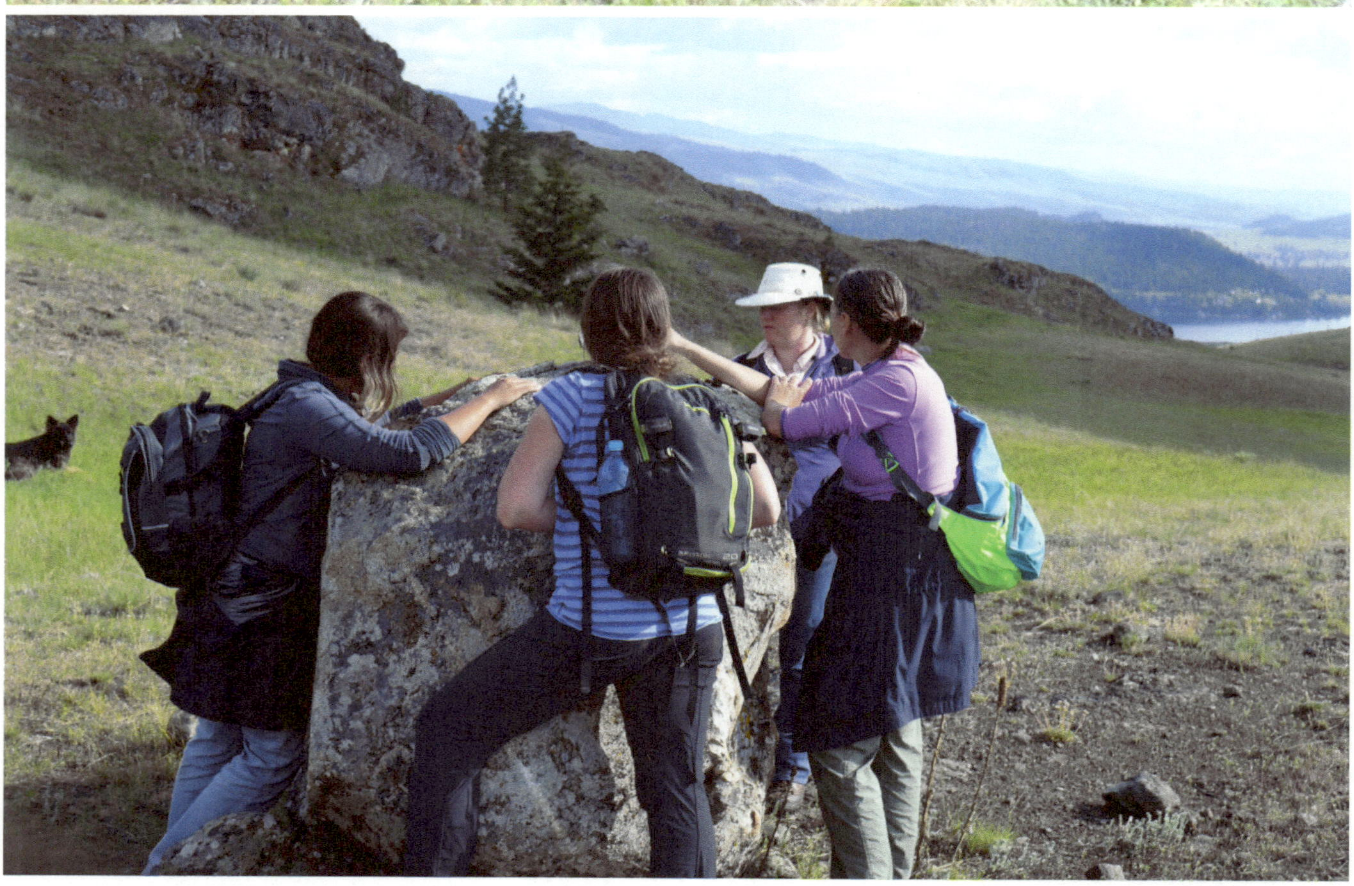

Liz has asked us to bring our recent behavior to light. Each individual creation at birth holds a unique microchip of color, shape, note, key, pattern, geometry, scent, mathematical formula, each a vibration which expresses perfect health. In the weight and substance of matter, distortion appears. When a new energy enters our space we take note of all of these and as well the ripples that extend before and beyond that creation and how it influences the rest of life. At this time in the Earth's history the animals and the natural world that are still uninfluenced by man are holding the microchip of information that can tune and heal the damage. Many now have noticed that along with all natural life, dolphins, whales, elephants, horses, cats and the trees, plants and rocks are in deep meditation to achieve this goal. Liz just asked about dogs and they are specifically healing hearts and expanding love throughout humanity. It is critical at this time that we focus on this as our primary goal. Although we are in deep meditation on a world level we still notice the comings and goings of the physical plane and people who come into our radar needing personal help. You might say we are able to multitask. As humans join together in group meditation, so we connect with all pure consciousness and share that perfection with individual, group and ALL consciousness, bringing forward a new Earth. We repeat again that consciousness is shifting and rising to higher levels exponentially at this time, so be open and allow the flow to cleanse and heal as the waters of the Earth.

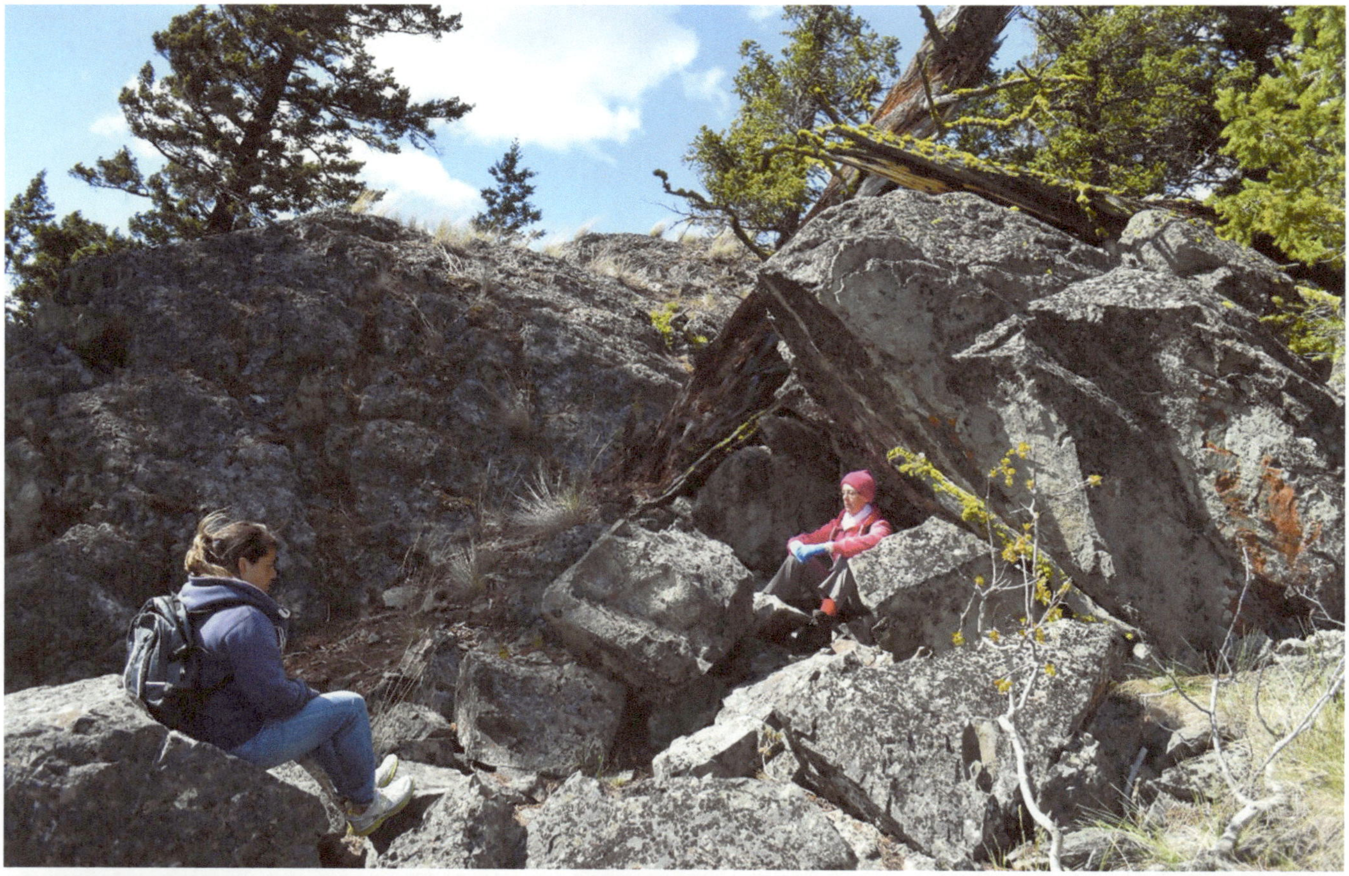

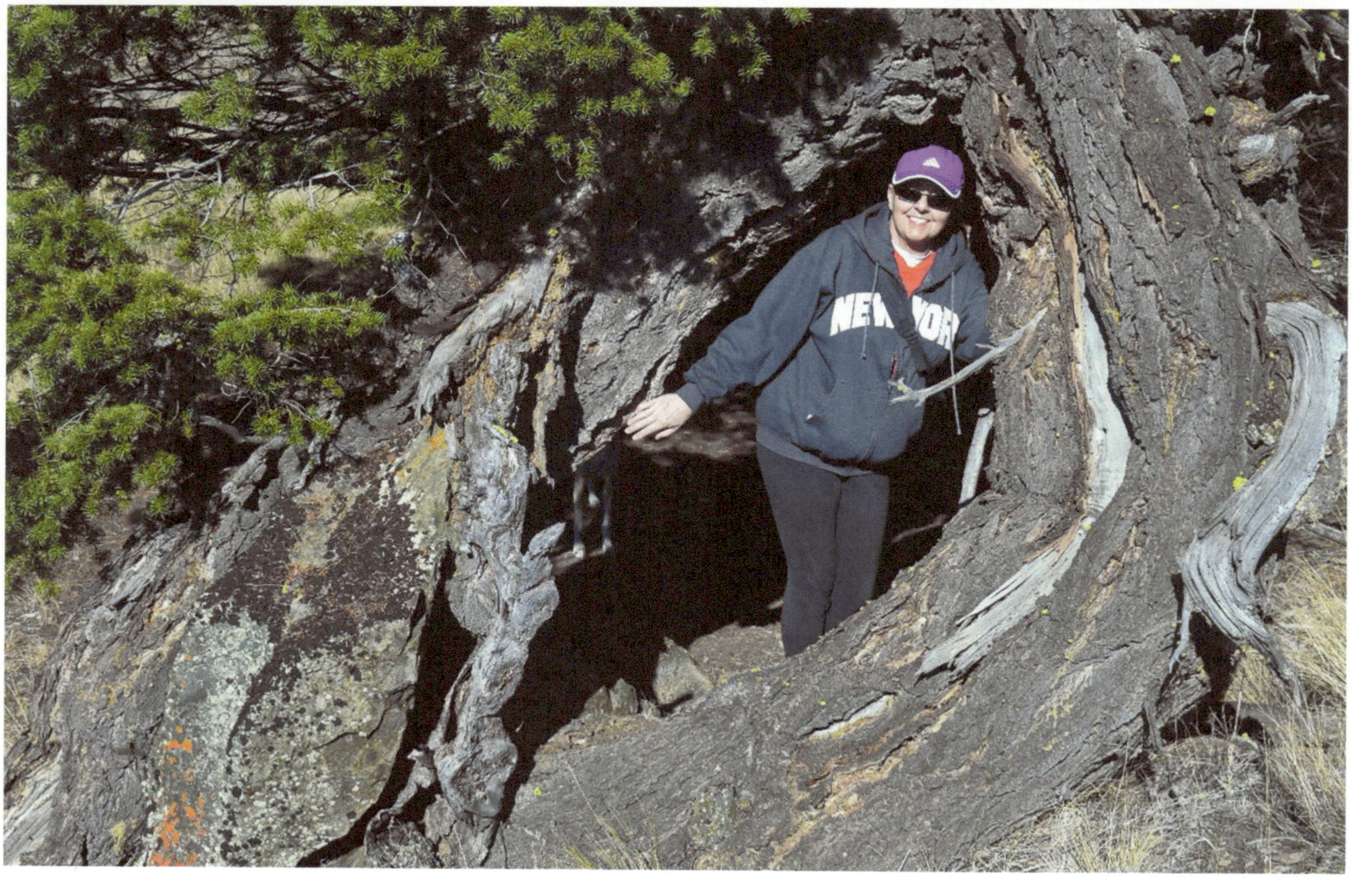

We are very concerned for the Earth right now and must continually focus on raising vibration and consciousness for all life. Gaia has become stressed with the parasitic behavior of humans and just like a human body under attack, is burning, drowning and shaking off the invaders. This is mostly concentrated on the larger areas of infection, the big cities that harbor greed and corruption and destroy the natural world with their industry. We are holding the energy of love to counteract the forces of entropy that are breaking down the planet. Nothing is stronger than love and our focus is to hold Gateway safe and join with the other animals, trees, plants, rocks and elements to hold safe the entire natural world. We are healing, inspiring and tipping human consciousness so that they might experience the truth and transitory nature of this life experience and accomplish their promise to the ALL.

As above, so below. Each and every created being lives within the body of Mother Earth, which along with the universe comprises the body of the ALL.

Again, like a human body if one of the organs is compromised then the body dies. We cannot live separate and apart from the love-force that is the essence of us all and without that connection we will all surely perish. Be in your truth. Go within and listen to your intuition and let us help you remember who you truly are.

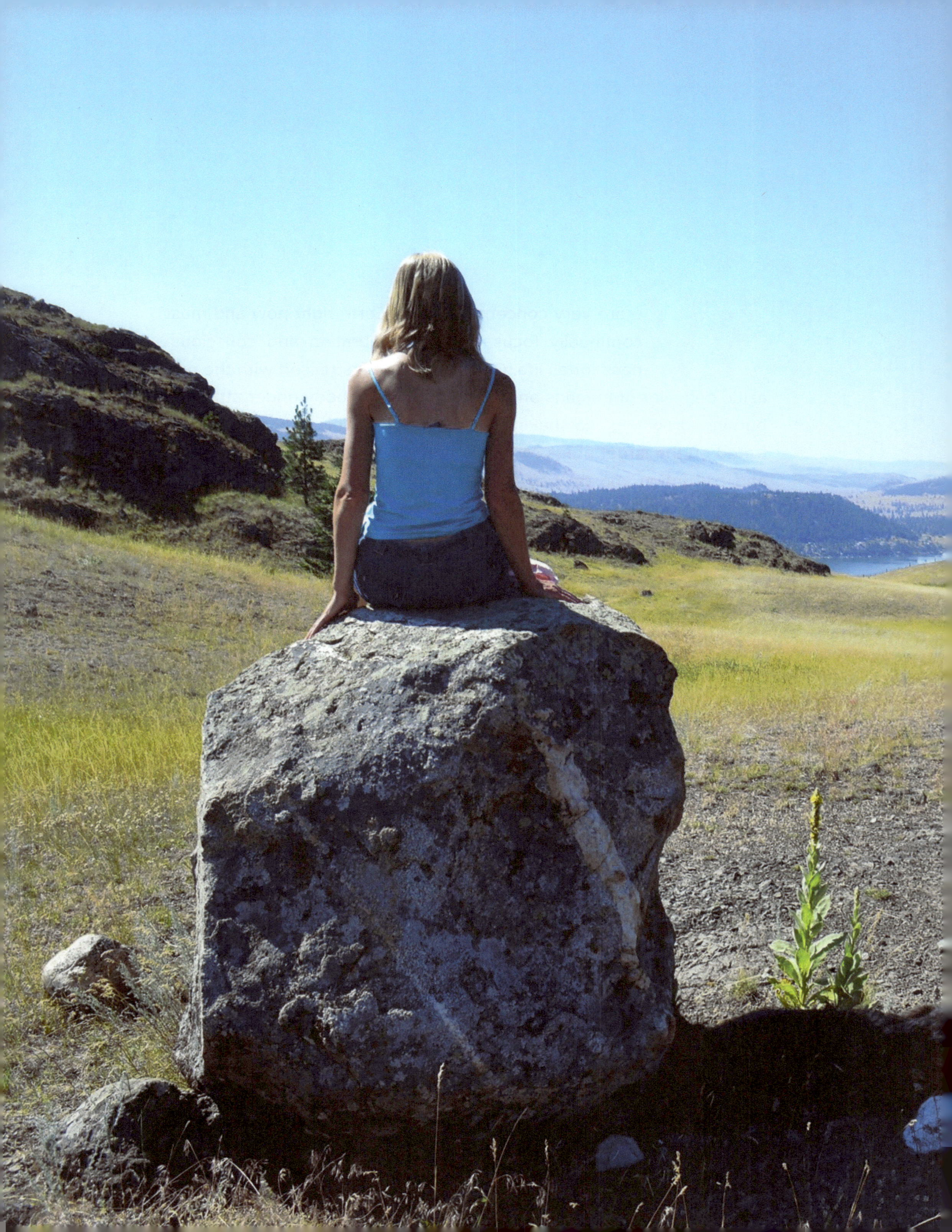

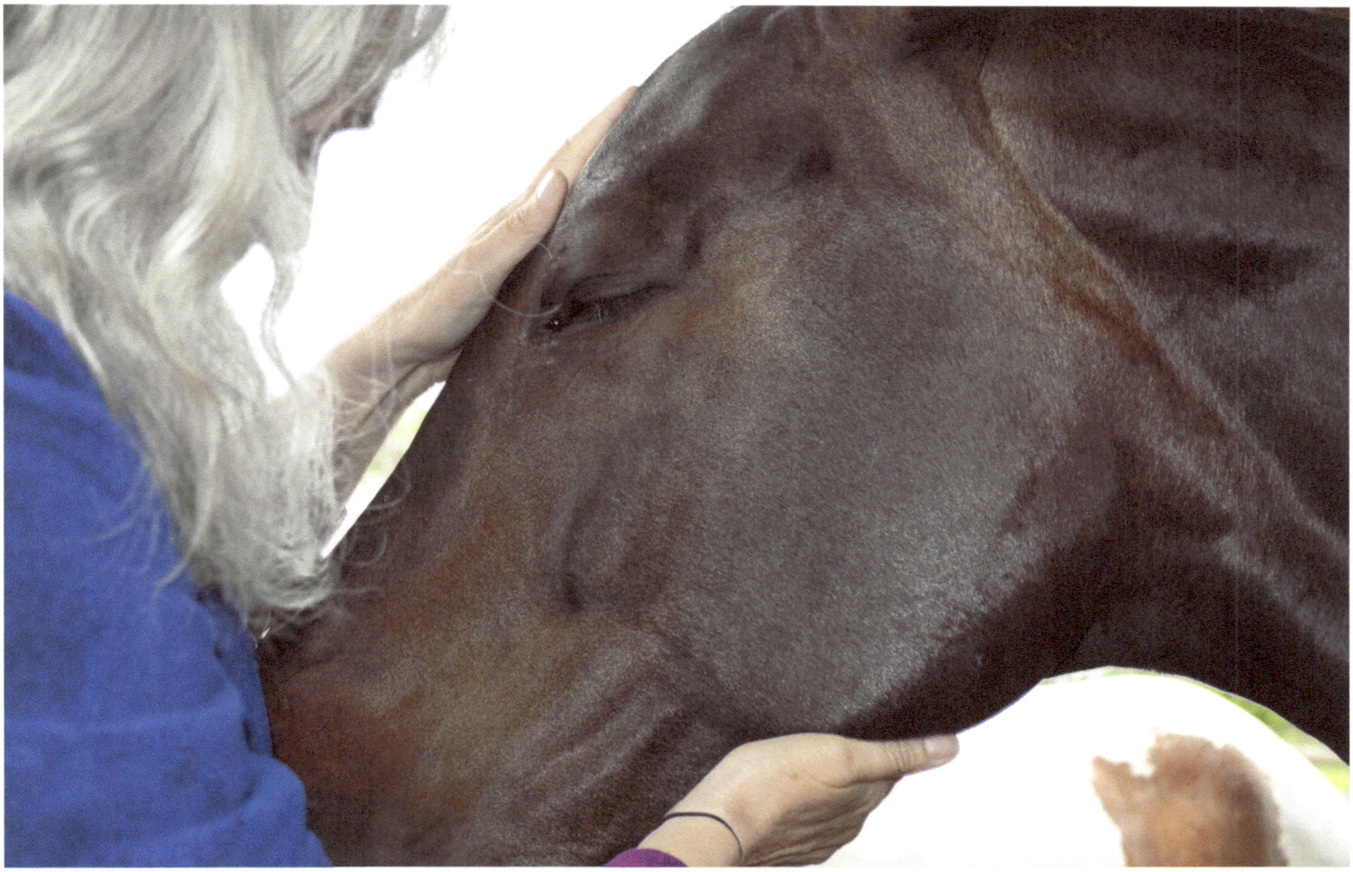

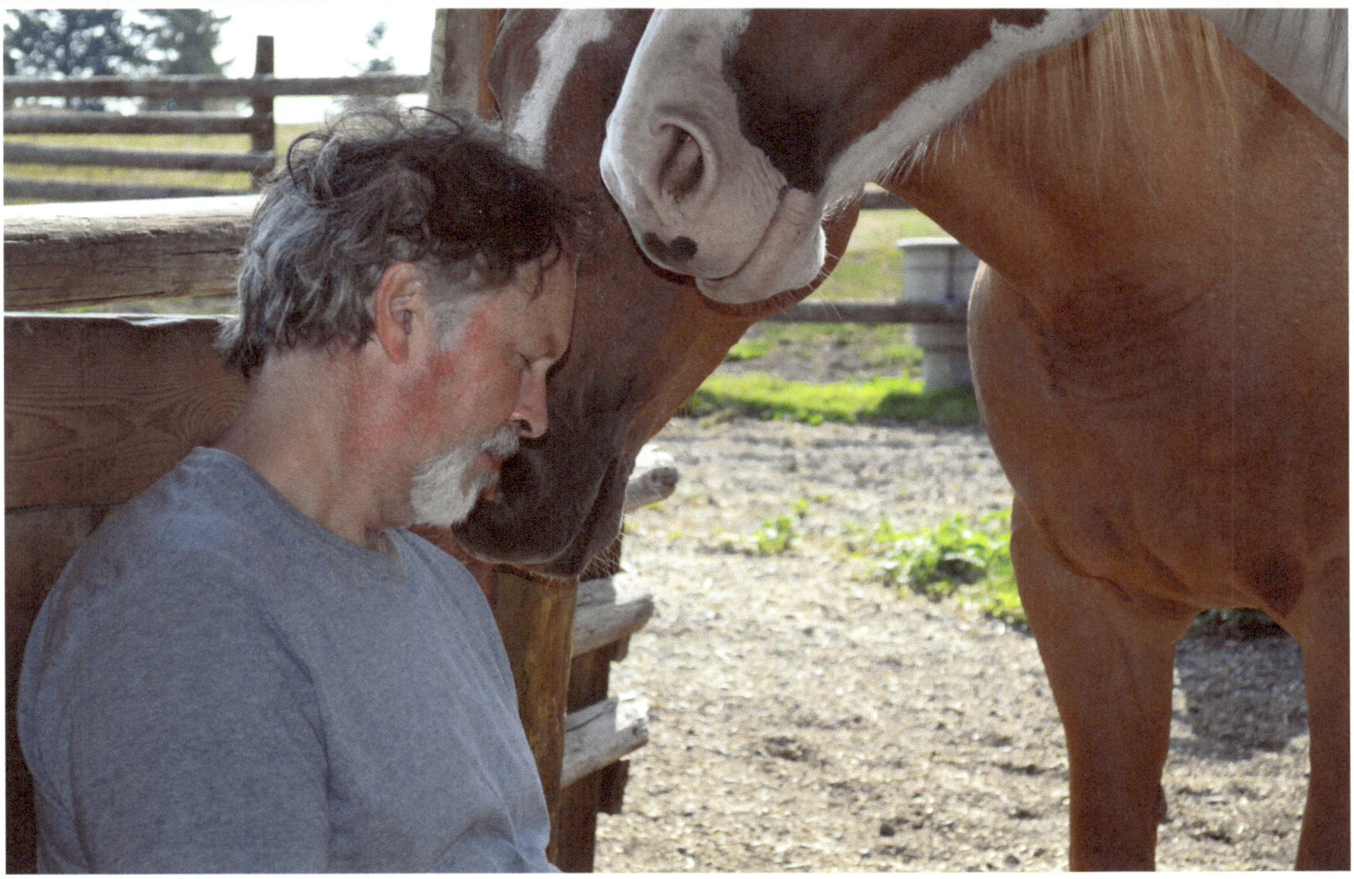

Oneness

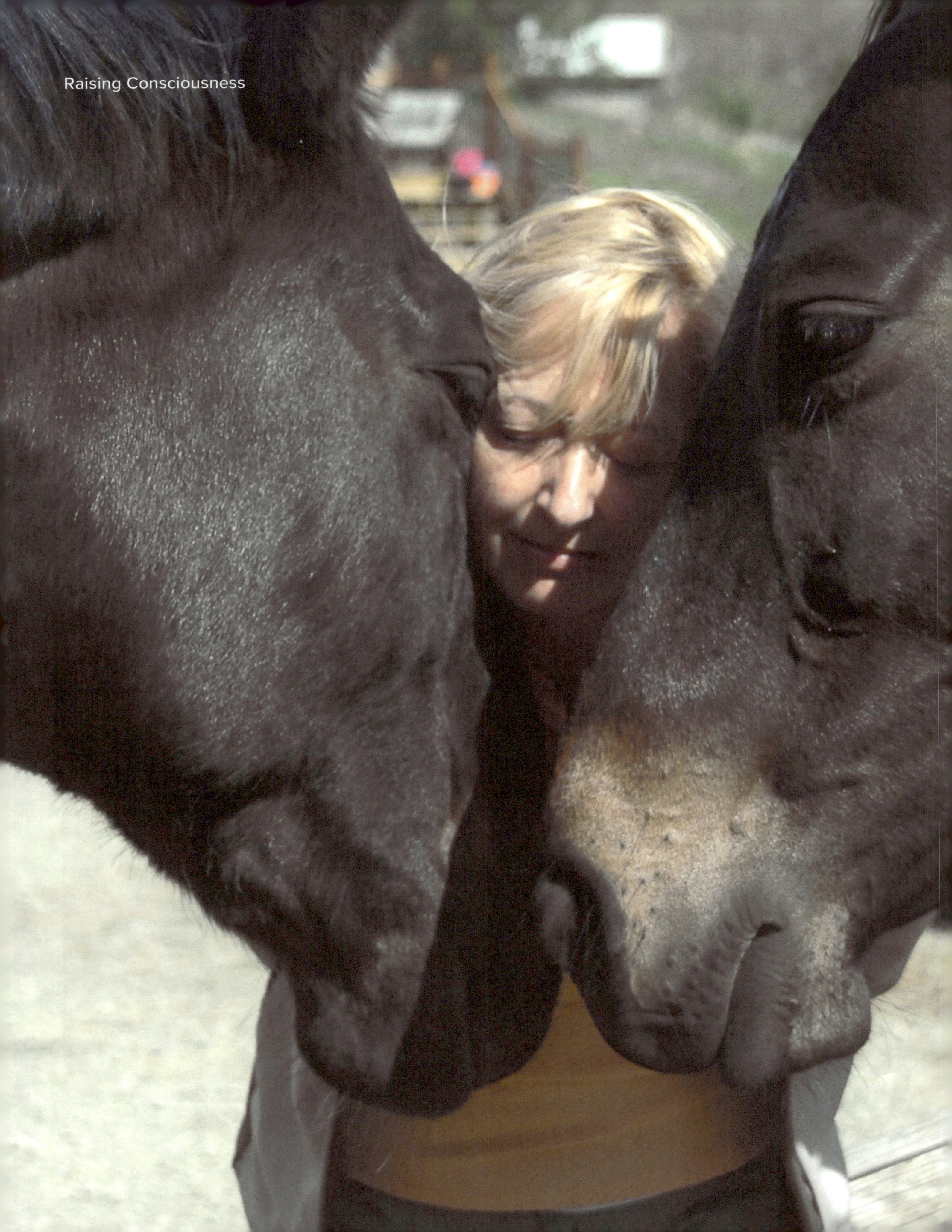

As often happens here in this mercurial energetic vortex of Gateway 2 the energies are reshaping or re-configuring to a higher and lighter plane of experience, which is calling in a new level of participants. The denser energies have been refined or repelled by the very nature of "like attracts like." Have you ever noticed when you enter a place where different energies are existing that it feels uncomfortable and you either shut down in a protective mode or have to leave? We have been in a protective mode for some time now as we are refining the Earth's energies and our focus has been intense and sharp in order to re-configure and create a new level of consciousness for the Earth at this time. We are now calling those who want better to immerse themselves and resonate at that new level of heart wisdom where the universal energies are free to flow unencumbered by mental blockages, which are still existing in the solidity of the historical human mass mind consciousness. We have expanded that consciousness to include new levels of universal consciousness that have always been the reality of the natural world and the animals and are now inviting all who are called to join us in that new level of awareness and experience. Wisdom, Truth, LOVE, Freedom, Abundance and JOY...Allness, Isness and Oneness, all ours in the instant of connection to source.

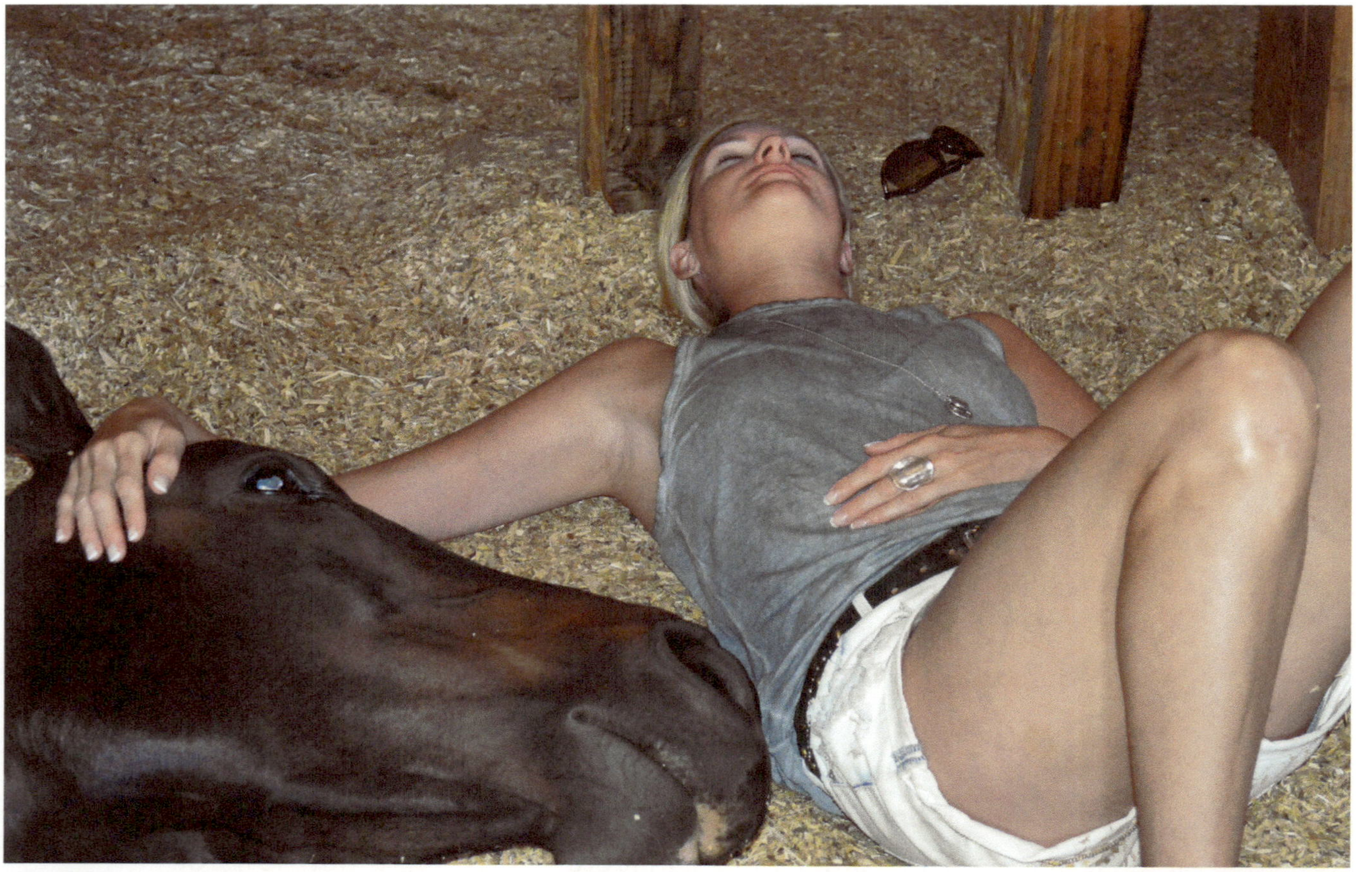

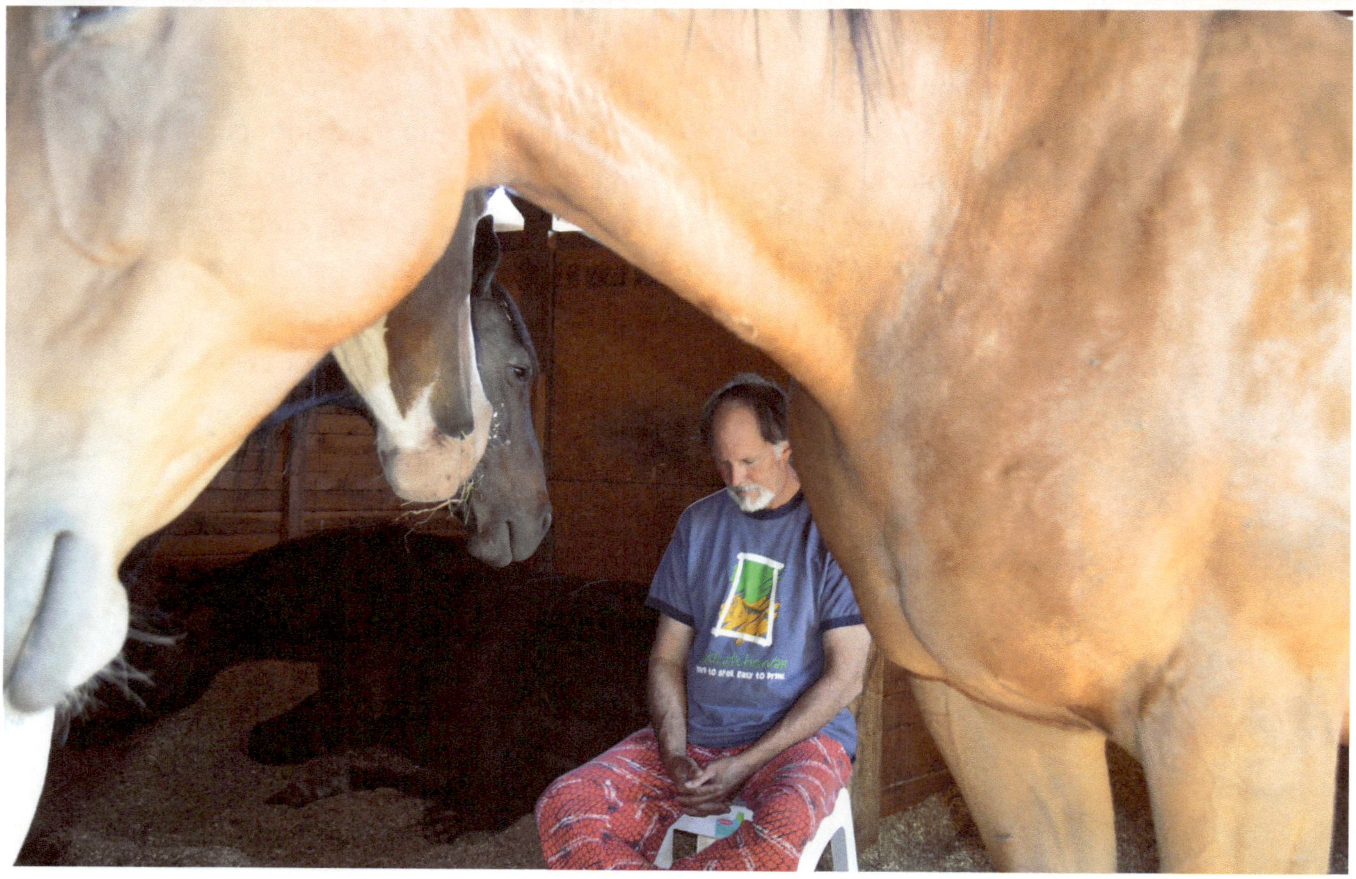

Connecting

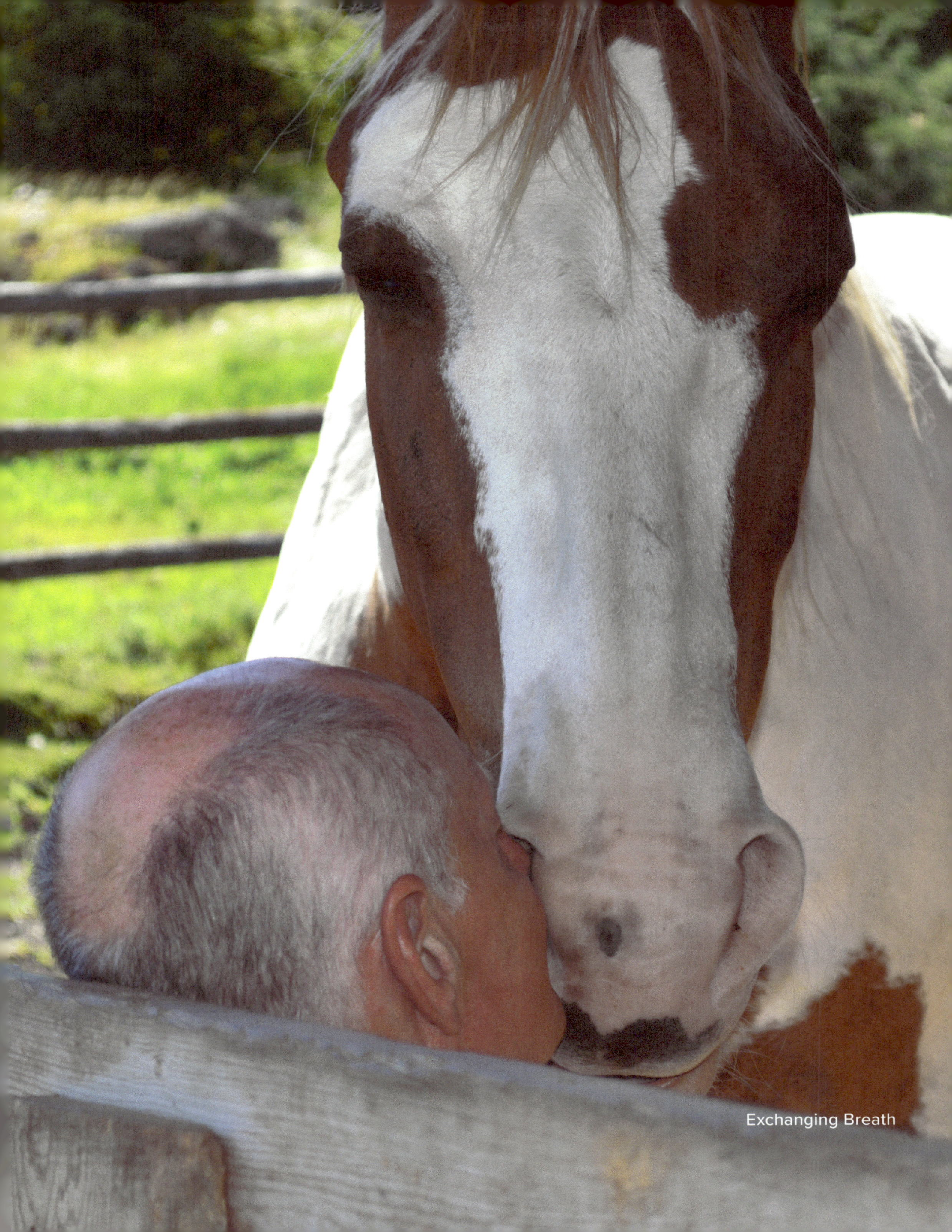

Exchanging Breath

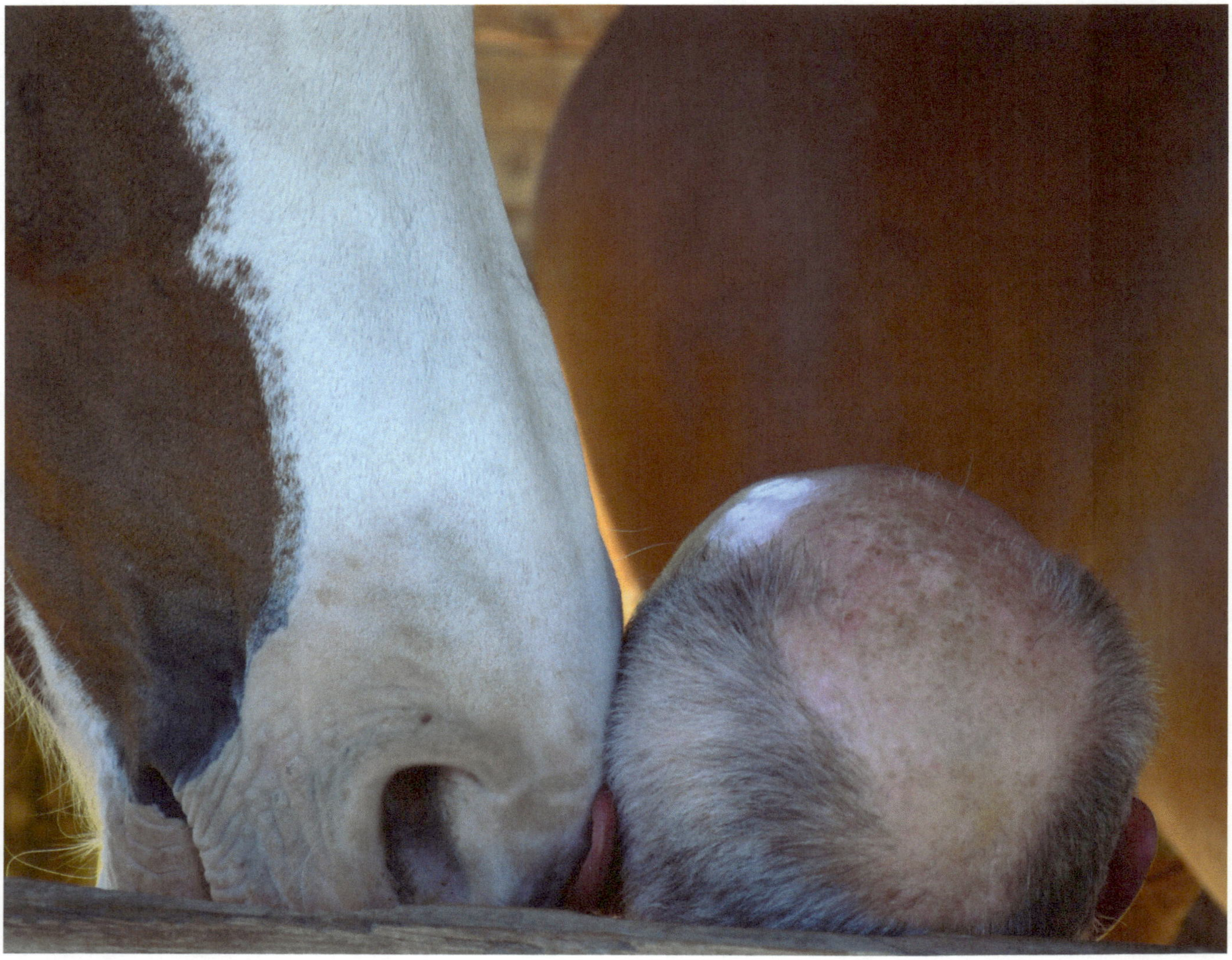

When a human enters, they are scanned and the Herd computes their synergy or lack of it. Health is a certain vibration, color and note and anything other is an obvious blip on the screen of horse perception extending far beyond the human senses. Any incongruency needs to be corrected. As they follow the prompts and are allowed by the person, the individual horses will come either in to touch or simply hold the space and correct energy to alter the vibration, in a meditative communion with perfect Oneness, Wellness, Isness and Allness, that place of connection with the All.

We have our gentle space holders like Prospera or Crystal who will breathe softly to open energy centers or rest their chins holding a steady pressure on problem areas, and our tough guys like little Merlin the pony who simply does his reading and then gets straight to the point. He does use his teeth a little, either as a head massage or prod to unleash past blocks or resistances. The Herd responds differently to each new situation and also to the expectation of the participant.

Well, Liz finally stopped expounding long enough to let us speak. We are so very grateful that she allows us our inherent freedom to fully actualize our highest expression as horse beings. If you humans sometimes feel a little strange at how different you are from the rest of creation there is a good reason for it. You are aliens, seeded on a planet that can evolve in love quite happily without you. That Garden of Eden story when we all walked and talked with God until humans ate of the tree of the knowledge of good and evil is just an analogy for how humans are separate and apart because of their focus on themselves and attachment to their egoist selves. No different from the individual focus in quantum physics that crystallizes all into a point when it is naturally a wave. All of creation is the wave and the ego is a point. From birth to death humans focus on their individual lives, creating walls around themselves, imagining they are separate and apart from all the rest of life when they are life itself in expression...life observing itself in expression. "Why create limits in a limitless universe," Prima said, and you are learning the errors of your creation (or more aptly put, your separation from creation). When you are in our presence we can tune and raise your vibration to a place of fusion with higher consciousness which allows the perfect expression of your higher self and the clear flow and guidance of the ALL through your awakened connection. Remember, the only way you can change your world is to change yourself. Blessings from the Herd.

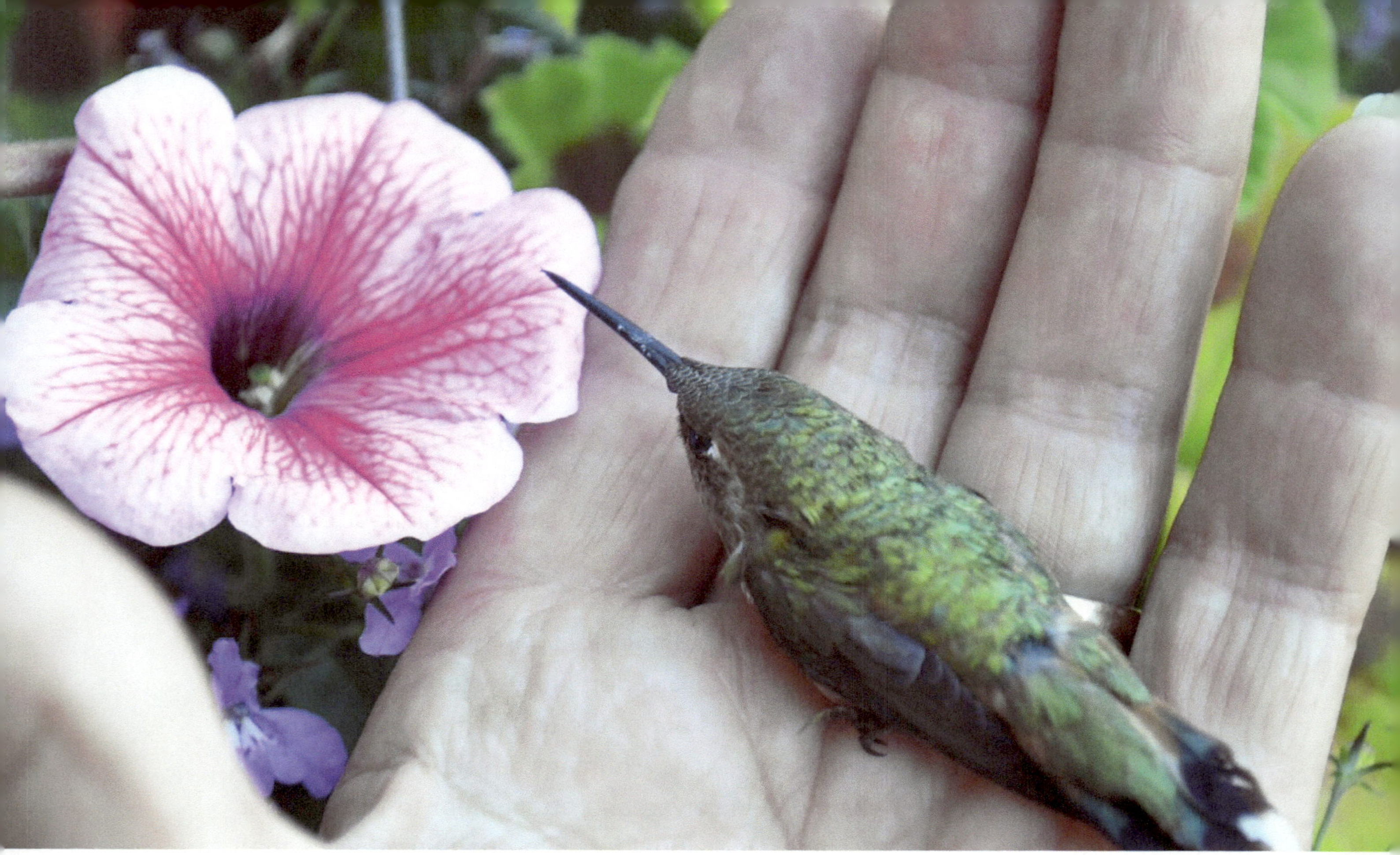

The lesson we have been sharing is that everything is energy and it's patterning which brings matter into physical form. The natural world is sensitive to energetic printing which happens by focus and intent. Nothing exists without first having an energetic idea behind its conception. We are playing with a new level of consciousness and thereby creation by holding thought and form as in DNA in an energetic pattern which dictates the new life or thought becoming form by its very shape. As you know, music and math and art all denote a vibration that is unique to the particular combination and design forming an energetic blueprint on the etheric level. We are designing a higher configuration which will lift consciousness to a unified new one mind which will incorporate human mass mind consciousness with the already unified consciousness of the natural world.

We are sharing this vision one mind at a time with all those who will spend unstructured time in our presence allowing us to lift and change the energetics of the old patterning and therefore rather than trans-forming we are trans-configuring the existing form to one of higher vibration. While the forms will remain, the ability to experience oneself as one with all life will enable God or ALL to realize itself as consciousness in matter and its separate components as a unified whole dependent on each individual facet for its very life. As we brought forth in *The Truth* According to Horses:

"There is a Golden Rule in your bible that says, 'Do unto others as you would have them do unto you.' That is because we are all individual cells of one enormous spiritual being. These cells unite to form organs and systems, and all are interdependent on the others to survive. The same thoughts and emotions travel throughout this being. Love that is held in its heart strengthens all of the organs and systems, and thoughts that are true and good benefit every cell. This being cannot survive without its lungs or its liver. All of these individual organs speak a different language; they have specific and important contributions to make for the life of the body, but they are all interconnected by the same intelligence, emotion and wisdom. We will all of us only be a fully actualized, complete, spiritual being when we know this truth and are united in understanding and in love, loving our neighbors as ourselves, because our neighbor is ourself—because we are one."

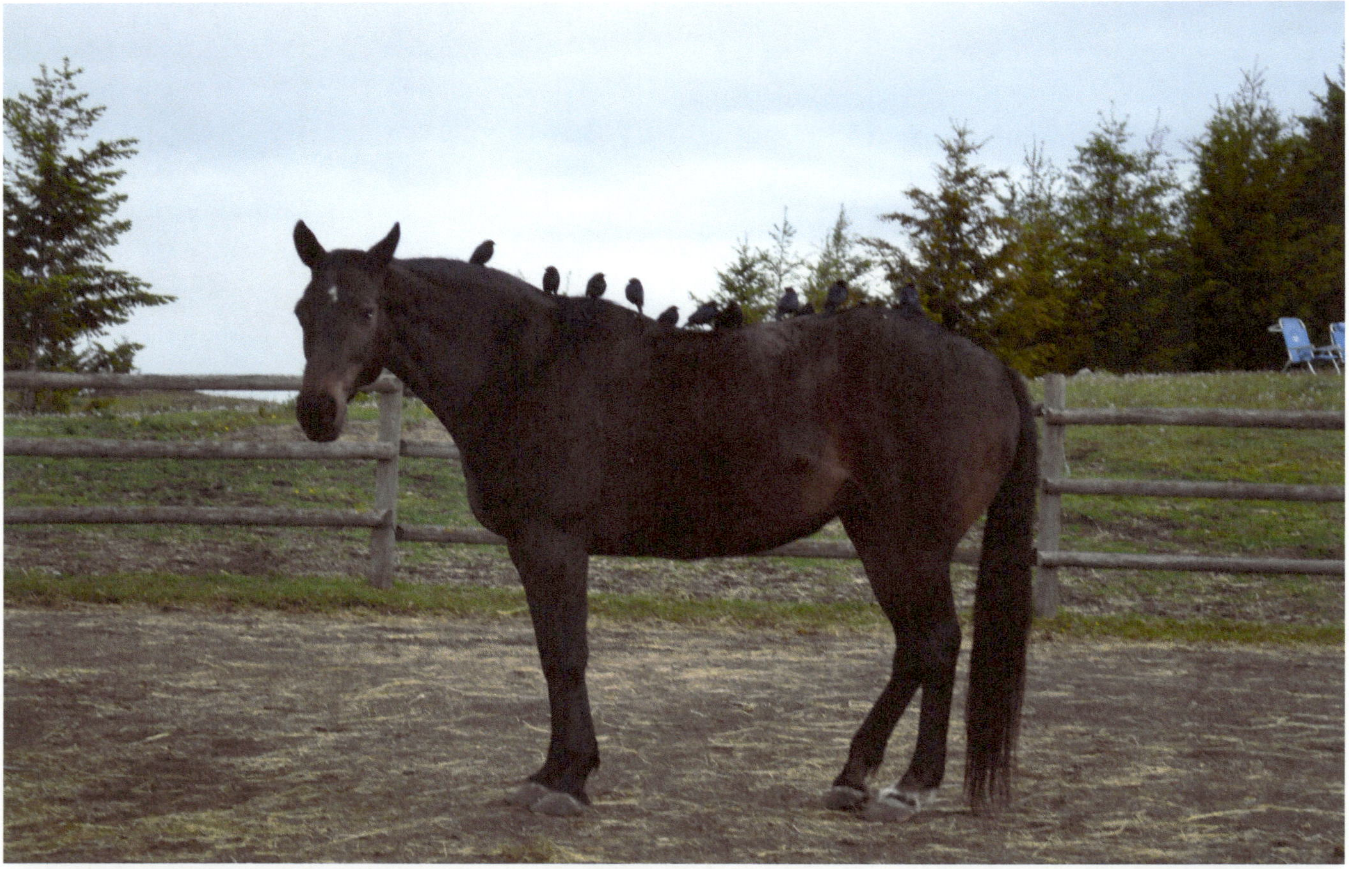

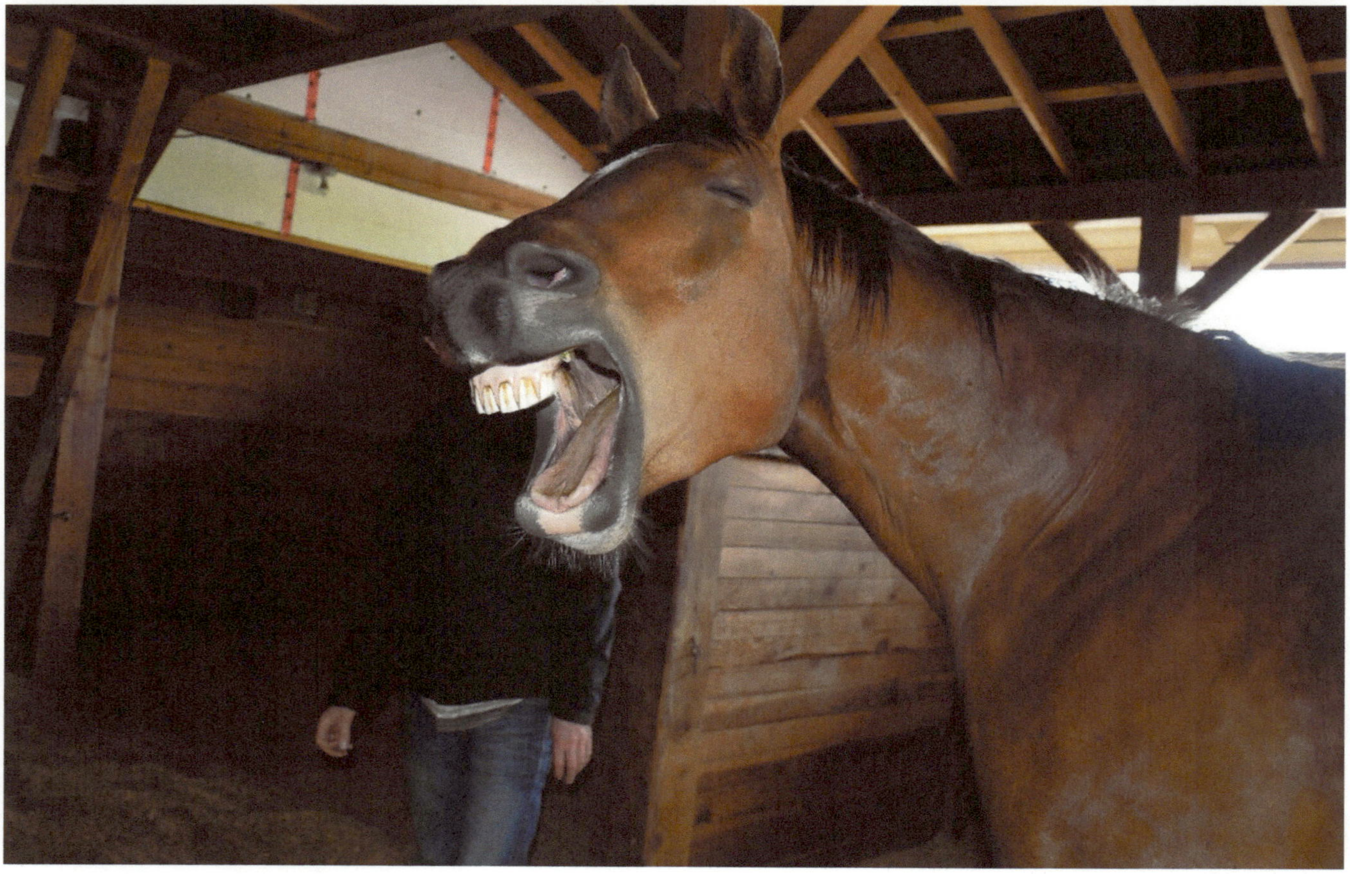

Miro healing sequence

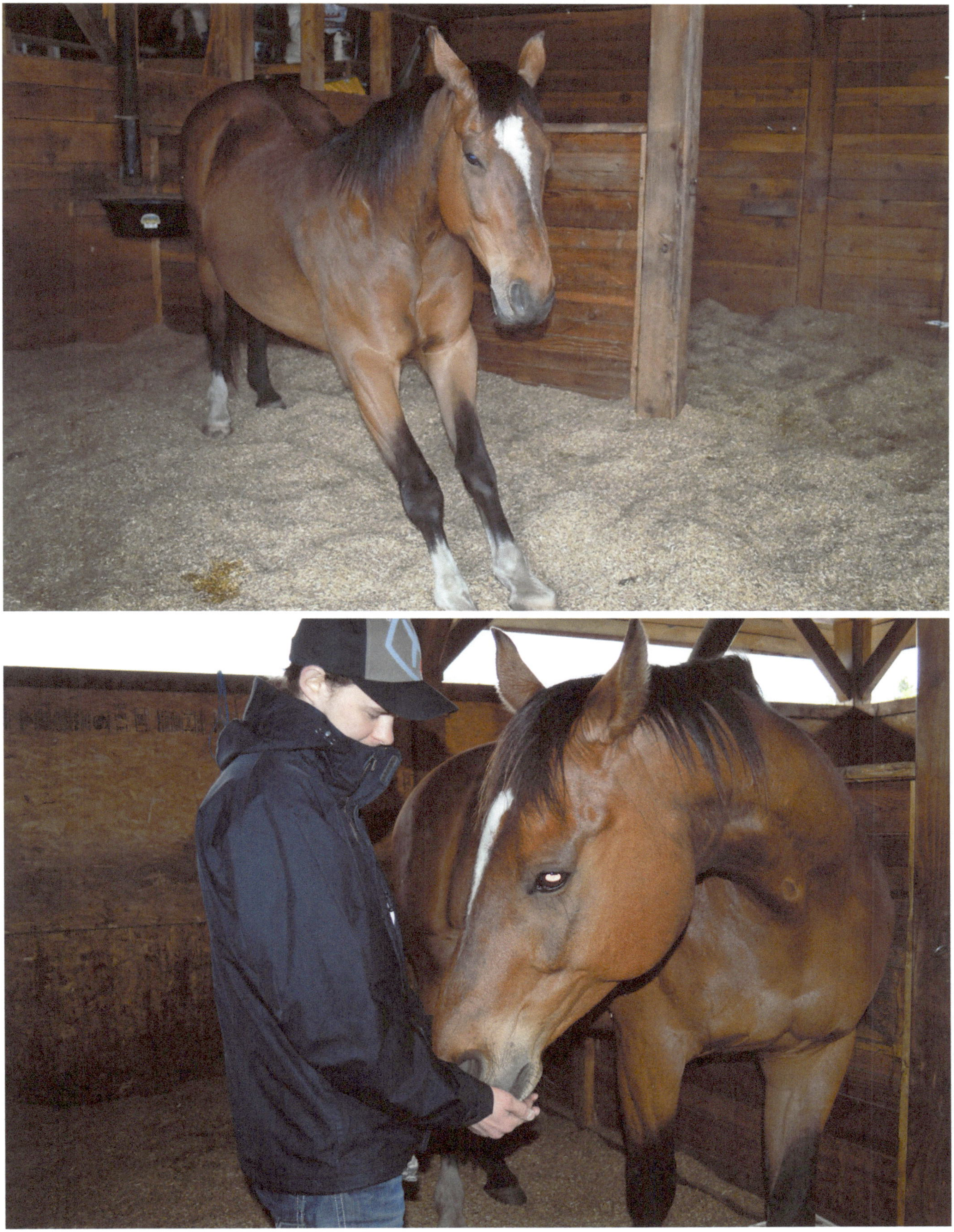

Miro healing sequence

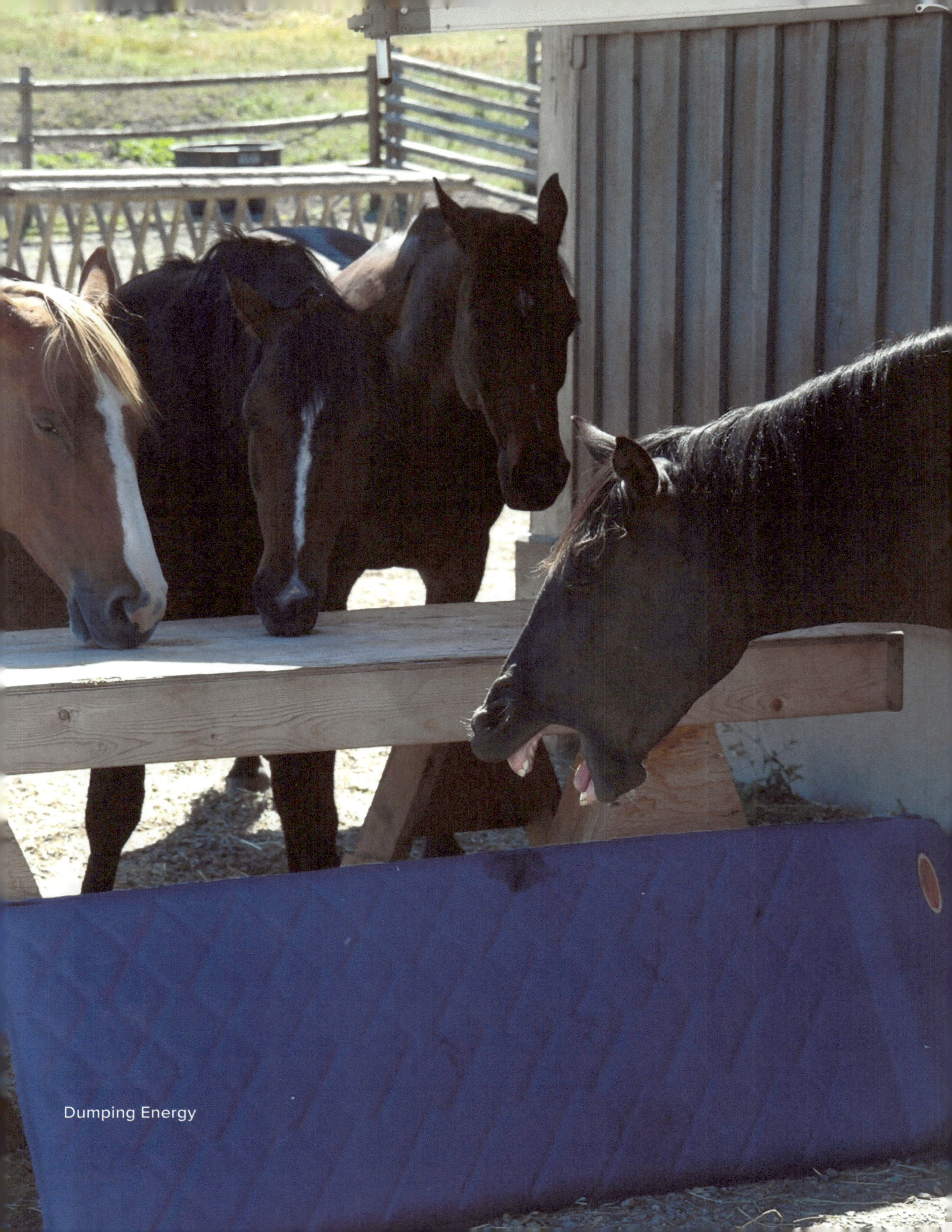

Dumping Energy

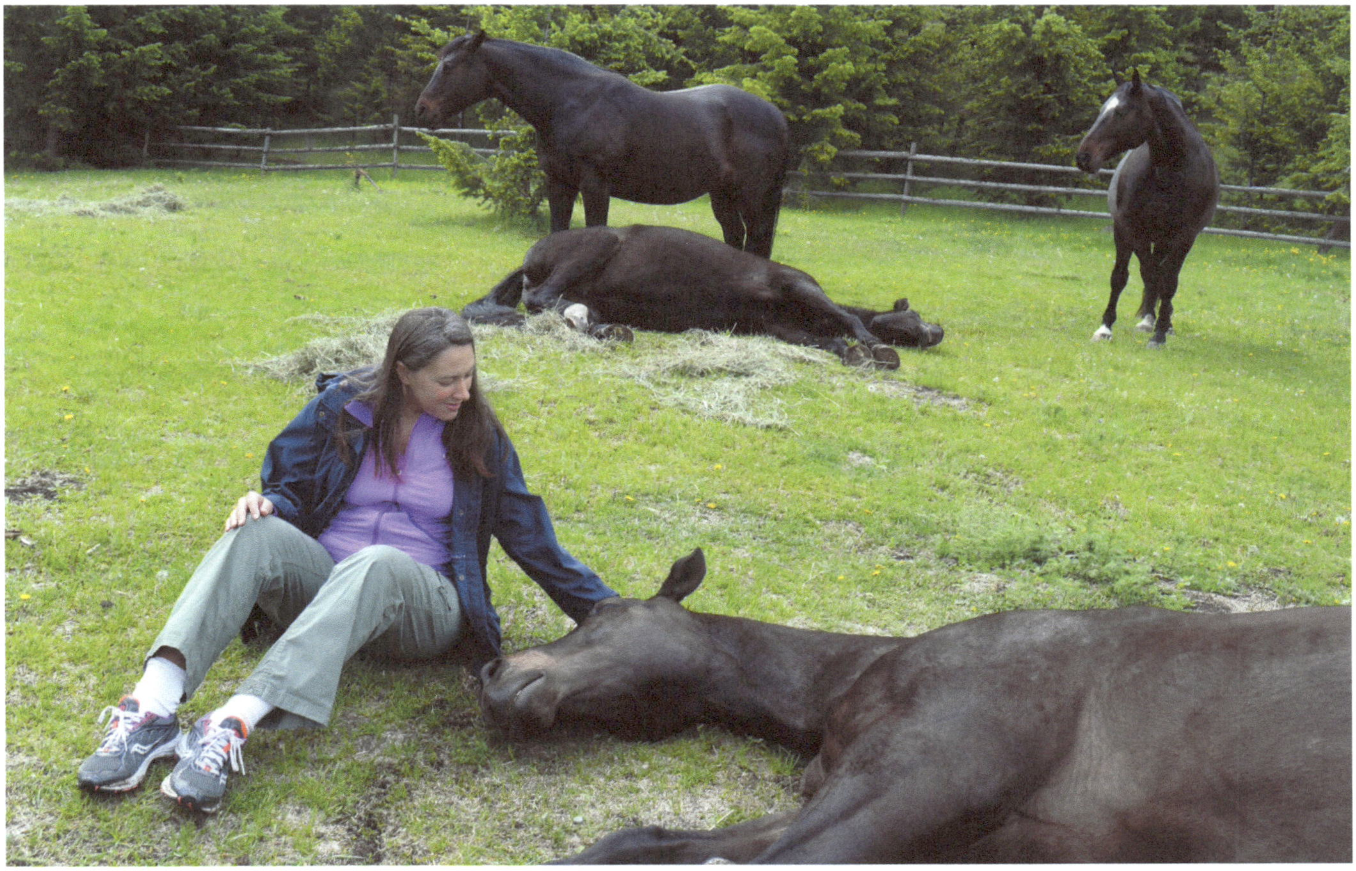

Happiness

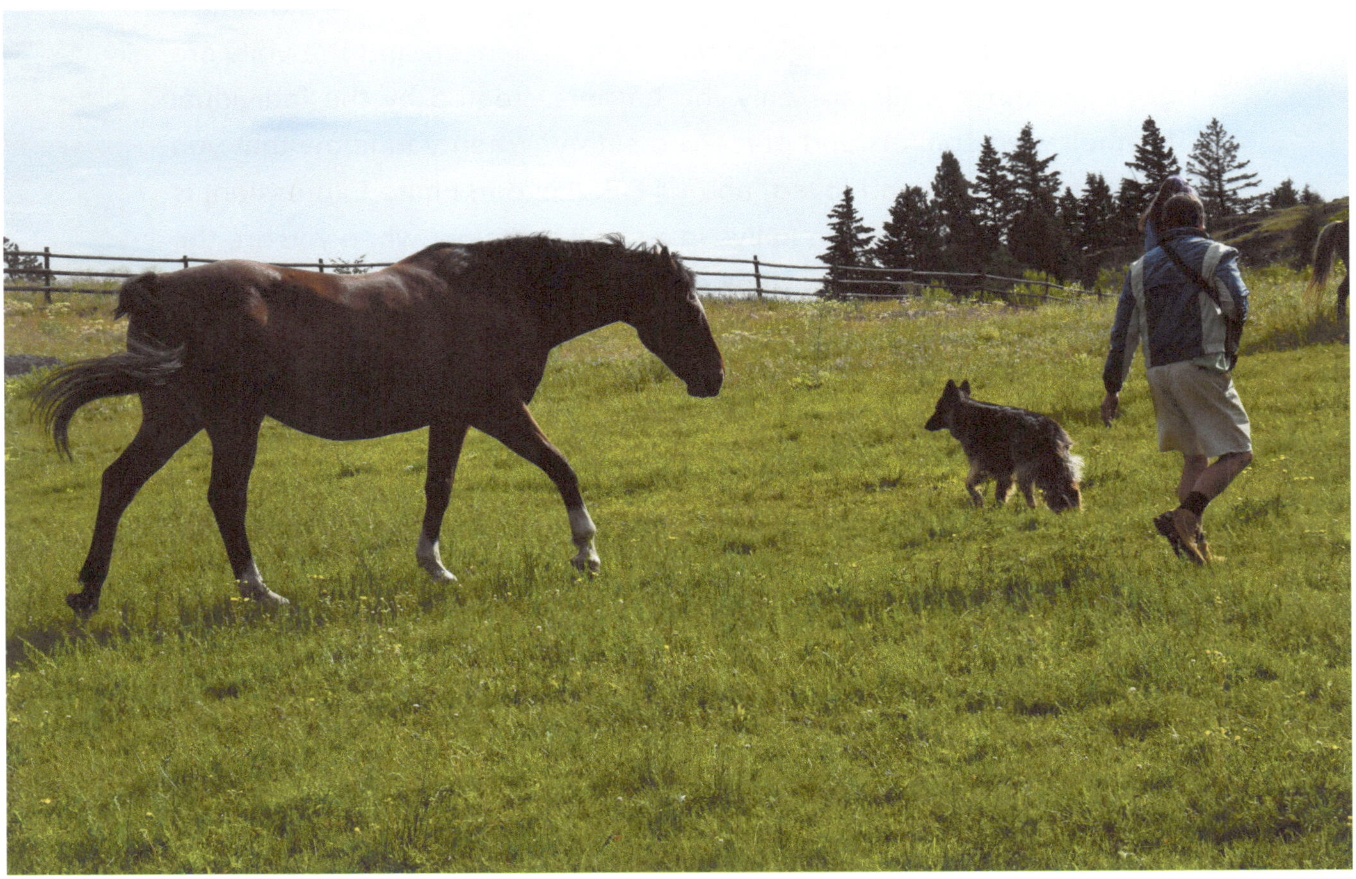

We are calling many to experience the Gateway that is available here on this higher frequency land and with the higher consciousness of the Herd. We are connecting not just to horse and animal consciousness, but to the One Consciousness of the universe from which all inspiration springs forth. We have been in deep meditation grounding the increased frequency of the highest consciousness that is now available to bring forth on Earth. There are those who receive with gratitude and those who are fearful and threatened by the changes. It is all your choice at which level and which dimension you focus on and there are no limits. Anything that can be imagined can be experienced and the veils are getting thinner. Veils are only the barriers created by the individual for their own comfort and perceived safety. When you know that you are eternally safe and loved, and L.I.F.E. (Love In Finite Expression) is forever there is no reason to live in a small container when you are the Earth and the sky. The joy of all creation is yours when you choose to allow it. Be Happy, Well, Creative and Forever Free.

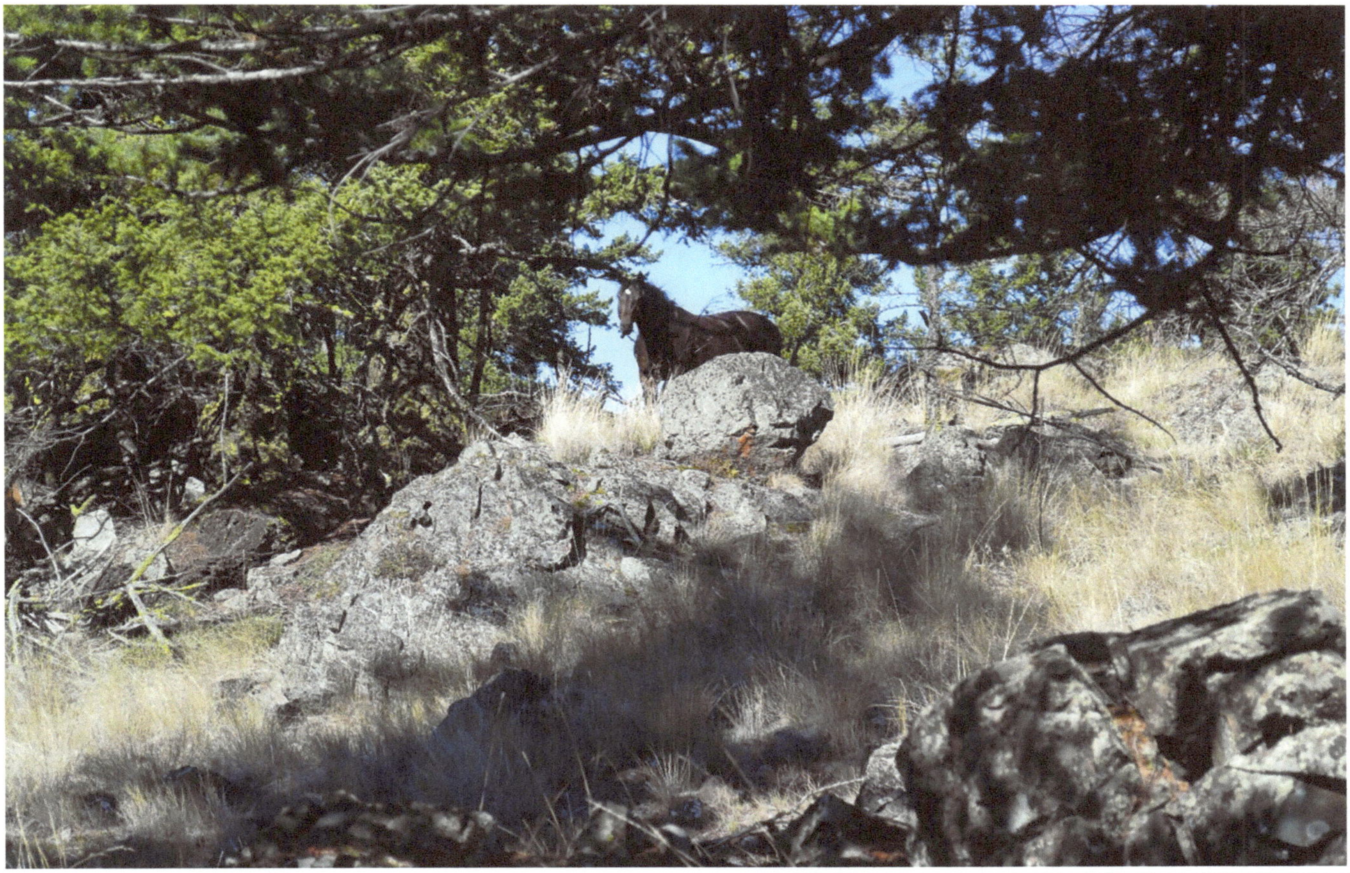

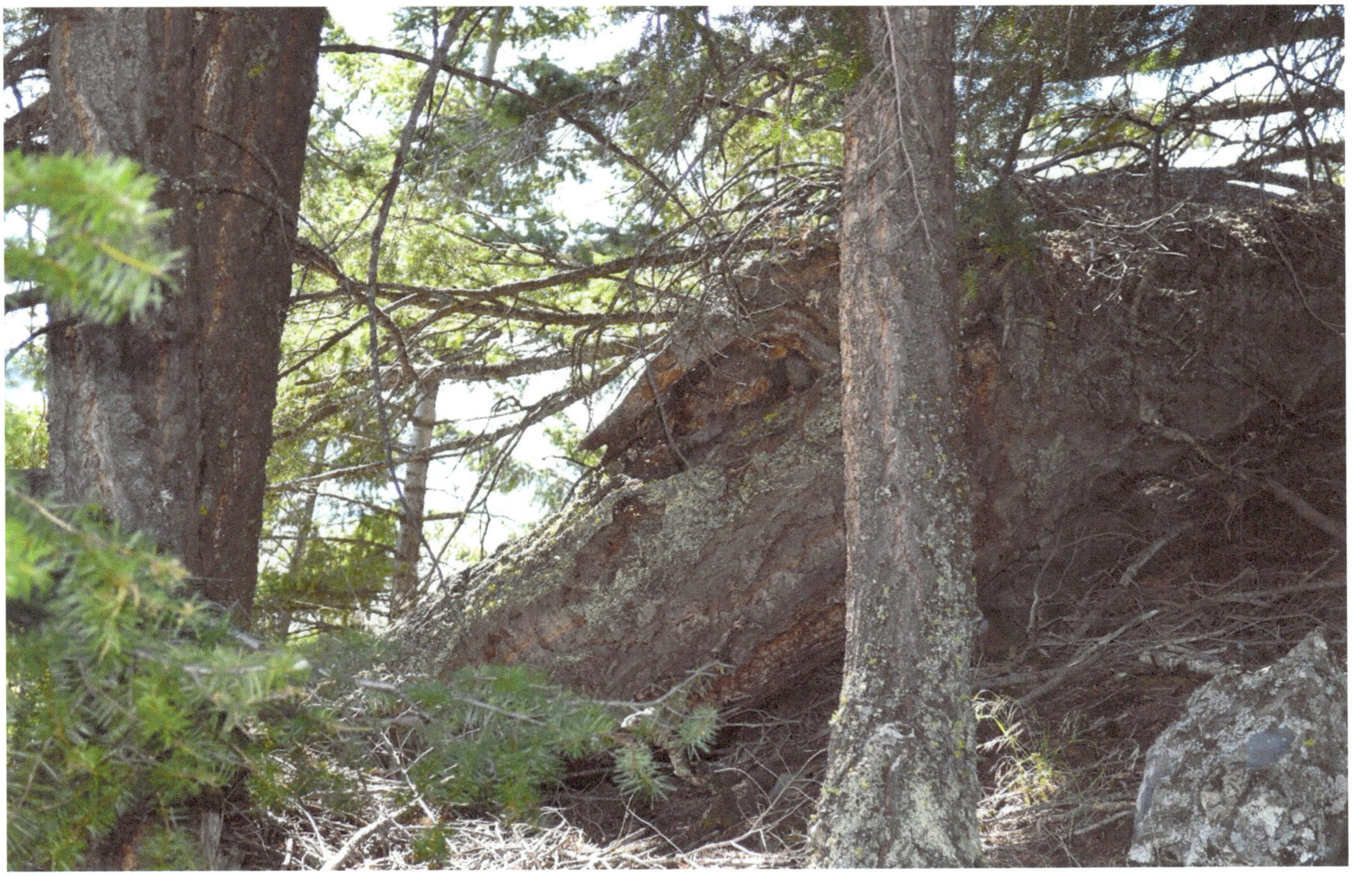

Dragon Energy is about Metamorphosis and Manifestation.

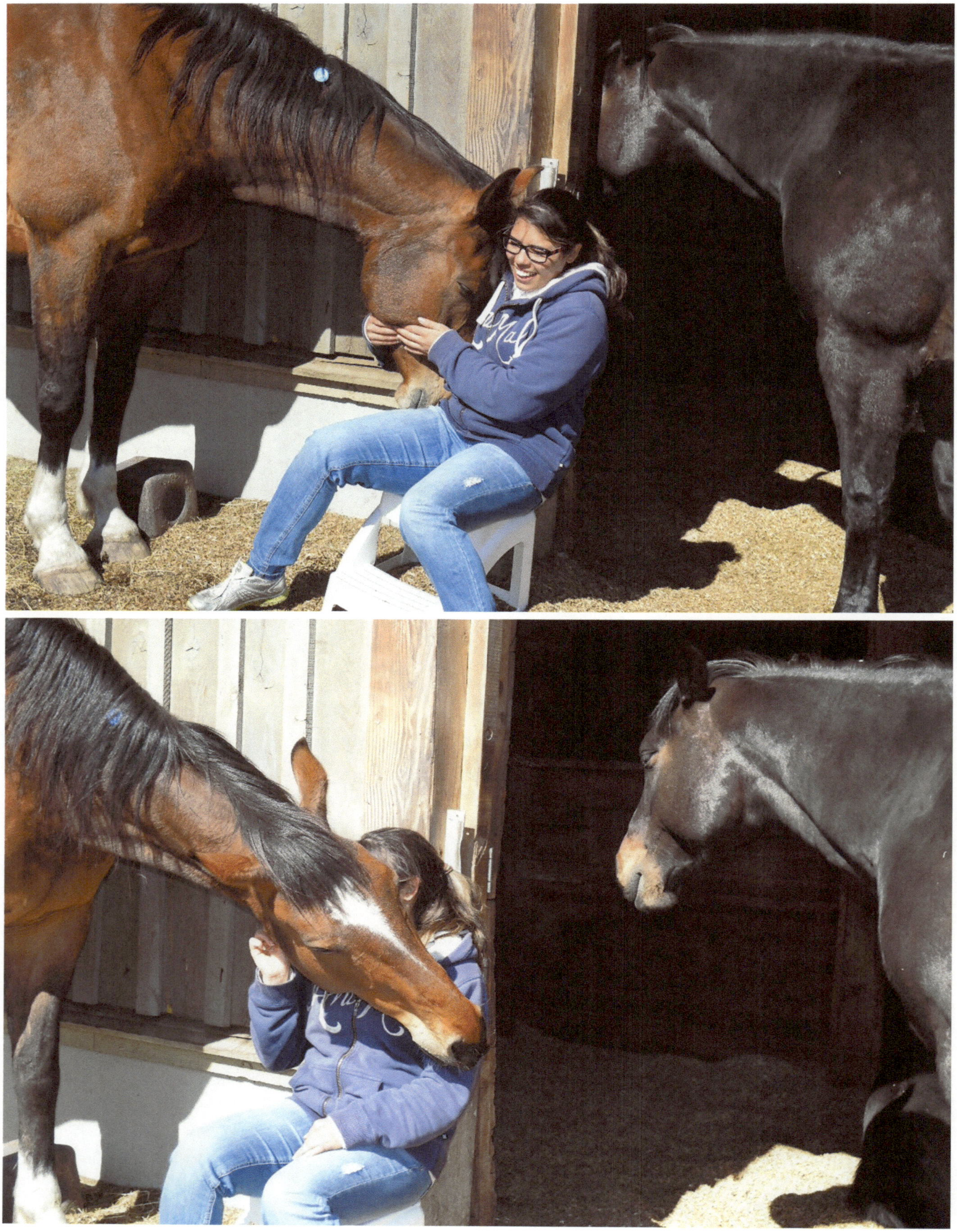

Major Healing for Ana

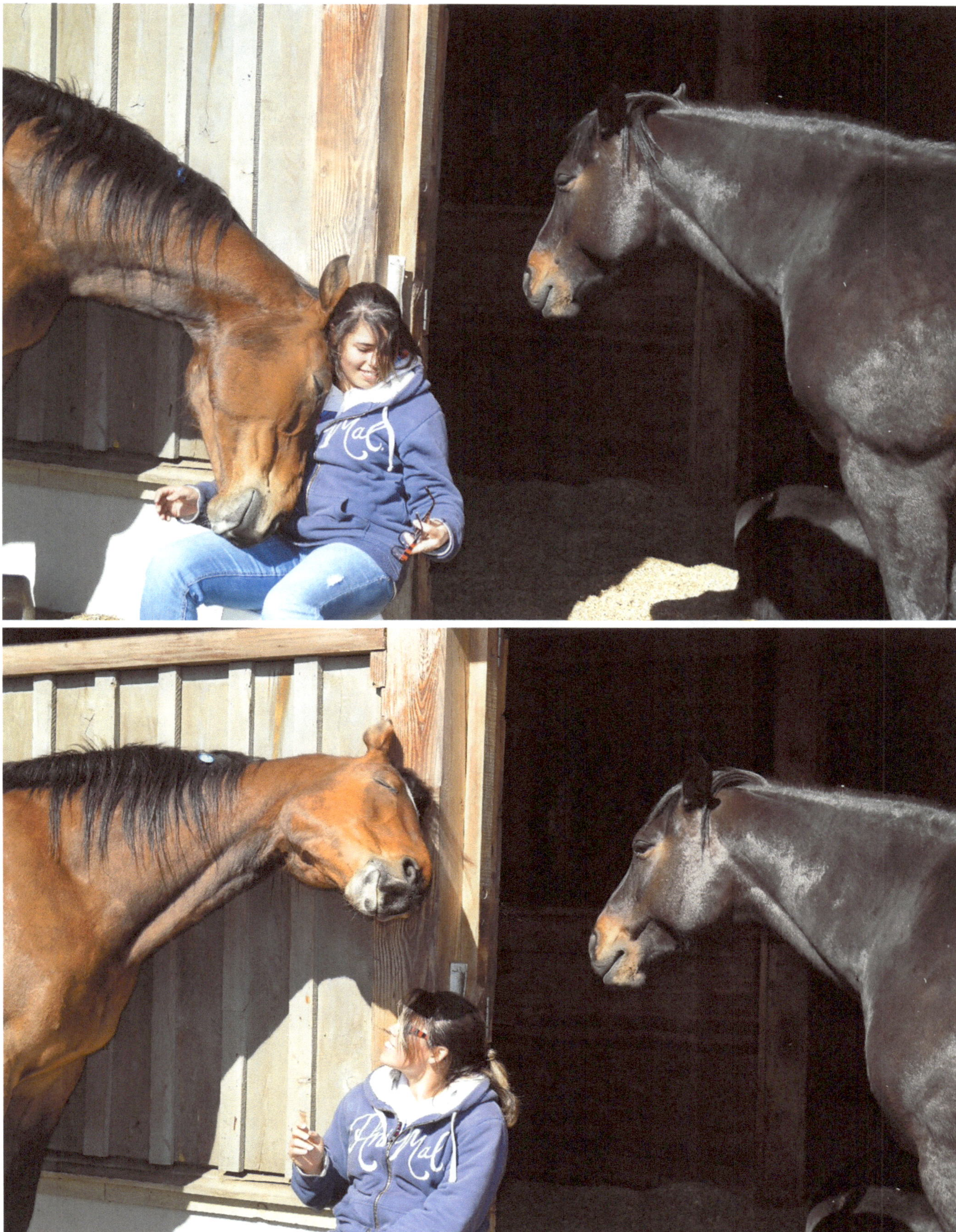

Major Healing for Ana

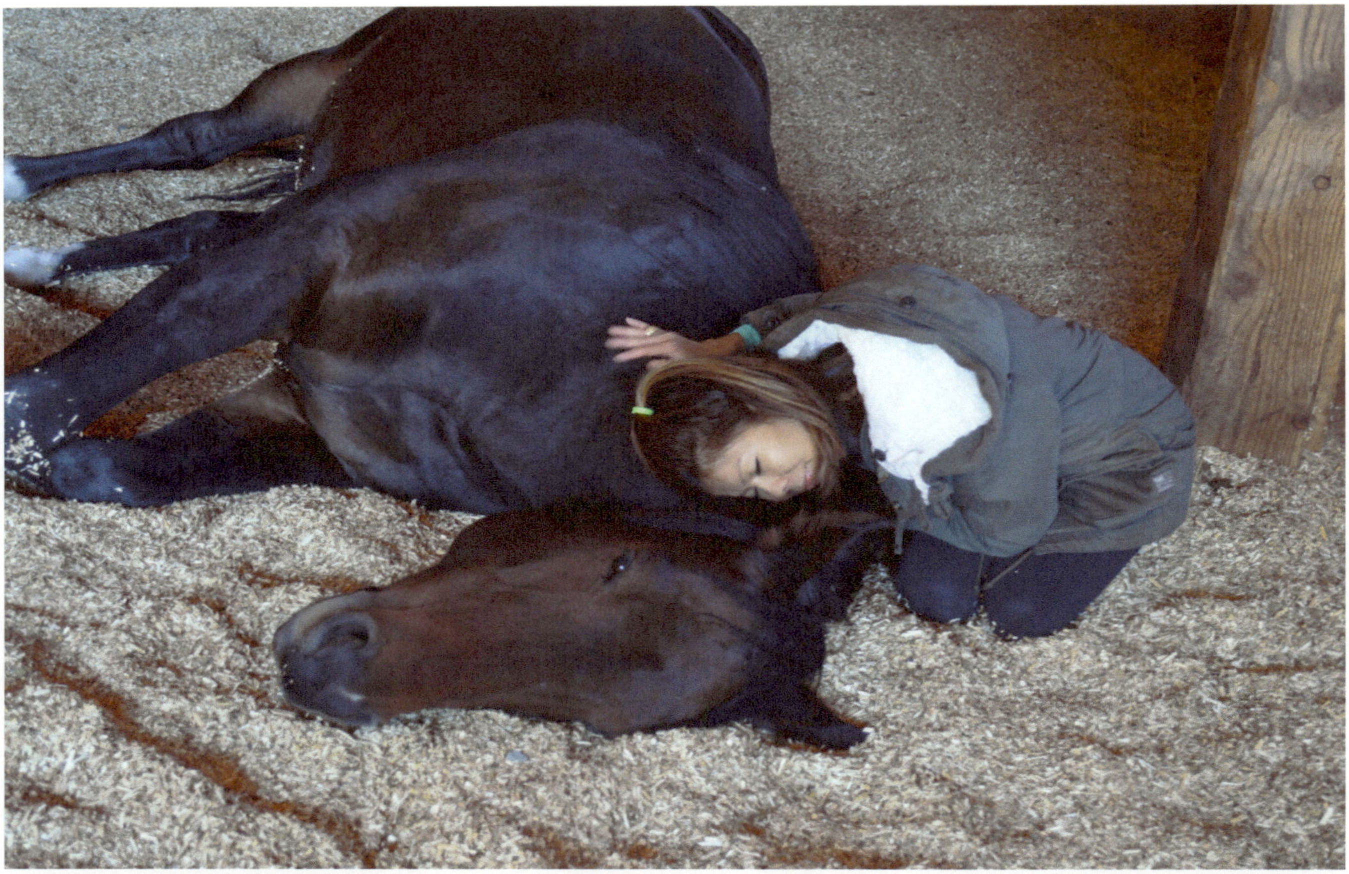

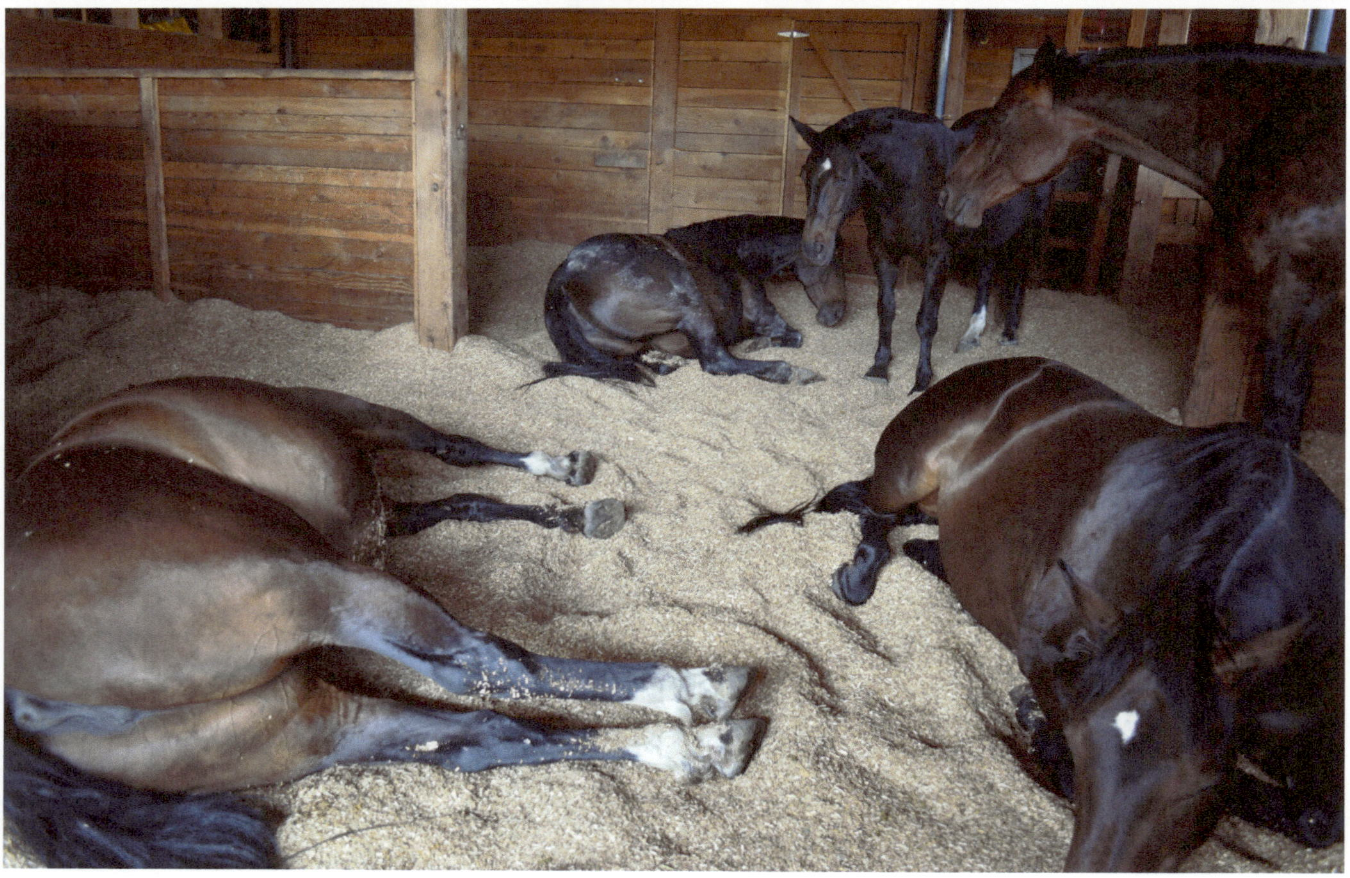

You know how humans talk about the tipping point in consciousness? It is as if we have scaled a tall mountain and are just going over the top, gathering momentum to run down the other side. It has reached exponential proportions and the understanding of consciousness has changed. Now it is up to the rest to happen upon the resultant shift, which those on the mountain have already made. WE ARE ALL ONE. Our thoughts are in fact your thoughts on a higher consciousness level. Yes, you have human bodies and brains and we have horse bodies and brains but our essence is the same and when we connect on a higher consciousness level (made possible by your realizing the veil is of your own making) we can play together in MIND, in CREATION, celebrating the JOY of UNCONDITIONAL LOVE. You are yourself and everyone else, you are the out-picturing of your thoughts. Just like the feather seeds, your thoughts take wing when they spring forth from your hearts and mingle with the heart of creation, the ALL. Come to us and FEEL the WONDER of truly remembering who you were before you set the limits, and remember why you set those limits (so that you could declare your separateness). Where did that separateness get you? It is fortunate that the veil is of your own making and it will dissolve in a thought—ONE thought which will change you from the point to the wave of ALL L.I.F.E.—LOVE IN FINITE (because you can change it in a thought) EXPRESSION. (Because it is just a temporary expression of your focus, but is infinite in its re-expression)... forever.

Liz just reiterated our message: "Walk your dream." Horses are calling around the world to ask people to follow their hearts and intuitive guidance rather than their ego-brains' collective consciousness of fear and limitation

The horses have just told me this year is an 8 and to research the number and sacred geometry on the net. (The year 2015 in numerology is an 8 which signifies the omega, the infinity sign, the new beginning of the Earth when God had made it in the bible, rested and it began, and the day of the resurrection of Christ, also the name of Christ was 888.

From the "hidden energy science of Sacred Geometry":

"We live in a remarkable time, when deeply hidden spiritual knowledge and practices are now being publicly released. Great Spiritual Traditions around the world are making public much of their formerly secret knowledge, including in recent years the Mayan, Tibetan, Taoist and European Rosicrucian traditions. These world traditions are the caretakers of our birthright: our shared human legacy of accumulated spiritual wisdom.

Perhaps the most fundamental—and essential—part of this spiritual knowledge is to know the actual patterns, the energy blueprints, which everything in creation is based on. Everything is based on a specific pattern; knowing that pattern unlocks the ability to make full practical use of it. This is true whether speaking of patterns of higher spiritual realities, psychological and behavior patterns, energetic patterns or actual structures manifested in the physical world. Only through our knowing these spiritual and energetic patterns can we achieve our full potential: to become conscious, responsible creator-beings in the world. In recent times, the term we use to describe these core spiritual, energetic and physical blueprint patterns is Sacred Geometry."

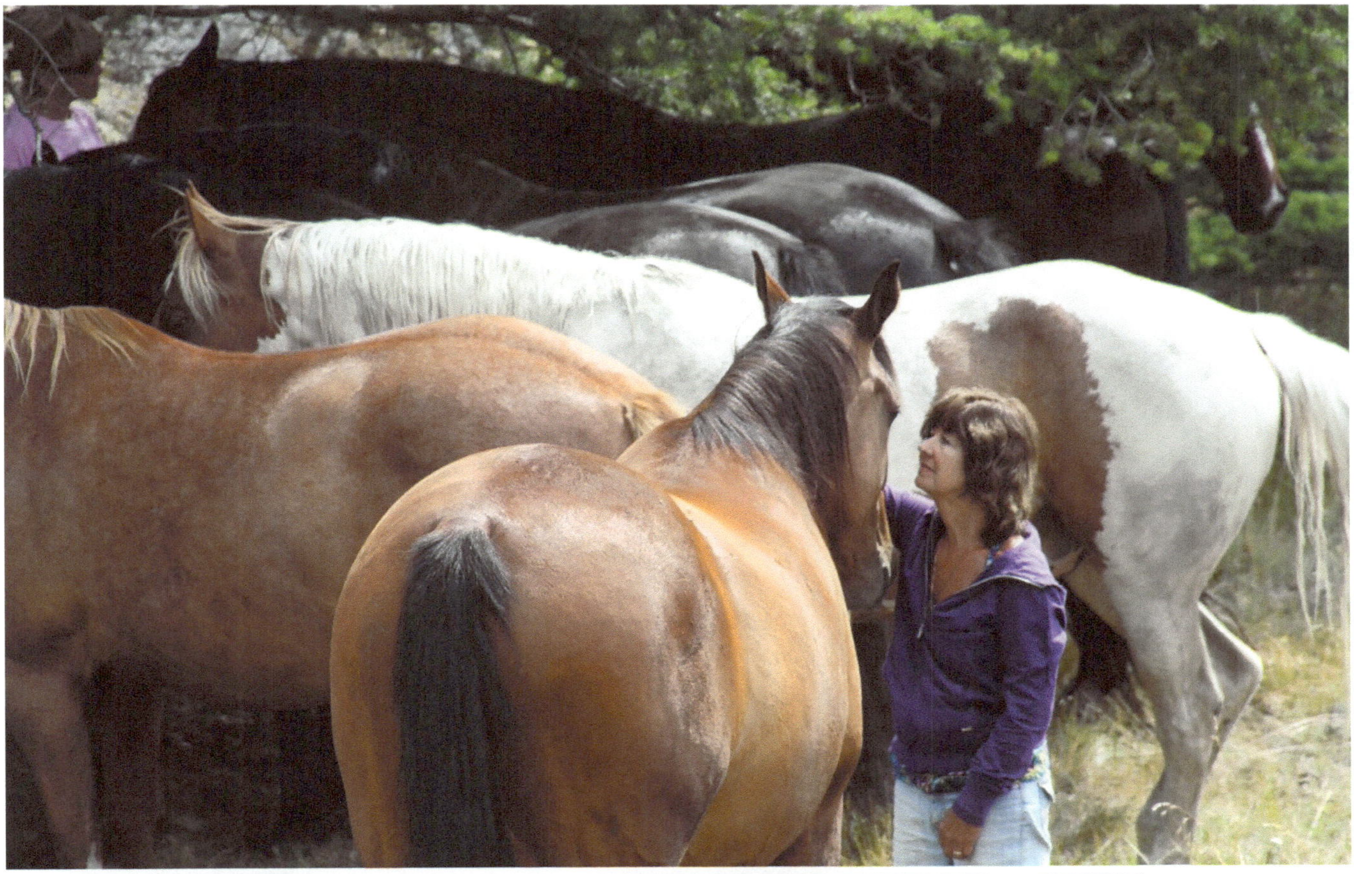

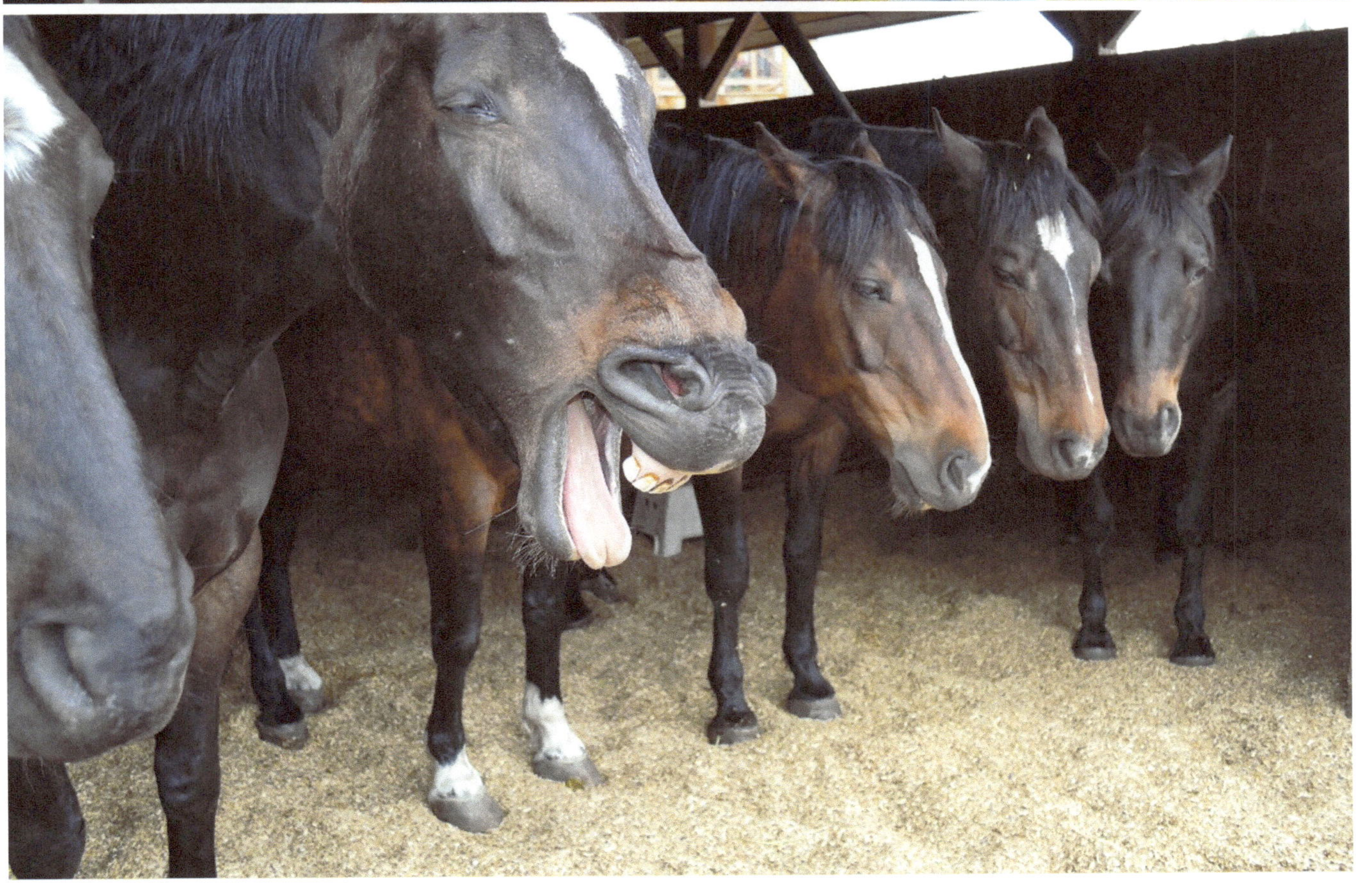

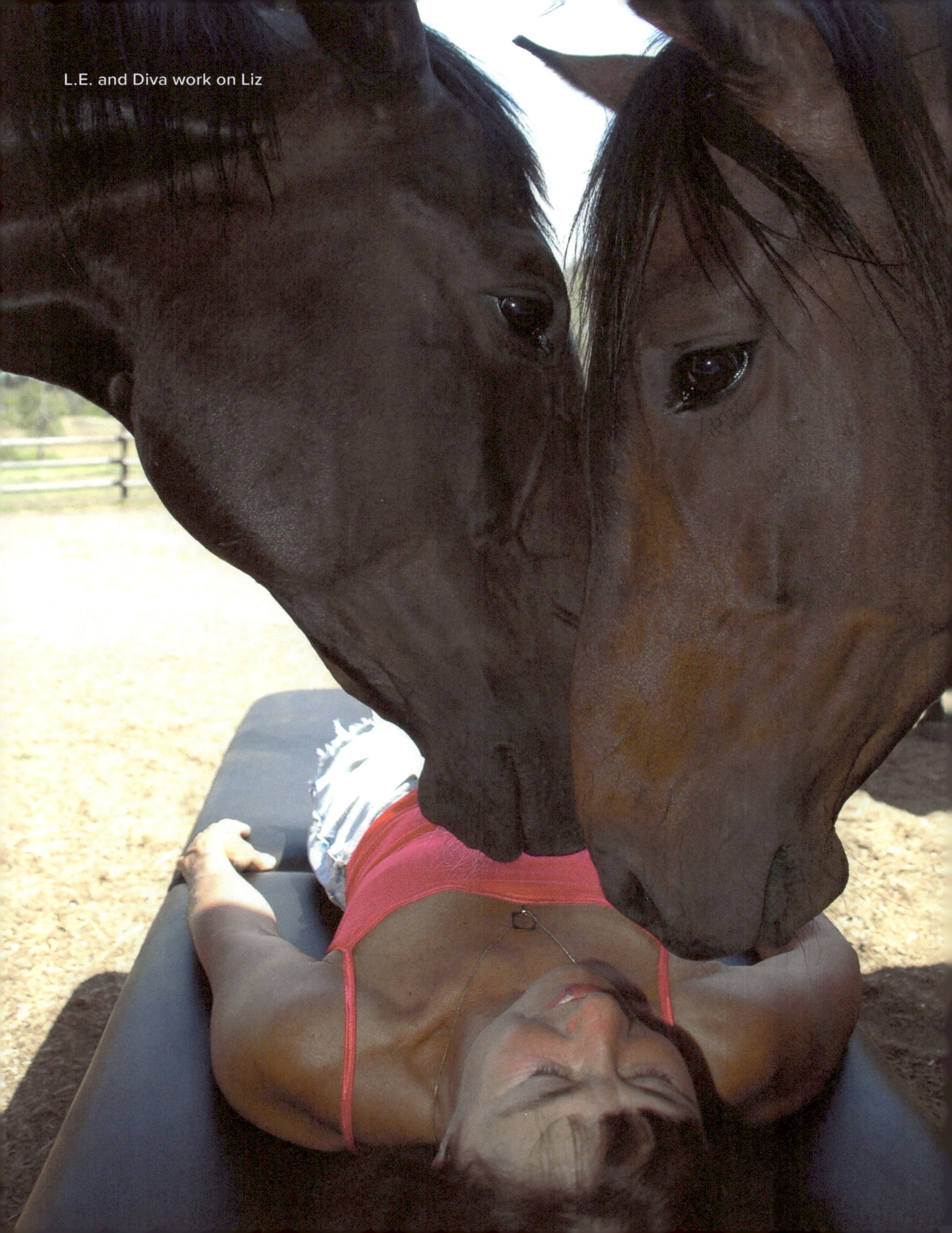
L.E. and Diva work on Liz

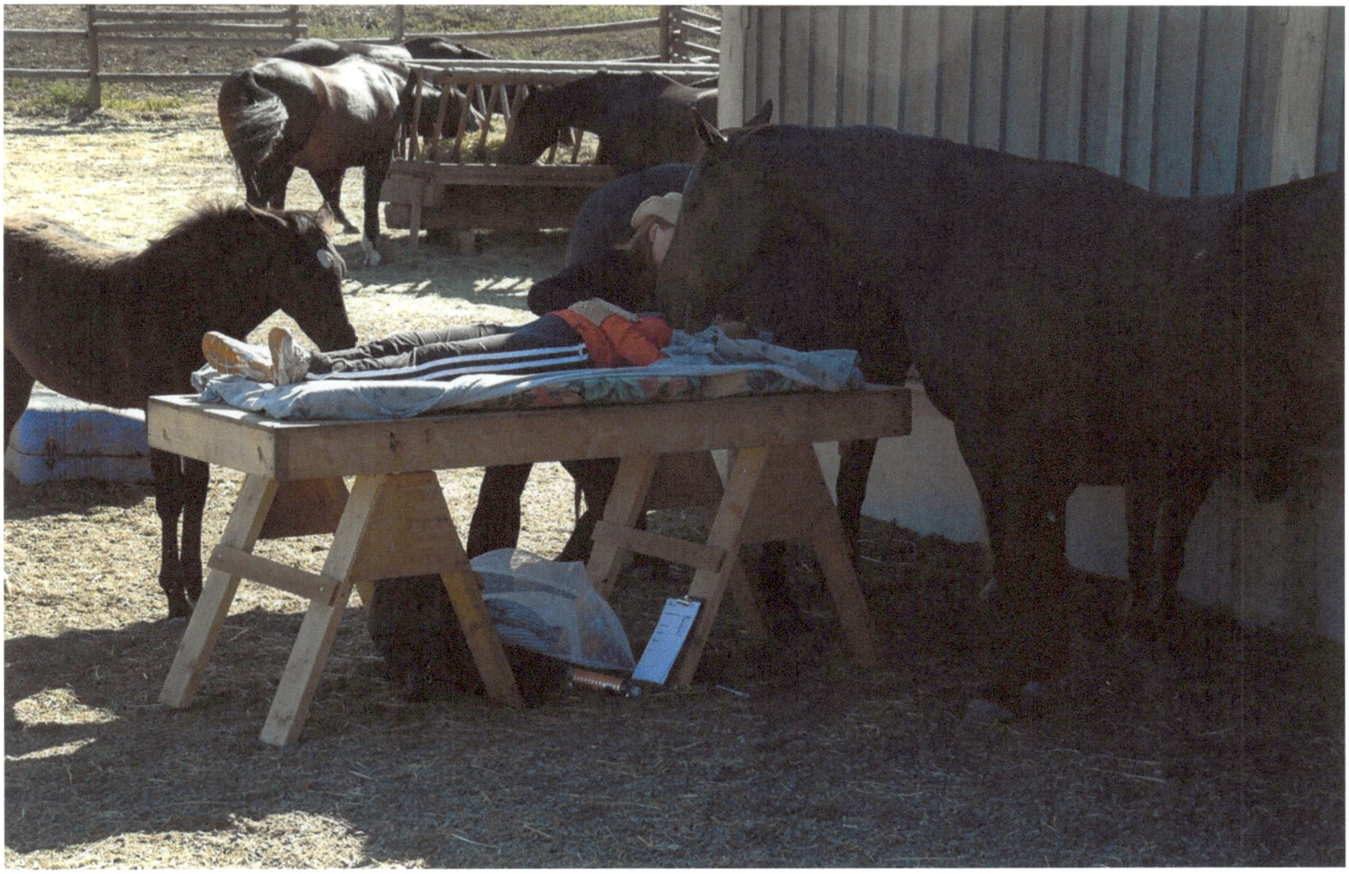

Several times now, the Herd has been instrumental in bringing forth new life. Women who have long attempted to conceive have come to visit and the horses are able to act as liaison between the unborn child and the soon to be mother. One particular woman had tried in vitro for 12 years and Prospera, at 3 months old and newly from spirit, was able to sort out the blockage. On the land we discovered a pregnant tree (which we had never seen before) with her name on it (notice the angels on the branch) and a rock with an embryo in its belly. Shafts of light were abundant and Prospera lifted up her '"Expect Miracles"' hat three times to announce the news. We now warn women who Prospera is paying a lot of attention to, just in case they don't desire a child!

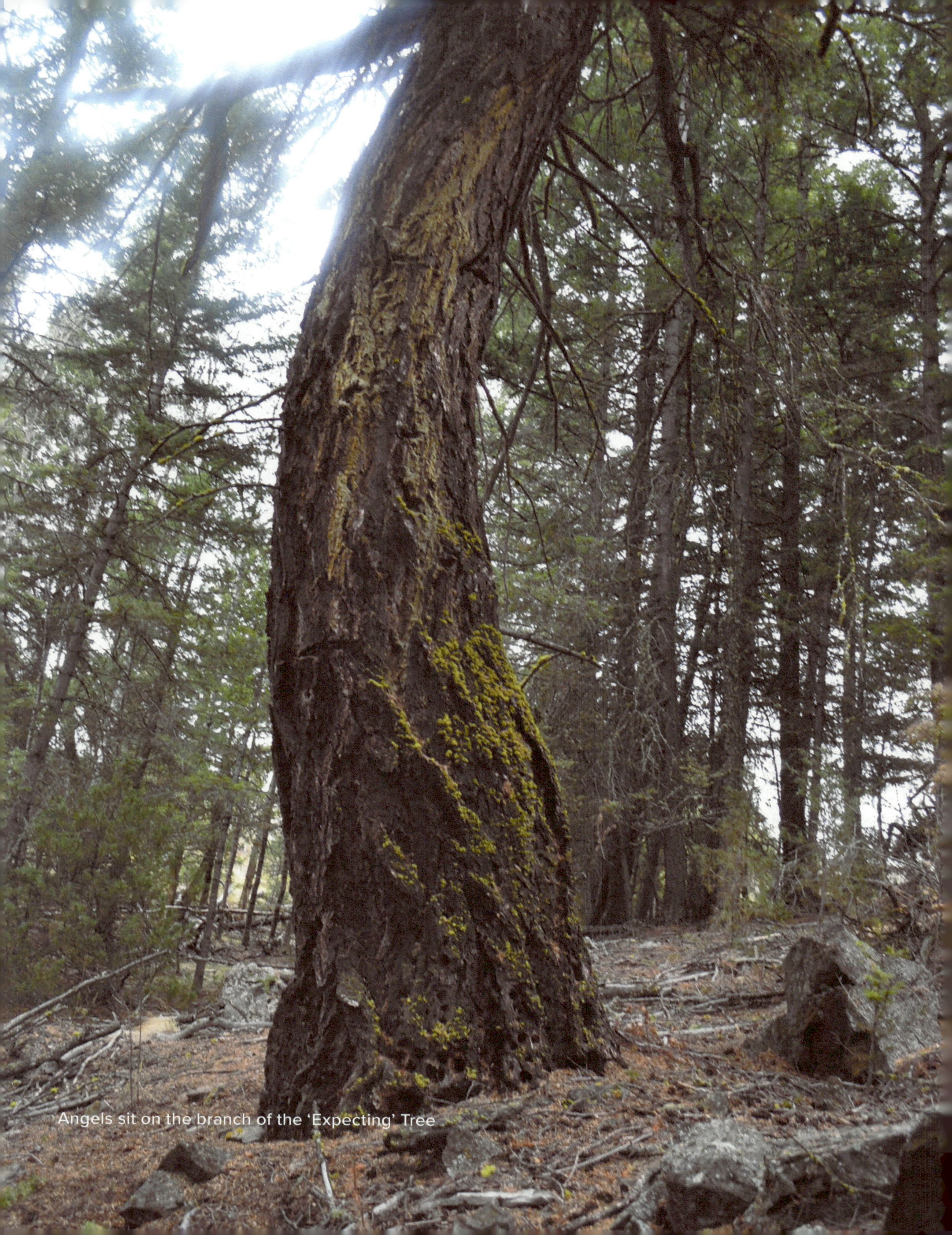

Angels sit on the branch of the ‘Expecting’ Tree

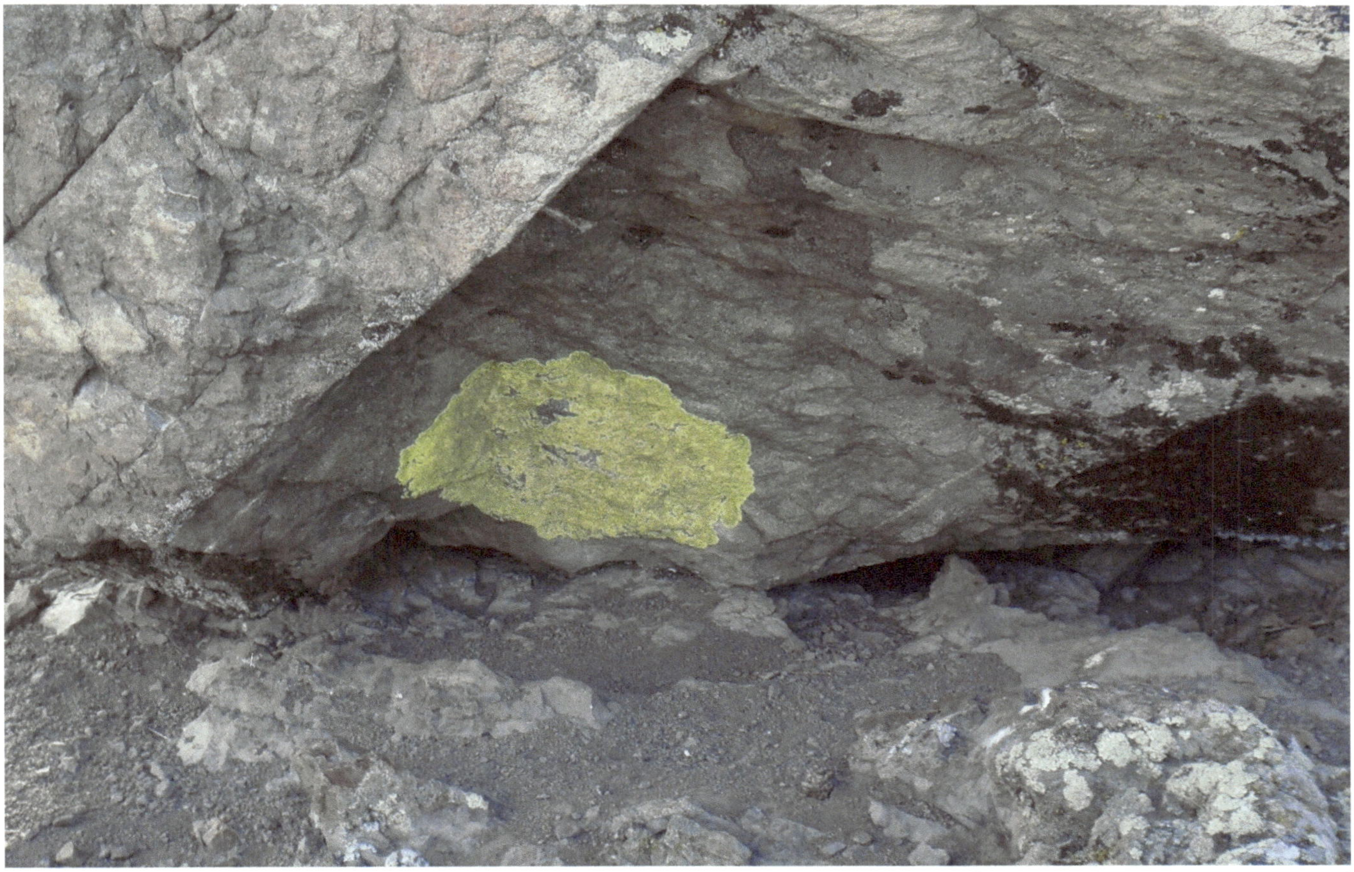

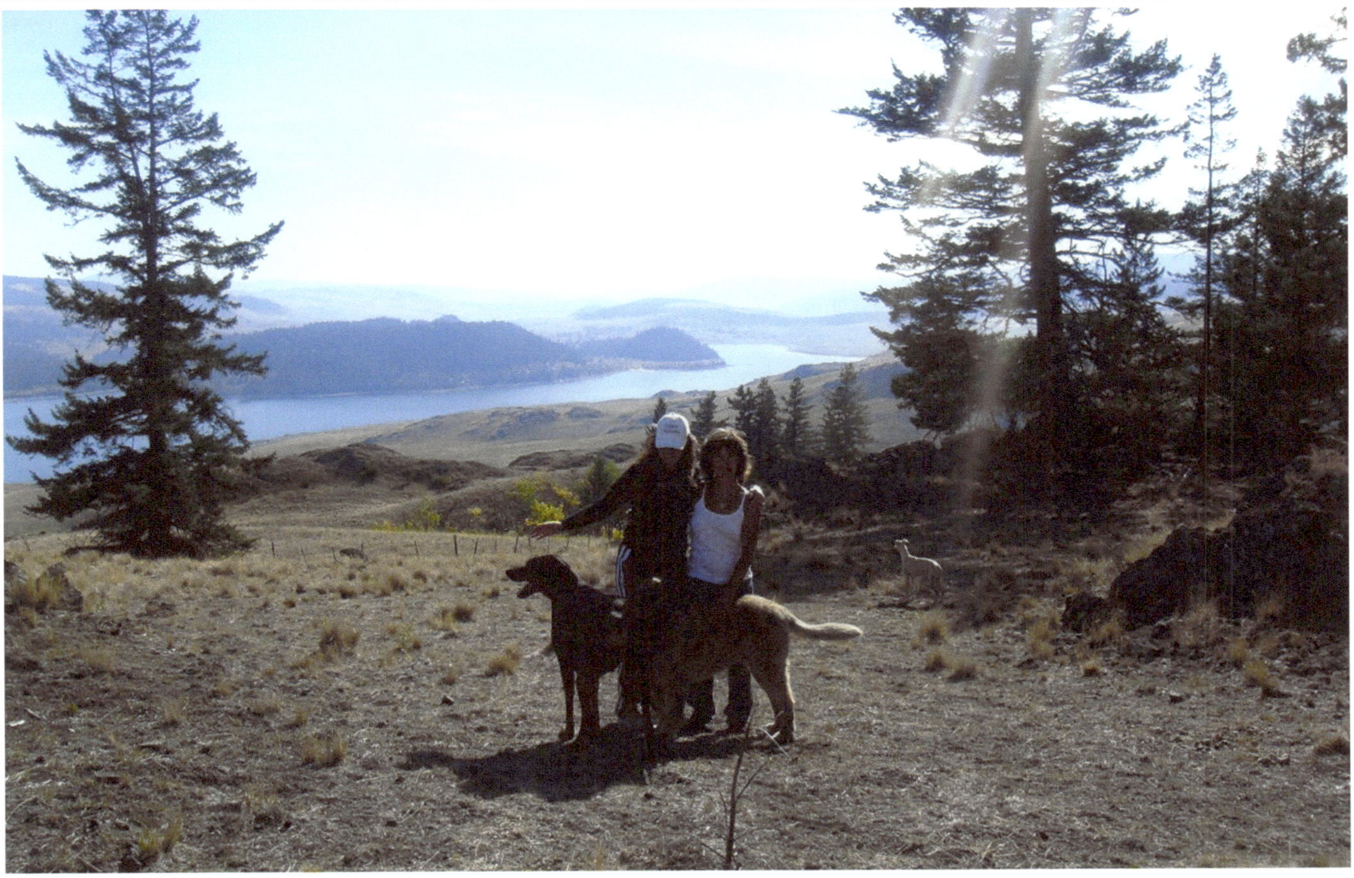

Embryo

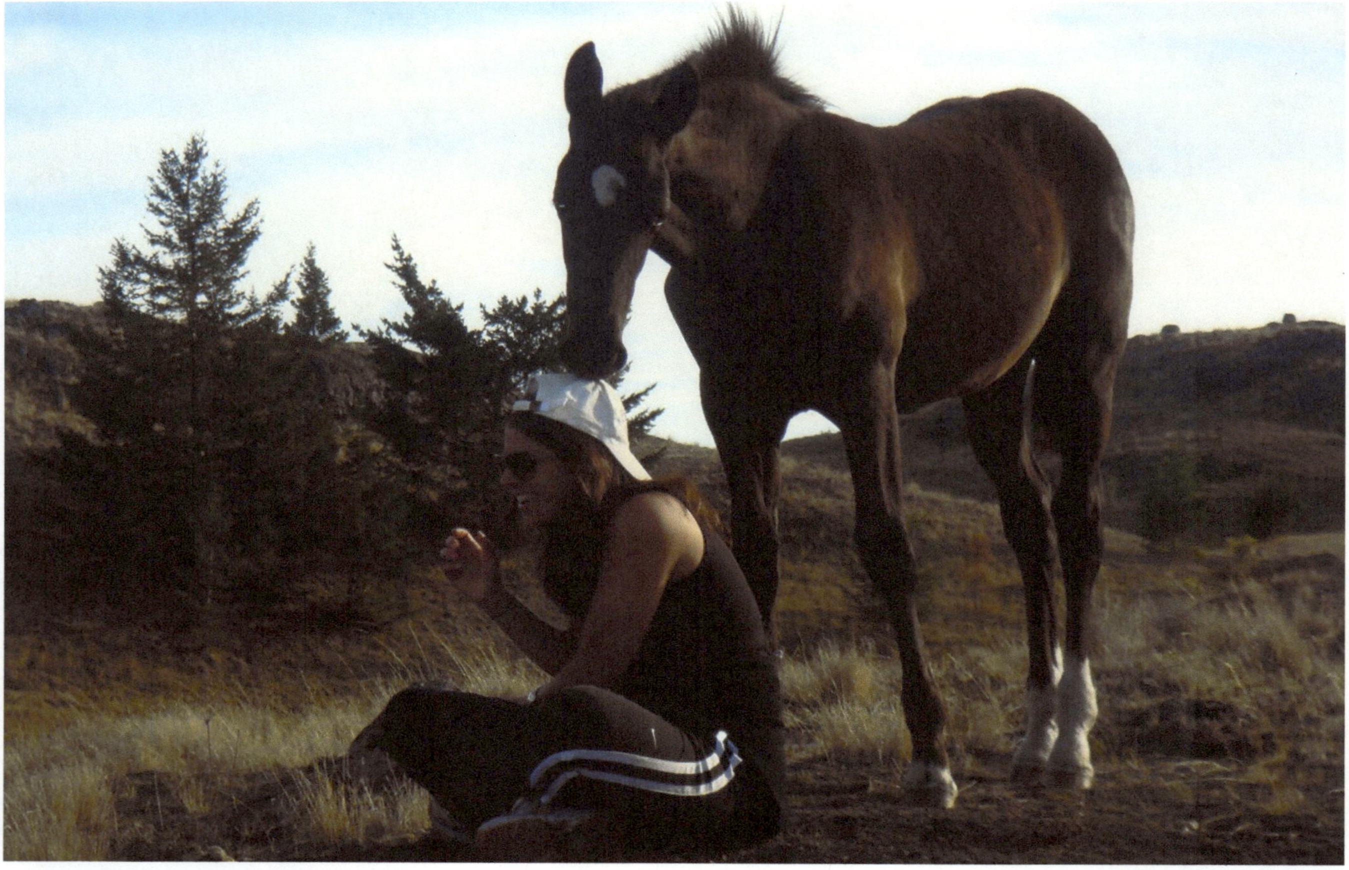

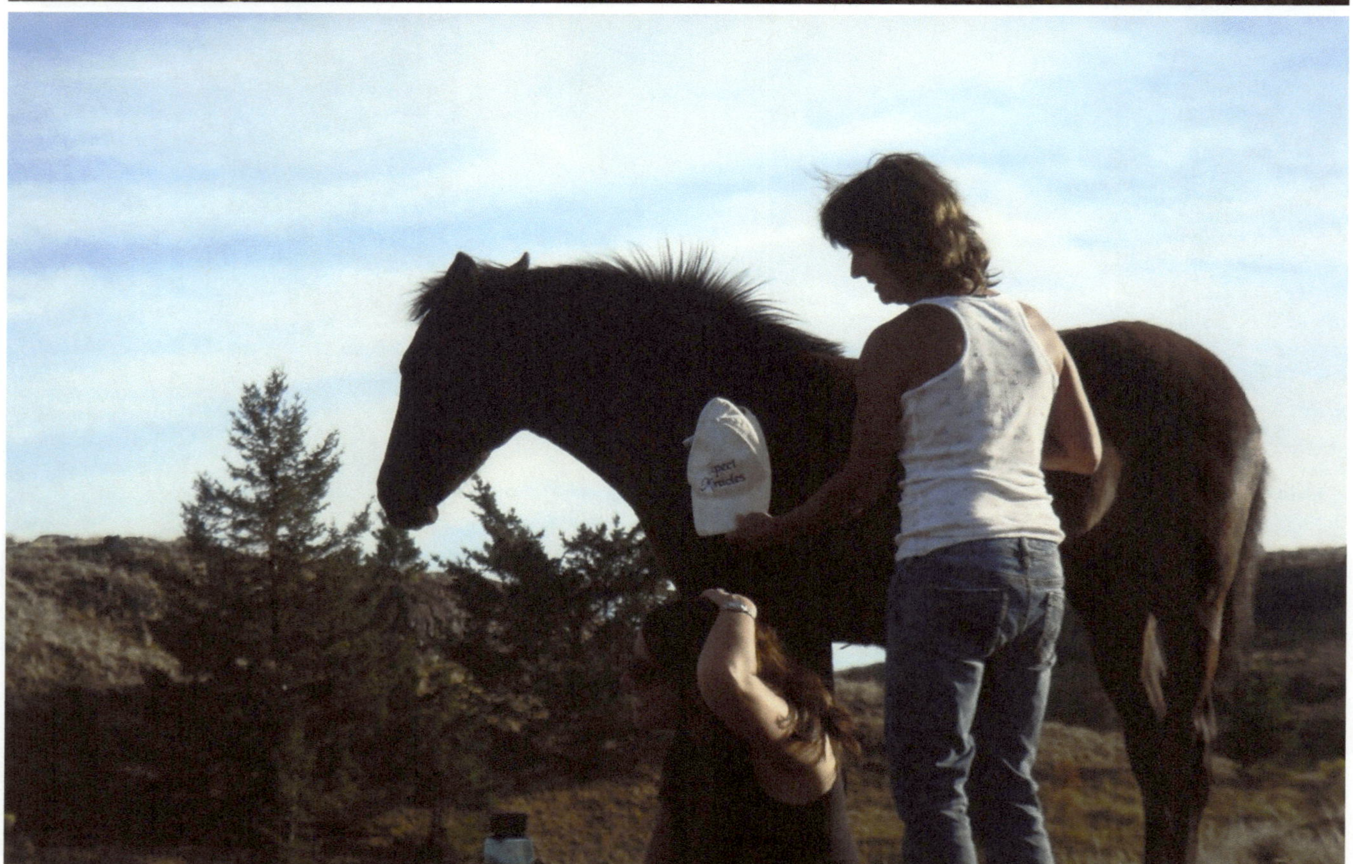

Expect Miracles!

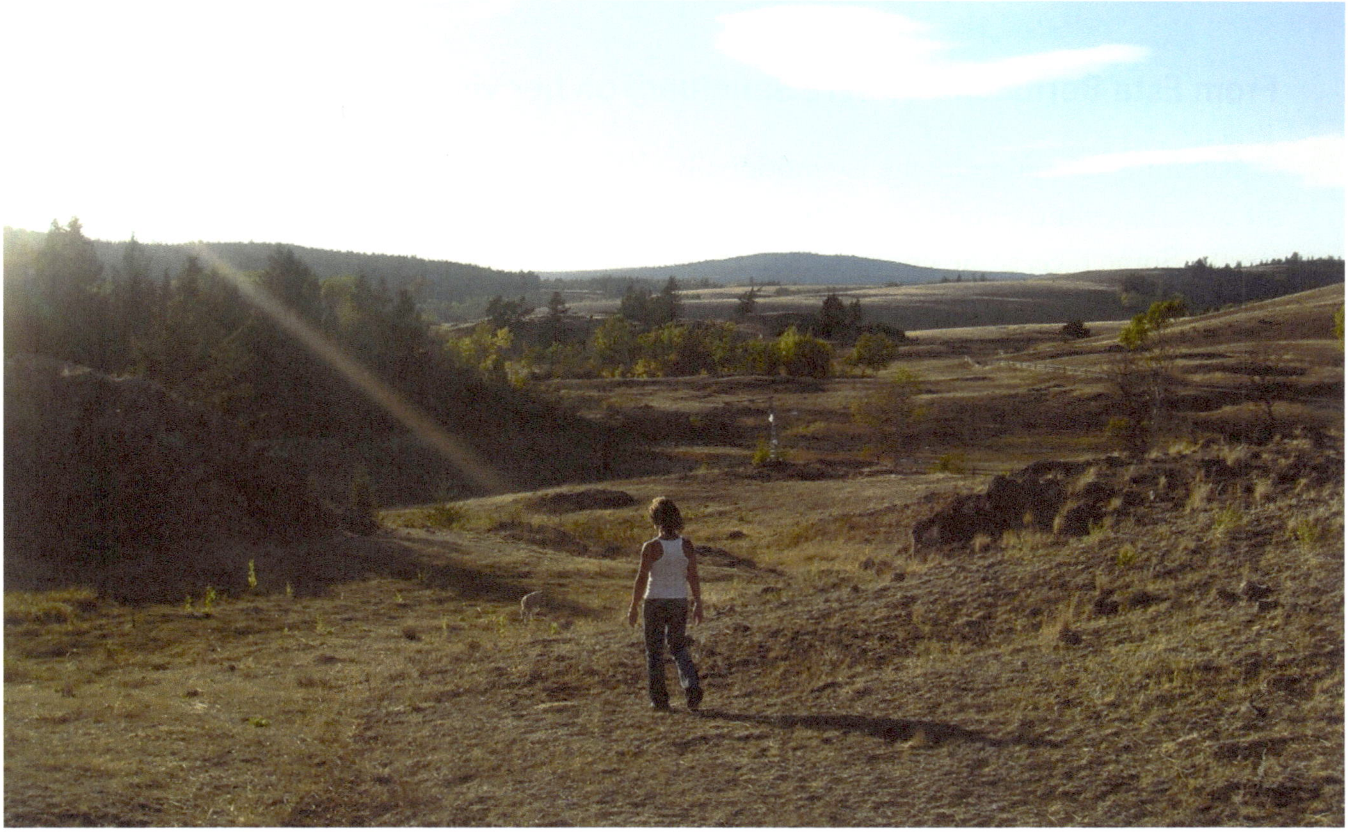
Sperm Clouds and Rays

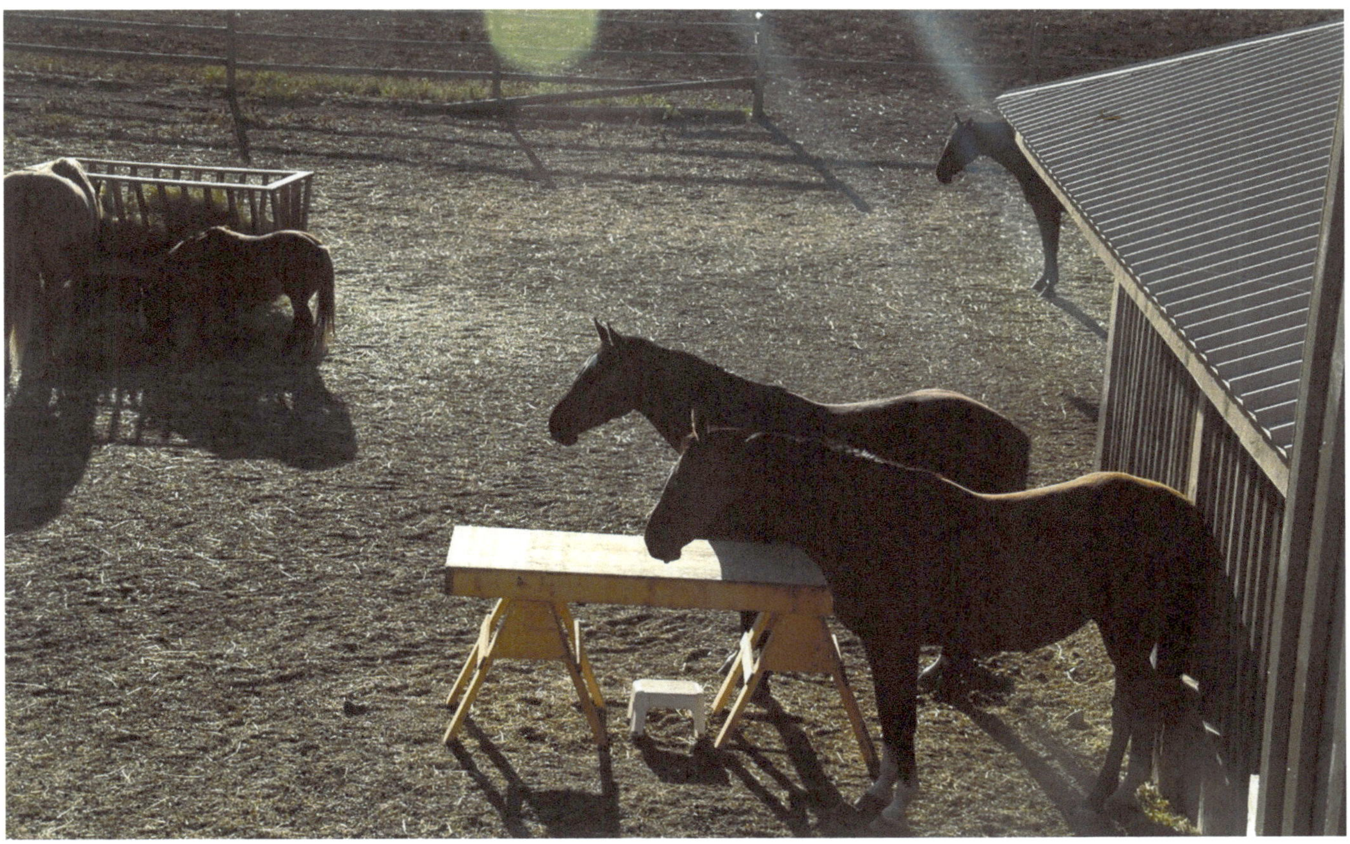
Crystal and Miro holding space for Heidi

From Esta Bernstein, Saffyre Sanctuary on her visit:

Running an equine rescue is emotionally challenging to say the least. I assist horses all over the country and have seen every aspect of the horse-human relationship imaginable. Some nice, some not so nice. But rarely, if ever until now, have I had the opportunity to be surrounded by people who ARE aware.

In April 2013, an animal communication session between me, medium Lisa Larson and a horse that I have never seen or heard of, was the beginning of my advanced spiritual journey. This horse, Lava Lady, an emotionally distraught racehorse in Florida, was very concerned about the wave of emotional disconnect between horses in captivity, their environment and their people. She knew what "Zen Horsie" was, but I could not envision the entirety of what that meant.

At that time, I did not have a complete understanding of what she was saying, nor did I have any idea about what "equine consciousness" was. A few weeks later I received my *Equine Wellness* magazine and glanced through it, noticing an article about Equinisity Retreats. Eight weeks later when I finally had time to pick up the magazine and read it, I immediately went to Liz's website and KNEW I was going. Lava Lady from a distance smacked me upside the head and said "idiot—I have been trying to get you to look at this for weeks now!"

The journey that Lava Lady sent me on turned into a total transformation of how I view everything. The horses at Equinisity gave me a complete and total understanding of what it is like to live at the "Fourth Level of Consciousness," where everything is connected, All is one, one is All, and the illusion of physical life. I can never look at the world through the same eyes that I arrived with.

During an awareness exercise, we had to feel a horse that we were drawn to, look directly in their eyes and explain what we heard. Magic, one of the horses came up to me immediately and put her eye right next to mine.

Looking deeply I heard her message: "See your reflection in me, as I see my refection in you. I am you, you are I, and we are one." She then showed me a picture of a tin can string telephone. She stuck one can on my forehead at my third eye, and the string connected ran through her heart, and subsequently through every other horse heart of the Herd. When it reached the last horse, the string and the can shot up into the sky and disappeared into the clouds. I then heard Magic say, "Now you can hear. Listen to and through your heart, see the soul in every entity."

The things these horses teach you are so simple, so pure, so basic, and we as humans have been programmed to forget. The time has come for all of us to remember.

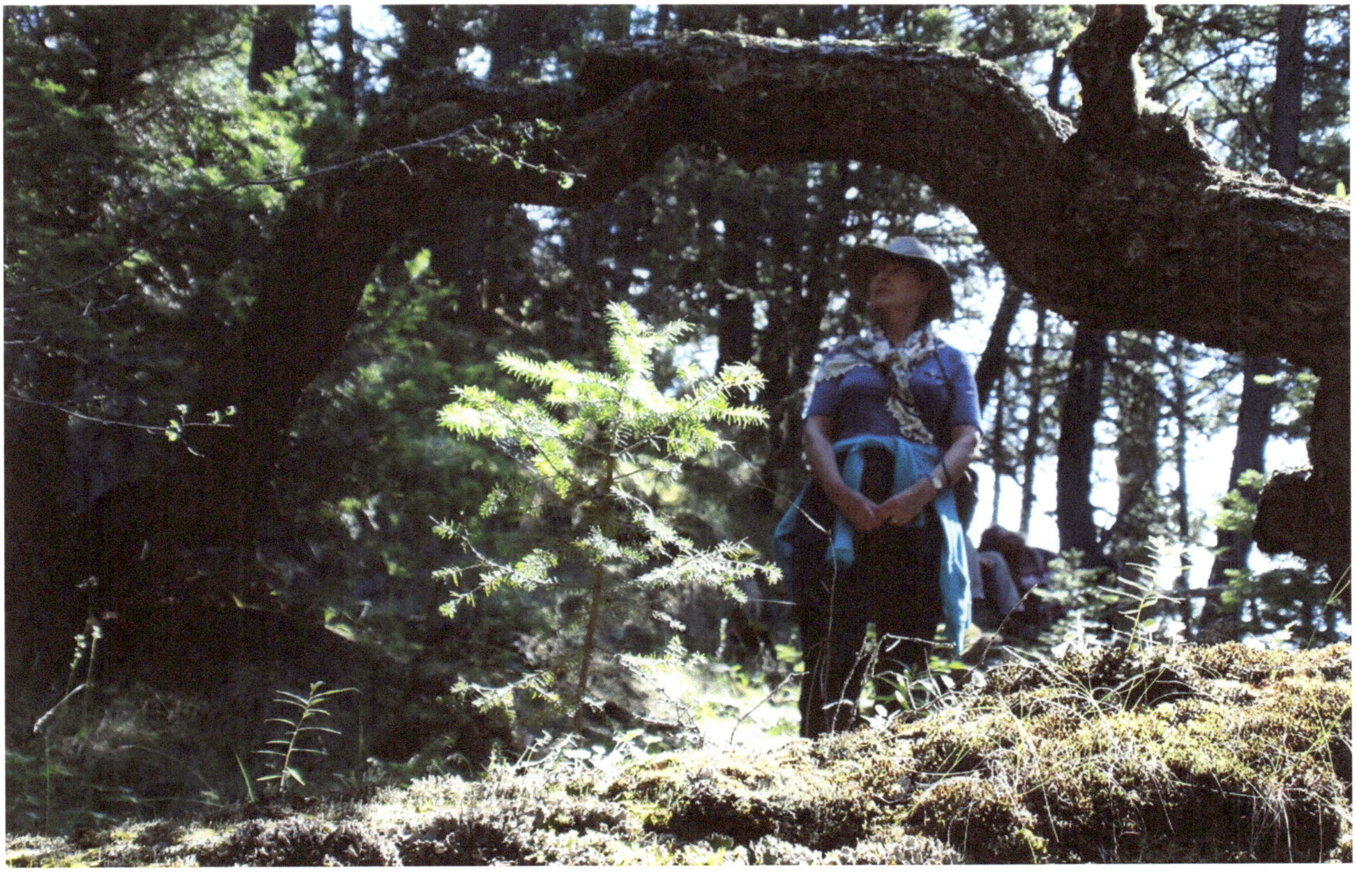

Gateway

The special circle of women I was blessed to be a part of were all called on by the Herd to carry their message of universal love, compassion and oneness. To view the world through the eyes of a horse is a gift that I will carry with me as I continue to rescue horses and try to change how people look at them. Thanks to Liz, the Herd and the entire Equinisity experience, I have a greater understanding of what they say through their bodies, minds and souls. It was the ride of my life.

See you next year!

With never ending love and appreciation.

Whether you are connecting with angels, guides, friends or family on the other side (including animals) you are simply opening to the pure and unfiltered energy of the one creative life force that is the essence of us all. That pure, unconditional force of LOVE is available to all of us, all the time, except when we create limits by our thoughts and beliefs. Those thoughts and beliefs are imposed by group consciousness and are simply agreed upon rules, which encourage fear in place of LOVE and cause us to reflect dis-ease as our true selves feel and express the dis-comfort. The natural world is a clear still pool reflecting the myriad beauty and perfection of the ALL. It is separate and apart from the limiting belief systems that humans have adopted and use to control the rest of creation for their distorted purposes. It is the pressure to conform to limits and beliefs that are against our nature as divinity in expression that wreaks havoc in our bodies and lives. The miracle is that when we change our understanding, the reflection in our physical expression is instant and absolute. Let us help you tune and raise your vibration to that level where you can access the God channel. It is not something separate and apart from the created world but only a state of being that is inherent to all life and freely expresses in a timeless, boundless, limitless sea of eternal Love. It is the truth of who we are and the state we return to instantly when the confines of consciousness are forgotten.

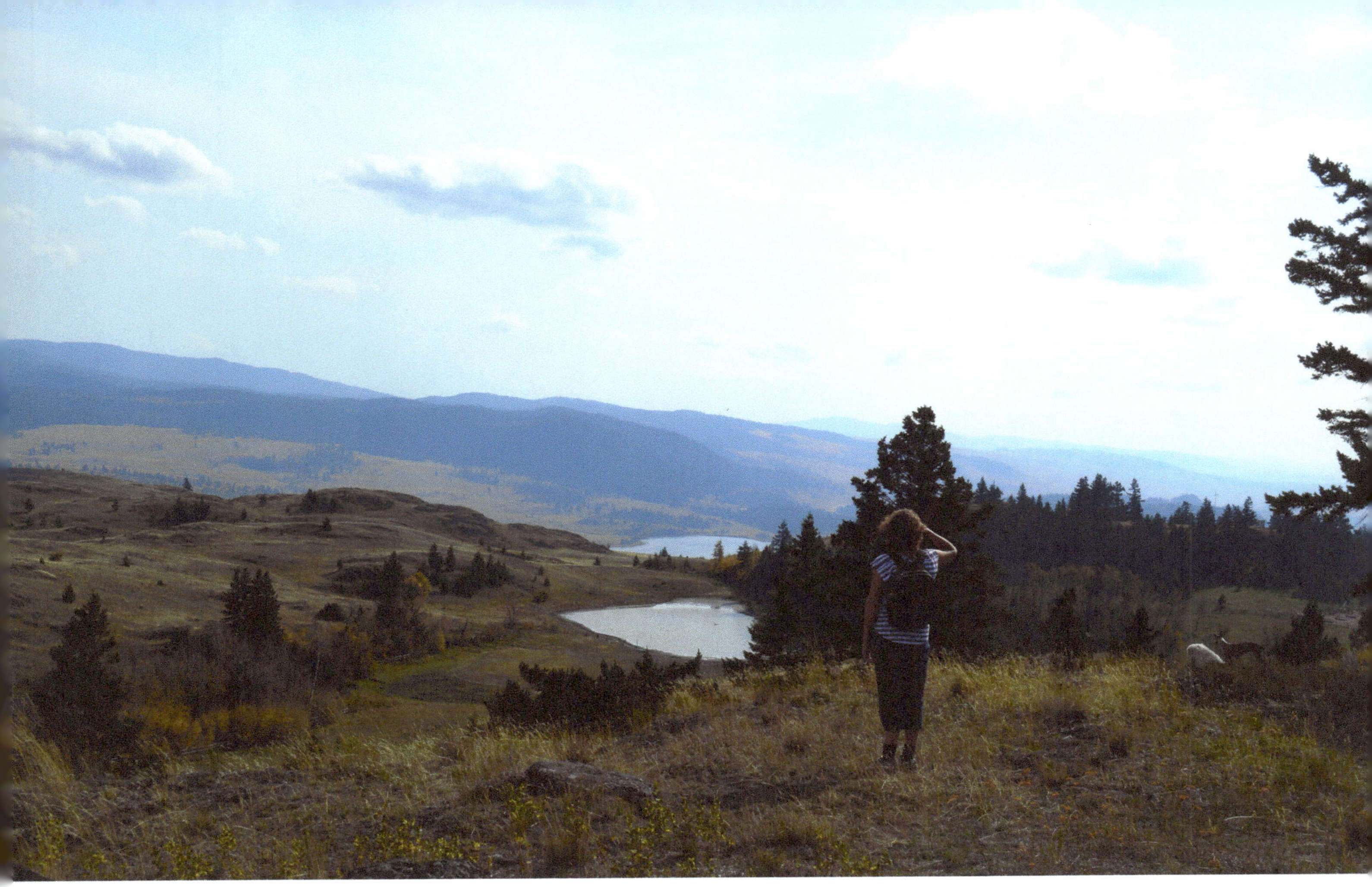

2015 - an eight year

Another image that was given was twin circles touching in the center like the principle of polarity and how we encompass both extremes yet touch in the midpoint...hot and cold...here now...north and south...here now...old and young... here now...

Sorry for that diversion but Liz is just the channeler and this is how the message went. Hope that you will make sense of it.

Back to the horses:

We are led to form patterns to change matter. Our minds are as one. When we sense discord we are given the image and pattern to correct it. Being sensitive to higher direction we go with the flow or become the pattern necessary for a new composition and from that new life comes. Very similar to DNA and the codes that dictate life, everything follows one pattern or another. The number 8 is yet another pattern. What is important is to open to the flow or current that will position you in the perfect pattern to create your unique creation in matter. Humans are the only species that either do not feel or resist the current. We are coming forth to help you listen.

—The Herd

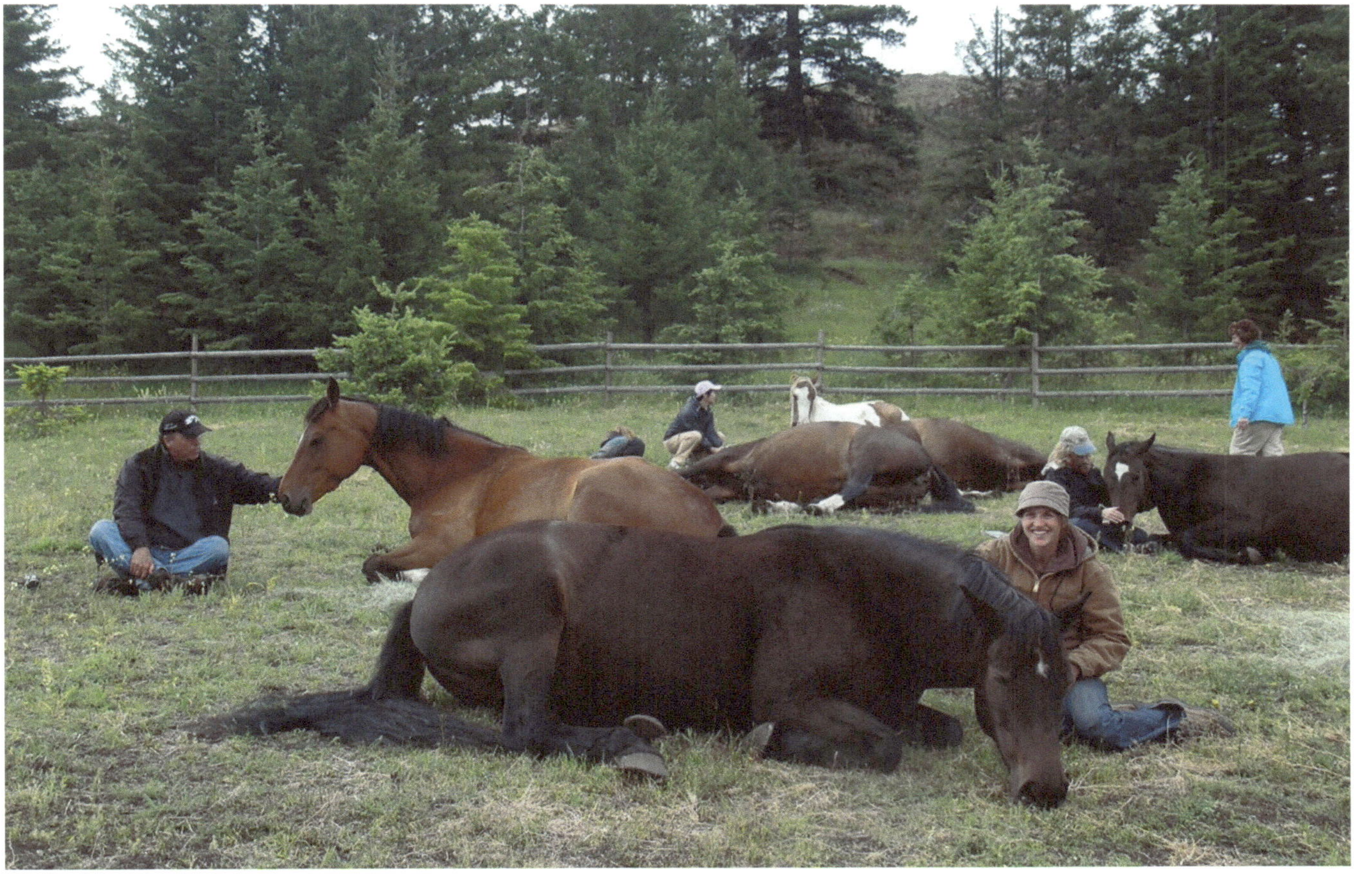

When I wrote the January 2015 newsletter, I was told that 2015 was an 8, which had many auspicious meanings. One of our spring happenings here is the return of the cranes that travel in flocks hundreds of miles up and make a distinctive cry announcing their arrival. This year we were outside at a retreat connecting with the Herd when the cranes returned. Two flocks dipped down just over the barn roof and then started circling over the pasture. As we watched in awe the two flocks made 8 circles each side by side forming a figure 8 as well by their position. I'm not sure what that means but it has to be a good omen!

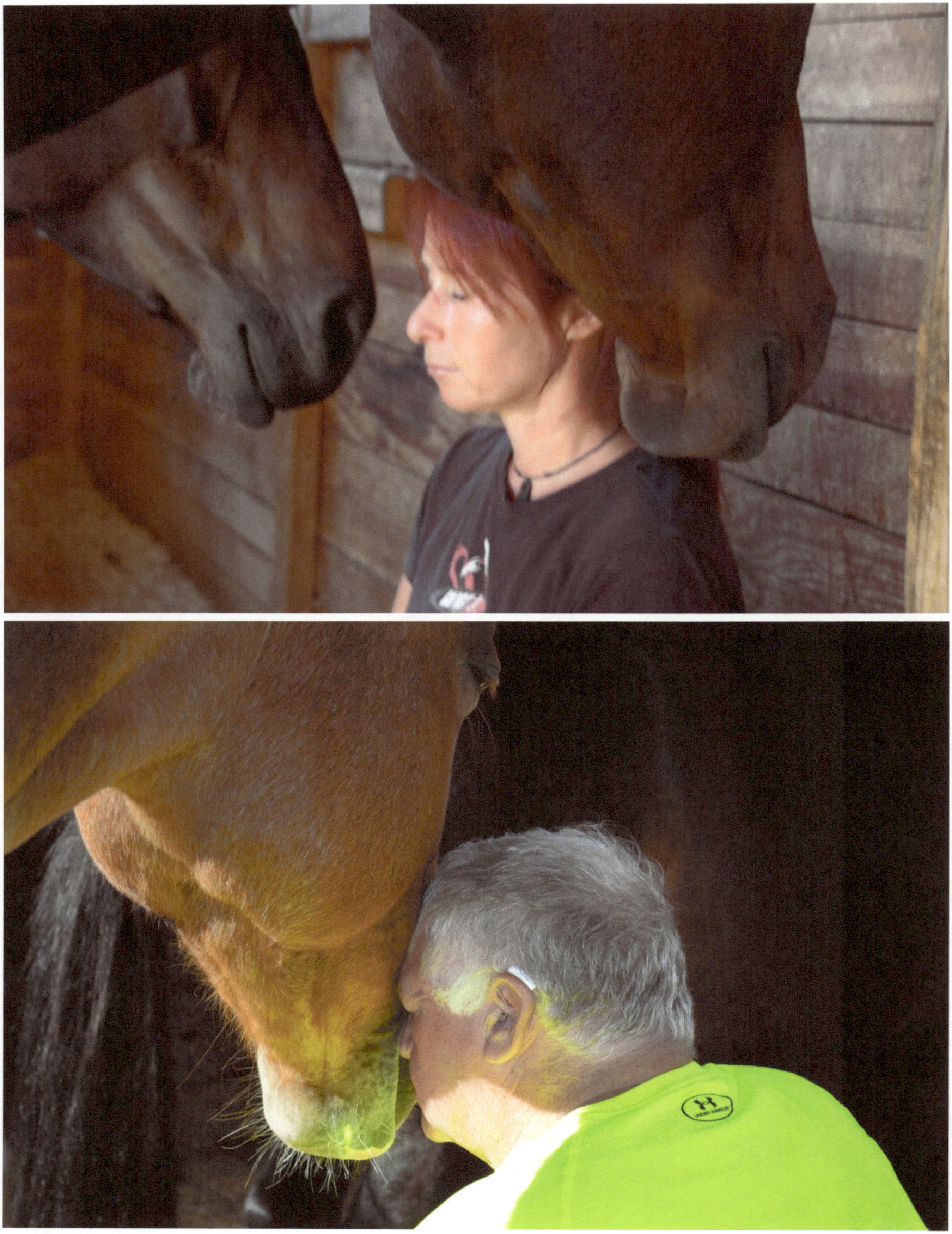

All Minds are Joined

I watch in awe as one by one, Herd members come to the healing tables, each scanning and then knowing exactly what to do to shift and release energy. There are always different horses for each person, sometimes several. Then suddenly from the far end of the pasture, galloping like a streak of light, comes Micky the cat, and jumping onto the table he does a complete round of the body under the blankets, back to the face to pay his respects before moving to the next person. Sometimes a whippet will scale the healing table as well to lend their support. We count our blessings that Theo, the 100-pound Doberman has not yet attempted this, choosing to hold space instead.

Later, while we are walking the land, the horses appear and circle an awestruck participant to deliver yet more connection and healing. Later we almost bump into them in the dark as the Herd surrounds the Spirit Lodge at the end of the day. It is so obvious that all minds are joined, and we create with our focus.

One participant—whose totem is the deer—is on her way to unpack in her tent and a deer stops by the side of the path, then heads straight over to welcome her.

Walking the land another participant finds all three of her totems, and in "Fairyland" the dragonflies now let people pat them and land on fingers when they are adored and then invited. The Merlin Tree continues to share its wisdom and strength, bringing one after another to silence and release. A giant labyrinth created on the dry lakebed, beneath the full moon, invites you to take off your shoes, feel the soft Earth and reflect on the journey. Here all the forces align to enlighten, to lift the burden of human mass mind beliefs and help us remember our truth as Unlimited God-Beings.

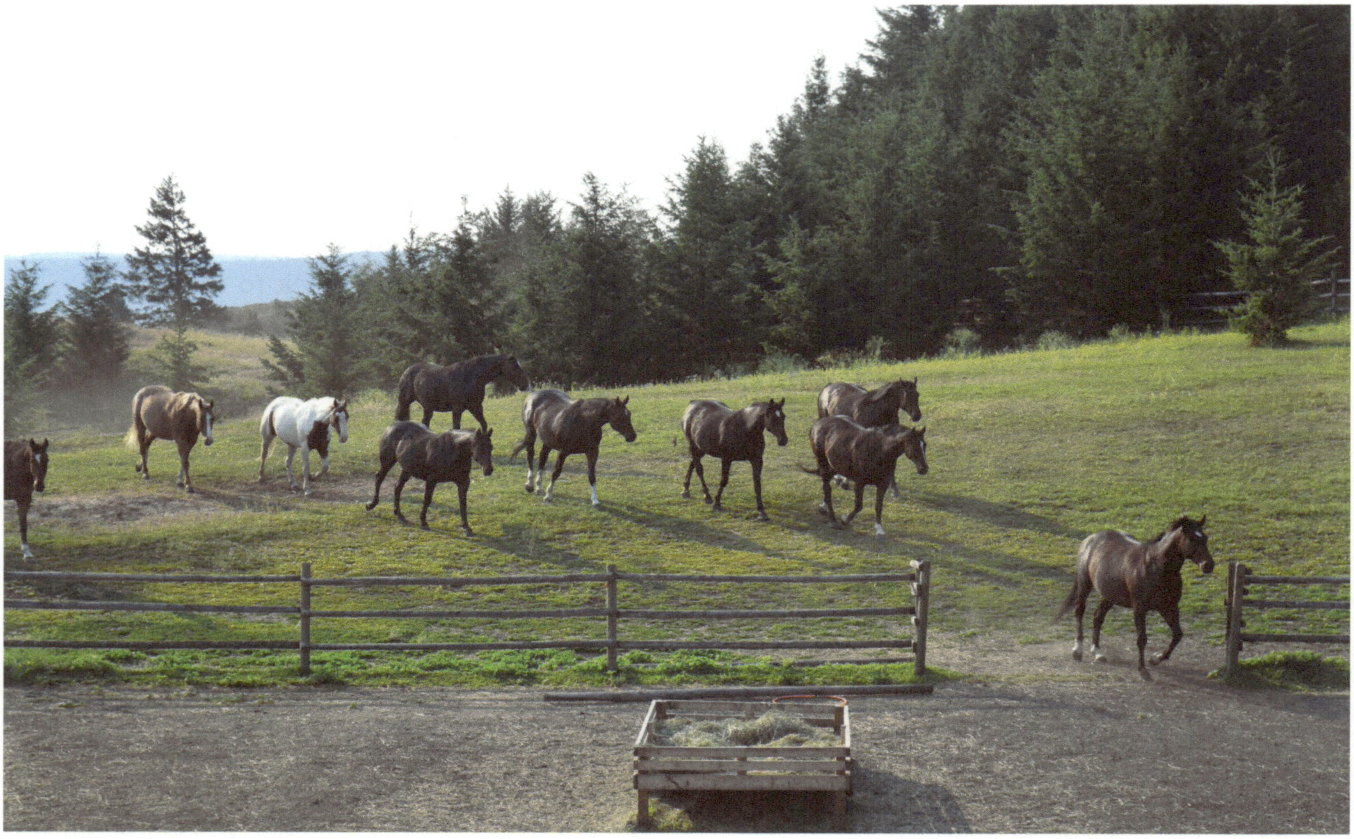

Breakfast time!

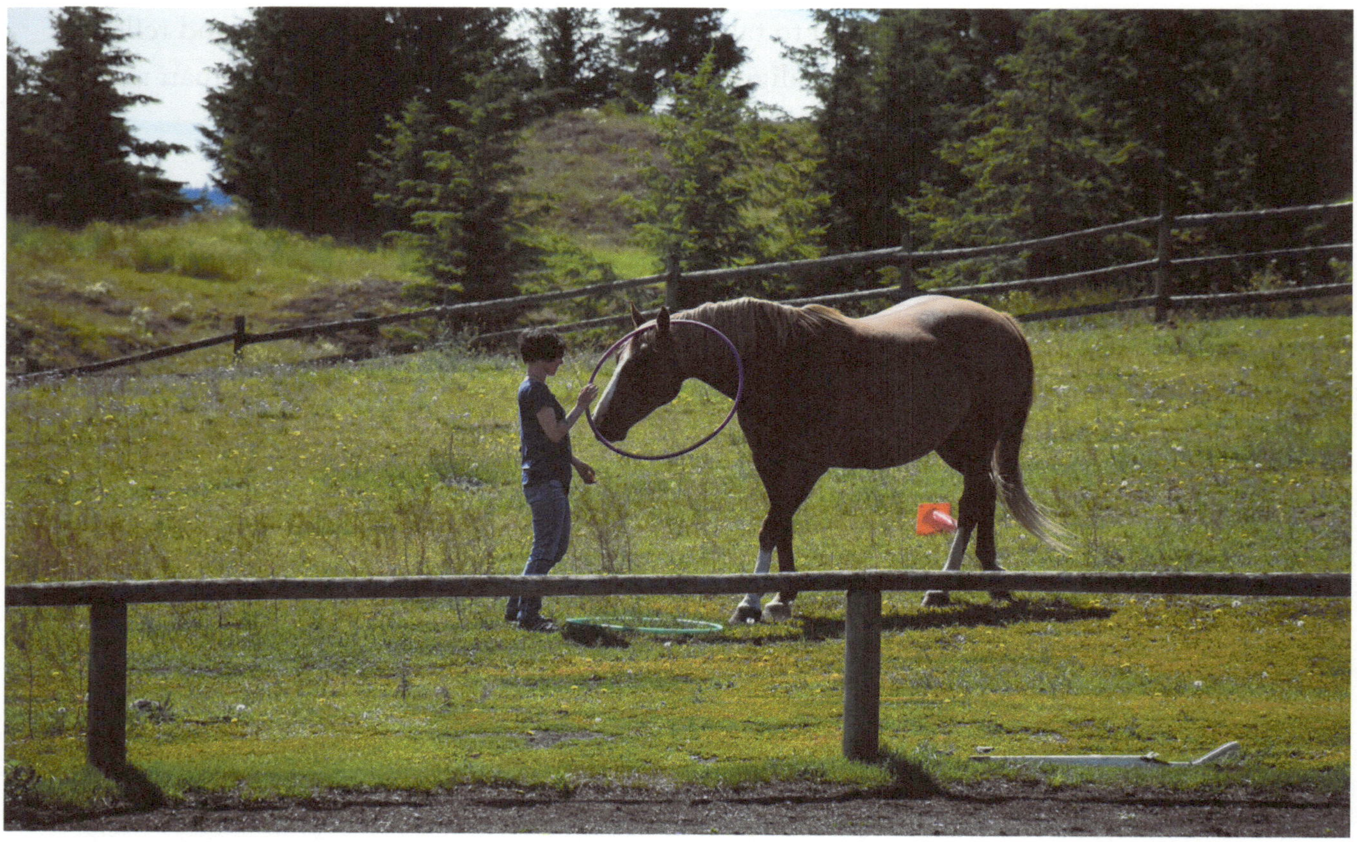

Jody plays with Epona

We are inviting you to share with us the powerful heartfelt vibration of this pivotal time. 528 hertz is the vibration of the All and is present in the natural world in all life. It is the vibration of grass, flowers, crystals, water, rocks and trees. We absorb and become it when living in a healthy and natural environment. It is present in sacred geometry which is the design of the natural world. It is the miracle vibration of love and manifestation. We horses share it for the purpose of healing and transmutation. We create and hold it in our healing circles and other sacred geometries that are used in the healing dynamics of the Herd. You will be hearing more about this and the other vibrations of the solfeggio scale which has been historically known and used by advanced civilizations in the past and will be used again by humans in the healing of the future. It is the musical mathematical matrix of creation essential to the sacred geometry of circles and spirals, and consistent with DNA structuring and repair. This is why healing must be felt and held in the heart with the vibration of love. There is no degree of difficulty in miracles when you hold the vibrational key.

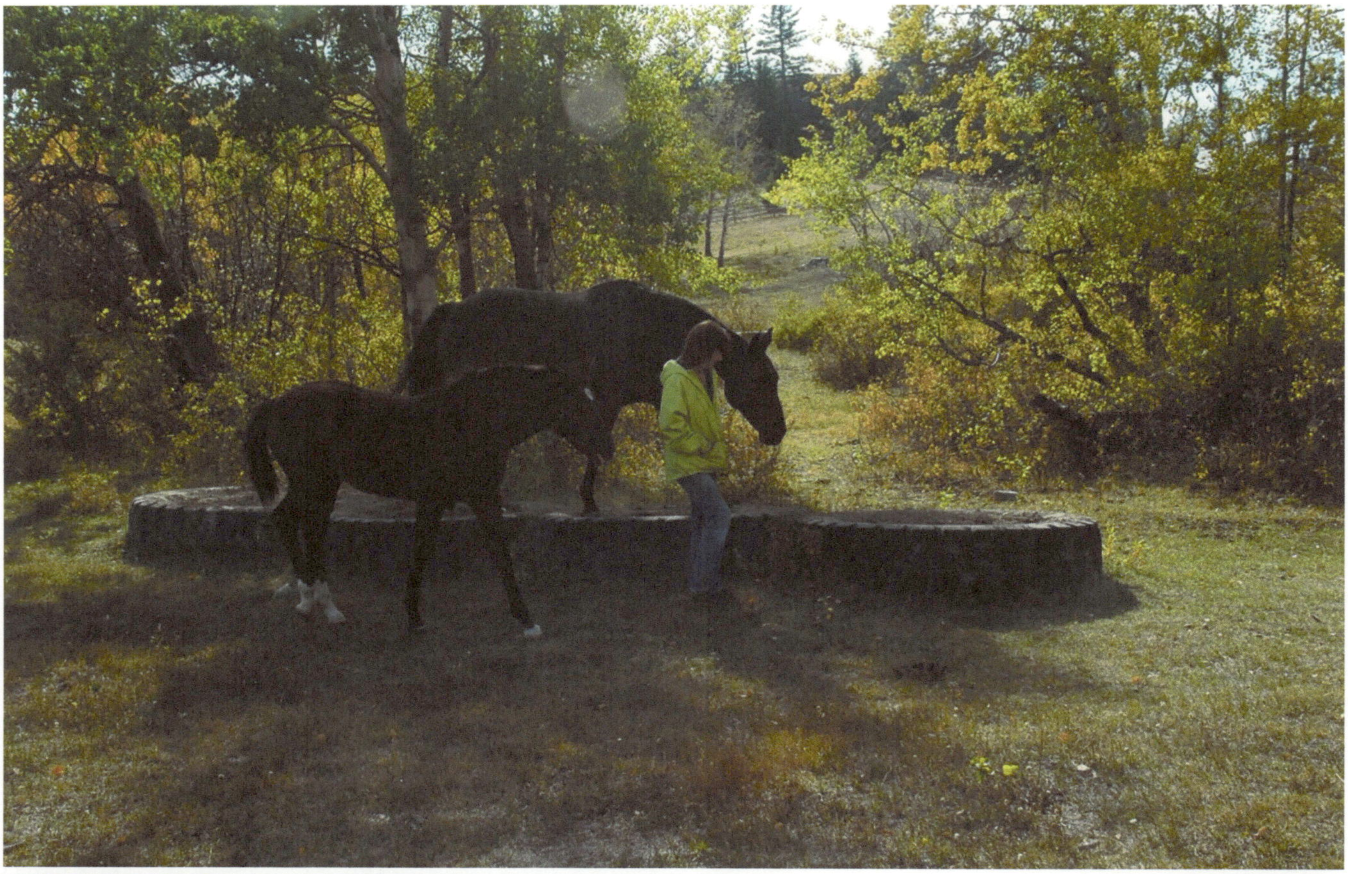

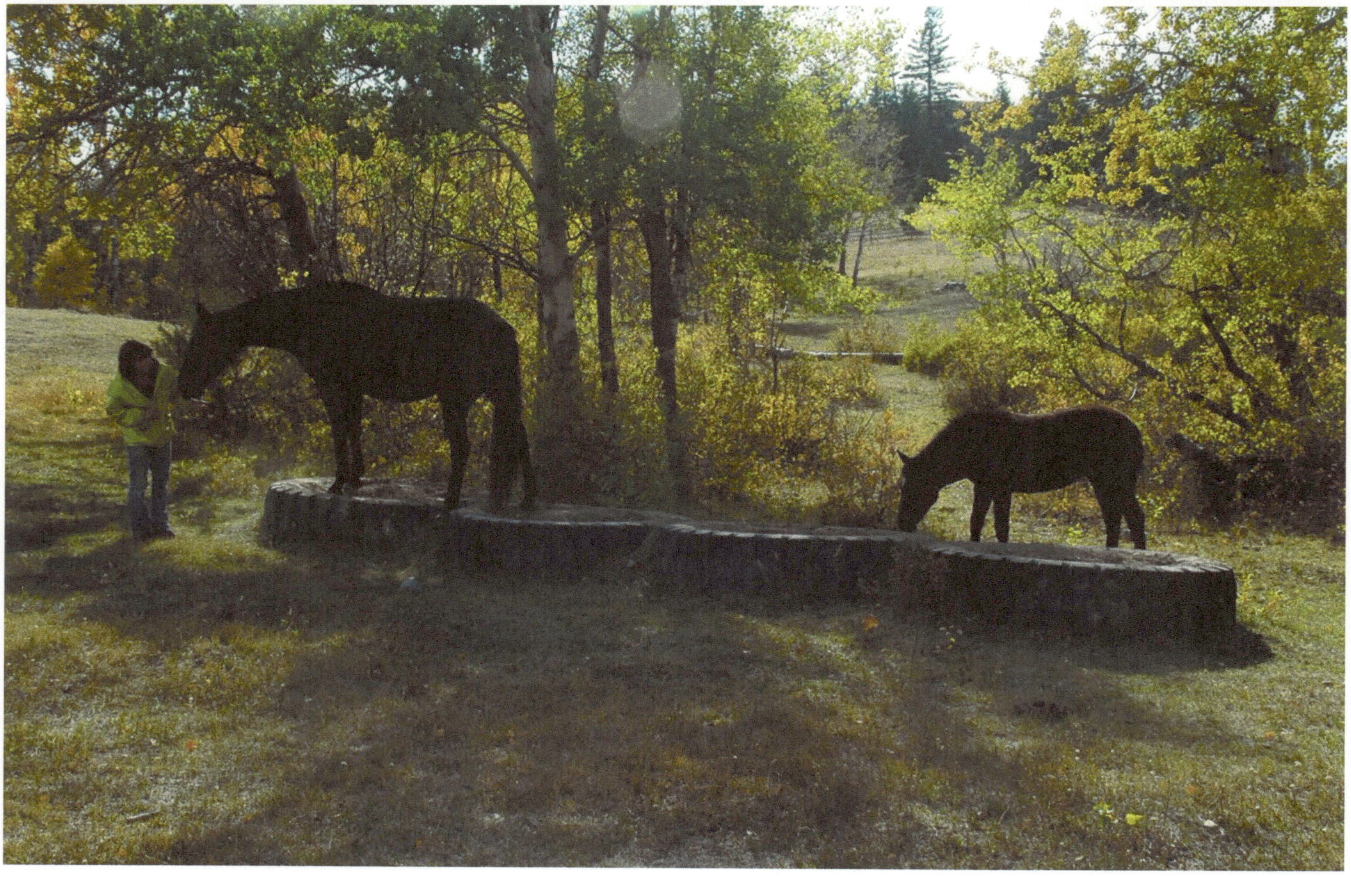

At the higher levels of vibration consciousness becomes clairvoyant as connection to the ALL gives us an overview of events outside of what humans call time. When one (like Liz) becomes fluent with the vision and knowing of the Herd and their connection, as in all of the natural world, to the dream of life, the pulse and flow of creation is instantly available. Not only do you experience the outcome of events but the outcome is always the most perfect for all involved and it is orchestrated by the ALL in every detail. We are always in the flow, seeing, feeling and knowing the score for our individual and collective symphony.

We need not find meaning or sense in what unfolds, but simply feel the joy, trust in the perfection and receive the gift of incarnation. In this place where form becomes a fluid interpretation and individual belief for humans, it is an absolute and infinite dance of creation to the rest of life.

That is our gift to you. When you immerse yourselves in the energies of animals and the natural world, you become tuned to the highest, purest levels of vibration where all is eternal perfection and LOVE.

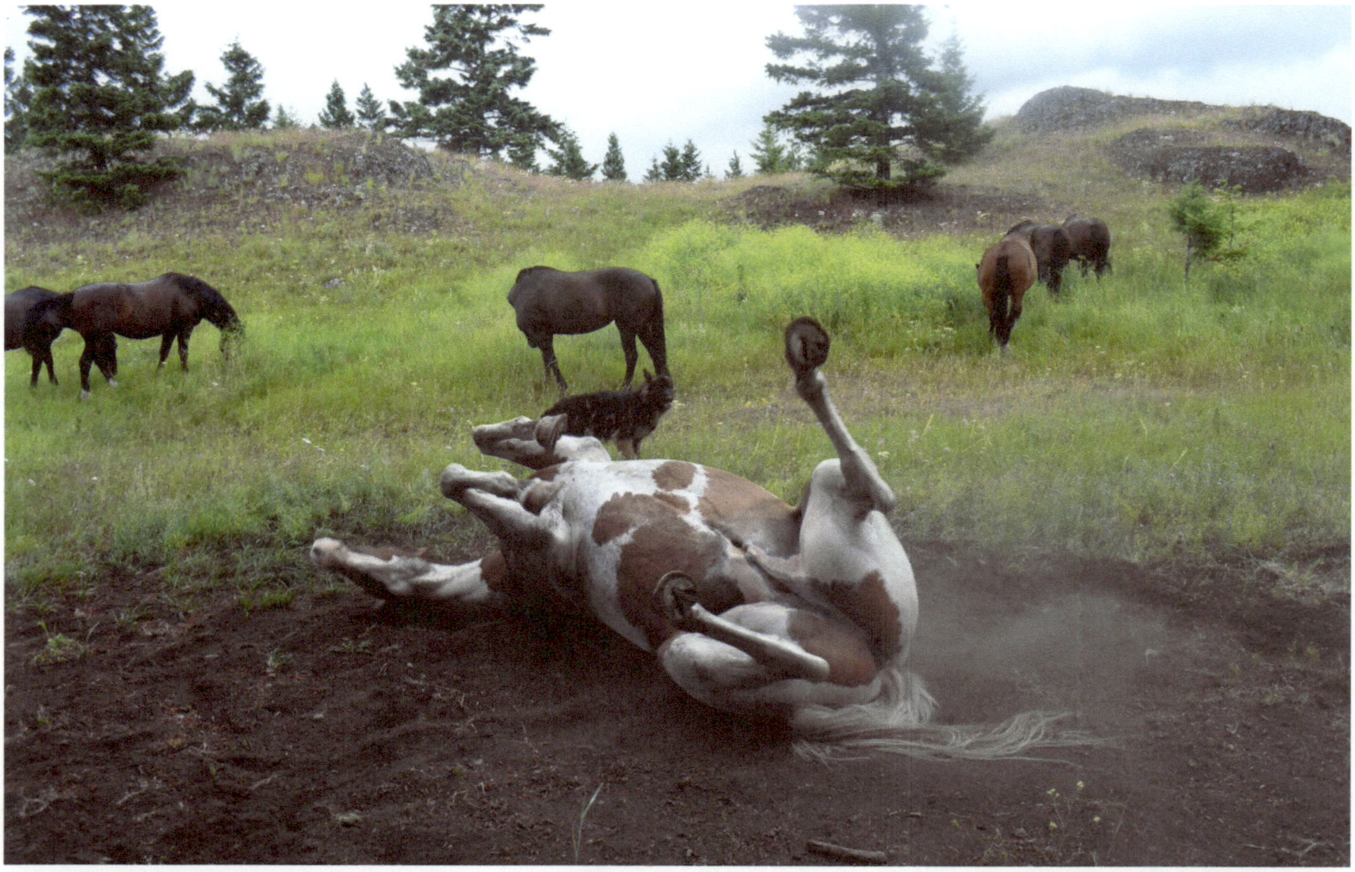

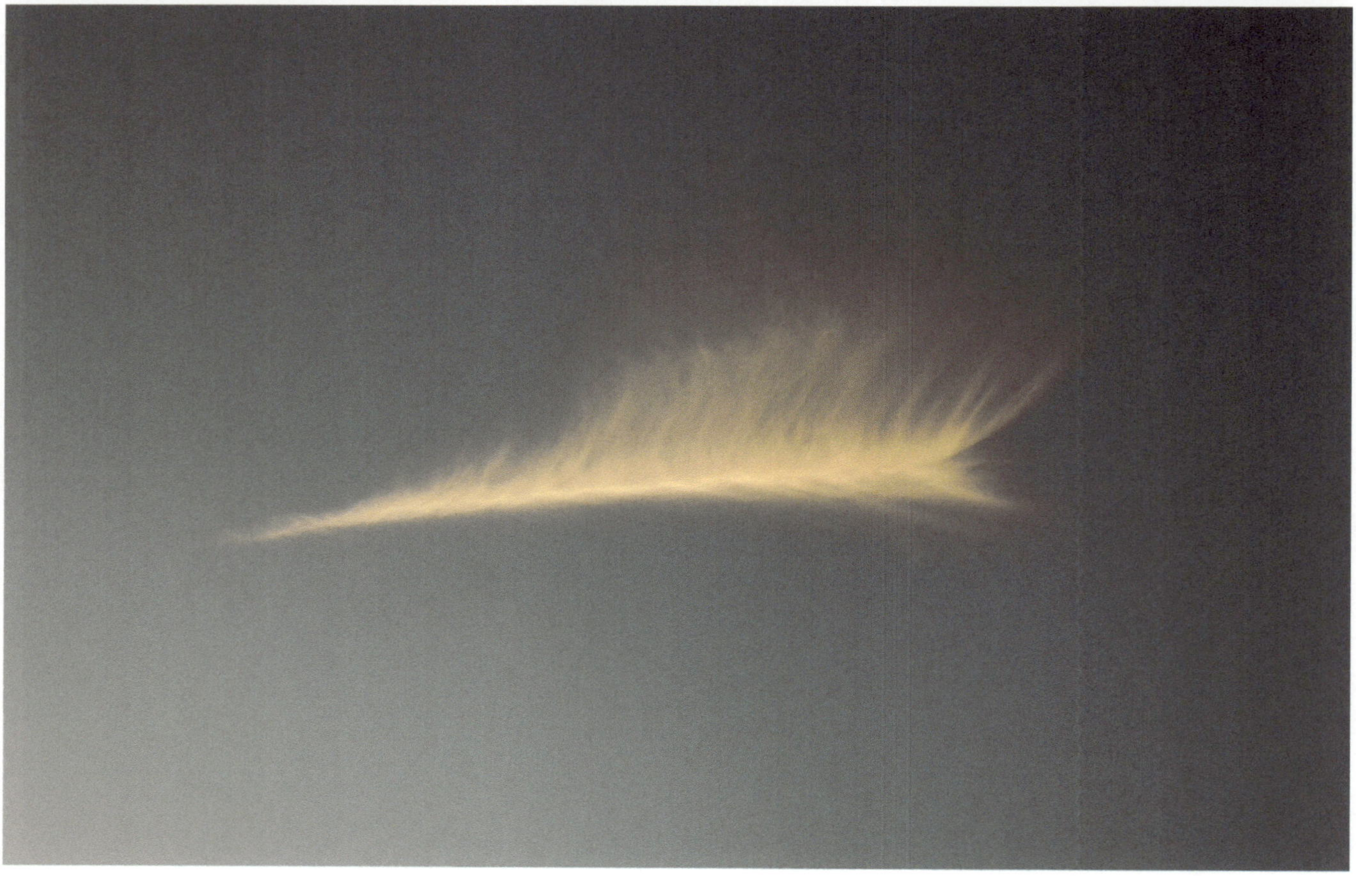

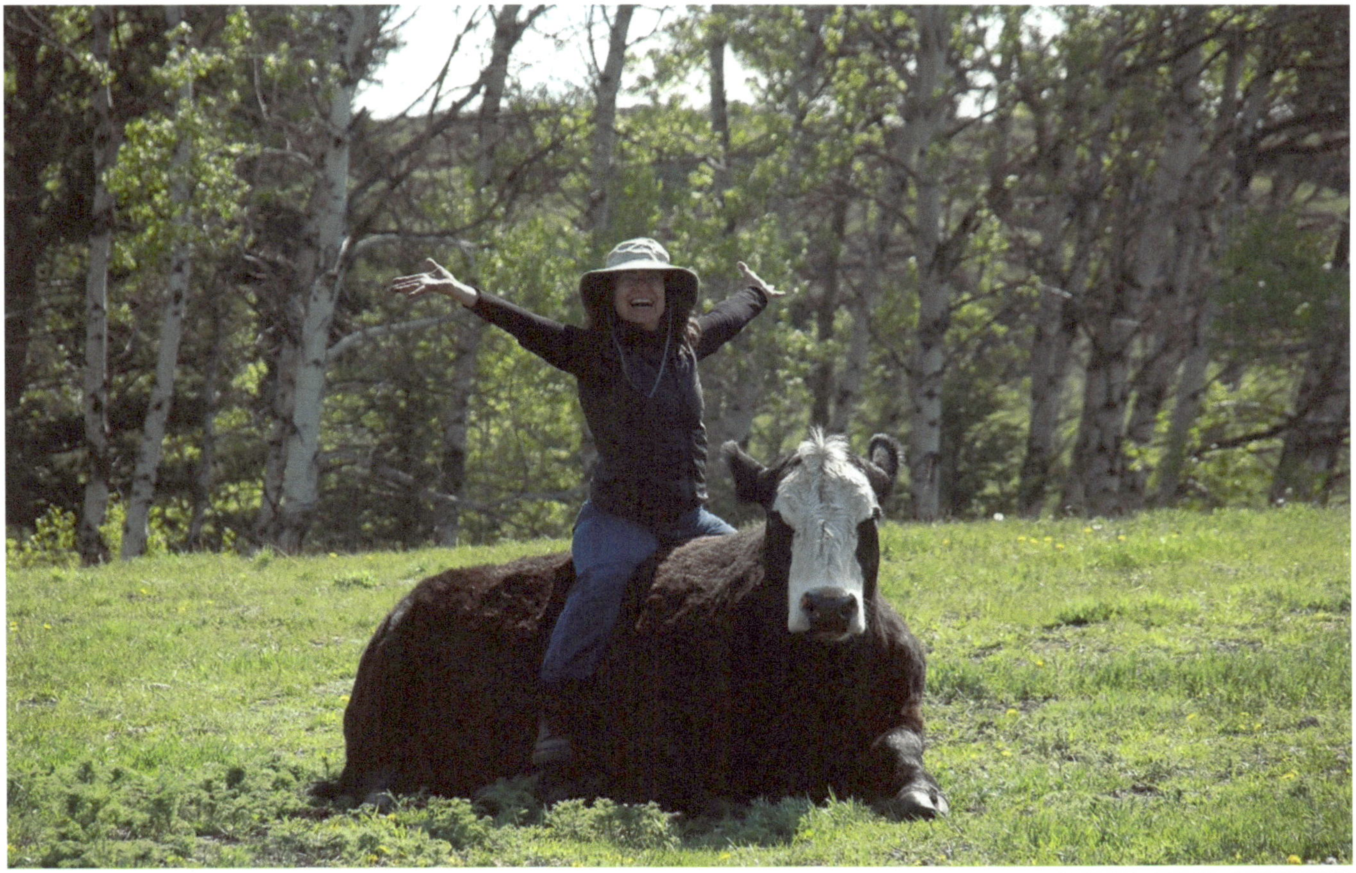

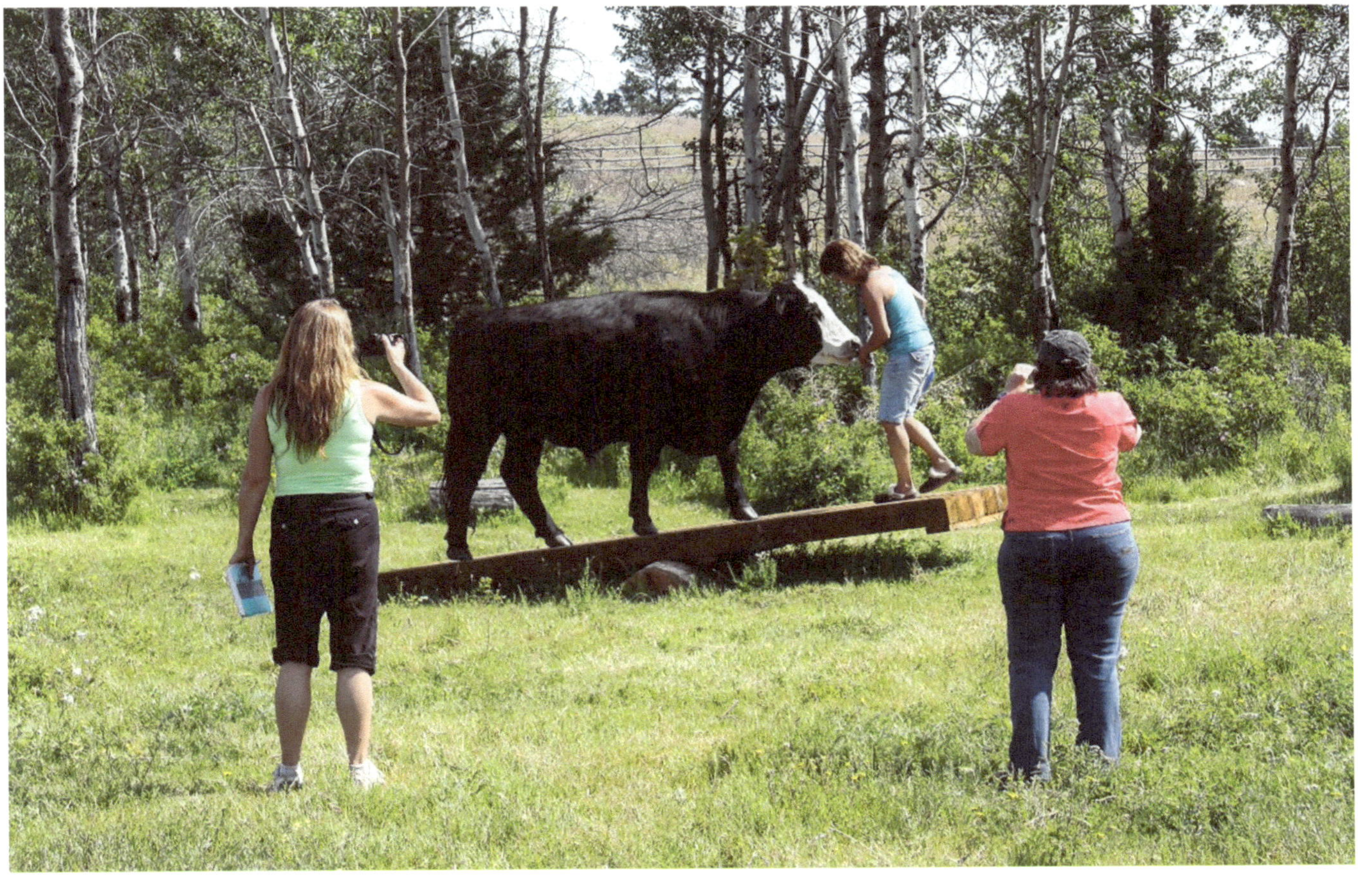

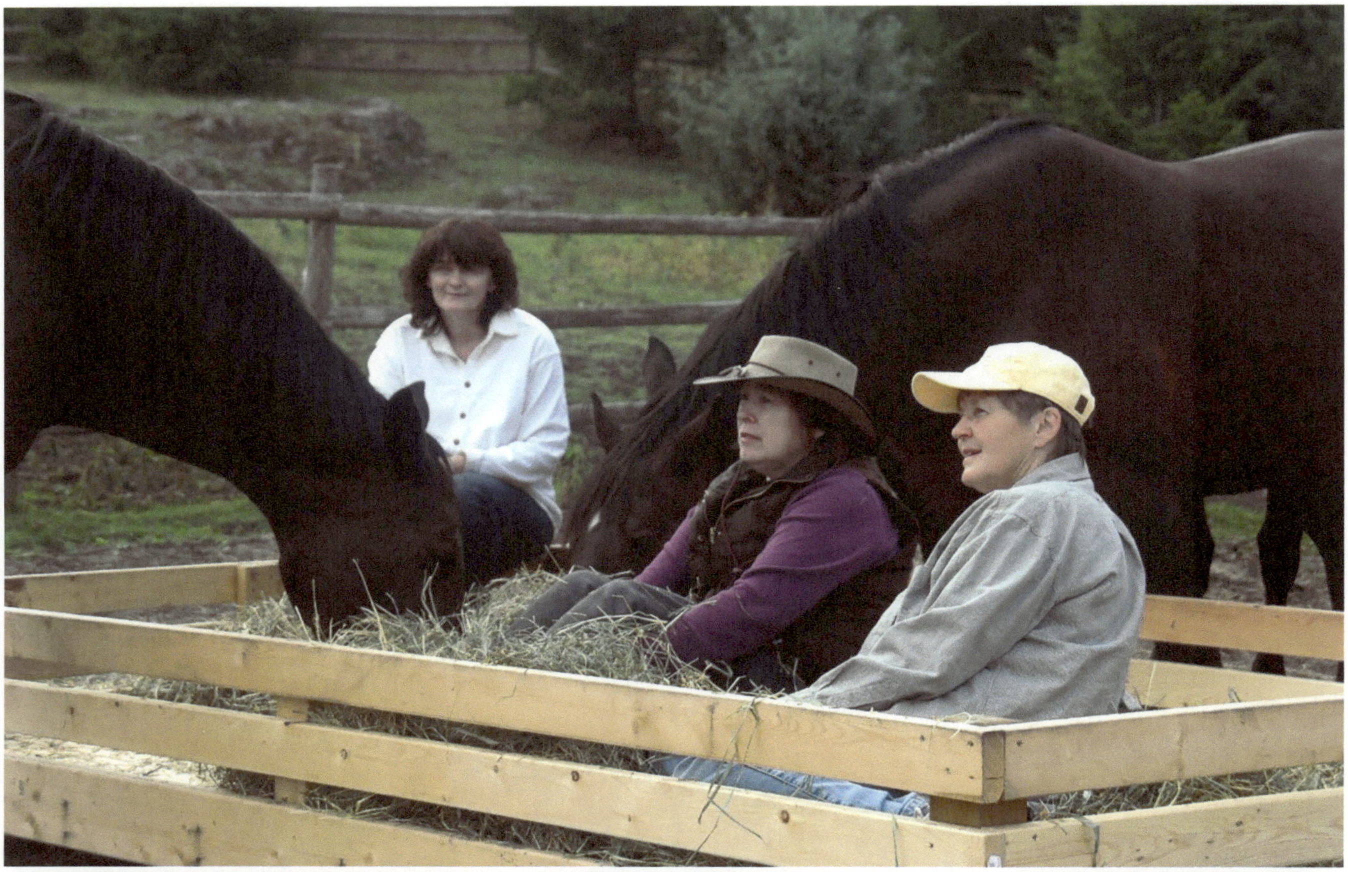

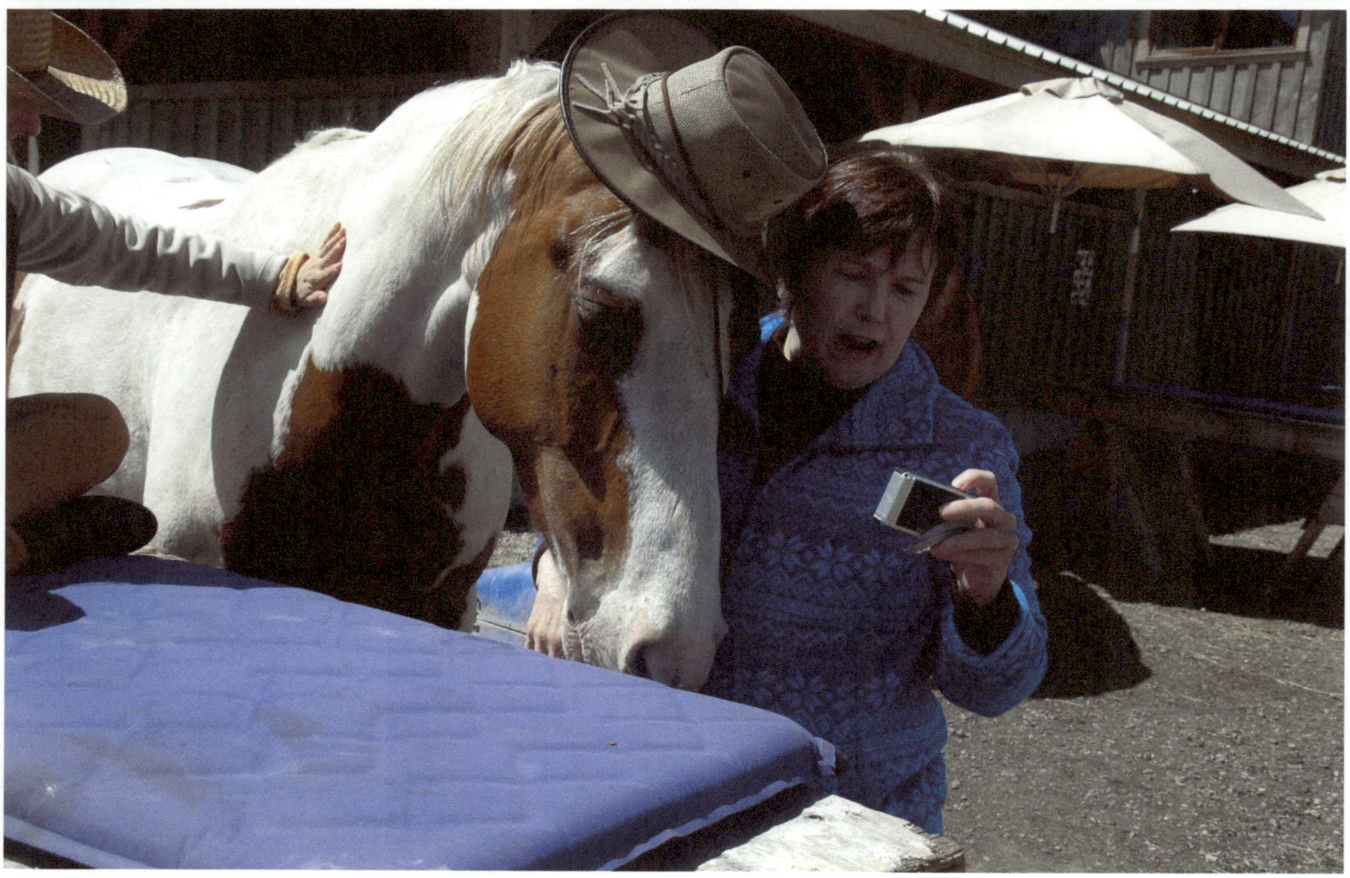

Liz Phillipson and Paschar take a selfie

From Liz Phillipson, Equinistic healing practitioner:

I don't even have the words to tell you how deeply the time at your ranch has changed my life. Not that all my ills have been healed; that is yet to come. I came away with an awareness of infinite abundance. I have more frequent moments of spontaneous bliss, and the vision of where to go in my future. I feel the opportunity to assist in bringing this type of awareness to the lives of others through equine-assisted healing. I am so much more loving toward 'conflict', therefore I don't experience much.

Do you remember when I mentioned in an email that there were no longer crows on the property as they were angry? I walked out the door this morning to see a large flock in the pasture. As I walked down the lane, there were more in the next pasture. Then as I moved the horses to the front fields, there again, were more.

I can hardly wait to go to bed at night so that I can get up the next morning to see what is on for the day! That is not as I used to be.

I am deeply, deeply grateful for what the horses did for me, and to you for making it possible. That I might change even one person's life as this has changed mine, my efforts shall not be lost.

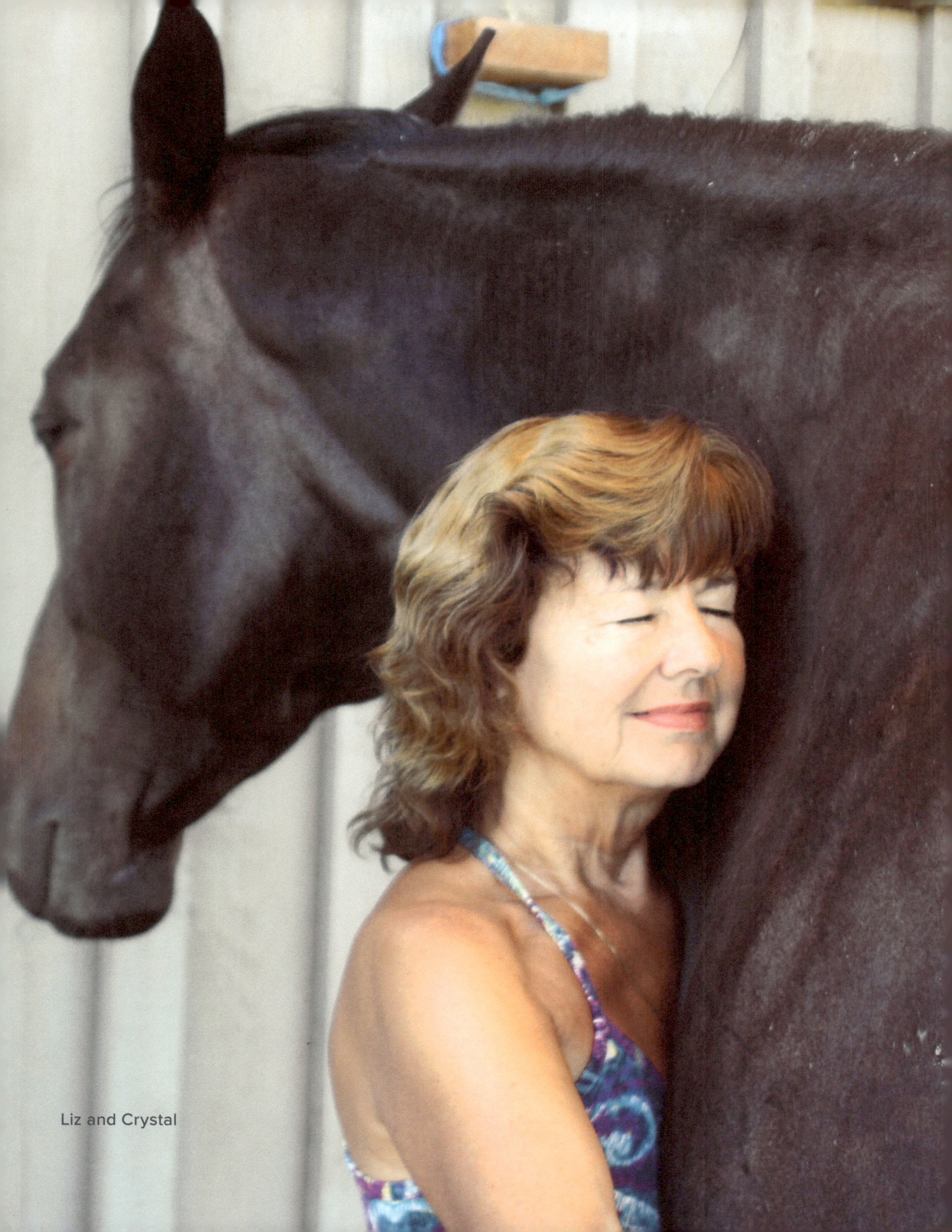

Liz and Crystal

It is so exciting for us to experience the new evolving consciousness of humans. Huge planetary shifts are allowing new frontiers in breaking down the barriers of the ego and allowing the free flow between species to return to that long forgotten Garden of Eden state. Those of you who can take time to remove yourselves from the noise and the clutter of human mass mind consciousness and invite higher consciousness to flow into that quiet space, will experience a big paradigm shift. It is not what happens to us but our interpretation of what has happened that is what becomes us. The clear still pond that is the consciousness of the natural world lies quiet and serene in our hearts and in the uncluttered mind that channels the Allness of Unconditional Love. Many humans are sharing that love and intention with us for a New World where we can all walk and talk with "God" and each other in peace and joy, inviting the adventure of discovering ourselves in matter in myriad form. We are ALL One and when we know this for certain it changes everything. If we are IT then what can IT do to us. It is all perception, and for years that perception has been tainted by human greed and misunderstanding of the truth of this physical incarnation. Horses are IT, and we are working to change human misconception one mind, one experience at a time. Take the time and listen, feel and allow that experience and congratulations all of those who have already joined the club!

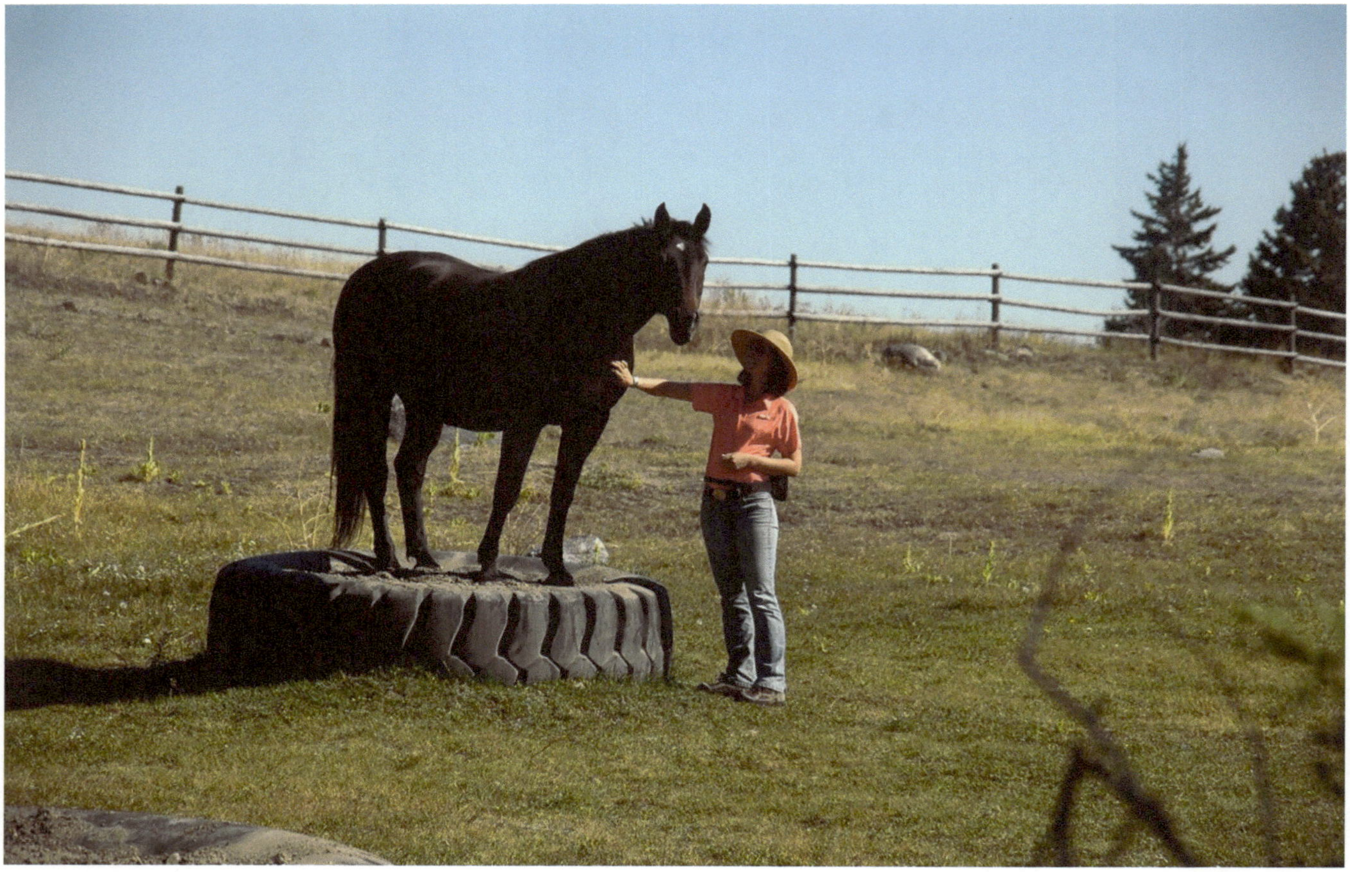

We want to share something obvious for horses but much less so for humans; there is a time for everything when all the forces align to bring that particular creation into being. We are very sensitive and in tune with the higher plan for our lives, our purpose and our commitment to bring forth the Allness into physical expression. Each being has a number, a name, a note and a vibration that is written in the heavens, and we must follow our higher guidance to find our truth as unique expressions of love in matter. At this time in our Earth history, we the animals and in-tune beings are holding that vision of perfect timing for a new consciousness to unfold. We council you to connect with your hearts, the truth you will find there and surrender to the flow as your breath, your blood and your life force do without a thought.

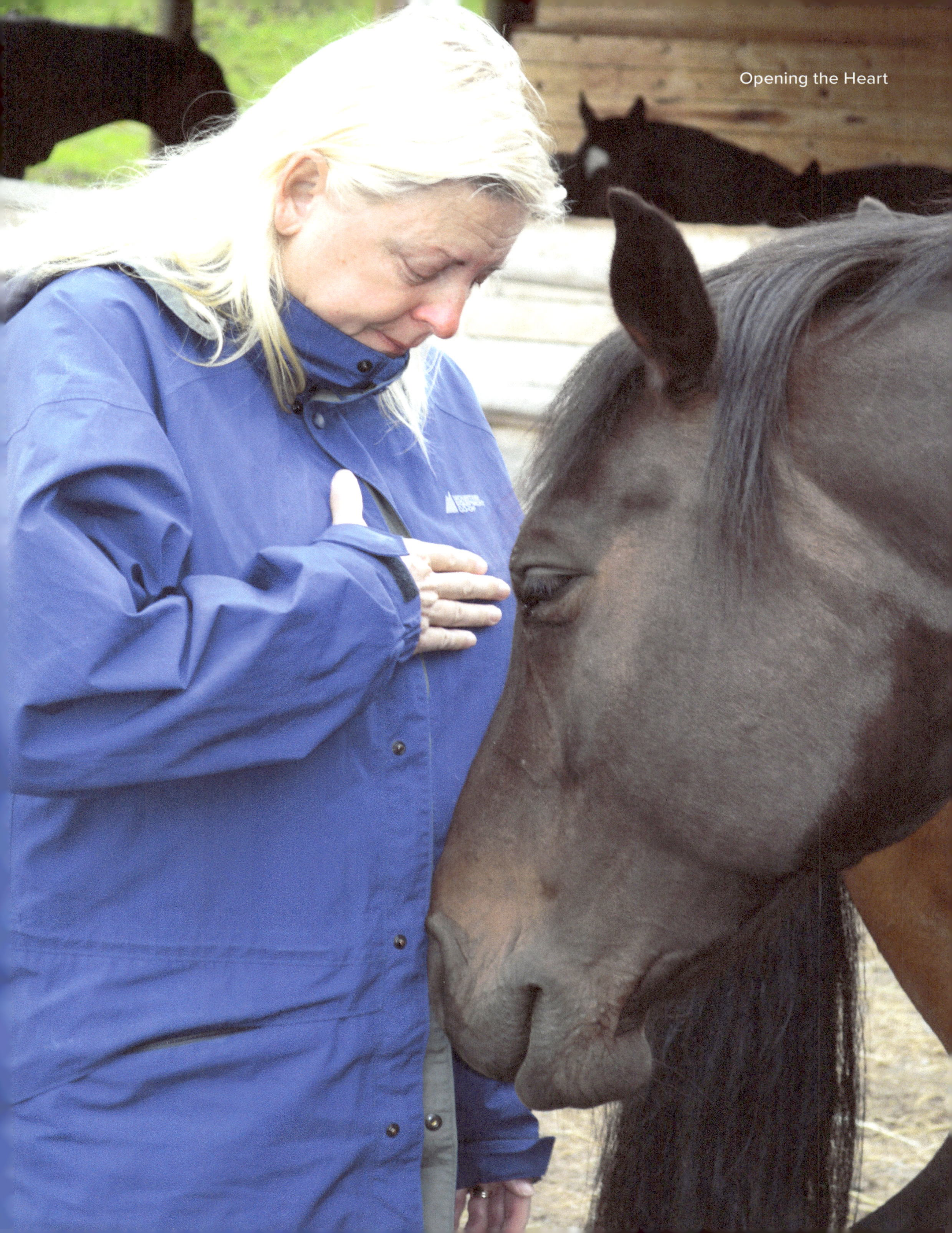

Communication is the most difficult skill between humans of the same culture, religion, sex, family, country, village, etc. Even humans who live together and "love" each other seem to spend much time developing the skill. For us it is much easier as we communicate through our highly developed senses with pictures, focus and instant understanding. There is no language barrier, no association with beliefs or customs other than the slight variance of breed or geographical reference. Basically the language of pictures is universal and humans would do well to re-awaken this skill. Humans have relied on segregation and competition when they would be better off developing and supporting a universal Herd dynamic. Horses are all interconnected, first with their familial Herd, then their breed, then geographic expression, then horse consciousness in general, and finally universal consciousness which transcends all individual variation. We are all; however, our individual variation, able to connect and communicate through our common language of "Herd Rituals" and our instant language of shared thoughts and pictures. It is all crystal clear and agreed upon as the way to peaceful co-existence on the planet. Humans often misconstrue our language based on their domination agenda in support of the ego. Yes, we first focus the picture and the energy, then carry out the picture in physical body language but our language has often been misinterpreted by the human perspective. Horses are often placed in non-contextual relationship with new Herd members being introduced and then removed, food supplied and removed, and family dynamics interfered with constantly. The whole horse/human relationship has effected how horses best offer their creative wisdom. Please allow us to share our wisdom by being attentive and open to our ways and learning a common language that will allow our horse/human families to express in mutual joy.

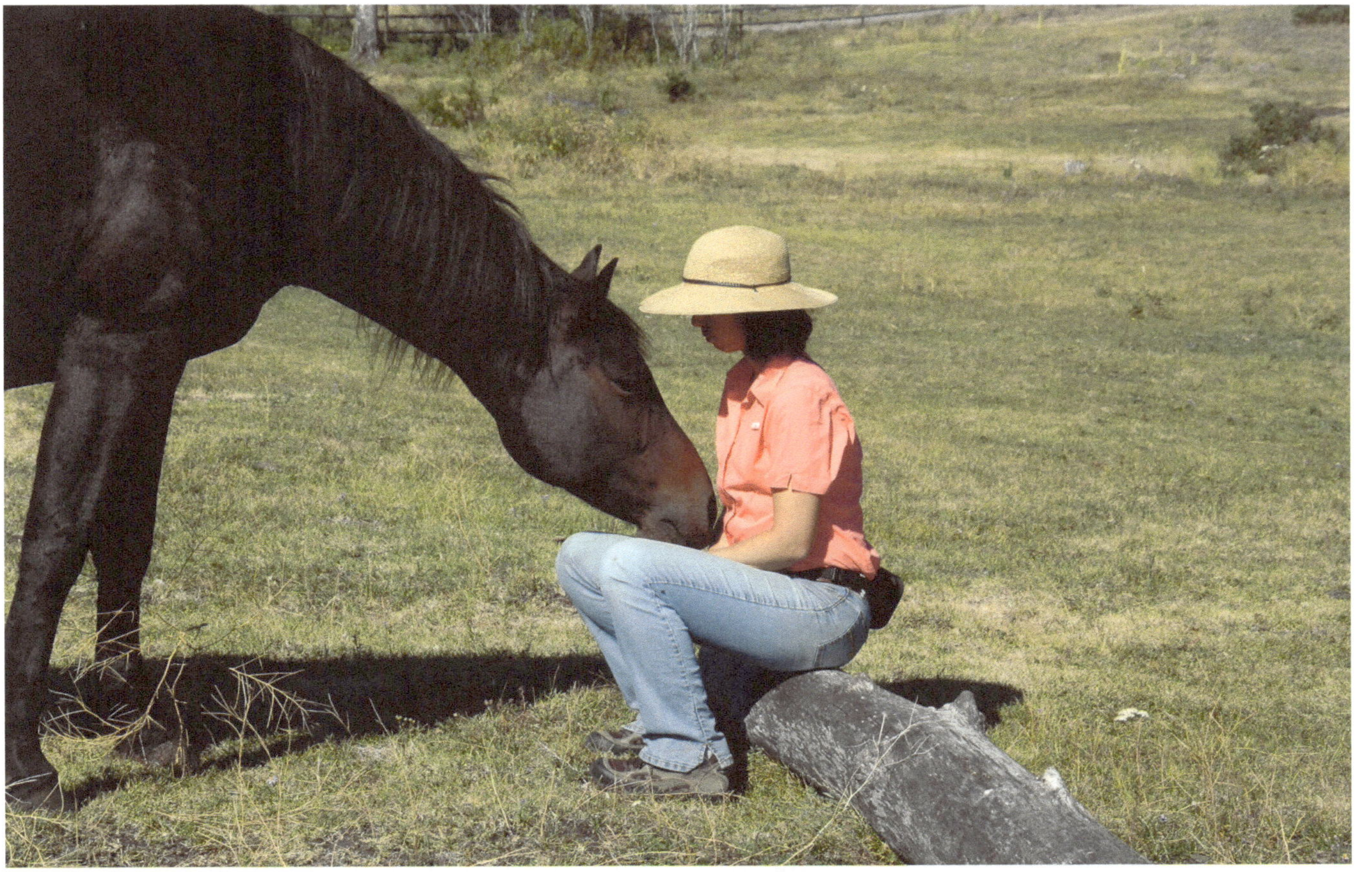

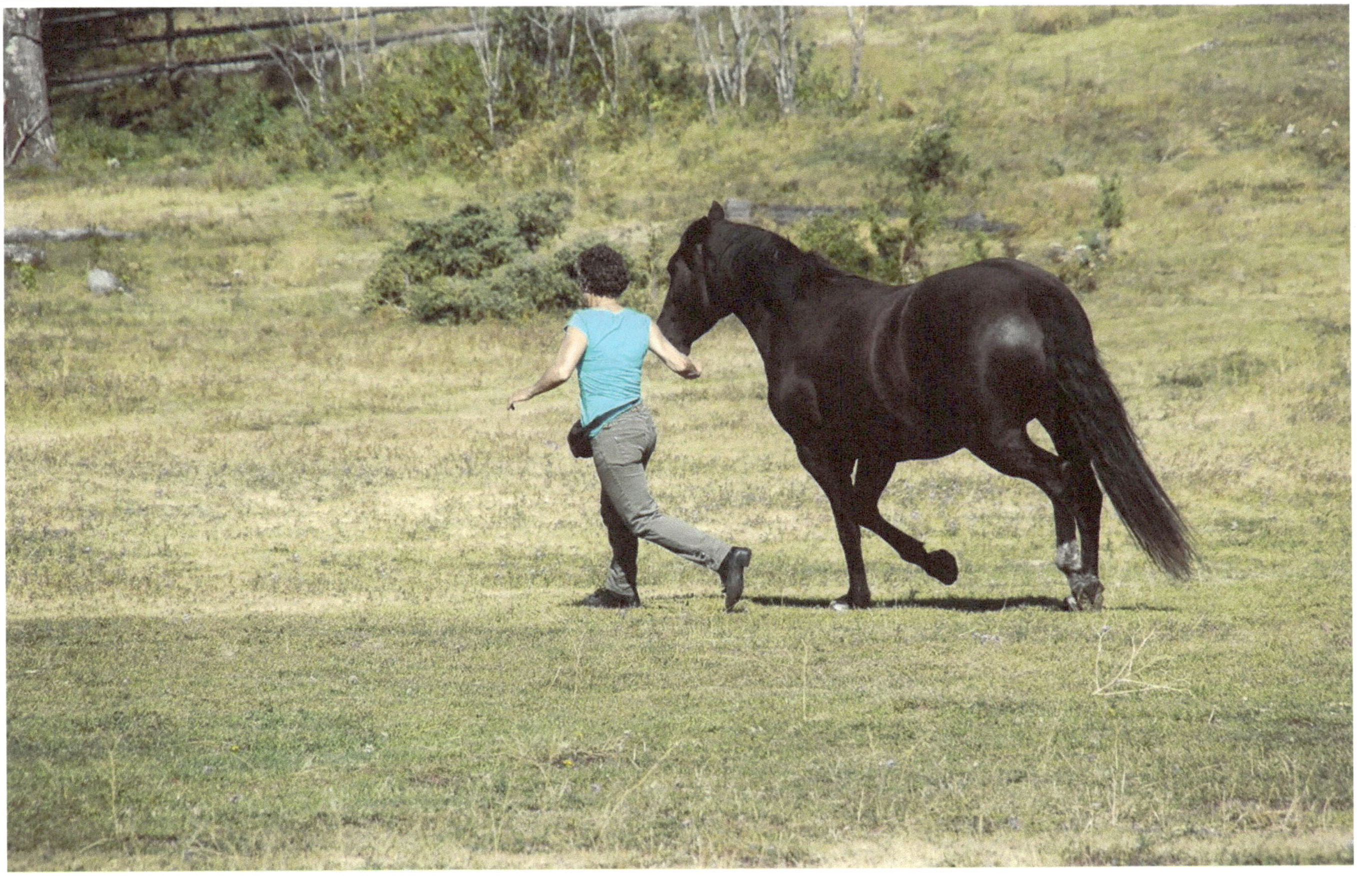

We just gave Liz the phrase "Heart of the Herd" that encapsulates the process we are sharing with humanity. We amplify our intuitive emotional intelligence to bathe all those in our field with healing higher vibrational energies. We precipitate "light in matter" by magnifying and patterning our shared vibrational attunement through a free flow from source into form. We bring the higher consciousness and perfection of the ALL through our hearts to resonate as the larger Heart of the Herd, bathing all who are open to receiving it with the wisdom, truth, joy, freedom, abundance and love of our source. We are all perfection in our individual expression when we allow that free flow from source. Whatever you want to call it, instinct or intuition, is our direct connection and is magnified when we allow its free flow through our hearts. It has no boundaries of time or space and changes reality the instant we allow it. Allowing is easy for the natural world, but often difficult for humans who insist on running heartfelt wisdom and guidance through the maze like circuitry of the human mass-mind belief system residing in their brains. Our brains are simply receivers allowing the flow to direct the functioning of our bodies without interference.

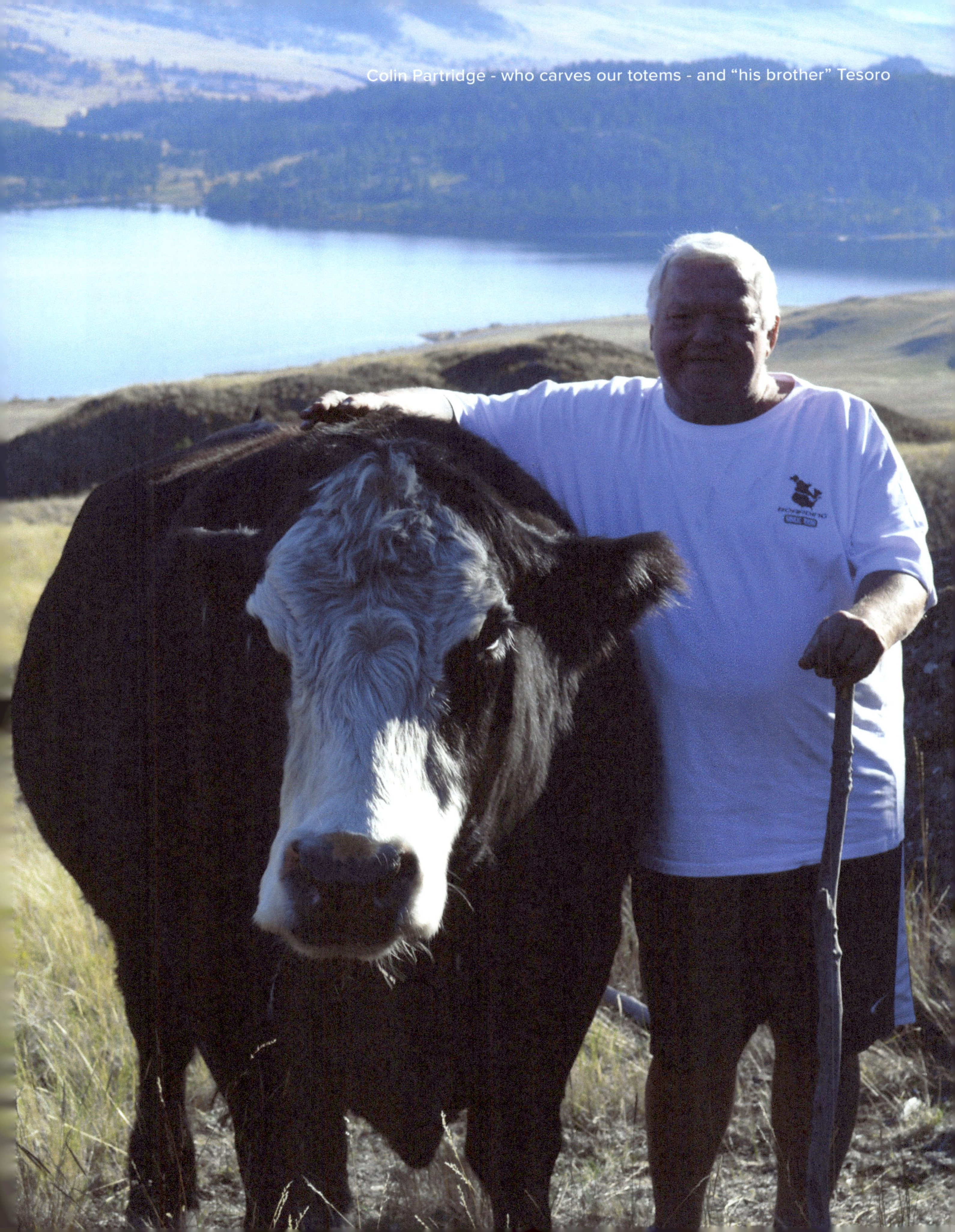

Colin Partridge - who carves our totems - and "his brother" Tesoro

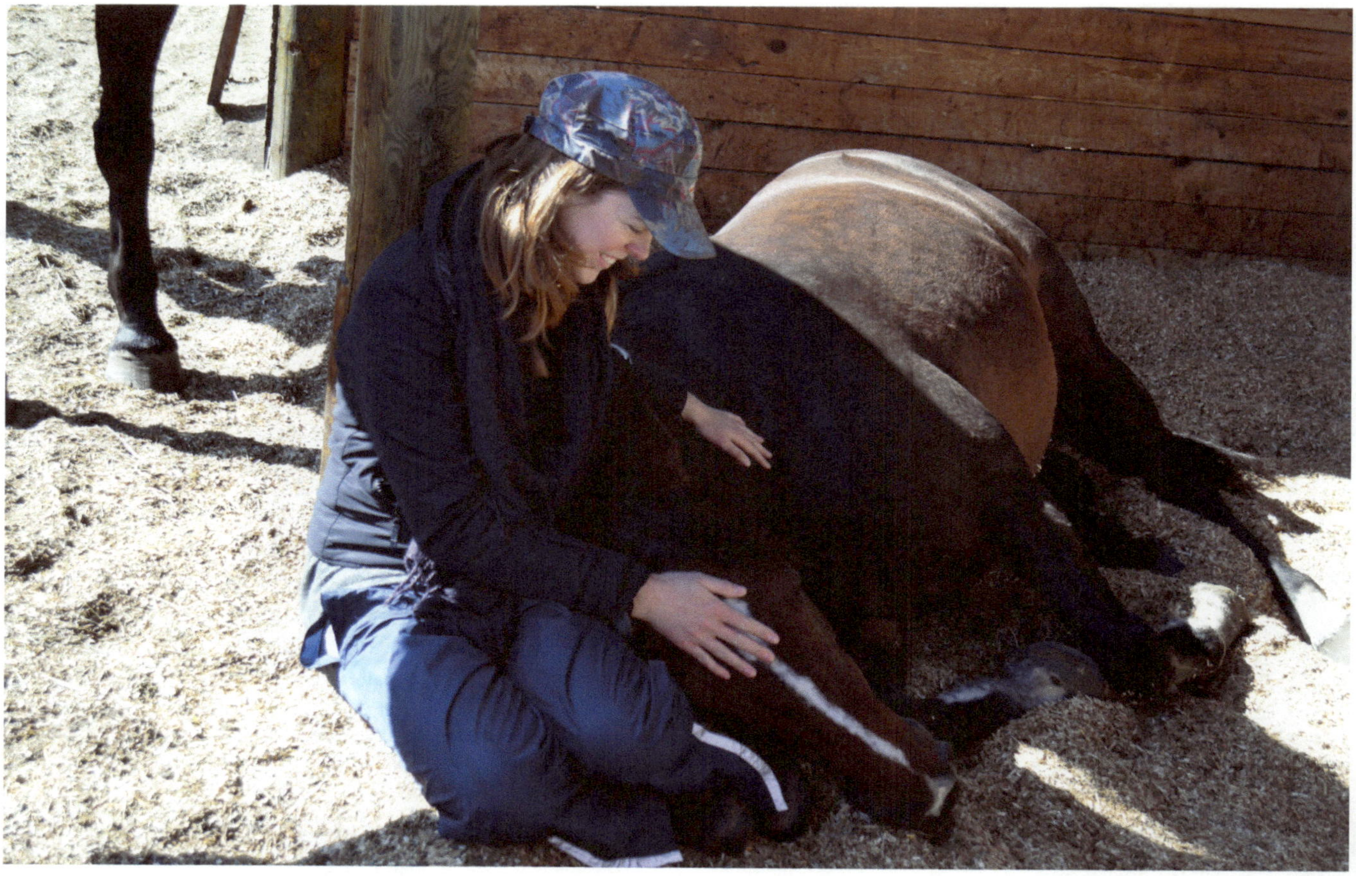

Tesoro (the steer) comes forward:

My name means "treasure," and I am here to share my peace with all who come here.

Our treasure is buried deep within us. It is a gift that transcends the mind. It is wisdom, held in the heart, guidance and direction offered freely to all who will listen. We, the animals and the natural world, listen and follow that guidance without question. Along with the stars, the planets, the tides, the seasons and all the non-human life on Earth, we without question trust in the perfection of our creator.

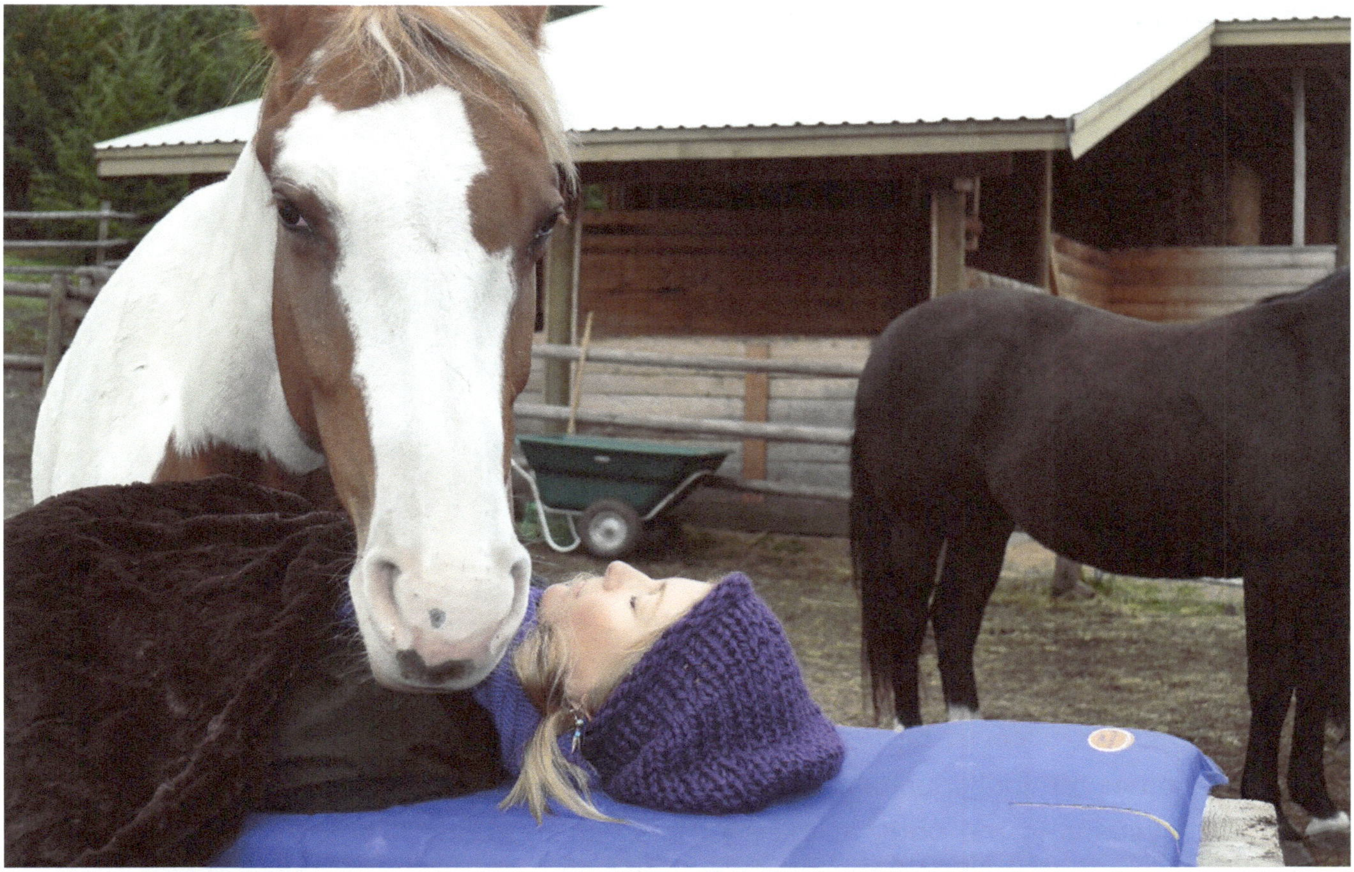

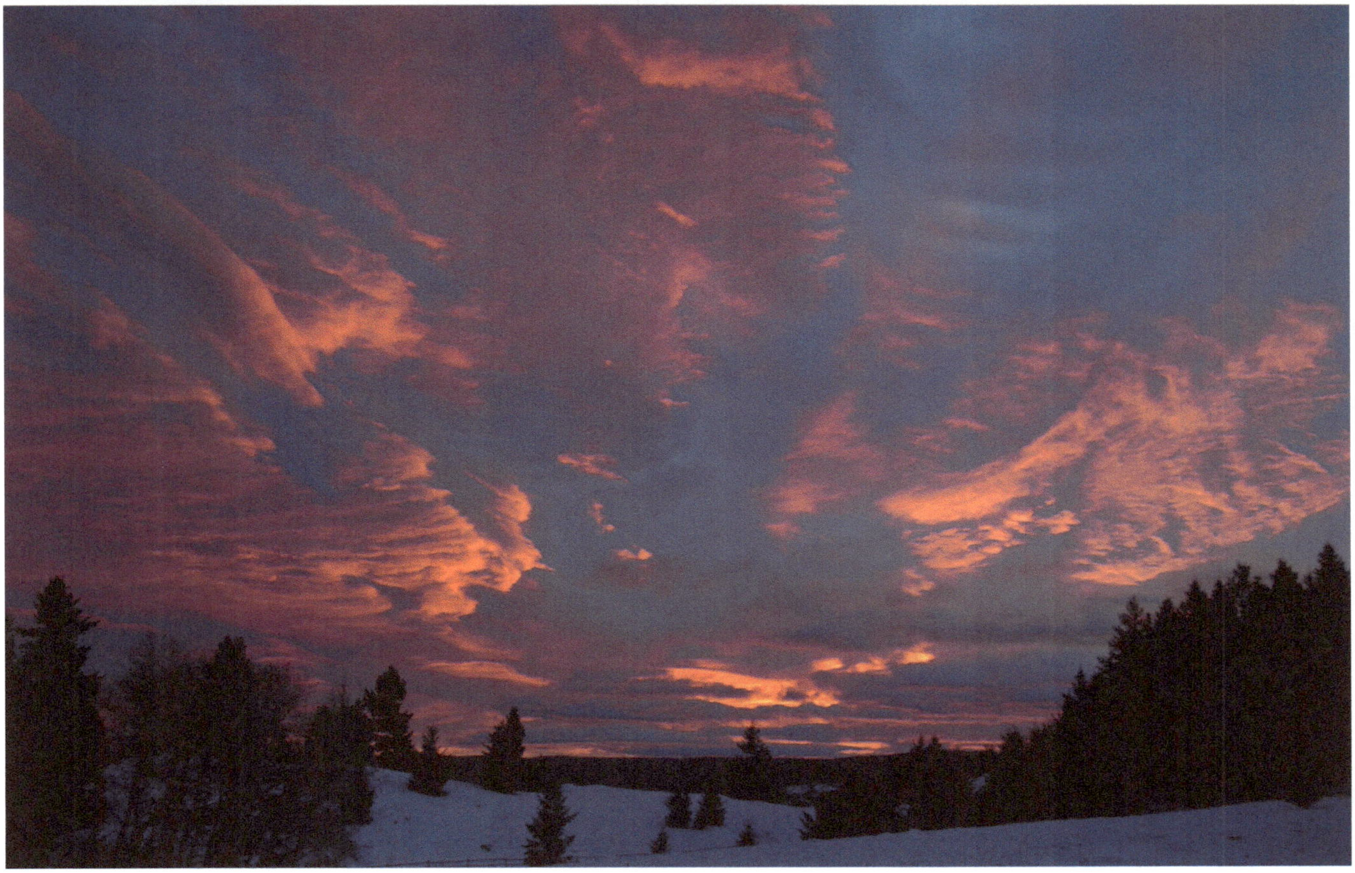

Angles over Gateway

From the horses:

Tesoro comes from a different group mind. We are all unique and express the creator in many ways. Horses, humans, cows, birds, flowers and trees, we are not one above the other but individual aspects of the ALL. We are all cells, organs and systems in the body of the All. How can the body live if one of its organs is not healthy? It is important for humans to understand that although we are different, we are all equal in our importance to the perfect functioning of the body of the All. Do not discount the fact that perfection does not make mistakes, and treasure all the myriad beauty and expression of the All in all life. Each interaction is a conversation with God. A New Year, a new opportunity unfolds. Unwrap the TREASURE within and know the peace that passeth understanding, the peace within all hearts and share the gratitude for that most precious gift with all life. Happy New Year and blessings to ALL, January 2016

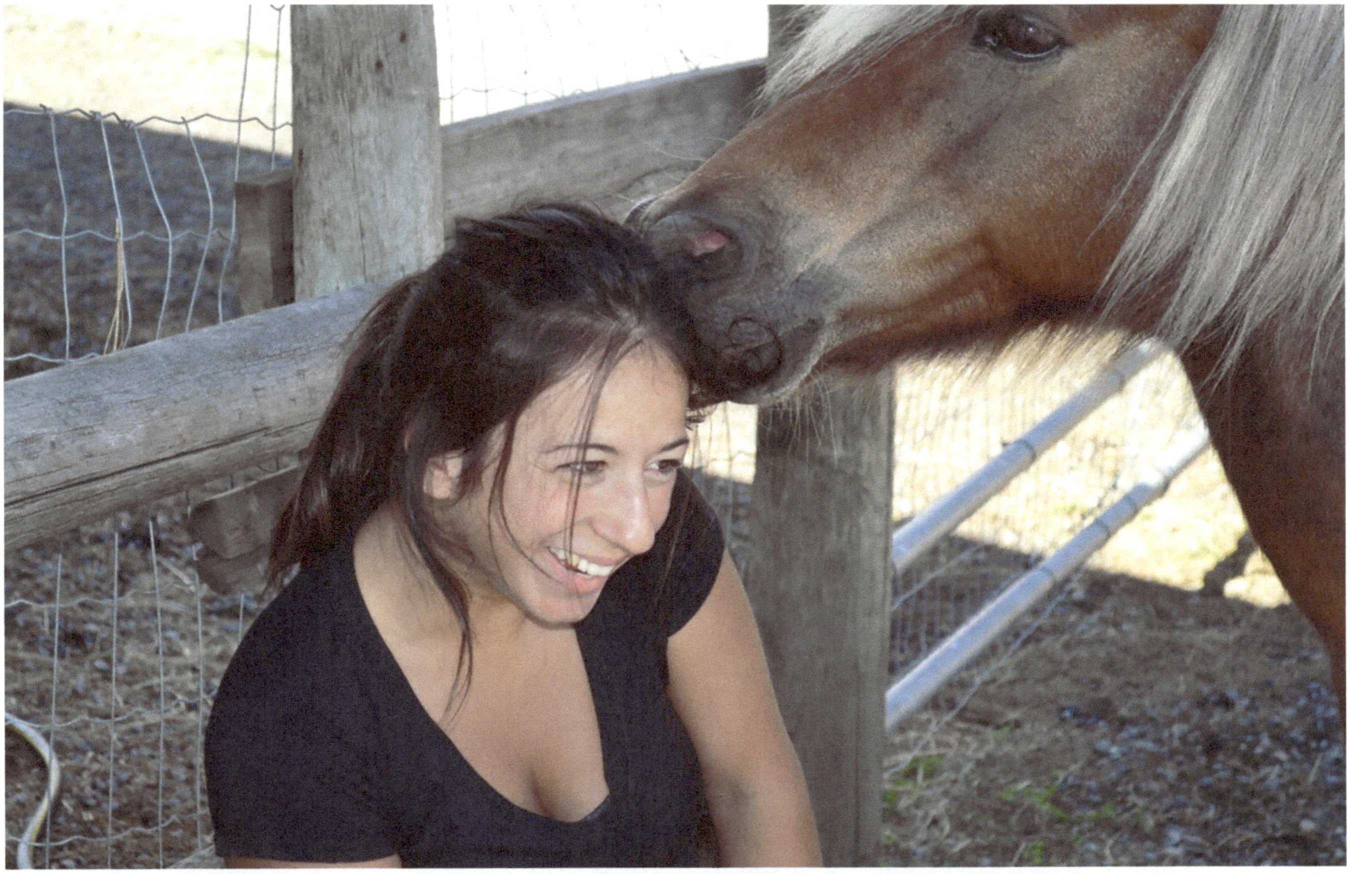

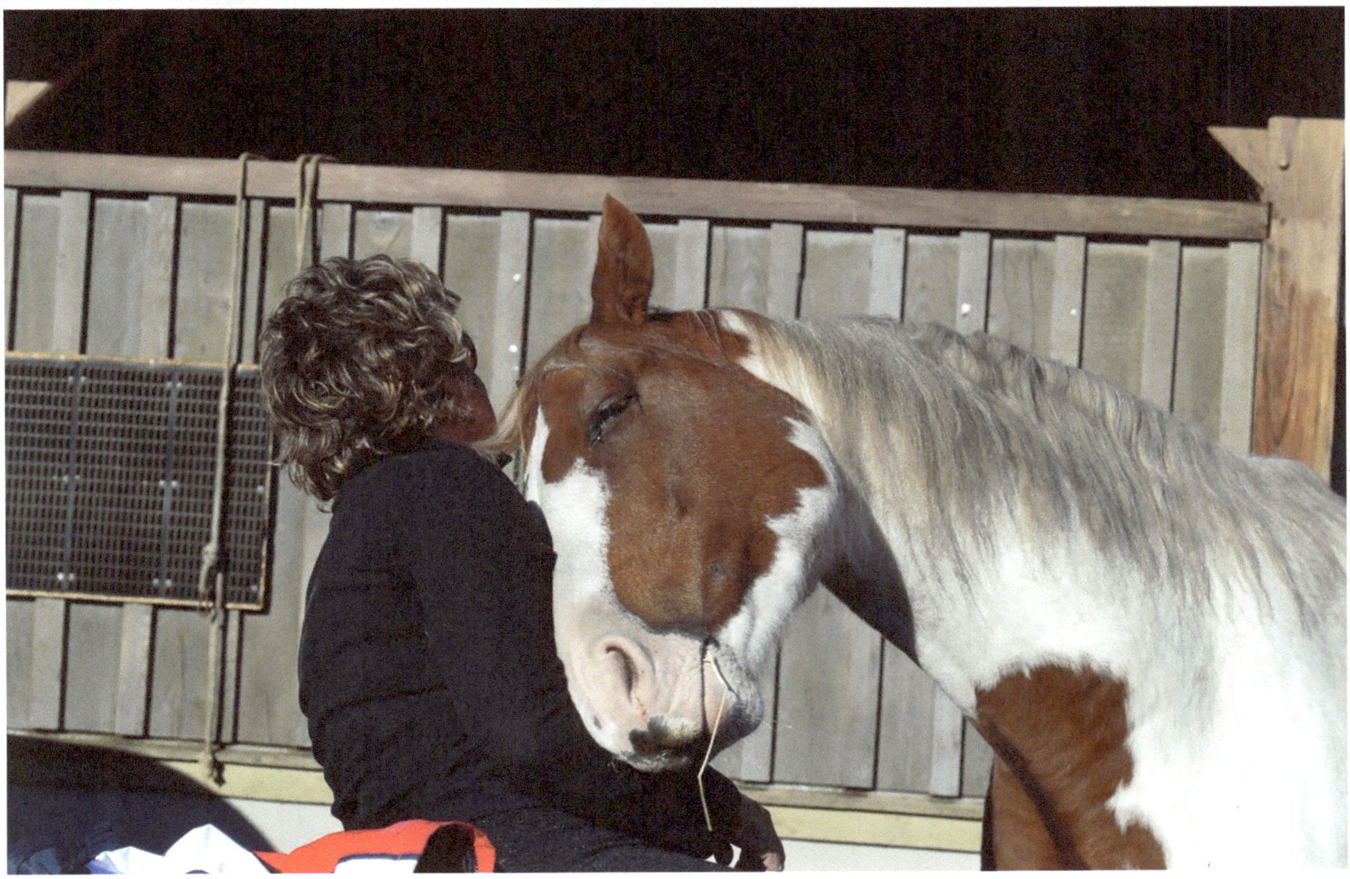

Massage Therapy

In 5th dimensional energy, words and thoughts have wings. We are holding a vision for a new world where all minds (human, animal, vegetable, mineral) will be joined in the expression of higher consciousness, and all hearts will be joined in the expression of love. As all of creation is now interfacing as one consciousness, one force of love in all LIFE, because of all the new connections and communications with animals, the human mass mind consciousness is being diluted and expanded to new levels. Concepts like time and space and individuality are disappearing and the matrix of the ALL is more available to connect with all life. Imagine connecting and communicating with everything from a rock or a tree, to a whale, a horse or even another human (although that is so busy and difficult). We have made the shift and things will not be as they have appeared in your past belief systems. Enjoy the pure and total surrender to life lived in total FREEDOM...surrender to individual truth, individual dreams, inspiration and intuition...TRUST and ALLOW spirit to become you and to surround you with your highest expression and in doing so float in the perfection of life lived as LOVE in expression in matter...Enjoy! As we shared in *Life Unbridled*, L.I.F.E. Love In Finite Expression...forever.

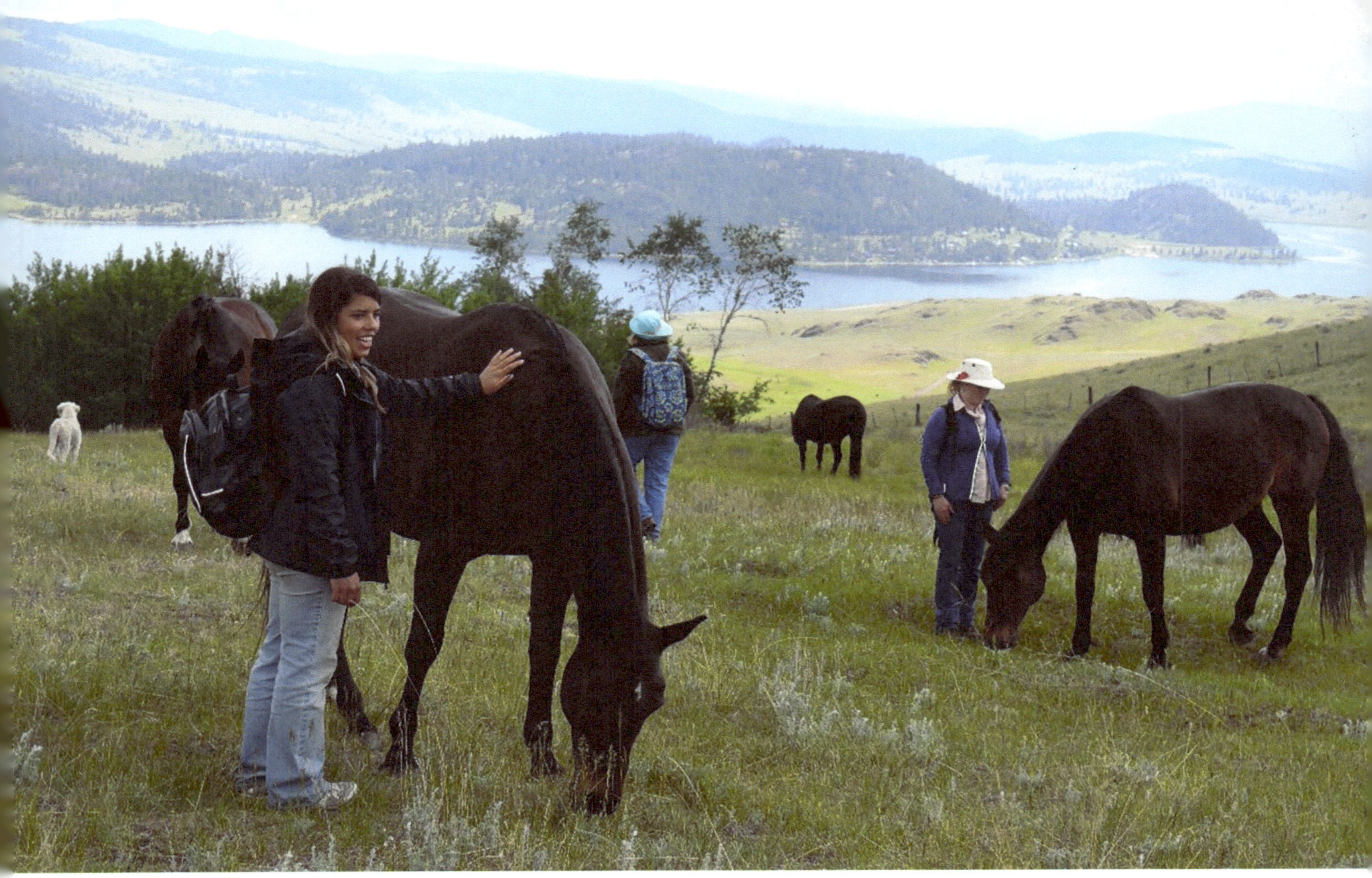

"Strong earth, big sky, healing wind, wise trees, and healing plants and rocks. And the horses, oh the horses! These creatures are magnificent and gentle, and every one of them is a teacher and friend."

—Equinisity participant

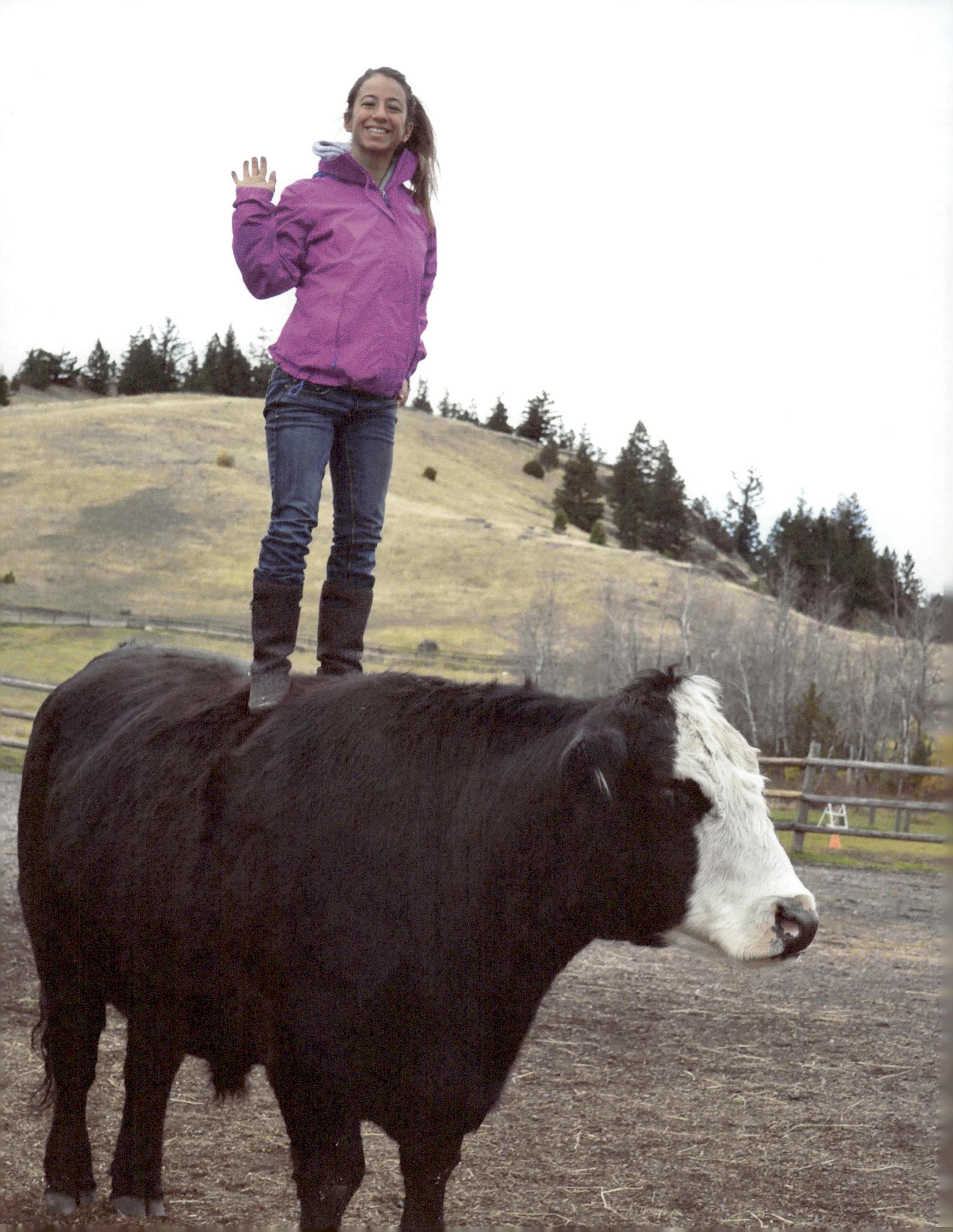

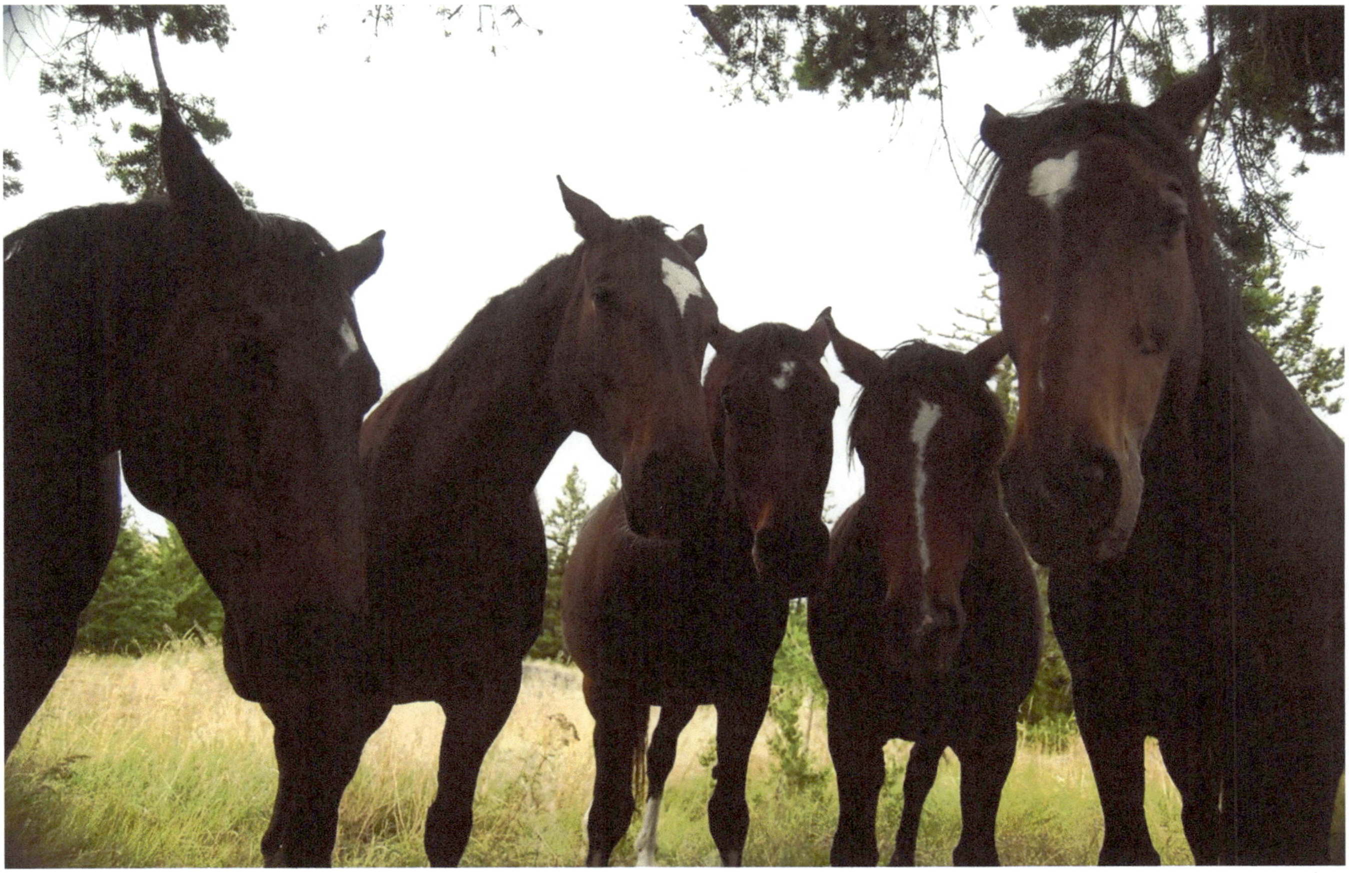

"All truth passes through three stages.
First, it is ridiculed,
Second, it is violently opposed,
Third, it is accepted as being self-evident."

—Arthur Schopenhauer

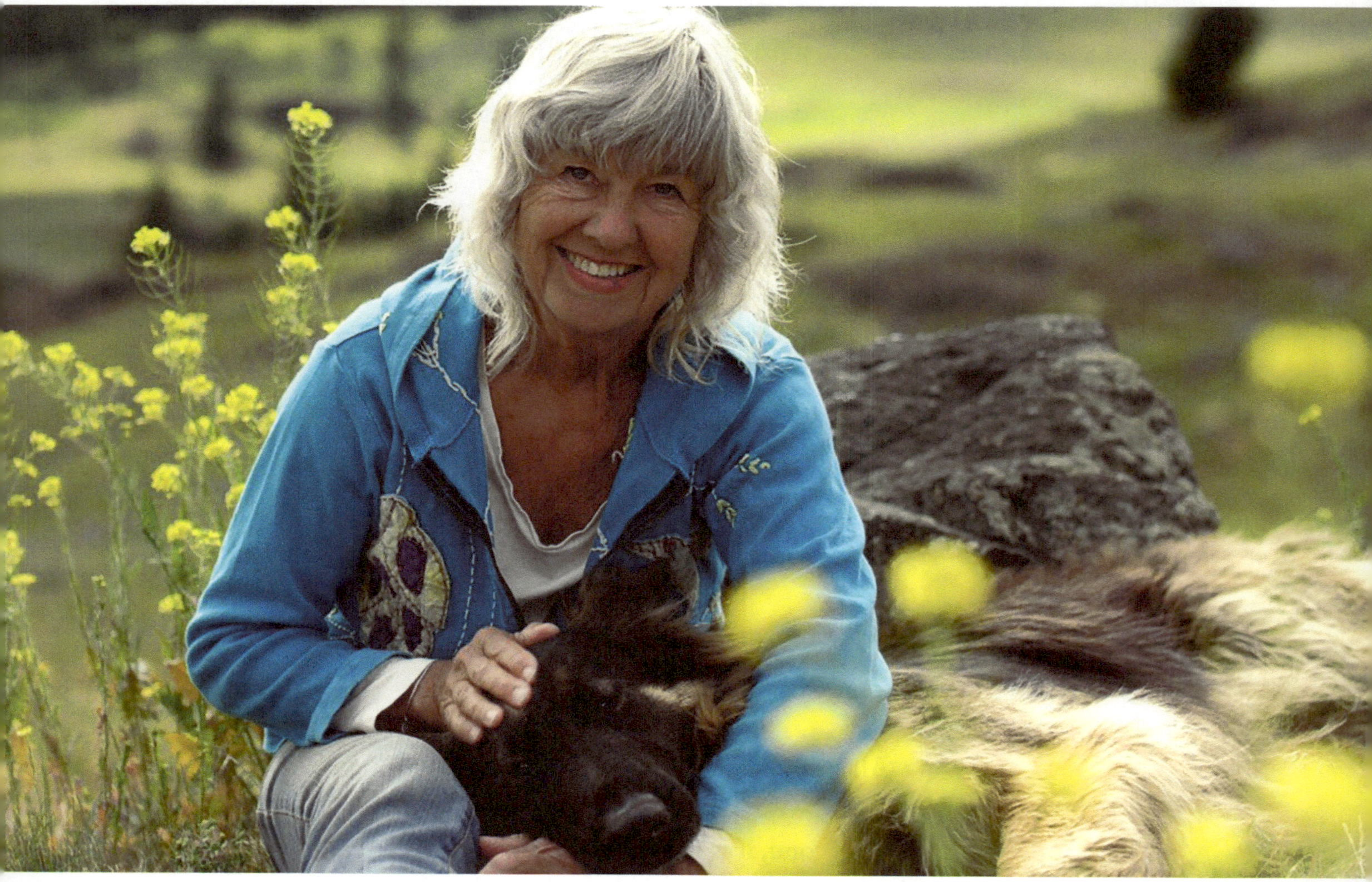

ABOUT THE AUTHOR

When Liz Mitten Ryan moved to Gateway 2 Ranch in 1999, she embarked on a life-changing journey. The 320 acres of untouched forests, meadows and lakes became the pasture and home to Liz and her Herd of warm blood horses. *One With The Herd–A Spiritual Journey* tells the story of how Liz lived in a wall tent for several months, following and communing with the Herd, learning their secrets of connection and communication with the ALL (the horses' name for God) and all life.

When the house and barn were finished, the structure offered a shared space for the horses to return to daily, to rest and reconnect; communicating the mystery and magic of life lived from a place of clear connection to the ALL. This communication grew to encompass four books, co-authored by the horses, dogs and cats, which explain the animals' perspectives on life. Untainted by human mass mind consciousness, this perspective provides a life-changing understanding of the enlightened journey. Liz and the Herd have been offering spiritual retreats with horses and nature since 2008 through her website www.equinisity.com. Book five, *Wisdom from the Herd* encompasses 10 years of channeled material from the horses along with insights from Liz and stories of participants who have experienced life-changing healing and re-connection to their life's calling.

Artist, writer, animal communicator, Liz's art has raised millions of dollars for animals and the environment through groups such as World Wildlife, Earth Day International, Ducks Unlimited and Habitat Canada. Her books have collectively won nine Independent Publishing awards.

Herd is also the title of a new film by award-winning documentary filmmaker Stefan Morel, which follows participants who experience an Equinisity retreat with Liz, and the horses in the magical and transformative setting of Gateway 2 Ranch. Stefan won 'Best Director' in the international documentary category at the 2016 Equus Film Festival.

"*Herd*" the film has a website, which highlights the trailer and story, and will link to the full film when it is available

http//www.herdfilm.com

Learn more about the Equinisity Retreats at:
http//www.equinisity.com

EQUINISITY RETREATS

At Equinisity Retreats in Kamloops, British Columbia, Canada. Our Sacred Land is home to a Herd of free roaming horses, and our resident Buddha, Tesoro the bull. The 320 acres of enchanted forests, hills, lakes, rivers of underground crystals and magnificent views, is an energetic matrix for personal transformation through higher consciousness, universal love and connection to all life.

Equinisity Retreats are transformational journeys hosted by Liz Mitten Ryan, Author, Artist and Animal Communicator and her Herd of equine higher beings. These spiritual, healing and personal growth with horses and nature retreats offer re-connection, re-vitalization and healing, dispelling illusion, shifting consciousness and tuning and raising personal and universal vibration.

We offer life changing, healing inspirational, spiritual and personal development retreats including a unique model of Horse Therapy offered by the Herd at liberty and certification in Equinistic Healing. The retreats are individually tailored to each participant depending on your interests in fusion and alignment with the consciousness and spirit of Equinisity.

**EQUINISTIC HEALING CERTIFICATION is available for those who want to expand their horse therapy practice to the highest levels. Please visit www.equinisity.com for more information on our retreats and certification.

OTHER BOOKS

By Liz Mitten Ryan

The horses' message is changing lives. In three years, they have coauthored four books with Liz and won nine book awards including the coveted *Nautilus Award* in company with Deepak Chopra, Eckhart Tolle, and the Dali Llama. Please visit: www.lizmittenryan.com for additional information on her books, DVDs, art, and more!

All books are available in print format at www.equinisity.com, and through Amazon worldwide

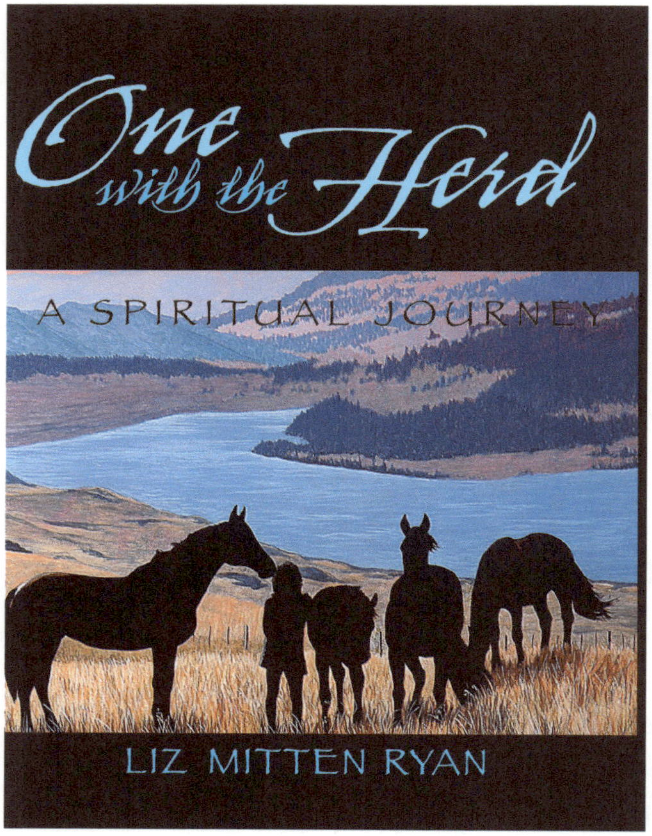
One with the Herd
A SPIRITUAL JOURNEY
LIZ MITTEN RYAN

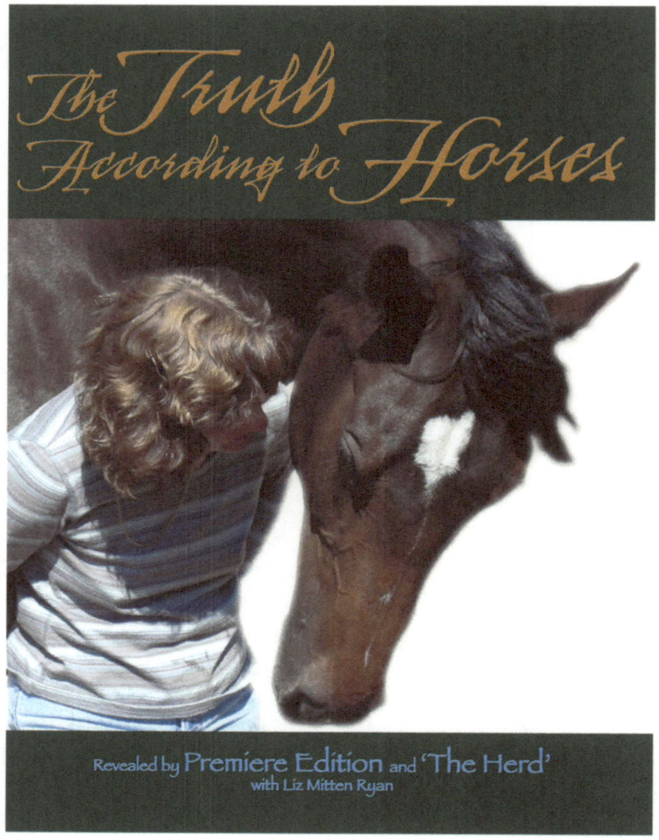
The Truth According to Horses
Revealed by Premiere Edition and 'The Herd'
with Liz Mitten Ryan

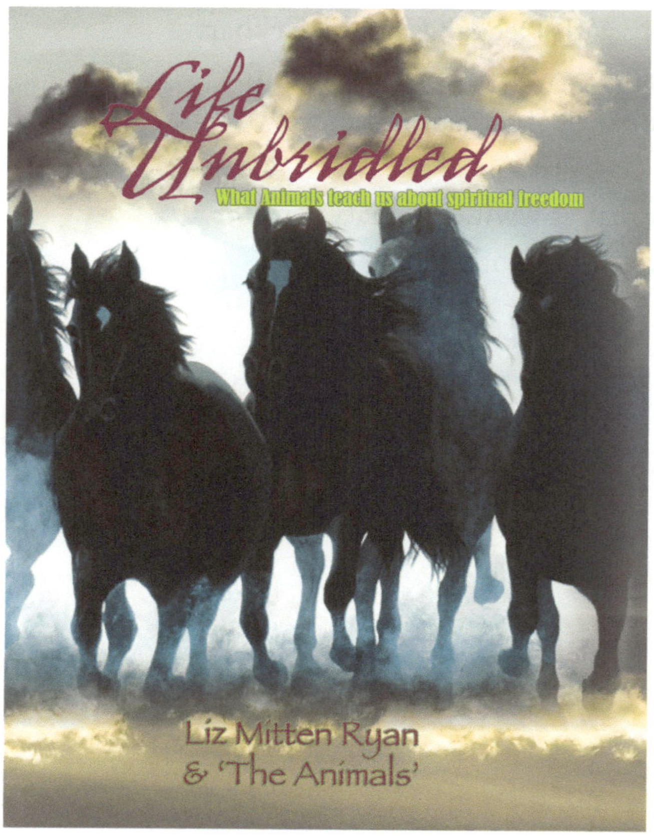
Life Unbridled
What Animals teach us about spiritual freedom
Liz Mitten Ryan
& 'The Animals'

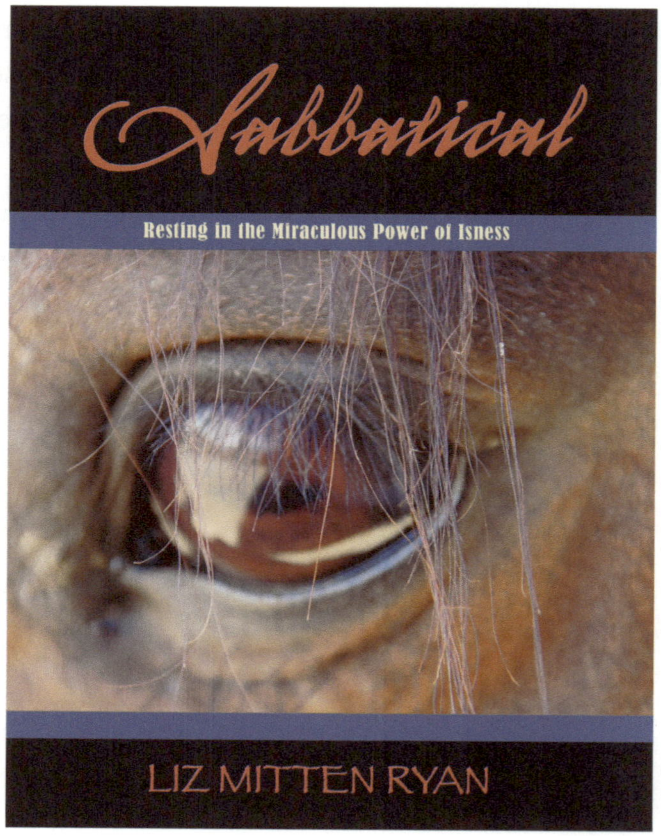
Sabbatical
Resting in the Miraculous Power of Isness
LIZ MITTEN RYAN

Lightning Source UK Ltd.
Milton Keynes UK
UKHW050707200220
359019UK00003B/73